GREAT AMERICAN AUTOMOBILES OF THE

BY RICHARD M. LANGWORTH · CHRIS POOLE

Credits

A Foulis Motoring Book

ISBN 0 85429 738 3

This edition first published 1989.

Published by:
Haynes Publishing Group
Sparkford, Nr. Yeovil, Somerset BA22 7JJ
England

Manufactured in Yugoslavia.

Principle authors

Richard M. Langworth
Chris Poole

Photography

The editors gratefully acknowledge the photographers who helped make this book possible:

Thomas Glatch—10, 11, 108, 109, 140, 141, 174, 175, 280, 281, 288, 289 **Bud Juneau**—12, 13, 24, 25, 30, 31, 36, 37, 44-47, 50, 51, 52-55, 64, 65, 100, 101, 102, 103, 140, 141, 158, 159, 168, 169, 180, 181, 194-197, 214, 215, 228, 229, 296, 297, 308, 309 **Sam Griffith**—14, 15, 52-55, 56, 57, 58, 59, 60, 61, 86, 87, 126, 127, 134, 135, 148, 149, 160, 161, 176, 177, 198, 199, 230-233 **Milton Gene Kieft**—16, 17, 70, 71, 80, 81, 134, 135, 146, 147, 170, 171, 172, 173, 202, 203, 224, 225, 292, 293 **Richard Spiegelman**—20, 21, 44-47, 68, 69, 74, 75, 120, 121, 170, 171, 192, 193, 256, 257, 258, 259, 260, 261, 298, 299, 316, 317 **Vince Manocchi**—22, 23, 64, 65, 78, 79, 88, 89, 110, 111, 128, 129, 130, 131, 136-139, 144, 145, 158, 159, 170, 171, 180, 181, 194-197, 198, 199, 204, 205, 222, 223, 230-233, 240, 241, 244, 245, 250, 251, 268, 269, 270, 271, 274-277, 282, 283, 284, 285, 286, 287 **Doug Mitchel**—26, 27, 42, 43, 56, 57, 84, 85, 106, 107, 112, 113, 136-139, 208, 209, 220, 221, 230-233, 242, 243, 256, 257, 266, 267, 278, 279, 290, 291, 292, 293 **Nickey Wright**—42, 43, 74, 75, 76, 77, 112, 113, 116, 117, 118, 119, 130, 131, 188, 189, 190, 191, 192, 193, 220, 221, 222, 223, 240, 241, 246, 247, 250, 251, 258, 259, 264, 265, 294, 295, 310, 311, 312, 313, 314, 315 **Kris Trexler**—88, 89 **Roland Flessner**—90, 91, 140, 141 **John L. Matras**—92, 93 **David Gooley**—92, 93 **Mike Mueller**—96, 97 **Steve Momot**—98, 99 **Bill Hill**—110, 111 **Bruce Wennerstrom**—114, 115 **Ned Schreiner**—122, 123 **Dave Patryas**—132, 133 **Robert Garris**—150, 151 **Bill Watkins**—150, 151 **Roy D. Query**—152, 153 **Rick Lenz**—178, 179 **Dennis Rozanski**—186, 187 **Ted Clow**—200, 201, 206, 207 **Lloyd Koenig**—202, 203 **Ed Lobit**—210, 211, 238, 239 **Joseph H. Wherry**—218, 219, 220, 221 **Greg Price**—234, 235 **Joe Bohovic**—262, 263, 264, 265 **Bill Bailey**—262, 263 **Bob Cavallo**—272, 273 **Mike Moya**—284, 285

Very special thanks to:

Tom Appeal of the Studebaker National Museum, South Bend, IN; **Helen J. Earley** of the Oldsmobile History Center, Lansing, MI; **Karla Rosenbusch** of the Chrysler Historical Collection, Detroit, MI; **Chuck Ordowski** of Ford Photo-Media, Dearborn, MI; **Betty Dworschack** of Nash Club of America, Clinton, IA; **Carlo Cola** of National Antique Oldsmobile Club, Elmont, NY; **Mr. Jim Gaylord; Steve Engeman** of Fomoco Owners Club, Loveland, CO

Owners

Special thanks to the owners of the cars featured in this book for their enthusiastic cooperation. Listed by car type, they are:

1950-52 Buick Roadmaster—Bob Adams Collectibles, Caledonia, WI **1953 Buick Skylark**—John H. White & Bill Knunson **1953 Buick Super**—Kurt Fredricks **1954 Buick Skylark**—Peter & Jane Schlacter **1958 Buick Limited**—Michael L. Berzenye **1959 Buick Electra**— Palmer Carson **1950-52 Cadillac**—Philip J. Kuhn **1954 Cadillac Eldorado**—Gary Robinson **1955-56 Cadillac Eldorado**—Joe Malta **1957-58 Cadillac Eldorado Brougham**—Mr. Gimelli **1959-60 Cadillac Eldorado Brougham**—Bob Waldock **1950-52 Chevrolet**—William E. Goodsene, John R. Vorva **1950-52 Chevrolet Bel Air**—Ralph Moceo, Denise & Charles Crevits **1953-55 Chevrolet Corvette**—Dave Stefun **1955-56 Chevrolet**—Gary Johns, Eugene R. Siuda, Jr., Bill Curran, James R. Cahill **1955-57 Chevrolet Nomad**—Ron Pittman, Bill Bodnarchuk **1956-57 Chevrolet Corvette**—Pete Bogard **1957 Chevrolet**—Bill Bodnarchuk, Roger & Betty Jerie **1958 Chevrolet Impala**—Gary Mills, John Cox **1959 Chevrolet**—Hugh Eshelman, E. Noggles **1959 Chevrolet El Camino**—Tom Stackhouse **1950 Chrysler Town & Country**—Bob Porter **1951-54 Chrysler New Yorker**—Virgil & Dorothy Meyer, Keith Cullen **1955-56 Chrysler New Yorker**—Bruce M. Stevens & Judy Wolfe **1955-56 Chrysler 300**—Richard Carpenter **1957-59 Chrysler New Yorker**—David L. Griebling **1956-57 Continental Mark II**—Robb Petty **1958-59 Continental Mark III/IV**—William R. Kipp, Kris Trexler **1950-52 DeSoto Sportsman**—M. Crider **1953-54 DeSoto**—Don Merz **1955-56 DeSoto Fireflite**—Jack Moore, Bob & Janet Nitz, Jeff & Aleta Wells **1956 DeSoto Adventurer**—Roger & Connie Graeber **1957-59 DeSoto Fireflite**—Jim Crossen, John & Susan Gray, Elmer & Shirley Hungate **1950-51 Dodge Wayfarer Sportabout**—Bill Bost **1953-54 Dodge V-8**—David Studer, William Rehberg, Bob & Roni Sue Shapiro **1955-56 Dodge D-500**—Harry A. DeMenge, Harry Magnuson, Jr. **1957-59 Dodge**—Daryl Thomsen, Harold Stabe **1956-58 Dual-Ghia**—Bruce Wennerstrom **1958 Edsel**—Dennis L. Huff, Andrew Alphonso **1959 Edsel**—Dennis L. Huff **1956-57 El Morocco**—Charles Davis **1950-51 Ford Crestliner**—Loren E. Miller **1951 Ford Victoria**—Gerald Hanson **1952-54 Ford**—Tom Howard **1952-59 Ford Station Wagons**—Fred & Diane Ives, Lynn Augustine, Charles L. Richards **1954 Ford Skyliner**—Dave Horn **1955-56 Ford Crown Victoria**—Donald Kish, Sr., Tom Risley **1955-57 Ford Thunderbird**—Alan Wendland, Paul Bastista, Leonard Nowosel **1957-59 Ford Ranchero**—Ted Maupin, Tom Lerdahl, Jerry Capizzi **1957-59 Ford Skyliner**—Jerry Magayne, George Richards **1958-59 Ford Thunderbird**—Ted Davidson, Herb Rothman **1959 Ford Galaxie**—William R. Muni **1950 Frazer Manhattan Convertible**—Art Sabin **1951 Frazer**—John Keck, William Tresize, Ray Frazier **1950 Hudson Commodore**—Dix Helland **1951-53 Hudson Hornet**—William D. Albright, Bob Hill, John & Minnie Keys **1953-54 Hudson Jet**—John Struthers **1956-57 Hudson**—Ed Wassmann **1955-56 Imperial**—Phil Walker, Brian H. Williams, Paul Hem **1957-59 Imperial**—Ray Geschke **1950 Kaiser Virginian**—Ken Griesemer **1951-53 Kaiser Dragon**—Jerry Johnson **1951-53 Kaiser Traveler**—Keith Zimmerman, Charles & Charlotte Watson, Jr. **1954 Kaiser Darrin**—Jerry Johnson, John Fawset, Ted Dahlmann **1954-55 Kaiser Manhattan**—Dennis Yauger, Kenneth G. Lindsey **1950-51 Lincoln Lido/Capri**—Fred Schillinger **1952-55 Lincoln**—Homer J. Sanders **1956-57 Lincoln**—Richard Nassar **1958-59 Lincoln**—David Showalter **1950-51 Mercury**—Roy Schneckloth, Jack Karleskind, Jerry & Jackie Lew **1952-54 Mercury**—Jay B. Jonagan **1954 Mercury Sun Valley**—Bob Botkowsky **1955-56 Mercury**—Ross Gibaldi, Bill & Lanee Proctor **1957-58 Mercury**—Bob Rose, James & Susan Verhasselt **1959 Mercury**—Eric Hopman **1951-54 Muntz Jet**—Joseph E. Bortz, Melvin R. Hull **1950-51 Nash Ambassador**—Larry Landis **1951-55 Nash-Healey**—Gordon McGregor, Gerald Newton **1953-55 Nash Rambler**—Roger & Barbara Stroud **1954-59 Nash Metropolitan**—Dale & Roxanne Carrington, Billy & Dorothy Harris, Dr. Roy V. Yorns **1955-57 Nash Ambassador**—Bud Hiler, Burt Carlson, Neil S. Black **1950 Oldsmobile 88**—Peter's Motorcars, Milan, OH **1953 Oldsmobile Fiesta**—Ramshead Auto Collection **1954-56 Oldsmobile**—Norman W. Prien, Bob Weber, Norb Kopchinski **1957-58 Oldsmobile**—Duane & Steven Stupienski **1959 Oldsmobile**—Ralph R. Leid **1950 Packard**—Larry Landis **1951-53 Packard Mayfair**—Edward J. Ostrowski, Greg Pagano **1951-54 Packard Patrician**—Chuck Beed **1953-54 Packard Clipper**—Fritz Hugo **1955 Packard Clipper/1956 Clipper**—Ken Ugolini, John Shulze, Steve Williams, Wayne Parson **1955-56 Packard Patrician/Four Hundred/Executive**—Harold Gibson **1957 Packard Clipper/1958 Packard**—Michael Wehling, Kevin Mullet **1958 Packard Hawk**—Gerald Revell, Thomas L. Karkiewicz **1951-52 Plymouth Belvedere**—Mr. Reinke **1953-54 Plymouth Belvedere**—Merv Afflerbach, James Bottger, Rex N. Yount **1955-56 Plymouth**—Andrew Nothnagel, John & Peggy Clinton **1957-58 Plymouth Fury**—Richard Carpenter **1959 Plymouth Sport Fury**—Richard Carpenter **1950-52 Pontiac Catalina**—Ronald Mack **1953-54 Pontiac**—Richard & Janice Plastino **1955-56 Pontiac**—Richard & Marilyn Bourgie, Ken Regnier **1955-57 Pontiac Safari**—Dennis M. Statz **1957 Pontiac Bonneville**—Dick Hoyt **1958 Pontiac Bonneville**—John Fitzgerald, Jerry Cinotti **1956-57 Rambler**—Bob Adams Collectibles **1957 Rambler Rebel**—Roger Fonk **1958-59 Rambler Ambassador**—Frank Wrenick, Gerald Srdek **1958-59 Rambler American**—Douglas Suter **1950-51 Studebaker Commander**—Roy Yost **1953-54 Studebaker Starliner**—Jim Ranage **1955 Studebaker Speedster**—Joseph R. Bua **1956-58 Studebaker**—Loger Hill, Jordan Morris, Ralph Mitchell **1956 Studebaker Hawk**—Donated by Srvislav Zivanovic, Theodore & Jeanette M. Diemer to the Studebaker National Museum; Jay Harrigan **1957-58 Studebaker Golden Hawk**—Bob Patrick **1959 Studebaker Lark**—Don & Bonnie Snipes **1959 Studebaker Silver Hawk**—Paul Warton **1950-51 Willys Jeepster**—James E. Dinehart

Contents

Introduction

Probably the hottest collector cars these days are those from the Fifties. That's perfectly understandable when you consider that the young men and women who grew up during that exciting decade are now at the point in their lives where careers are established and the children are beginning to leave the nest. That gives Mom and Dad the opportunity to indulge themselves in a nostalgic trip back to the days when they were courting, when America seemed invincible, and when the annual model change stirred excitement in every U.S. city and hamlet.

When viewed through misty eyes, the Fifties are remembered as years of promise. Most Americans then enjoyed greater prosperity than they had ever known, and so the parents of the "baby-boom" generation began a massive trek to the suburbs. Industry, also booming, soon followed. The automobile made this massive shift possible—most families could afford one now—and it was during this era that the two-car family began to emerge.

Most of the world envied America in those days. A "Made in U.S.A." label carried great prestige, especially on an automobile, any one of which was considered "great" in most corners of the globe.

And so it is in modern-day America, for the passage of time has a way of making the "good old days," and the "good old cars," seem better than they really were. It should be remembered that for years cars of the Fifties were assailed for being overstyled and underdeveloped, needlessly large and thirsty, poorly built, and tastelessly gimmicky. A closer look reveals that there were notable exceptions to these criticisms, even though the cars of that era are often best remembered for fins and flash.

Yet, there was progress—lots of it. Consider the reliable fully automatic transmission, perfected in the Fifties and universal today. The short-stroke overhead-valve V-8 also came to the fore in these years, a clear advance for power and fuel efficiency over traditional L-head engines. The best of the breed powered some of the most memorable performance machines ever built, many of which are recalled

1953 Buick Super

here: the original Oldsmobile 88, Chrysler's 300B of 1956, the first and last of the "classic" Chevrolets, the '57 Corvette, and Pontiac's first Bonneville. Of course, V-8s aren't as numerous in today's four-cylinder world (though they've been making a comeback), but it's significant that Chevy's landmark 265-cid powerplant is still with us, albeit in much-modified form. Good things do endure.

Other good things we remember from the Fifties were simply premature. Fuel injection—on the aforementioned Bonneville and '57 Chevrolets—got its production impetus in this decade. So too did unit construction. Though it wouldn't catch on until much later, its advantages were recognized even for such dissimilar cars as the 1950 Rambler and the 1958-59 Ford Thunderbird. The former was predictive as the first successful postwar compact, the latter as the pioneer of "personal-luxury," two concepts that would sweep the auto industry in the Sixties. And it shouldn't be forgotten that the Fifties ushered in the all-steel station wagon and the hardtop coupe and sedan, body styles that would dominate for a quarter of a century.

The Fifties may have produced some of the industry's worst styling excesses, but it also left us its share of design milestones: the Continental Mark II, the two-seat Thunderbird, the second-generation Kaiser, Studebaker's "Loewy coupes," and others. You'll find them all within these pages. You'll also find the original Cadillac Eldorado and Hudson's short-lived Italia, recalling the Fifties as the age of "dream cars," some of which you could actually buy.

However "great" is defined, every car within these pages can lay claim to that description, from the humble compacts that foretold the future to the most blatant, befinned creations of that era, which simply reflected—with some exaggeration—the optimistic mood of a great country.

Significantly, young people nowadays are showing more than a passing interest in cars of the Fifties, just like their folks. Which just goes to prove that even if you didn't grow up with the *Great American Automobiles of the 50s*, you're sure to enjoy the ride.

The Auto Editors of CONSUMER GUIDE® *January 1989*

1952-53 Allstate

Sears, Roebuck & Company usually goes to great lengths to hide the origin of proprietary products—those built by some other famous company but wearing a Sears brand. But there was no disguising the origins of the Allstate. It was, of course, Sears' version of Kaiser-Frazer's compact Henry J. Most people, however, got their first look at it in the ubiquitous Sears catalog, and many never actually saw a real one. With a total production run of about 2400 units, Allstates weren't exactly the most common automobiles on the road.

Theodore V. Houser, a Sears executive who also owned some Kaiser-Frazer stock, had been asking Henry Kaiser to build Sears a car since the west coast construction tycoon had entered the auto business in 1945. (This was not the first attempt by Sears to produce cars: a pretty little high-wheeler had carried the Sears name back in 1912.) Houser and Kaiser had earlier collaborated when the latter's steel mills produced pots and pans for Sears' kitchenware department. Design renderings of early, slab-sided Kaiser-Frazer sedans with Allstate labels were completed, but nothing came of the idea until K-F produced the Henry J, announced in early 1950 as a 1951 model.

The Henry J looked ideal to Sears because of its middle-class, economy-minded clientele, and Henry Kaiser agreed to produce a version for Sears. This decision caused dismay within the Kaiser-Frazer dealer organization, which fretted about competition from the giant department store and catalog merchandiser. Henry's son Edgar, K-F's president, was sent to mollify them: Allstates would be produced in small quantities, he told the dealers, and would be marketed mainly on a test basis in the southeast part of the country (where K-F's dealer network was notably sparse). The dealers remained unconvinced. As things turned out, Edgar was right.

K-F designer Alex Tremulis was asked to contrive a hardware shuffle to give the Allstate a different look. This involved, as Tremulis recalled, mainly "a new face. I did a hurry-up remake of the grille, putting in two horizontals and a little triangular piece, made up a jet plane-type hood ornament that looked nice, and put on the Allstate logo with a map of the U.S. *Voilá*, there it was!" Other distinguishing exterior details were: smooth hub caps or wheelcovers without the "K," special door locks, standard decklid (this was *not* standard on all Henry Js!); under the hood the Willys-designed flathead engines were painted blue with orange "Allstate" lettering.

Allstate departed more from Henry J design on the inside, which Houser had wanted to be of slightly higher quality. Kaiser-Frazer's interior trim specialist, Carleton Spencer, developed a colorful plaid Deluxe interior using a new material: coated paper fibers soaked in vinyl—an impervious material that had proven its durability in none other than the transatlantic telephone cable! This Spencer combined with quilted saran plastic. The idea was to save Allstate owners the cost of slipcovers, which almost every new car buyer installed in those days. Of course you had to order the Deluxe to get this interior; cheaper models had more austere upholstery. Other unique interior features included plain (no "K") horn button, standard glove box (again, not always found in Henry Js), and special armrests and sunvisors.

Everything automotive that Sears, Roebuck sold was naturally applied to the new car: tires, tubes, battery, spark plugs, each with their generous Sears guarantee. The Allstate as a whole was guaranteed for 90 days or 4000 miles by K-F—"which was as long as anybody would want to guarantee one of the things," as one critic of the Henry J put it. That's being unfair, since the Allstate, like the Henry J, had a good service and repair record.

If you can find a 1952 Sears catalog, you'll find the Allstate on the back cover. It didn't reappear in the 1953 catalog because the project was already winding down. Technically available anywhere, the Allstate was delivered almost exclusively in Dixie; if you lived, say, in Minnesota, you would have had a hard time getting one. Price was against it, too: the lowest you could pay was $1395, and in practice most sold for about $1600. At a time when a two-door Ford V-8 cost $1500 and a Chevrolet about $1550, the Allstate was up against very tough competition. Of the minuscule production, about three of every five cars were fours and the rest sixes.

The 1952 Sears, Roebuck catalog featured a new offering on the back cover, the Allstate automobile. It was basically a Henry J with a different grille and other trim changes. Despite Sears' marketing muscle, the Allstate sold poorly, partly because people weren't used to buying cars from a catalog and also because the price was too high compared to Ford and Chevy. A few cars were sold into 1953, after which Sears abandoned the ill-fated Allstate project.

SPECIFICATIONS

Engines: flathead I-4, 134.2 cid (3.11 × 4.38), 68 bhp; flathead I-6, 161.0 cid (3.13 × 3.50), 80 bhp

Transmission:	3-speed manual; overdrive optional
Suspension, front:	independent, coil springs, tube shocks
Suspension, rear:	live axle, leaf springs, tube shocks
Brakes:	front/rear drums
Wheelbase (in.):	100.0
Weight (lbs):	2300-2455
Top speed (mph):	**4** 75, **6** 80
0-60 mph (sec):	**4** 25.0, **6** 20.0
Production:	**1952** 1566 **1953** 797

COLLECTOR
245 A
WISCONSIN

245 A

1950-52
Buick Roadmaster

"Valve-in-head, ahead in value." Buick's traditional slogan was still being touted prominently in 1950, although the rest of the industry (led by soul mates Cadillac and Oldsmobile) was finally coming round to the conclusion that overhead valves were going to replace side valves. Still, as recently as 1947, Chevrolet, Buick, and Nash had been the only major American producers to espouse the valve-in-head engine. By the mid-Sixties, everybody would be using it.

"Roadmaster"—what a wonderful name for a car! It had emerged during 1936 and would last until it was foolishly removed for 1959. It was the perfect term for the top of the Buick line, a car bordering on Cadillac price territory, preferred transport for the up-and-coming professional—the doctor, the lawyer, and anybody else who could not quite afford a Caddy. Buick catered to this clientele with flashy styling—far and away the flashiest of the GM divisions—plus luxury and a host of novel design ideas: the famous pop-art grille, the gun-sight hood ornament, the hardtop convertible, the sweepspear, and the porthole. The latter three all arrived in 1949, when Buick sales correspondingly increased by 50 percent, and then doubled in 1950. In that long-lost halcyon era, this was the kind of car America wanted—and bought.

At a time when the annual model change was an act of faith, Buick chief designer Ned Nickles responded in the ordained manner by adding chrome, and the early-Fifties Buicks were not as purely beautiful as Ned's '49, the first all-new postwar design. The buck-tooth grille extended down over the bumper in 1950, but this was too strange even for Buickfolk (but much coveted today), and promptly receded in 1951.

Every account of Buick in those days invariably mentions the origin of the porthole which—variously bent, squeezed, elongated, wiped out, and restored again—has been part of the Buick styling tradition since '49. It was part of that design lexicon

which took inspiration from the wonderful new jet aircraft (the basic Buick shape had evolved from the propellor-driven Lockheed P-38), along with the rounded "fuselage" of car body sides, the big scoop grilles, and the aileron-like tailfins (Buick's first "fins" came in 1952, well ahead of Virgil Exner and Chrysler). When Nickles whimsically mounted little colored lights inside the portholes of his own Roadmaster, wired through the distributor to flash in firing order, Flint managers stared at it wide-eyed in open admiration; the wonder is that they didn't make it standard.

This is not to imply that these Buicks were all fluff and lightheaded frippery. They were very serious automobiles, built with integrity, of a quality and durability that vanished around 1955 and has not been around since. It has often been remarked that there was probably more steel in the dashboard of an early-Fifties Buick than in an entire Suburu: undoubtedly an exaggeration, but the photos reveal what's implied. Like most other cars of 1950, '51 and '52, these Roadmasters were *built:* hoods clang down like manhole covers, doors shut with a solid clunk on bank vault-like hinges, radios wrap you in that kind of "fat" sound you just don't get from transistors. Maybe it was clumsily executed, but it is this kind of sheer integrity that makes cars like the Roadmaster appeal to people today.

Roadmasters in all three years were offered as a four-door sedan, Riviera hardtop, convertible, and wagon, the latter making extensive use of real tree wood. (The last woodies made by anyone were built by Buick, in 1953.) In 1950 there were also Deluxe versions of the Riviera and sedan, the latter confusingly called the "Riviera" too, plus the last Roadmaster sedanets. These pretty fastbacks were dropped because of slow sales—only 2968 in their final '50 model year—which renders them highly desirable by collectors today.

These Buicks also represent the last, or almost the last, of the long-running overhead valve straight eight, which still pumped out creditable horsepower in the Roadmaster. The smaller Buick Special retained its straight eight in 1953; then the entire line received V-8 power for '54.

In its final year, the straight-eight Roadmaster convertible—the most expensive Buick save for the woody wagons—had a base price of $3453, which means it typically cost about $4000, or just under $20,000 in today's money. That's quite a lot of car for the dollar.

SPECIFICATIONS

Engine: overhead valve I-8, 320.2 cid (3.44 × 4.31) **1950-51** 152 bhp **1952** 170 bhp

Transmission:	Dynaflow automatic
Suspension, front:	independent, coil springs, lever shocks
Suspension, rear:	live axle, coil springs, lever shocks
Brakes:	front/rear drums
Wheelbase (in.):	125.2
Weight (lbs):	4150-4400
Top speed (mph):	95-100
0-60 mph (sec):	17.0 using Lo/Hi ranges
Production:	**1950** 78,034 **1951** 66,058 **1952** 46,217

Practically every teenage male growing up in the early Fifties knew that cheaper Buicks—the Special and Super—got three "Ventiports" per side, and that only the top-of-the-line Roadmaster got to wear four. The Roadmaster also boasted a larger valve-in-head straight eight—320.2 cubic inches and, in 1952, 170 horsepower. Although the four-door sedan sold best, the sportier Riviera hardtop (below) *attracted 11,387 buyers in that production-restricted year.*

1953 Buick Skylark

The Skylark shared with Cadillac's Eldorado and Oldsmobile's Fiesta the status of a show car come to life. All three, from GM's luxury and near-luxury divisions, were limited-production, top-of-the-line convertibles with every conceivable accessory as standard. Buick's Skylark sold better than the other two combined in 1953, however, and to many eyes it also looked better. Likewise it doubled as a commemorative edition: Buick celebrated its 50th anniversary that year (as did Ford), and the $5000 Skylark seemed an appropriate way to mark this milestone.

Like any one-off Motorama showpiece, the Skylark prefigured mass-production designs to come on later Buicks: the wraparound windshield, full wheel openings, two-way sweepspear extending fore and aft from a point ahead of the rear wheels. The Skylark also eliminated Buick's famous portholes, which were destined to be dropped from all models in 1959 (although they would return later).

At that lofty price, customers expected—and got—everything standard: tinted glass, "Selectronic" radio (with floor button control), power antenna, whitewalls, power seats/windows/steering/brakes/top, two-tone full leather upholstery; even expensive chrome plated Kelsey-Hayes wire wheels carrying red, white, and blue "50th Anniversary" emblems in their hubs (repeated in the horn button). The signal-seeking radio was neat: stabbing the floor button changed stations, and by adjusting a "more/less" knob it stopped at more or fewer stations at the whim of the operator.

The Skylark also benefited from Buick's first modern over-square V-8. Though it had only about 10 percent more horsepower than the '52 straight eight, it also provided a stump-wrenching 300 lbs/ft of torque at a low 2400 rpm. The Skylark and other Roadmasters were capable of cruising all day at nearly 100 mph.

New engine notwithstanding, the Skylark's main impression was visual: unabashedly big, but somehow more deftly styled than the Eldo and not overdone like the Fiesta. The rakish lines were achieved by its bold open wheel wells and drastically lowered beltline, along with a four-inch-chop from the standard Roadmaster convertible's windshield—a well-known trick customizers had been using on their Fords and Mercs in the early Fifties. In a day when every new Detroit gadget was treated like one giant leap for mankind, a top that retracted out of sight behind a metal boot was a mini-wonder. Wire wheels, of course, transformed any big Detroiter into a "sports car" in the eyes of Joe Average.

Buick stylist Ned Nickles and GM chief of design Harley Earl were apparently so sure their formula was right that they never made a full-size styling mock-up or considered any alternative shapes. Writer Michael Lamm revealed that, "This was highly irregular—perhaps even unique...the Skylark went straight from a 3/8-scale clay to blueprints and then into metal."

According to *Buick Magazine,* "We are bringing this special, ultramodern car to the market for several important reasons. First, we found that Buick's experimental sports car, the XP-300, excited tremendous public interest when it was exhibited more than a year ago. Many wanted to place orders, though the XP-300 was not for sale. We also observed that there existed in America a...demand for sports cars that was being partially satisfied by...various European automobiles. So we designed the Skylark [as] an American-built sports car. Response was immediate, positive and strong...giving Buick another significant styling first."

Maybe so, but Buick's focus was skewed. A half dozen similar limited-production "flagships" were launched at about this time—the aforementioned GM models, Packard's Caribbean, Kaiser's Dragon, and the later Chrysler 300/DeSoto Adventurer/ Plymouth Fury brigade. With only one exception—the Eldorado—none sold well enough to justify their manufacture (and Cadillac had to work hard for several years to establish the Eldorado). Detroit did not recognize then, nor did it until much later, that the motivations of, say Jaguar buyers, had nothing to do with those Detroit nurtured in its entirely different milieu.

SPECIFICATIONS

Engine: overhead valve V-8, 322 cid (4.00 × 3.20), 188 bhp

Transmission:	Twin Turbine Dynaflow
Suspension, front:	independent, coil springs, lever shocks
Suspension, rear:	live axle, coil springs, lever shocks
Brakes:	front/rear drums
Wheelbase (in.):	121.5
Weight (lbs):	4315
Top speed (mph):	105
0-60 mph (sec):	12.0
Production:	1690, plus one experimental hardtop

Buick celebrated its 50th Anniversary with a new V-8 engine and a limited-production luxury convertible, the Skylark. At $5000 even, it came with every conceivable accessory as standard. Output reached 1690 units, modest to be sure, but more than the equally luxurious Oldsmobile Fiesta and the even-pricier Cadillac Eldorado combined.

1953 Buick Super

Two great American automakers celebrated their 50th birthdays in 1953. Ford indulged in a splashy year-long party; Buick simply issued a more changed group of cars.

Long a prewar symbol of upper-middle-class affluence, Buick ran its traditional fourth in postwar industry production by continuing to offer attractive styling, smooth performance, and near-Cadillac luxury at competitive prices. The 1946-48 models, continuations of the smart all-new '42 design, were followed by all-new postwar '49s. Just a year later, the top-line Roadmaster and mid-range Super acquired a bulkier, reskinned General Motors C-body, shared with Cadillac and the senior Oldsmobiles. The low-priced Special got a new B-body for 1950—and quickly displaced the Super from its late-Forties status as Buick's best-seller.

As ever, early postwar Buicks were big, solid, and comfortable, powered by the division's reliable "valve-in-head" straight eight that by 1952 reached 320.2 cubic inches/170 horsepower for Roadmaster and 263.3 cid/124-128 bhp for Super. Division chief designer Ned Nickles had enhanced the traditional Buick look by giving the '49s front-fender "Ventiports" and rakish "sweepspear" bodyside moldings. Both were perfect complements to the make's usual toothy grille, and would be much in evidence through 1958.

Two popular postwar innovations contributed to Buick's success in this period. One was the pillarless "hardtop convertible," which Buick pioneered in mass production (along with Olds and Cadillac) with its 1949 Roadmaster Riviera. A Super version arrived for 1950 and sold better than 56,000 copies. Abetted by Special models from 1951, Buick would sell vast numbers of hardtops through decade's end.

Equally popular was Dynaflow automatic, introduced as standard for the '48 Roadmaster and made optional for other models the following year for about $200. Dynaflow multiplied torque via a drive turbine that was made to rotate through an oil bath by a crankshaft-driven power turbine. Though a smooth operator, Dynaflow did nothing for performance (leading some to call it "Dynaslush") but was immensely popular. By 1950, it was being fitted to some 85 percent of total Buick production.

At first glance, the Golden Anniversary '53s didn't seem all that, er, special, retaining the basic 1950-52 bodies for one final year. Yet these were arguably the most changed Buicks since 1949. Aside from the glamorous limited-edition Skylark convertible (covered elsewhere) and improved Twin-Turbine Dynaflow (with dual power turbines), the big attraction was Buick's first-ever V-8: a modern short-stroke, high-compression design aptly dubbed "Fireball." Sized at 322 cubic inches, it boosted the Super to 164/170 standard horsepower with manual/ Dynaflow; higher compression (8.5 versus 8.0:1) gave Roadmaster 188 bhp. Accompanying it was a new 12-volt electrical system. This year's Special retained the 263.3-cid straight eight but would get the V-8 for '54.

Though Buick was later with a postwar V-8 than most rivals, the Fireball was a fine engine: smooth, efficient, and as time would prove, extremely elastic. With successive increases in displacement, compression, and output, it would serve the division well into the '60s.

Buick's 1953 styling was recognizably evolved from 1950-52, but more impressive with a lower, wider grille; bigger front bumper guards; and a reprofiled hood/front-fender ensemble that imparted a lower look. Headlamps were newly combined with parking lights in oval nacelles, an idea lifted from the 1952 XP-300 show car that would return for '54. One surprising difference: a shortish 121.5-inch wheelbase for all models, save the smooth Super and Roadmaster Riviera sedans that remained on a 125.5-inch span. Recent Roadmasters had measured 126.3 inches between wheel centers (130.3 for the four-door Riviera).

This change should have helped the Super, and did; series volume rose more than 40 percent for '53. But Special nearly doubled its 1952 sales and Roadmaster went up almost 70 percent. Still, the Super Riviera hardtop was the second best-seller in the '53 line (after the four-door Special). Skylark aside, Super continued with the same four models as Roadmaster—Riviera sedan and hardtop, convertible, and a four-door Estate Wagon with vestigial wood structure—at prices about $500 lower model-for-model.

But Super was on the wane, ever overshadowed by the Roadmaster in prestige, the Special for value and, from 1954, the revived Century for performance. By 1958 the line was down to just two- and four-door Riviera hardtops. It then disappeared, along with Buick's other longtime series names. So in a way, the '53 was the last Buick Super that really was.

SPECIFICATIONS

Engine:	ohv V-8, 322 cid (4.00 × 3.20), 164/170 bhp
Transmission:	3-speed manual; 2-speed Dynaflow automatic optional
Suspension, front:	upper and lower A-arms, coil springs
Suspension, rear:	live axle, semi-elliptic leaf springs
Brakes:	front/rear drums
Wheelbase (in.):	121.5 **Riviera sdn** 125.5
Weight (lbs):	3845-4150
Top speed (mph):	100
0-60 mph (sec):	14.5

Production: Riviera 4d sdn 90,685 **cvt** 6701 **Riviera 2d htp** 91,298 **4d Estate wgn** 1830

Buick celebrated its 50th Anniversary in 1953 by bringing out its brand-new overhead-valve V-8 engine and revised styling that included a new grille and squared-up rear fenders. The mid-range Super series (with three "portholes" per side) listed four models, including a dashing convertible that 6701 customers found enticing at a list price of $3002.

ILL 1953
2302 648

1954
Buick Skylark

Car collectors have come to look upon the 1954 Skylark as either a retrograde effort or a purposeful downgrading of the singular, semi-custom 1953 model. Neither contention is true. The evidence is that Buick had as high a hope that the '54 Skylark would grow into a minor profit maker as did Cadillac with the '54 Eldorado. Both cars were intentionally made more conventional this year, and both saw their prices cut. GM hoped they would carve out a decent market of 5000 to 10,000 units per year in order to justify all the extra effort they had cost the two divisions. (Oldsmobile had summarily abandoned the Fiesta, after 1953.)

While Cadillac had the right kind of moneyed clientele to sustain this sort of product, Buick didn't, and the difference was soon apparent. The cheaper and more conventional Eldo now outsold Buick—by almost three to one. Result: Cadillac kept the Eldorado, while Buick gave up on the Skylark. In those years it was almost physically impossible for General Motors to make a mistake—they just didn't know how. Time soon proved that both these decisions were the right ones. Cadillac went on to carve a niche for the Eldo, which broke 5000 units in 1956 and became a separate model in 1959. Buick took aim at the Big Three, and knocked Plymouth out of its traditional third place in the 1955 model year. The plain fact was that Buick simply didn't need the Skylark after 1953.

The 1954 Skylark, now listed as a separate "Series 100," was based on the Century convertible. Although a rather smaller model, it surprisingly weighed only about 50 pounds less than its big predecessor and was only incrementally quicker. Still, it was a pleasant car to drive, a heavy and ponderous beast to be sure, but entirely manageable with full power accessories. The Dynaflow automatic hesitated—not between shifts but between the time the driver selected a new position and the time it engaged. Holding "Lo" to 35 mph consistently delivered 0-60 times in 11 or 12 seconds, very good for a big 1954 car, if a bit rough on the transmission.

In keeping with the more conventional game plan, the beltline and windshield were not lowered on the '54, but it did feature unique deep-scoop wheel wells, the cavities of which were painted red on some cars at the factory. That was an interesting styling fillip, but the effect was spoiled by the enormous tack-on tailfins inspired by the Wildcat II Motorama show car. According to stylist Ned Nickles, these chrome plated taillight housings were adopted because Harley Earl saw and liked them in a studio sketch. Automotive styling was simpler in those days....

Horsepower was up only slightly in 1954, but a significant suspension change occurred when Buick shifted to tubular front shocks in place of its long-running levers. The '54 was a more solid car, too, thanks to a beefier X-member frame. Its problem was certainly in the price—$4483 base. Although there were few options to add, it still cost 50 percent more than a standard Century convertible. And, aside from those enormous tailfins, the Skylark didn't offer much distinction for this premium. Furthermore, Buick needed the distinctive Skylark less in 1954. Its entire line had been restyled, and *Motor Trend* had judged the result the best of the year. The baseline Century won a reputation as the "hot" Buick, and at only $400 or $500 higher than a comparable model Chevy, the standard Century had undeniable appeal.

Thus the dealers shook their heads and shrank from ordering the Skylark, saying the customers just weren't there. The Buick Motor Division took the hint and dropped the posh convertible out of hand after only 836 '54s had been built. The Skylark name was shelved but not forgotten, and returned in 1961 in a way no one expected—on Buick's first "compact."

SPECIFICATIONS

Engine:	overhead valve V-8, 322 cid (4.00 × 3.20), 200 bhp
Transmission:	Twin Turbine Dynaflow
Suspension, front:	independent, coil springs, tube shocks
Suspension, rear:	live axle, coil springs, lever shocks
Brakes:	front/rear drums
Wheelbase (in.):	122.0
Weight (lbs):	4260
Top speed (mph):	105
0-60 mph (sec):	11.5
Production:	836

The Skylark created an incredible publicity bonanza for Buick in 1953, even though only 1650 copies actually left the factory. This was followed up with another Skylark, based this time on the all-new 1954 platform. It cost a towering $4483 ($962 more than a Roadmaster ragtop), and some thought the rear-end styling a bit curious. After a dismal 836 sales, Buick decided to concentrate instead on its mainline models, leaving the specialty market to Caddy's Eldorado.

BUICK

1954-58 Buick Century

Performance sold cars even in the hard-luck Thirties, especially if it was affordable. Henry Ford proved that with his immensely popular low-cost V-8 of 1932. The lesson wasn't lost on Harlow Curtice, who became Buick general manager in 1933. Perhaps taking his cue from Dearborn, Curtice okayed a hot new addition for Buick's totally revamped 1936 line: the Series 60 Century.

Named for its near 100-mph top speed, the Century was as neat a combination as peanut butter and jelly: the larger of Buick's two straight eights in a slightly stretched version of the lightweight Special chassis. The results were go-power anyone could appreciate and extra cash in Buick's bank account.

But only for a time. A more potent Special and a revived Super hurt sales of the Century after 1937, and the line was deemed expendable by the time World War II came along. The temporary suspension of civilian manufacturing gave Buick a convenient excuse to forget it, and the Century did not return when peace did.

Things were different by the early Fifties. A horsepower war was on throughout Detroit, with V-8s the weapon of choice. Buick had one ready for 1953 and all-new styling for '54, so that seemed like a good time to revive Flint's "factory hot rod." Curtice was now GM president, but still strongly interested in Buick's fortunes, and the deed was done with his enthusiastic blessing.

Though prewar Centurys were always longer and heavier than Specials, many remembered the "Special with the Roadmaster engine." The reborn Century was exactly that: the low-priced line's new 122-inch-wheelbase B-body carrying the premium series' 322-cubic-inch "Fireball" V-8. Packing 195 horsepower with manual shift or 200 with optional Dynaflow automatic, the '54 offered spectacular performance: less than 11 seconds in the 0-60 mph dash and a 110-mph top end—making this the quickest Buick ever and one of America's hottest production cars.

Century returned with just a sedan and Riviera hardtop coupe, but a convertible arrived in April to replace the slow-selling, high-priced '54 Skylark (see entry). Bowing with it was the first Century Estate Wagon, sharing new all-steel bodywork with a counterpart Special. Of course, engineering and Buick's squarish new '54 look (featuring the wrapped "Panoramic" windshield) were as for other models. Options included power steering and the Skylark's handsome 40-spoke Kelsey-Hayes chrome wire wheels.

Though late introduction held '54 output to fewer than 82,000 units, Century zoomed to near 159,000 for record-setting '55, helped by Buick's handsome line-wide facelift and 36-41 more horsepower. Offerings expanded to include a two-door sedan and new four-door Riviera hardtop, the latter an instant hit. A 0-60-mph dash now came in below 10 seconds and top speed nudged 115 mph, yet the Century could still approach 20 miles per gallon with right-foot restraint.

A less ambitious facelift marked the '56 Buicks. Volume was down throughout Detroit, but Century regained its runner-up spot in division sales—nearly 20,000 above Super at about 102,000. Improved "Variable-Pitch" Dynaflow returned from '55, but Century two- and four-door sedans didn't. Horsepower was up again, to a thrilling 255. A dual-exhaust "Power Kit" with chrome extensions was newly optional, though it didn't change rated output.

Retaining their existing wheelbases, the '57 Buicks were rebodied on a new X-member "Contour" chassis, looking longer, lower, and heavier—which they were. Styling was quite conservative, but not performance. An enlarged 364-cid Fireball with 10.0:1 compression provided 300 bhp for all but Specials. Despite its added bulk, the '57 was the fastest Century yet—0-60 mph took only about nine seconds—but it swilled premium gas at the rate of 15 mpg or less. The four-door sedan was reinstated, the wagon shorn of B-posts and retitled Caballero (see separate entry).

Alas, quality and engineering woes were catching up with Buick. Total division sales slumped 30 percent from '56, but Century's plunged by nearer 40 percent. Aggravated by a deep national recession, the hulkier, overchromed "B-58" Buicks fared even worse, Century falling to less than 38,000 units. Adding insult to injury, the '58 was not only slower (11.2 seconds 0-60), but thirstier (less than 10 mpg "economy" in town).

It was thus just as well that Flint retired its familiar series names for 1959. The Century name would again return in the Seventies and Eighties, but on Buicks that have been nothing like the smooth and speedy mid-Fifties models—great American cars one and all.

The 1954-58 Century was a "banker's hot rod" by Buick. Based on the Special's lighter body but using the Roadmaster's more powerful V-8, it sported three "portholes" in 1954, four in 1955 (top row) *and 1956* (bottom). *It also sported four for '57, but discarded them for 1958.*

SPECIFICATIONS

Engines: ohv V-8 **1954-56** 322 cid (4.00 × 3.20) **1954** 195/200 bhp **1955** 236 bhp **1956** 255 bhp **1957-58** 364 cid (4.13 × 3.40), 300 bhp

Transmissions:	3-speed manual; 2-speed Dynaflow automatic
Suspension, front:	upper and lower A-arms, coil springs
Suspension, rear:	live axle, semi-elliptic leaf springs
Brakes:	front/rear drums
Wheelbase (in.):	122.0
Weight (lbs):	**1954-55** 3805-3975 **1956** 3890-4080 **1957** 4081-4423 **1958** 4241-4498
Top speed:	110-115
0-60 (sec):	9.0-11.5

Production: **1954 4d sdn** 31,919 **cvt** 2790 **Riviera 2d htp** 45,710 **4d Estate Wagon** 1563 **1955 4d sdn** 13,269 **Riviera 4d htp** 55,088 **cvt** 5588 **Riviera 2d htp** 80,338 **2d sdn** 270 **4d Estate Wagon** 4243 **1956 Riviera 4d htp** 20,891 **Riviera Deluxe 4d htp** 35,082 **cvt** 4721 **Riviera 2d htp** 33,334 **4d Estate Wagon** 8160 **1957 4d sdn** 8075 **Riviera 4d htp** 26,589 **cvt** 4085 **Riviera 2d htp** 17,029 **2d sdn** 2 **Caballero 4d htp wgn** 10,186 **1958 4d sdn** 7241 **Riviera 4d htp** 15,171 **cvt** 2588 **Riviera 2d htp** 8100 **2d sdn** 2 **Caballero 4d htp wgn** 4456

Buick
1955

1957-58 Buick Caballero/Special Riviera Estate

The all-steel station wagon and the pillarless hardtop were the two major body innovations of the early postwar years. Both found a ready market—hardtops enormously so—though for different reasons. Steel wagons were nowhere near the hassle their structural-wood predecessors had been, demanding much less upkeep and proving far more resistant to squeaks, rattles, and loosening-up with age. Bereft of B-posts, hardtops offered the sort of style and airiness associated with convertibles, plus sedan-like safety and weather protection—a well-nigh irresistible combination.

It was thus only a matter of time before these two influential ideas were combined in one car, and it didn't take long. General Motors, which pioneered mass-production "hardtop-convertibles" in 1949, showed the way with its new Chevrolet Nomad and Pontiac Safari for 1955 (see entries). Though both had B-posts, they were the sleekest wagons ever: two-door models with thin C- and D-pillars and vast expanses of side glass wrapped around to one-piece tailgates with drop-down windows.

But it was tiny American Motors that offered the first true hardtop wagon: the four-door Rambler Custom Cross Country of 1956. It was a logical follow-up to the 1955 arrival of pillarless hardtop sedans—another GM innovation—though AMC had already planned the Cross-Country as well as Rambler four-door hardtops.

Other makes fielded hardtop sedans for '56—most everyone, in fact, save Lincoln, struggling Studebaker-Packard, and Nash/Hudson at AMC. A few followed AMC by venturing into pillarless wagons for '57, among them Oldsmobile and Mercury—and Buick. Buick, of course, was no stranger to hardtops. It had shared honors with Olds and Cadillac for the first series-production pillarless coupes of 1949, with Olds for the first four-door hardtops of mid-1955. In the process, Buick helped start the period practice of special names for hardtop models, which produced such romantic appellations as Victoria (Ford), Bel Air (Chevrolet), Catalina (Pontiac), Belvedere (Plymouth), Starliner (Studebaker), and of course the original trio of Holiday (Olds), Coupe de Ville (Cadillac), and Buick's own Riviera.

Flint weighed in with two hardtop haulers for '57. One was the inevitable Riviera Estate Wagon, a $3167 entry in the low-priced Special series and all but identical with a pillared counterpart costing $120 less. The other debuted as the colorfully named Century Caballero, much the same thing save a $3706 price tag, four instead of three front-fender "portholes" (as used on Centurys since '55), and a more potent version of the division's newly enlarged 364-cubic-inch V-8 with 300 instead of 250 horsepower. On all three, the rear half of the roof bore longitudinal indentations, inspired by stylist Carl Renner's crosswise ribbing on the Nomad/Safari, and an aft superstructure with a slightly curved liftgate window mated to a graceful hardtop-style main greenhouse.

Though pleasantly breezy and as practical as any wagon, the Caballero and Riviera Estate suffered the usual hardtop handicap of noisy air leaks with the side windows up—reflecting the relatively greater flexibility and poorer weather-sealing of pillarless bodies—and Buick's growing reputation at the time for poor brakes and indifferent workmanship. Neither model was much help in a year when Buick fell from third to fourth in the industry on volume that fell to half of what it had been in banner '55. Of course, wagons have never sold as well as closed models with trunks, but these Buicks were harder to move than most. The Riviera Estate attracted only 6817 buyers, versus 23,000-plus for its pillared sister. Perhaps because of its better performance, the Caballero saw 10,186 built—still nothing to rave about.

Output fell even further for '58: just 3420 and 4456 respectively. The reason wasn't so much their faults as either hardtops or wagons as the "Air Born B-58 Buicks" in general—as wrong for that recession year as any medium-price car. Not that it mattered, because the public quickly tired of hardtop wagons—which only makes Chrysler's belated early-'60s models seem all the more curious. Buick bailed out after '58 as new managers began bringing General Motors to its senses—and more sensible cars.

Despite higher production, the Caballero has greater collector appeal than the pillarless Special because it's a Century, though like all wagons it's less desired than a convertible or hardtop. Still, these Buicks are worth seeking out as a nostalgic reminder of a time when Detroit thought it could get away with almost anything.

Buick received a tasteful, if somewhat heavy-handed, restyling for 1957. Although the fins on Chrysler products were the "in" thing, Buick had a lot going for it, too, including a four-door hardtop station wagon (a body style introduced by Rambler the year before). Although available as a Special, the more powerful Century Caballero (seen here) proved more popular.

SPECIFICATIONS

Engine: ohv V-8, 364 cid (4.13 × 3.40) **Special** 250 bhp **Century** 300 bhp

Transmissions:	3-speed manual; 2-speed Dynaflow automatic
Suspension, front:	upper and lower A-arms, coil springs
Suspension, rear:	live axle, semi-elliptic leaf springs
Brakes:	front/rear drums
Wheelbase (in.):	122.0
Weight (lbs):	**Caballero** 4423 **Special Riviera** 4309
Top speed (mph):	100-110
0-60 mph (sec):	10.0-10.5

Production: Century Caballero 4d htp wgn 10,186 **Special Riviera Estate Wagon** 6817

1958 Buick Limited

Everyone remembers the Edsel as the Great Mistake of 1958, but established medium-price brands faltered too, none more than Buick. Having ousted Plymouth as Detroit's number-three producer for 1955-56, Buick dropped to its usual fourth for '57 on a third less volume. This despite a major restyle and its broadest-ever postwar model lineup. Then, in 1958, Flint stumbled again, and came limping in fifth.

Of course, a sudden, sharp national recession made 1958 difficult for most every make save Rambler, but Buick had additional problems. Despite several attempts at improving it, the division's Dynaflow automatic still couldn't hold a candle to Hydra-Matic for efficiency or performance, and Buick brakes had gained a reputation as some of the industry's worst. Quality wasn't what it had been. Neither was styling. Where the newly rebodied '57s had been merely flashy, the '58s were, as division chief Ed Ragsdale accurately proclaimed, "dazzling." Bill Mitchell, who succeeded Harley Earl as GM design chief in '58, later admitted that company stylists in this period slathered on chrome "with a trowel"—doubtless because management had come to equate more brightwork with more sales. But considering the handsome 1954-57 Buicks, the '58 came as a garish shock—even for its day—matched only by an equally glittery Oldsmobile.

The new top-of-the-line Limited series symbolized Buick's troubles in 1958. It replaced the previous year's Roadmaster 75 and revived a name that Buick hadn't used since 1942. Like its prewar forebear, this new "Super Buick" took aim at the heart of the luxury market. Conceived in the salad days of 1954-55 when the medium-price field was booming, its growth potential seemed...well, unlimited. Writer Dick Reddy described the Limited as "Buick's answer to the USS Forrestal, measuring eight inches longer than the king-size Roadmaster for a total of 227.1 inches. Wheelbase is 127.5 inches, same as the Roadmaster's, and the extra length has been made up by stretching out the rear overhang until the car almost needs a tail-wheel like an airplane. 'Limited' owners should be good potential buyers of Cadillacs as little, second cars!"

Indeed, despite a two-inch shorter wheelbase, Buick's new biggie measured about that much longer than Cadillac's new-for-1958 extended-deck Series Sixty-Two hardtop sedan. More expensive too—$5112 for the Riviera four-door hardtop versus $5079—and almost as heavy. (Limited also came as a convertible and Riviera hardtop coupe).

Brightwork covered both cars liberally, to put it kindly, but Buick took a more heavy-handed approach. Smiling broadly below heavily lidded new quad headlamps rode a "Fashion-Aire Dynastar" grille composed of no fewer than 160 little chrome squares. Each had four facets for maximum sparkle, a long-favored Earl technique carried to extremes. Equally gaudy were the bomb-like parking-light housings, massive chrome stone shields on the lower rear fenders, a huge back bumper with suggestive bullet outriggers, and the 15 hashmarks (in three groups of five) on each Limited rear flank. With all this and the traditional bodyside sweepspears, no one probably even noticed the absence of Buick's trademark portholes.

Testers quickly noticed the extra weight of the '58s, which made them somewhat slower—no surprise as they used an unchanged version of the 364-cubic-inch V-8 from 1957. Buick spent some $86 million to improve its Dynaflow automatic, adding yet another drive turbine to produce a new "Flight-Pitch" transmission (called Triple-Turbine from '59). But it didn't much help performance or fuel efficiency. One writer reported "extreme slippage somewhere between the engine and the rear wheels" of his test Super, and 11.3-mpg "economy" on the highway. In-town mileage sank to 8.5 mpg. The heavyweight Limited drank even more heavily.

Like other GM divisions, Buick peddled an optional air suspension system in 1958. Flint called its version "Air-Poise," but it was the basic GM system that substituted air bladders (pressurized by a trunk-mounted compressor) for conventional coil springs at each corner. Some testers thought Air-Poise really did improve cornering, and pulling an under-dash lever lifted the car 5.5 inches for clearing road hazards or changing a tire—a nifty feature. But like other air-ride setups, Buick's proved a monumental service headache and soon went the way of other Fifties gimmicks.

The Limited saw only limited production, and so Buick dropped it after that one brief year. The problem wasn't so much the vastly reduced market of recession '58 as the fact that a Limited cost more than a "real" luxury car, yet wore an upper-middle-class nameplate. Its 1959 successor, the Electra 225, sold far better, helped by more attractive styling, more realistic upper-middle-class prices, and an improving economy. Buick has since revived the Limited name for its top-line models. Most have been far more rational than the '58, which remains an instructive artifact of a time when Detroit too often got too carried away with itself.

Buick moved into Cadillac territory in 1958 with the Limited, but few seemed interested in paying Cadillac money for a Buick. Sales were thus predictably limited. The $5125 ragtop, for example, saw only 839 units sold.

SPECIFICATIONS

Engine:	ohv V-8, 364 cid (4.13 × 3.40), 300 bhp
Transmission:	Flight-Pitch Dynaflow automatic
Suspension, front:	upper and lower A-arms, coil springs; air suspension optional
Suspension, rear:	live axle, coil springs; air suspension optional
Brakes:	front/rear drums
Wheelbase (in.):	127.5
Weight (lbs):	4603-4710
Top speed (mph):	110
0-60 mph (sec):	9.5
Production:	**Riviera 4d htp** 5571 **Riviera 2d htp** 1026 **cvt** 839

58 LTD
AMERICA

58 LTD

1959 Buick Electra

One thing about the '59 Buick—it was different. From slanted quad headlamps to huge canted fins, it was Flint's most flamboyant car ever, a complete break with Buick's styling past. Seldom had a make changed character so dramatically or abruptly. Compared to the chrome-encrusted "B-58s," the '59s looked like something from tomorrow—and more tasteful at that. "Buicks so new even the names had to be new," blared the brochures. And for once they were right.

Model year 1959 marked the third time in as many years that General Motors completely redesigned its corporate fleet—impossible for any U.S. automaker today, even GM. This extravagance had less to do with Detroit's longtime devotion to the annual model change than with GM's desire to lower production costs by reducing the number of unique components among its five divisions. Management thus decreed closer body sharing beginning with the '59s. As former Chevy stylist Clare MacKichan explained to author Pat Chappell: "The idea was to make the outer surfaces different so that nobody would know [that the bodyshells] were shared, but the things underneath that cost the major amount of money would be shared." The upshot of this decision was that GM had to junk its all-new 1958 Chevy/Pontiac A-body and the new-for-1957 B- and C-bodies used by Buick, Olds, and Cadillac.

But the change did usher in a new corporate look that in Buick's case was definitely for the better. Its main elements were rounded lower body contours, long rear decks and thin-section rooflines with glass areas so vast as to give new meaning to the design term "greenhouse." Buick wore this styling better than any other '59 GM car save Pontiac, avoiding Cadillac's vulgarity and the downright oddities of this year's "bat-wing" Chevy. In contrast, Buick's canted fins made a clean sweep from the windshield to the tip of the rear. Aside from the Buick name, about the only holdover from '58 was the grille, still composed of tiny bright squares, though there were fewer of them.

To emphasize how new its '59s really were, Buick rearranged and renamed its lineup. The low-end Special became the LeSabre, riding a 123-inch wheelbase shared with the mid-range Invicta, which carried the Century's mantle as "the most spirited Buick." Replacing the old Super was the 126.3-inch-wheelbase Electra, offering a sedan and a pair of hardtops. An extended-deck companion named for its overall length, the Electra 225, took over for Roadmaster and the 1958-only Limited. It offered a convertible and, like Cadillac, hardtop sedans with different rooflines: a flat-top model with a vast wraparound backlight, and a six-window Riviera with a curved rear superstructure. Both Electras cost $800-$1000 less than comparable '58s, ranging from $3856 for the pillared four-door to $4300 for either 225 hardtop sedan.

The '59 Buicks also boasted a lot of new engineering. The '57-vintage X-member chassis gave way to a K-braced frame with boxed side rails, and finned brake drums were adopted across the board, with aluminum used for the fronts. Yet another rework of Buick's hoary Dynaflow automatic had produced "Flight-Pitch" or Triple-Turbine Drive as a 1958 optional alternative to the familiar Twin-Turbine unit. Both returned for '59, mated to a still-larger Buick V-8 in Electra/Invicta, this time stretched to 401 cubic inches and 325 horsepower. LeSabre used the 364-cid version introduced for '57, still rated at 250 bhp. Left unimproved was 1958's new Air Poise suspension, a trouble-prone $188 option that found few takers among '59 buyers.

Being new and different was generally a sales asset in the '50s. Yet for all their changes, Buick found only mixed success with its '59s. The division built 42,000 more cars than it had for recession-wracked 1958 but slipped from fifth to seventh in industry production. It had been third as recently as 1956.

Still, these Buicks—especially the long and lush "Deuce and a Quarter"—are at last garnering collector attention. That doesn't necessarily make them great American cars, except maybe for those who like to be...different.

The 1958 Buick turned out to be a sales disaster. The recession that year was partly to blame, but so was the styling. The '59 model was all-new and, like some of its other GM stablemates, sported some of the wildest fins Detroit would ever see. Buick's were canted, as were the headlights, and shot rearward from just aft of the windshield. The top-of-the-line Electra 225 series included a convertible listing at $4192; only 5493 were built for the model year.

SPECIFICATIONS

Engine:	ohv V-8, 401 cid (4.19 × 3.64), 325 bhp
Transmission:	Twin-Turbine/Triple-Turbine Dynaflow automatic
Suspension, front:	upper and lower A-arms, coil springs
Suspension, rear:	live axle, coil springs
Brakes:	front/rear drums
Wheelbase (in.):	126.3
Weight (lbs):	4465-4562
Top speed (mph):	110-115
0-60 mph (sec):	11.0

Production: Electra 4d sdn 12,357 **2d htp** 11,216 **4d htp** 20,612 **Electra 225 Riviera 4d htp (6-window)** 6324 **4d htp (4-window)** 10,491 **cvt** 5493

YRP 884

YRP 884

1950-52 Cadillac

Sometime during the 1940s, Cadillac replaced Packard as the leading American luxury car. Some say the transformation had begun during the Depression, when manufacturers were forced to produce middle-priced volume models. Packard built the One Twenty, but still called it a Packard; Cadillac called its lifesaver a LaSalle, and thus did not tarnish its image.

Another theory has it that Packard really abdicated its luxury role *after* the war, when its volume-besotted management opted to continue producing middle-priced cars of the Olds-Mercury class, while Cadillac quickly reverted to total luxury. This point of view has merit: one of Packard's first new models after the war was a station wagon; Cadillac's, the Coupe de Ville.

At any rate, by 1950 the "Standard of the World" had also become the Standard of America. The new, tailfinned styling, ushered in during 1948 and based on inspiration of prewar aircraft, at once made Cadillac distinctive and recognizable—from the rear as well as the front. The fine new overhead valve V-8 engine of 1949 completed a mechanical transformation, and the development of the Coupe de Ville gave Cadillac one of the first hardtop convertibles, a model so popular that Chuck Berry sang a song about it: "Maybelline."

Chuck caught Maybelline at the top of the hill, but Packard never caught Cadillac, and neither did Lincoln, nor Chrysler Imperial, nor indeed all three combined. By 1952, Cadillac's share of the luxury market was an all-dominating 80 percent. In 1950 and '51 Cadillac built an astonishing 100,000 units annually, unprecedented for it or any other luxury marque. It would have done so again in 1952, but the Korean conflict caused production allocations which favored the independents, so "only" 90,000 Caddys were produced.

The lineup was impressive, starting with the elongated series Seventy-Five limousines and seven-passenger sedans, and chassis for the commercial body trade;

the elegant, long-wheelbase Sixty Special with its "body by Fleetwood"; the best-selling line of Sixty-Two sedans, hardtops, and convertibles. Through 1951 there had also been a cheaper range of Sixty-One four-door sedans and club coupes, but these garnered decreasing sales and were deemed expendable by 1952.

The basic styling theme conjured up by Harley Earl, Bill Mitchell, and Art Ross for 1948 was generally left alone in the early Fifties. The fabled "dollar grin" announced a ponderous, round, chrome-swathed land yacht, while the unique sharkfin taillights gave definition to the rear. For 1950 they'd come up with a dummy scoop at the leading edge of the rear fender, which became a long-running Cadillac hallmark. The '50 models retained trisected rear windows; the '51s were identified by small auxiliary grilles under the headlamps; the '52s had a winged badge in that spot.

Despite all its chrome and weight and roundy-round looks, this period piece should not be regarded as a wallowing pig. The relatively light Sixty-Two could clock 0-60 mph times in the 12-second range, and much better performance could be had by careful tuning. It hardly seems possible, but a 1950 Cadillac driven by Sam and Miles Collier finished tenth overall at the world's greatest road race, Le Mans—a performance never matched by any other luxury make. Briggs Cunningham also raced a streamlined Cadillac special that year, which was even faster than the Collier brothers' stock car, but he lost top gear and slid in the corners, finishing only 11th.

Granted, these were specially prepared Cadillacs, but even off the floor the cars were serious performers. A light-weight Sixty-One, which you could still get with a stickshift in 1950, could pace a Jaguar XK-120 to 90 mph and the only thing quicker in those days was probably the Olds 88.

The secret to Cadillac's success was to concentrate on a relative handful of models, and to build those cars extremely well and of the finest materials. In 1952 there were only seven different body styles in the entire Cadillac line, and two of these were limited production Seventy-Fives. The big gun was always the Sixty-Two four-door sedan, which usually sold around 50,000 units per year all by itself. But 15,000 to 18,000 Sixty Specials were sold annually in this period, and Cadillac regularly produced over 6000 convertibles. Nobody ever caught this company manufacturing station wagons.

SPECIFICATIONS

Engine: overhead valve V-8, 331 cid (3.80 × 3.63) **1950-51** 160 bhp **1952** 190 bhp

Transmission:	Hydra-Matic
Suspension, front:	independent, coil springs, tube shocks
Suspension, rear:	live axle, leaf springs, tube shocks
Brakes:	front/rear drums
Wheelbase (in.):	**Sixty-One** 122.0 **Sixty-Two** 126.0 **Sixty Special** 130.0 **Seventy-Five** 146.8
Weight (lbs):	3800-4600
Top speed (mph):	100-110
0-60 mph (sec):	11.0-14.0
Production:	**1950** 103,857 **1951** 110,340 **1952** 90,259

By 1950, Cadillac had pretty well established its number one position in the luxury-car field. And for good reason—it boasted more modern styling than the competition and it had an up-to-the-minute overhead-valve V-8. Not only that, Cadillac had introduced the hardtop Coupe de Ville the year previous. At $2761, the 1950 Series Sixty-One coupe seen here was a bargain.

1953 Cadillac Eldorado

In its first year, it looked like a mistake. Priced at a truly monumental figure, Cadillac's Eldorado barely saw 500 copies. But within a few years the Eldo had established itself as the ultimate, most desirable, *ne plus ultra* Cadillac. It quickly became the car of stars and politicians, the one machine everybody from Marilyn Monroe to Dwight Eisenhower wanted to be seen in, and usually was.

All this came as the result of deft product planning and management by a heads-up company which spent a lot of time measuring what the American public wanted—a question not always easy to answer. When Cadillac saw this megabuck ragtop ($7750 when a Chevy started at $1524) lay an egg in 1953, it revised the recipe, cut the price by 50 percent, and scored several thousand sales the following year. In 1956, the Eldorados (a hardtop had by then joined the convertible) broke the 5000-unit mark, and from that point on their future was secure.

On arrival it was one of many. Everybody, it seemed, had jumped into the "flagship" business. At GM, along with the Riviera and Fiesta, Chevrolet had run off the first Corvette. Ford was planning both the 1955 Thunderbird and the '56 Continental Mark II. Chrysler was getting ready to produce the limited-production Chrysler 300, DeSoto Adventurer, Plymouth Fury, and Dodge D-500. Kaiser debuted the Dragon, Hudson was readying the Italia, Nash offered its Nash-Healey sports car, Packard its Caribbean.

Why and how, then, did the Eldorado emerge as absolute ruler of this glittering company? First because it was a Cadillac—by the mid-Fifties the bluest of automotive blue chips, the car every red-blooded American aspired to own. Second, because its makers, as already observed, knew exactly what they were doing.

Like the Buick Skylark and Oldsmobile Fiesta, the '53 Eldorado was a "production show car," with notable Motorama features which more mundane GM products would display in future years. It boasted the most powerful V-8 yet developed by Cadillac, plus a host of special features: a leather-cowled instrument panel (later with vinyl) that become a Caddy trademark, wraparound windshield (ubiquitous by 1956), wire wheels (which everybody wanted but few could afford), an ultra-low beltline, and a soft top that vanished beneath a metal boot painted the body color. Tops came in black or white Orlon; body colors shined in Aztec Red, Azure Blue, Alpine White, or Artisan Ochre; interiors were color-keyed to match.

All the "standard extras" and *grand luxe* trim bits meant the final product weighed some 300 pounds more than the standard Sixty-Two convertible, making the Eldorado the slowest Caddy in the line, save for the long-wheelbase commercial cars. This is relative, however: with an advertised 210 horsepower there was plenty of off-the-line power, and the Eldo driver could cruise at any feasible speed up to 100 mph.

The Eldorado's nearest rivals in 1953 were the Buick Skylark and Packard Caribbean, both of which outsold it handily, but were eclipsed the following year. The Caribbean's problems are easily explained: Its parent company was in deep trouble, and it had only conjured up the Caribbean as a hasty effort to add some allure to a mundane, aging body style. Indeed, the Caribbean wasn't even built on a senior Packard chassis, and its straight-eight powerplant had fallen out of fashion.

The Riviera ostensibly posed a more serious threat, despite its intra-mural status—but that's exactly why Cadillac didn't have to worry about it. "I had the definite understanding that one of the reasons Buick dropped the Skylark after 1954 was a corporate desire to give the 'flagship' business to the Eldorado," a longtime Cadillac executive explained. Whether or not this is completely accurate, there is no doubt that Buick took aim at other game after 1954, leaving the super-car field to Cadillac.

So the fabulous Eldo lived on, gained its famous shark fins in 1955, blossomed into the Continental-rivaling Eldorado Brougham in 1957, and switched to front-drive in 1967. Today it is impossible to think of the Cadillac line without one. But the pioneering was all done back in 1953.

The Cadillac Eldorado bowed in 1953. It was intended as a limited production model, and at $7750 it was (the regular Series Sixty-Two ragtop sold for $4144). Features included Cadillac's most powerful V-8 yet, leather-covered instrument panel, wraparound windshield, wire wheels, an ultra-low beltline, and a flush metal boot to hide the convertible top.

SPECIFICATIONS

Engine: overhead valve V-8, 331 cid (3.81 × 3.63), 210 bhp

Transmission:	Dual-Range Hydra-Matic
Suspension, front:	independent, coil springs, tube shocks
Suspension, rear:	live axle, leaf springs, tube shocks
Brakes:	front/rear drums
Wheelbase (in.):	126.0
Weight (lbs):	4800
Top speed (mph):	100+
0-60 mph (sec):	13.0-14.0
Production:	532

CALIFORNIA
MY53LDO

1954
Cadillac Eldorado

To the uninitiated, the '54 may seem like the forgotten Eldorado. Packing much less exclusivity than its predecessor, and selling in not-that-much-greater quantities, it appears to fall into a hole between the all-out-luxury 1953 original and the wild, sharkfinned '55. Neither are there many of them left in the field; probably for similar reasons, people did not cling to the '54s quite as tightly as they did the '53s and subsequent Eldorados.

To Cadillac fanciers, it's a different story. The '54 Eldorado was an historic car—the model that guaranteed Cadillac's long-running premium series a permanent place in the lineup. The low production figures are of course a point in its favor, as far as present day enthusiasts are concerned. Besides all that, it stood as a very attractive car in its own right, combining the flair of the line-wide restyle of 1954 with many special features exclusive to the Eldorado. (As in 1953, it still fell within the Sixty-Two model series.) Today, a 1954 Eldorado in prime condition carries a very high premium indeed, and one price guide—optimistically, perhaps—shows it worth even more than the vaunted '53 model.

The market game plan of down-pricing the Eldorado worked much better for Cadillac than it did for Buick's Skylark—perhaps because the price cut was much more significant. While the Skylark dropped $500 for 1954, the Eldorado saw its price slashed by $2000. This altered their relative sales positions: while the Skylark recorded only 836 units, the Eldorado notched 2150. At a base price of $5738, the Eldo still cost a colossal amount of money (the standard Sixty-Two soft top listed at only $4400)—but not much more than the original '53 Skylark, and it had the measureless advantage of the Cadillac name.

What was left to distinguish it from run of the mill Cadillacs? The most obvious feature was a broad, ribbed panel of bright metal along the lower rear fender, flowing backward from the dummy airscoop in the leading fender edge, and the characteristic metal boot (instead of the conventional fabric) to cover the top when folded. There was also a full leather interior and chrome plated wire wheels. What had disappeared was the chopped windshield and beltline of 1953, whose deletion was largely behind the drastic cut in price.

The Eldorado was testimony to the longer-lower school of design, three inches longer in wheelbase, eight inches longer overall (though no wider). It received the expected horsepower boost, going from 210 the year before to 230. The increase stemmed mainly from improved intake manifolding and slightly increased valve lift, with appropriate changes to timing. But as more than one tester pointed out, there was no improvement in torque or compression ratio, and at the rear wheels the '54 registered 122 horsepower, against 120 for the '53.

A more genuine improvement came in handling: All '54 Cadillacs had a redesigned, wider-track frame that took some of the mush out of the handling. The frame had more extensive bracing, sturdier engine-steering-suspension mounts, and channel-section side rails to reinforce the "X" member. To this was added new angled telescopic shock absorbers. "It's not easy to break loose the rear wheels, even considering the '54's lower center of gravity (which does away with much of the heel-over common to past Cadillacs without making the car hard-riding or too prone to broadsliding)," wrote *Motor Trend,* whose editors rated the 1954 Cadillacs among the best handling American cars.

Cadillac Division celebrated an extremely good year in 1954 by producing 123,746 cars—a new record for any January-December period. The cars themselves were good ones, but were beginning to exhibit unaccustomed quality problems that would multiply later. They became notorious for allowing gas fumes into the passenger compartment (through a hard-to-seat gas filler cap); there were uneven gaps around the doors, and too much plastic in the dashboard area. Eldorados were less prone to such problems, since a great deal more time was spent producing them. Though not priced quite as high as the Seventy-Fives, Eldo was the unchallenged top of the Cadillac line, and certainly the classiest in the fleet that year.

The 1954 Cadillac Eldorado sold for $5738, $2000 less than the '53 model, and was more closely related to the regular production Cadillacs. Nonetheless, it could be quickly told by the ribbed bright metal panel on the lower rear quarters, the metal boot, leather interior, and chrome wire wheels. There was no finer way to travel—or to impress the neighbors—in '54.

SPECIFICATIONS

Engine: overhead valve V-8, 331.0 cid (3.81 × 3.63), 230 bhp

Transmission:	Hydra-Matic
Suspension, front:	independent, coil springs, tube shocks
Suspension, rear:	live axle, leaf springs, tube shocks
Brakes:	front/rear drums
Wheelbase (in.):	129.0
Weight (lbs):	4815
Top speed (mph):	115
0-60 mph (sec):	11.0
Production:	2150

BAB 087

HILLS BROS
COFFEE

1955-56 Cadillac Eldorado

Watching General Motors in the Fifties, evolving a long shot like the Eldorado into a profitable part of the Cadillac lineup was like observing a piano virtuoso playing a difficult piece with faultless precision. That incidentally is a reminder of how often the same company has missed the mark lately. This is not so much another GM bashing as a statement of honest truth. The General had the confidence born of a generation's dominance of the industry in those days; in present times things are not so simple, the right decisions not so obvious.

The Eldorado game plan unfolded like a well planned military campaign. In 1953 came the original, stalwartly priced spin-off, a Motorama show car in every respect save the fact that anyone with a lot of money could buy one. In 1954, with the name established, the Eldo was dropped $2000 in price, tripling its sales and commensurately widening its recognition. In 1955 Cadillac gave it the unique sharkfin tail end, and in 1956 they added a two-door hardtop to the formula.

The fins, of course, pre-date Chrysler Corporation's by two years, though Chrysler is still considered to have touched off the tailfin craze—probably because the Eldorado was such a limited production model. Here was Cadillac's first departure from the aircraft-inspired tail end that had prevailed since 1948. Taillights were now carried in little round pods underneath the fins, flanked inboard by similar back-up lamps.

On the body sides, the '55 parted company with 1954's broad, bright metal rear fender appliqué, but flashed something new that caught the public's imagination: "Sabre Spoke" wheel covers instead of the previous genuine wire wheels. Though Sabre Spokes cost plenty, they were still a lot cheaper than wires. Eldorados also had a bright metal appliqué along the beltline under the windows, and a new rear wheel treatment: fully arched wheel openings with skirts omitted.

SPECIFICATIONS

Engines: overhead valve V-8, **1955** 331 cid (3.81 × 3.63), 270 bhp **1956** 365 cid (4.00 × 3.63), 305 bhp

Transmission:	Hydra-Matic
Suspension, front:	independent, coil springs, tube shocks
Suspension, rear:	live axle, leaf springs, tube shocks
Brakes:	front/rear drums
Wheelbase (in.):	129.0
Weight (lbs):	**Seville** 4665 **Convertibles** 4850
Top speed (mph):	120.0
0-60 mph (sec):	10.0

Production: **1955** 3950 **1956 Biarritz** 2150 **1956 Seville** 3900

Another Eldorado feature established in 1955 was mechanical: higher-than-normal performance from the big-block V-8, still unchanged from its 1949 dimensions. While conventional Cadillacs had 250 bhp, Eldorados had twin Carter or Rochester four-barrel carbs that helped churn out 270 horses. Likewise in 1956, when Cadillac bored the engine out to 365 cubic inches, the Eldorado developed its 20 extra horsepower, now 305. This translated to a small improvement in acceleration compared to standard Cadillacs, but didn't make any apparent difference in top speed.

Production nearly doubled for the 1955 model year, and shot up another 50 percent in 1956—the year the Eldo finally broke the 5000 mark and the first time it offered a hardtop, which bore the now-familiar name "Seville." Not surprisingly, the closed model actually outsold the traditional convertible by nearly two to one.

Curiously, DeSoto had also named its lower-priced Firedome two- and four-door hardtops Seville, a neat tie-in between the Spanish explorer after which the car was named and the well-known Spanish town. Nonetheless, after a little hasty consultation DeSoto abandoned the name for 1957. Cadillac kept Seville through 1960, dropped it, and then brought it back again in 1975 for a new "international size" four-door sedan. When Cadillac had an Eldorado Seville in the line, it called the convertible counter-part Biarritz.

In 1956, another component of the Eldorado marketing plan clicked into place: once established and desirable, up went the price! Even in those inflationless times, Eldorado prices were galloping. The '55 convertible ($6300) listed at $500 more than the '54; in 1956 it rose another $300—and the new Seville hardtop came in at exactly the same figure even though it obviously cost less to build than a ragtop.

It is instructive to compare this canny marketing of what had started as a limited-volume publicity stunt with that of less successful automakers. Ford Motor Company had nothing like the Eldorado. Chrysler, while it did field the 300 in 1955, aimed at a different buyer—the 300 was fast, but rode like a truck and appealed to a very selective customer, as did the '56 DeSoto Adventurer, Dodge D-500, and Plymouth Fury. Packard never considered the Caribbean more than a toy, and none of the other independents had anything close. The Eldorado was both unique— and uniquely successful.

The quickest way to tell the 1955-56 Eldorado was by the sharp pointed fins and "Sabre Spoke" wheel covers. The '56 model (this page) *sported a finer-mesh grille than the '55* (opposite). *The latter sold for $6286, the '56 for $6556—big money back in the mid-Fifties.*

1957-58 Cadillac Eldorado

Cadillac's flagship went through hard times in the late Fifties, but so did just about every other Detroit glamor boat—along with the industry as a whole. The recession of 1958 conveniently arrived around the same time that Volkswagen got its dealer network and vehicle supply problems sorted out, and these two factors came together like a nuclear reaction. Overnight the bottom dropped out of the traditional, middle-priced American car market. Among 1958 Detroiters, only Rambler bettered its sales.

Cadillac, in its more stable and secure luxury market sector, appeared to suffer less from this rapid change in buying preferences: sales were down, but not a lot by Caddy's relatively low volume standards. But the Eldorados—Biarritz convertible and Seville hardtop—fell off by heavy margins, especially in '58. Perhaps the problem arose because they didn't seem as special as they had been earlier. Although each retained its tailfinned individuality, both were upstaged by the *grand luxe* Eldorado Brougham. Also, Eldo prices had taken another big jump upward to $7286 in 1957 and $7500 in '58, really serious money back then.

Remaining technically within the Sixty-Two series, the Eldorados shared that model's 129.5-inch wheelbase. The sharkfins and Sabre Spoke wheels were their chief distinguishing characteristics, although students of detail noticed they also lacked hood ornaments. A feature revived from the '54 model was the broad bright metal appliqué on the lower rear fenders; as in the past, Eldorados wore fully, or almost fully, exposed wheels.

Aside from the Biarritz/Seville, incidentally, Cadillac records indicate the production of four model 6239S Seville four-door hardtops, nominally priced at the same $7286

The 1957 Cadillac was redesigned, and along with it the '57 Eldorado. The rear-end styling of these models was unique—and striking. The '57 Biarritz (opposite) *came in at $7286 (as did the hardtop), while the '58 model* (this page) *listed at an even $7500. These Cadillacs weighed two and a half tons, but a 325-horsepower V-8 (310 bhp in 1958) assured good performance—and terrible gas mileage.*

that fetched a convertible. But these appear to be special models built either for show purposes or trial marketing. Of the seriously produced models, sales dropped off by 50 percent—nothing compared to where they'd be after 1958.

Really, it seems that Eldorado sales varied directly with the amount of visual difference each model had from the rest of the Cadillac line. In 1955-56 the difference had been blatant and obvious, and sales were huge. In 1957 it was less apparent, and sales plunged; in 1958, when all Cadillacs adopted the sharkfin tails of Eldorados past, Eldo sales almost disappeared. True, the Biarritz and Seville looked entirely unique at the rear: tapered, rounded, and sprouting distinctively tall fins. But up front they wore the same chromey smile of the other Caddys—and after all, a dealer could sell Sabre Spoke wheels to the buyer of a plain Sixty-Two model. The leather and chrome-swathed interiors did not of themselves render this package so desirable.

Another factor in the slowdown may have been mechanical, since the '58 Eldorado was the first in several years that didn't pack at least a token bit of extra horsepower. A less intriguing trade-off for the sudsy engine was air suspension, a little-ordered option that gave some ride/handling benefits, at least when it worked. In practice the air bags were prone to leaks, and one can only imagine the feelings of the Eldorado's wealthy owner upon arriving in the garage to find the family pride collapsed on its flat suspension like a dead Citroën.

None of which means these cars have been written off by collectors—quite the contrary, as they were the last really "custom styled" Eldorados for some time. Both Seville and Biarritz are now recognized as Milestone cars, which has enhanced their collectibility. The convertibles, of course, are fast ascending the price scale at auctions, in the wake of the astonishing increases in bids for 1959 ragtops.

Mechanically, the 365 was a very good engine indeed, far more reliable than the 390 which would follow; the cars too seem better hung together than later models, and those that have eluded the dreaded tinworm remain in remarkably good original condition. Massive, smooth, and powerful, they are at their best in highway cruising, which they will do all day at 100 mph in exchange for large doses of premium fuel.

SPECIFICATIONS

Engine: overhead valve V-8, 365 cid (4.00 × 3.63), **1957** 300 bhp **1958** 310 bhp

Transmission:	Hydra-Matic
Suspension, front:	independent, coil springs, tube shocks **1958** central compressor and accumulator, self-leveling with air bags optional
Suspension, rear:	live axle, coil springs, tube shocks **1958** central compressor and accumulator optional, self-leveling, with four-link rear suspension and air bags
Brakes:	front/rear drums
Wheelbase (in.):	129.5
Weight (lbs):	4700-4850
Top speed (mph):	115-120
0-60 mph (sec):	11.0-12.0

Production: **Biarritz 1957** 1800 **1958** 815 **Seville 1957** 2100 **1958** 855 (four Seville four-door hardtops built experimentally in 1957)

1957-58 Cadillac Eldorado Brougham

It has been said and endlessly repeated that there would never have been an Eldorado Brougham had there not been a Mark II Continental. Everybody believes this, even though it's probably wrong. Limited production showroom traffic builders were not new to the industry by 1957—and certainly not new to Cadillac. Superficial comparisons often fail to comprehend the three-year gestation period that attends most new Detroit models. In fact, the Brougham first began to take shape in 1955, before the Mark II had been announced (though there were rumors of it). At any rate, the two cars were vastly different. The Mark II coupe bespoke elegance and understatement, cost the buyer $10,000 and Ford a grand on every sale. The Eldorado Brougham sedan was blatant, overstated, mid-Fifties chrome-luxe; it cost $13,000, and Cadillac lost ten grand on every sale.

If they had anything in common it was that final fact: both were conceived at least initially as publicity makers, not profit earners. On the other hand, nobody expected them to lay such colossal eggs, either. Business being business, neither car—however interesting—could survive as a money loser. In the Brougham's case, the original recipe ran only two years, was then farmed out to be built by Pinin Farina in Italy, and disappeared forever after 1960.

But what a car it was! Consider what Uncle Harley, Duke of Earl, offered the moneyed buyers of the 704 Broughams built: Motorama-style brushed stainless steel roof with matching panel on lower rear fenders; full power everything including door locks and trunklid; dual heating system with independent controls front and rear; a glove box packed with magnetized silver tumblers, cigarette and tissue dispensers, lipstick and Arpegé cologne in a special atomizer; 45 choices of interior colors and trims, including Karakul or lambskin carpeting; the industry's first production quad

The 1957-58 Eldorado Brougham was Cadillac's response to the ultra-expensive 1956-57 Continental Mark II. At $13,074, it outpriced the Mark by some $3000, and sold in even tinier numbers. But it served nobly as Cadillac's flagship, letting the world know that Cadillac was still "The Standard of the World," and had every intention of remaining so.

headlamps (a distinction shared with Nash, who made hardly more '57s than Cadillac made Broughams); standard air suspension; full pillarless hardtop styling with center-closing doors (there was not even the stub of a "B" pillar showing with both doors open). All this for only $13,000? Remarkable...

And remarkable it has remained. Today the 1957-58 Eldorado Brougham is the most desirable closed Cadillac of the postwar era, maybe of any era, its price (when you can find one) gamey and high-pitched, vying with the fortunes paid for similar-period Cadillac convertibles. A Brougham Owners Club has done yeoman service for owners (magnetized silver tumblers don't grow on trees or even at swap meets), and people just seem to love the Eldorado Brougham, whoever they are.

As the late Michael Sedgwick told an admiring audience of Milestone Car Society members: "Those of you who worship these rare motorcars today did not have to put up with them when they were new." The Brougham's air suspension, though unique (four rubber domes replacing the springs; air chambers fed by a small motor regulated by three levelers to maintain constant body height), was unreliable to the point of embarrassment, leaving one down (literally) at every possible opportunity, thereby causing many Broughams to be converted by dealers to conventional coil spring suspensions. Baubles like Arpegé atomizers and cigarette dispensers tended to disappear rapidly and were impossible to replace. When trade-in time came, owners found the Brougham had depreciated almost out of sight; 1961 average loan value, for example, was only $2540. The folks who bought them when the market was at such rock-bottom levels are the ones who can chuckle—and they don't have to drive them every day.

History will say that in the end the Cadillac Eldorado Brougham was a striking example of over-engineering and under-development. But despite its faults it was a fabulous automobile, the kind of all-out statement the industry is either afraid of or can't afford to make anymore. Since the 1949 Cadillacs with their revolutionary new V-8, there had not been such total change in one Cadillac product. If the product proved a failure, it also gave the Eldorado name a reputation for advanced engineering as well as unique styling. This reputation would continue into the Sixties, when Cadillac produced another landmark, the first front-wheel-drive Eldorado.

SPECIFICATIONS

Engine: overhead valve V-8, 365 cid (4.00 × 3.63), **1957** 300 bhp **1958** 310 bhp

Transmission:	Hydra-Matic
Suspension, front:	independent self-leveling with air bags
Suspension, rear:	four-link self-leveling with central compressor and air bag units
Brakes:	front/rear drums
Wheelbase (in.):	129.0
Weight (lbs):	5315
Top speed (mph):	115
0-60 mph (sec):	12.0
Production:	**1957** 400 **1958** 304

1959 Cadillac

Superficial thinkers constantly describe the strident tailfins of the unforgettable 1959 Cadillac as a "reply to Chrysler." True, at least on the basis of much else that was good from the hand of Virgil Exner, combined with a period of malaise at the GM styling staff in the final years of Harley Earl, for Chrysler stole design leadership from GM in 1957.

The problem is, of course, that the '59 Cadillac took shape in 1956, when Exner was himself only beginning to reveal tacked-on tailfins with the '56 Chrysler cars, which had perforce been designed (in private) in 1953. Furthermore, Cadillac itself had started the whole business back in 1948 with a sensational restyle, just one of whose interesting components had been the tailfin (inspired by a viewing of a then-secret Lockheed fighter by Cadillac stylists...in 1941).

Cadillac, goes the story, saw how ridiculous it had all become and hastily trimmed its tailfins in 1960, cut them further in later years, until they disappeared altogether by mid-decade. But again, the three-year design lead time intervenes, and we realize that Cadillac cut its '60 model's fins back in 1957—with Chrysler at its finny peak. Obviously, other factors besides a GM-Chrysler styling war were at work here.

One Cadillac stylist willing to talk about the period (and they are not all willing to talk) said that "by 1957 we felt the fins had gone about as far as they could go, so we began to evolve a less ostentatious shape. Then, the following year, Mr. Earl retired and Bill Mitchell took over—and we threw everything we were doing out the window." (Enter the crisp, extruded look evident by 1961, in full force by 1963, replacing the rounded, torpedo shapes beloved by Harley Earl.)

So much of the stuff written about this heroically proportioned Caddy is rubbish. It matters little, anyway. What is significant about the '59 Cadillac is its position as an artifact, an exemplar of its times: the last years of unabashed optimism and confidence in American institutions and ingenuity. It matters even less that as Cadillacs go, the 1959 model wasn't a particularly good one. It's all in those tailfins. Today, 1959 Cadillac convertibles painted "resale red" command upwards of $50,000 at car auctions, while tailfinned Buick Electra convertibles, to take one example, cost a third as much. Doesn't make sense. If it's fins you want, the Electra's run nose-to-tail.

The 390 V-8 was a reasonably good engine, but there were other problems that made the '59s mechanically deficient. Front ends were notorious for vibration and chatter—one report from the service department itself was entitled something like "Rattles, Shakes, Sonic Booms and Things That Go Bump in the Night." Another problem was rust, '59s being more susceptible than any Cadillac to date. And of course there were still air bag suspensions, though in diminishing quantity. Finally, the quality of fit and finish was mediocre, and even the materials not up to traditional standards. "There was a lot of printed aluminum trim that just looks tacky," says one Cadillac collector.

Cadillac had a new market orientation this year. The old standard Sixty-Two series was accompanied for the first time since 1951 by a mate: the de Ville series. Unlike the old Sixty-One, however, the de Ville was an up-market model, and it soon began to outsell the Sixty-Two. A curiosity, too, was the '59 Sixty Special, no longer mounted on a slightly longer wheelbase. Still, Cadillac sold its traditional 12,000 copies, so perhaps what people liked was not the car's length but its "Fleetwood" name on the trunk. There was also the usual Seventy-Five nine-passenger sedan and limousine on the 149.8-inch wheelbase, and a three-model Eldorado lineup consisting of Seville, Biarritz, and Brougham. (The Eldo regained its performance edge with a 20-bhp boost over standard output.)

Cadillac was on a roll in those years, racking up big production, closing on a 150,000-car annual average, finishing as high as 10th in the annual production race. In retrospect, the '59 couldn't have been all that bad. But there were many better years, so in the end what distinguishes the '59 must be those tailfins. There was nothing else quite like them, in 1959 or any other year.

Back in 1959, the spectacularly finned Cadillac was considered garish by many observers. Some still think that, but it is this very quality that makes the car so desirable to collectors from all over the globe today. The convertible is the model most in demand, of course, but the supply is strictly limited, and asking prices are soaring. Back in 1959, a Series Sixty-Two ragtop (as pictured) cost $5455, and 11,130 were built. How many are left now?

SPECIFICATIONS

Engine: overhead valve V-8, 390 cid (4.00 × 3.88), 325 bhp **Eldorado** 345 bhp

Transmission:	Hydra-Matic
Suspension, front:	independent, coil springs, tube shocks; air suspension optional
Suspension, rear:	live axle, coil springs, tube shocks; air suspension optional
Brakes:	front/rear drums
Wheelbase (in.):	130.0 **Seventy-Five** 149.8
Weight (lbs):	4690-5570
Top speed (mph):	120
0-60 mph (sec):	11.5

Production: **Sixty-Two** 70,736 **de Ville** 53,390 **Eldorado** 2,394 **Sixty Special** 12,250 **Seventy-Five** 1,400 **Chassis** 2,102

DOY 534

1959-60 Cadillac Eldorado Brougham

Not all 1959 Cadillacs wore towering tailfins, but you needed $13,075 to avoid them. That was the price of the new, Italian-built Eldorado Brougham, manufactured by Pinin Farina in Torino as a sort of rear-guard action while the Brougham was being quietly laid to rest. Production was infinitesimal.

Unlike the 1957-58 variety, these Broughams look quite conventional—until you realize that what they most resemble are the later Sixties Cadillacs, not the '59. Though it shared the same 130-inch wheelbase with other Cadillacs, the Brougham was obviously different. Even the roofline varied, crisp and formal, rather than rounded at the rear and without the severely wrapped windshield and dog-leg "A" post of the standard models. All this was a statement of things to come from a more conservative Cadillac in the Sixties. (Another way to tell one at a glance: these Broughams lack the horizontal divider bar in the grille, which has an all-of-a-piece look.)

At such low production there were few changes in the second model year. The Pinin Farina badge was apparently removed, and hubcaps were changed slightly. Cloissoné emblems were used on the rear of the back fenders, and there was a low creaseline in the body sides. Both the 1959 and '60 Eldorado Brougham featured narrow-band whitewall tires, exclusive to this model at the time.

Like their predecessors, the Broughams were delivered as standard with air suspension. Also like the earlier cars, many had it replaced with conventional all-coil

Cadillac gave up on the 1957-58 Eldorado Brougham after only 704 units, then turned to Pinin Farina in Italy to build the 1959-60 edition. The Farina car, avoiding the towering fins of 1959, sported modest blades, more akin to those on the '61 Cadillac to come. The roofline and windshield also predicted the '61. With a price as high as the fins on the other '59s, demand was small: 99 units for 1959, 100 for 1960. But the Brougham nonetheless helped maintain Cadillac's image as "The Standard of the World."

springs. Italian Broughams were also subject to corrosion. The Italians liked to use a lot of body filler, and rust was a serious hazard. A problem for today's collectors is the Brougham-only body sheetmetal, replacement pieces being almost impossible to find, let alone buy.

Cadillac would not build so expensive a car until the late 1970s, and certainly never again with the kind of individual custom construction of the Eldorado Brougham. Frankly, it was not in the Cadillac mold, or what would come to be the pattern for the 1960s and '70s. *Volume* was now the name of the game, and every Cadillac had to sustain a given volume level to stay in the line.

One could see in this new Cadillac philosophy the roots of disaster. Today the division searches, thus far in vain, for its lost heritage, having been replaced in the hearts of the wealthy by Jaguar, Mercedes, and BMW. The one-time "Standard of the World" awoke in the middle Seventies to find itself relegated to the ranks of the ordinary, the mundane. Was it because Cadillac stopped turning out the kind of all-out luxury machine the Eldorado Brougham had been—while Mercedes-Benz won fame with its "Grosser 600," BMW with its 6 and 7 series, Jaguar with its V-12s?

It would be simplistic to say this abandonment of the top percentile of the luxury car market alone cost Cadillac its reputation. There were other factors, especially quality problems, which have to be considered. But there is no doubt that Cadillac began its long downhill slide around the time the Eldorado Brougham disappeared.

Mercedes-Benz, after all, has generally built a lot more cars than Cadillac, and a good number of them are plebian taxicabs. It is not, therefore, simply high volume and production of conventional machinery that costs a luxury car points in its competitive market. It has been observed that Packard maintained its reputation for some years after building the One Twenty by continuing also to produce custom-bodied Twelves and Super Eights—but when Packard stopped building such singular models after the war, it lost its fabled reputation.

Perhaps that's what happened to Cadillac, and why the division is hoping so hard that cars like the new Allanté will return it to the pinnacle. But reputations take years to build up. They can be lost in a matter of months.

SPECIFICATIONS

Engine: overhead valve V-8, 390 cid (4.00 × 3.88), 345 bhp

Transmission:	Hydra-Matic
Suspension, front:	independent self-leveling with air units
Suspension, rear:	four-link self-leveling with central compressor
Brakes:	front/rear drums
Wheelbase (in.):	130.0
Weight (lbs):	5200
Top speed (mph):	120
0-60 mph (sec):	10.5
Production:	**1959** 99 **1960** 101

1950-52 Chevrolet

The 1950-52 Chevrolets evolved from the all-new '49, part of the first all-postwar General Motors fleet launched with the 1948 Cadillac and Oldsmobile. Except for a heavy 1953 restyle, Chevy's basic '49 design would see few major changes until the equally new, but far more exciting, '55 came along (see entry).

Chevy emphasized styling for 1949, mechanicals being largely unchanged from 1946-48. The division's venerable "Stovebolt Six," last enlarged to 216.5 cubic inches for 1938, returned with the 90 horsepower it had delivered since '41. As ever, it mated to a three-speed manual transmission with column shift. Also retained was a ladder-type chassis with independent coil-spring front suspension and a live rear axle on semi-elliptic leaf springs—old stuff for Chevy but big news on the completely redesigned '49 Ford. Despite this dull familiarity, the '49s handled better than previous Chevys because their sleek new bodywork conferred a lower center of gravity, aided by fractional reductions in wheelbase (cut an inch to 115), overall length, and weight.

After three years of mostly rehashed prewar cars, buyers craved new styling in '49, and Chevy had some of the best: smoother and obviously lower than the 1946-48 models—and longer-looking despite the trimmer dimensions. It's generally accepted that elements of GM's first postwar designs owed much to the Lockheed P-38 "Lightning" pursuit aircraft, which had fascinated styling chief Harley Earl and some of his staffers ever since they got a sneak peek at it just before America entered the war. Yet, this influence seemed far less evident on Chevy than other '49 GM cars, except possibly for the prominent "pontoon" rear fenders and a larger, slightly curved windshield.

Model offerings came in for a revamping for the first time since 1942. The low-end Stylemaster series was retitled Special and the upper-range Fleetmaster became the DeLuxe. Each offered a pair of fastback sedans, still called Fleetline, plus a notchback sport coupe and sedans with two or four doors, all named Styleline. A business coupe was exclusive to Styleline Special; Chevy's convertible and a four-door wagon came only in Styleline DeLuxe trim. The wagon was initially a true "woody," though its structural body timber was now confined to the rear corners. Mid-model year brought an all-steel replacement with pseudo-wood trim but near-identical looks and the same $2267 price. At $1413, the Special business coupe was Chevy's most affordable '49.

With record production of 1.01 million, the '49 became the most popular Chevy ever, but Ford topped the model year totals by a mere 8300 units on the strength of its more competitive new design and traditional V-8 advantage—and a longer model year. For 1950, however, Chevy reclaimed the top spot and wouldn't again surrender it to Ford until 1957—and not by much.

Though both rivals wore only the mildest of facelifts for 1950, Chevy regained the production lead partly by introducing two innovations a full year ahead of Ford, both of them instant hits. One was the first low-priced "hardtop-convertible," the smart Styleline DeLuxe Bel Air (see separate entry). The other was optional two-speed Powerglide, the first fully automatic transmission among the "Low-Price Three." To compensate for power losses to the new transmission's torque converter, Chevy teamed Powerglide with a modified version of the 235.5-cid "Stovebolt" from its truck line, with slightly higher compression and 105 bhp. The smaller six was bumped up 2 bhp that year. Production jumped to nearly 1.5 million as Chevy bested Ford by over a quarter-million cars.

Much the same story unfolded for '51, when Chevy and Ford matched heavier facelifts on their '49 platforms. Longer and higher rear fenders, revised trim, and a reshaped grille identified an unchanged lineup of Chevys. The following year brought a squarish new Ford that was slightly larger but looked smaller. Chevy countered by mounting "teeth" on its grille crossbar and thinning out the Fleetline fastbacks, which hadn't been selling that well, to a single DeLuxe two-door. Restrictions stemming from the Korean conflict limited 1952 production throughout Detroit, but Chevy remained "USA-1," leading Ford by a still-substantial 146,500 units—remarkable for a four-year old design against a brand-new one.

In retrospect, the '49 Chevy and its 1950-52 evolutions reaffirmed the make's prewar tradition of stylish, dependable family transportation, while hinting that more exciting Chevys were on the way. They were, but the early-'50s models have deservedly attracted their own enthusiastic followers as the last of a noble breed: the solid, practical Chevy—as faithful as a best friend.

After introducing the Bel Air hardtop and Powerglide for 1950, Chevy stood pat for a while. The 1950 lineup included the $1529 Styleline DeLuxe Sport Sedan (above)*, that year's best-seller. The soft top* (opposite, top)*, in the same series, cost $1847 and saw 32,810 built. The '52 DeLuxe Fleetline fastback* (bottom) *was in its last year.*

SPECIFICATIONS

Engines: ohv I-6, 216.5-cid (3.50 × 3.75), 92 bhp, (manual shift); 235.5 cid (3.56 × 3.94), 105 bhp (Powerglide)

Transmission:	3-speed manual **Deluxe** 2-speed Powerglide automatic optional
Suspension, front:	upper and lower A-arms, coil springs
Suspension, rear:	live axle, semi-elliptic leaf springs
Brakes:	front/rear drums
Wheelbase (in.):	115.0
Weight (lbs):	3025-3475
Top speed (mph):	85
0-60 mph (sec):	16.0

Production: 1950 Styleline Special 2d Town Sedan 89,897 **4d Sport Sedan** 55,644 **business cpe** 20,984 **sport cpe** 28,328 **Fleetline Special 2d sdn** 43,682 **4d sdn** 23,277 **Styleline DeLuxe 2d Town Sedan** 248,567 **4d Sport Sedan** 316,412 **4d wgn** 166,995 **sport cpe** 81,536 **cvt** 32,810 **Bel Air 2d htp** 75,662 **Fleetline DeLuxe 2d sdn** 189,509 **4d sdn** 124,287 **1951 Styleline Special 2d Town Sedan** 75,566 **4d Sport Sedan** 63,718 **business cpe** 17,020 **sport cpe** 18,981 **Fleetline Special 2d sdn** 6441 **4d sdn** 3364 **Styleline DeLuxe 2d Town Sedan** 262,933 **4d Sport Sedan** 380,270 **4d wgn** 23,586 **sport cpe** 64,976 **cvt** 20,172 **Bel Air 2d htp** 103,356 **Fleetline DeLuxe 2d sdn** 131,910 **4d sdn** 57,693 **1952 Styleline Special 2d Town Sedan** 54,781 **4d Sport Sedan** 35,460 **business cpe** 10,359 **sport cpe** 8906 **Styleline DeLuxe 2d Town Sedan** 215,417 **4d Sport Sedan** 319,736 **4d wgn** 12,756 **sport cpe** 36,954 **cvt** 11,975 **Bel Air 2d htp** 74,634 **Fleetline DeLuxe 2d sdn** 37,164

3490

1950-52 Chevrolet Bel Air

Business tends to approach new ideas with a mixture of hope and skepticism. Depending on public response, an innovative product or feature can mean either high sales, busy factories, and windfall profits—or big losses, employee cutbacks, and damaged reputations.

Car companies are no less cautious, but General Motors no doubt felt quite sanguine about its new "hardtop-convertibles" of 1949. Soft-top cars had traditionally been a pain in the rain—and winter—and the advent of better roads and higher speeds made open-air driving increasingly less practical after World War II. This suggested that the public might go for a sedan without B-posts but with windows that still rolled down completely—a hybrid style providing convertible airiness when opened up, closed-car comfort and weather protection when buttoned up, and the safety of a fixed steel roof all the time.

It seemed like a fine idea—so much so that others thought of it besides GM. Most recently, in 1946, Chrysler had built seven prototype hardtops by grafting steel club-coupe roofs onto Town & Country convertibles, but decided not to proceed with series production right away. This left GM to pioneer the concept in anything approaching significant volume, though Kaiser spun off an interesting variation the

SPECIFICATIONS

Engines: ohv I-6, 216.5-cid (3.50 × 3.75), 92 bhp (manual shift); 235.5 cid (3.56 × 3.94), 105 bhp (Powerglide)

Transmission:	3-speed manual **Deluxe** 2-speed automatic optional
Suspension, front:	upper and lower A-arms, coil springs
Suspension, rear:	live axle, semi-elliptic leaf springs
Brakes:	front/rear drums
Wheelbase (in.)	115.0
Weight (lbs):	3215
Top speed (mph):	85
0-60 mph (sec):	16.0
Production:	**1950** 76,662 **1951** 103,356 **1952** 74,634

Chevy was the first low-priced make to bring out a hardtop, the swanky trimmed 1950 Bel Air (both pages). It was part of the top-of-the-line Styleline DeLuxe series and sold for $1741, just $106 less than the convertible. Buyers loved it, snapping up 76,662 copies the first year, many of them equipped with the newly available Powerglide automatic transmission.

same year with its Virginian "Hard Top," basically that firm's convertible sedan with its curious little fixed, glass-filled B-posts, to which a canvas-covered steel top was welded.

Detroit automakers typically introduce new ideas on lower-volume models to minimize the risk of lost design, tooling, and marketing funds should the innovation bomb. Thus, GM tested the hardtop waters with senior Buick, Cadillac, and Oldsmobile models. Though mid-year introductions and highish prices kept 1949 sales modest—respectively, 4343 Roadmaster Rivieras, 2150 Series Sixty-Two Coupe de Villes, and 3006 Futuramic 98 Holidays—they were sufficient to encourage the company to proceed with the lower-priced, higher-volume junior versions planned for 1950.

These duly arrived as the Chevrolet Styleline DeLuxe Bel Air, Oldsmobile Futuramic 88 DeLuxe Holiday, Buick Super Riviera, and no fewer than four Pontiac Chieftain Catalinas. Bel Air proved to be the most popular by far, scoring 74,634 sales to help Chevy regain supremacy over Ford as "USA-1." It probably helped more than that figure suggests, since many prospects undoubtedly came in to see the Bel Air but drove out in other Chevys. Rival Ford and Plymouth hardtops were a full year away.

Outside, the Bel Air looked much like any other 1950 Chevy, which meant the basic new-for-'49 styling with a different winged hood emblem, vertical bars below the parking lamps, no "teeth" below the grille's center crossbar, raised taillight lens,

The modestly facelifted '51 Chevy received a new grille, squared-up rear fenders, and revised side trim. The '52 seen here added five "teeth" to the grille and extra chrome trim over the rear wheels. Skirts were a popular extra on the Bel Air, which continued with its deluxe interior. After a run of 103,356 Bel Airs for 1951, output slipped to 74,634 for '52, but this was a result of government forced production cutbacks resulting from U.S. involvement in the Korean conflict. After 1952, the Bel Air would expand into a multi-model series listing four body styles.

and other minor changes. Its roofline followed the Riviera/Holiday/Coupe de Ville style in having chrome-framed side windows and a wraparound backlight with a pair of bright vertical dividers near the outboard ends. The interior treatment was similar, too, and lusher than on other Chevys. Handsome pile-cord fabric surrounded by genuine leather covered the seats, and the headliner sported chrome crossbars suggesting the top mechanism of a true ragtop. Convertible-type frame reinforcements helped make up for the loss in structural rigidity from the missing B-pillars, but some body flex remained, a characteristic of most every hardtop ever built. Mechanicals were stock 1950 Chevy (see entry), but that year's new Powerglide automatic surely lifted sales as much as the Bel Air's fresh, sporty looks.

Priced in the $1750-$2000 range, about halfway between its convertible and sport coupe linemates, the Bel Air changed in parallel with other Chevys while racking up over 103,000 sales for 1951, and close to 75,000 for '52. This success prompted Chevy to apply the Bel Air name to its convertible and top-line sedans for 1953, an arrangement that would persist through 1958. Then came the Impala and, in the mid-Sixties, the even more-luxurious Caprice, which pushed Bel Air down the series hierarchy until it disappeared in the early Seventies, by which time it had become merely the baseline four-door sedan.

But it's the early Bel Airs that Chevy fans remember most today, especially the pioneering 1950-52 models with their jaunty looks and spiffy interiors. And who can blame them? Few cars, let alone trend-setters, have been more pleasant.

1953-54 Chevrolet Bel Air

In the Fifties, you made an old car look new without changing its basic structure by applying different outer panels, a process designers call "reskinning." Nobody did this better at the time than General Motors, and the 1953 Chevrolet proved it.

Swift managerial changes in the late Forties had ushered in Thomas H. Keating as Chevrolet general manager, brimming with confidence about the future and filled with expansive plans for it. By 1952, the division was hard at work on an all-new V-8 for an equally new group of 1955 passenger cars. Meantime, they faced the problem of how to extend the sales life of the basic 1949 platform, then looking pretty long in the tooth. Reskinning was the obvious answer.

The result appeared for 1953 as the most changed Chevy in five years. Singer Dinah Shore, Chevy's TV pitchperson in those days, introduced it as "a glamorous new star," paused while the camera cut to a close up, then gushingly asked: "Isn't that about the prettiest thing you ever saw?"

We tend to laugh at this commercial now, but the '53 Chevy *did* look pretty good in its day. Stylist Carl Renner dressed up the old bodies with fresh sheetmetal below the belt, one-piece windshields (replacing twin-panes), and a prominent oval grille whose three vertical "teeth" provided a familial resemblance to the forthcoming Corvette sports car. Rear ends on hardtops and sedans gained a bulkier, more "important" look, and introduced bodyside two-toning on Bel Air rear fenders. Artful die changes also reshaped rear side-window openings.

Model-wise, the sole remaining Fleetline fastback sedan disappeared, and the lineup was reordered. At the bottom came the low-price One-Fifty, replacing the previous Special; DeLuxe gave way to the mid-range Two-Ten. This year's top-of-the-line series took the Bel Air name from Chevy's 1950-52 hardtop coupe (see entry), which now became a Sport Coupe with two sedans and a convertible as running mates. Lower-series offerings comprised sedans, pillared club coupe, and Handyman wagon, plus One-Fifty business coupe and Two-Ten Townsman wagon, convertible, and Sport Coupe.

Bel Air became a four-model top-line Chevy series for 1953, the costliest being the $2175 convertible (this page)*. It saw 24,047 units built. Bel Air picked up a fifth model for 1954, a Townsman wagon, but the $1884 four-door sedan* (opposite) *was easily the most popular with 248,750 built. Bel Air output that year nudged a half-million units.*

SPECIFICATIONS

Engines: ohv I-6, 235.5 cid (3.56 × 3.94) **1953** 105/115 bhp (manual/Powerglide) **1954** 115/125 (manual/Powerglide)

Transmissions:	3-speed manual; 2-speed Powerglide optional
Suspension, front:	upper and lower A-arms, coil springs
Suspension, rear:	live axle, semi-elliptic leaf springs
Brakes:	front/rear drums
Wheelbase (in.):	115.0
Weight (lbs):	3230-3540
Top speed (mph):	90
0-60 mph (sec):	15.0

Production: **1953 2d sdn** 144,401 **4d sdn** 247,284 **cvt** 24,047 **Sport Coupe 2d htp** 99,028 **1954 2d sdn** 143,573 **4d sdn** 248,570 **Townsman 4d wgn** 8156 **cvt** 19,383 **Sport Coupe 2d htp** 66,378

On the mechanical side, Chevy scrapped its smaller "Stovebolt" six and adopted the 235.5-cubic-inch Powerglide unit for all models. Higher compression boosted it to 105 horsepower with stickshift or 115 with Powerglide. The latter version received aluminum pistons (replacing cast iron) and insert-type rod bearings plus a more modern, pressurized lubrication system. Manual-transmission engines would get these changes for '54, when the six was retitled "Blue Flame." All this reflected the presence of new chief engineer Edward N. Cole, who'd arrived from Cadillac in May 1952 after working on that division's milestone 1949 V-8.

The '53 Chevy arrived none too soon. Ford, determined to regain sales supremacy, launched an all-out production "blitz" that year as the industry shifted back into high gear with the end of the Korean hostilities. Forced to sell cars they hadn't ordered, Ford dealers resorted to heavy discounting. Chevy had no choice but to follow, and the race was on, though Chrysler Corporation and the independents ended up the losers.

For 1954, Ford again facelifted its new-for-'52 bodies, but stole a march on Chevy with a new 239-cid overhead-valve V-8 and ball-joint front suspension. Chevy replied with more chrome, a wider grille with more teeth, new taillights, brighter colors, new interior trims, and a fortified six running 115 horses with stickshift (same as that year's 223-cid Ford six), or 125 with Powerglide (versus the Ford V-8's 130). The One-Fifty business coupe was renamed Utility sedan, while a spiffy two-door sedan called Delray replaced the Two-Ten convertible and hardtop. Finally, the Two-Ten Townsman was upgraded into a Bel Air, bringing the series up to five separate models. New options, most often installed on Bel Airs, included power brakes ($38) and power front seat and front door windows ($86 for either).

Despite Ford's hard press, Chevy had added just enough pizzazz in 1953 and '54 to remain "USA-1", producing nearly 1.35 million cars for '53 (about 100,000 more than Ford) and 1.166 million for '54 (about 20,000 ahead). The Two-Ten emerged as the volume leader in both years, but the Bel Air finished a creditable second, rare for a flagship line even in those heady days. It also indicated that buyers were ready for more upmarket Chevys with colorful "living room" interiors; chromier, two-tone exteriors; and ever more convenience options. Indeed, the 1953-54 Chevy pointed toward the future more than anyone probably realized at the time.

As collector cars, the 1955-57 Chevys will probably always overshadow the 1953-54 models, but the latter—especially the Bel Airs—are being discovered by enthusiasts as very pleasant cars with significance as the last of the low-suds "pre-classic" Chevys, an important transition in the make's history. That's reason enough to include them here—that and the bow-tie badge they wear.

1953-55 Chevrolet Corvette

Dream cars made big news in '50s Detroit, but only General Motors built some you could actually buy. Take 1953, when a quartet of sporty convertibles from the traveling Motorama show went on sale. Three of them—Buick Skylark, Cadillac Eldorado, and Oldsmobile Fiesta—were big and flashy. But the fourth bowed as a trim two-seat roadster with a body made of that new wonder material, fiberglass. It was, of course, the Chevrolet Corvette.

Its genesis is well known. In late fall of 1951, Harley Earl, GM's legendary design chief, began sketching ideas for a simple, two-seat sporty car priced to sell at around $1850, about what a Chevy sedan cost then. Within a year he'd convinced company brass that his idea merited a full-blown, super-secret development program. Perhaps to confuse the press, it was dubbed "Project Opel," after GM's German subsidiary.

To hold down cost, veteran Chevy engineer Maurice Olley, with an assist from Bob McLean, cut down a standard Chevrolet passenger-car chassis to a 102-inch wheelbase, identical with that of the XK-120 (one of Earl's favorites). Next, Olley coaxed 150 horsepower from Chevy's aged "Blue Flame Six" via triple carburetors, higher compression, solid (versus hydraulic) valve lifters, and high-lift camshaft. Chevy didn't have a manual transmission that could handle this power, so two-speed Powerglide automatic was used instead. Despite all the parts borrowing, the eventual production Corvette had its own X-member frame with box-section side rails, outboard-mounted rear leaf springs for better cornering stability, Hotchkiss instead of torque-tube drive, and an engine set 13 inches further back than in other Chevys, for better weight distribution and thus handling.

It also looked considerably different, which was the Corvette's main mission: to reverse Chevy's image as a builder of mundane people-movers. By the time of the 1953 Motorama, in January at New York's Waldorf-Astoria Hotel, Earl had penned a sleek, rounded body with a toothy grille, mesh stone guards over inset headlamps,

The '53 Corvette (this page) *bowed with a fiberglass body mounted on a cut-down, 102-inch-wheelbase passenger-car chassis and a hopped-up 150-bhp Chevy six. It was built in Flint, Michigan. The '55* (opposite) *boasted a 265-cid, 195-bhp V-8 and was built in St. Louis.*

a trendy wrapped windshield, and thrusting "jet-pod" tail lamps. A soft top folded out of sight beneath a solid lift-up panel, while European-style side curtains replaced roll-up windows.

That Motorama Corvette generated lots of interest, not least because it looked like a production prototype. It was, and Chevy Division general manager Thomas H. Keating duly announced that it would be built, albeit in limited numbers, though this may have been planned all along. Regardless, the show car was little altered for production, which began June 30, 1953 on a small auxiliary line at Chevy's Flint, Michigan plant. Fiberglass was retained for its lower cost and greater manufacturing flexibility compared to steel bodywork, though the decision came quite late.

Alas, this dream-car-come-true quickly turned into something of a nightmare for Chevy. Assembly-line problems with the complex body (no fewer than 46 separate pieces) and lack of plant capacity kept 1953 production to just 315 Corvettes. Yet you couldn't really buy one because they were earmarked for VIPs and dealer promotion. Purists, meantime, chided the "plastic" body, tepid six-cylinder performance, and gimmicky styling, while practical types disliked the side curtains, small trunk, and two-passenger seating.

Without changing it much, Chevy made the Corvette more readily available for 1954, transferring production to larger facilities in St. Louis. But though 10 times '53 volume, 1954 output reached less than a third of the projected total, leaving Chevy with some 1500 unsold cars at year's end. The Corvette might have died right there had it not been for pleas by Earl and Edward N. Cole, who'd arrived from Cadillac in 1952 to become Chevy chief engineer.

And Cole had what would prove to be the Corvette's salvation: the brilliant overhead-valve V-8 he'd developed for Chevy's all-new 1955 passenger cars. It gave the Corvette almost 30 percent more horsepower, yet weighed 30 pounds less than the old six. Even better was a new three-speed manual transmission for 1955, plus some adroit chassis tuning by recently hired Belgian-born engineer Zora Arkus-Duntov. The result was a much faster, more exciting, and more roadable Corvette. For all that, and a price cut from $3513 to $2799, only 674 of the '55s were built.

Better things were coming, but the 1953-55 Corvette is still revered as the progenitor of America's first truly successful sports car. That, and as a happy accident for which we can all be grateful.

SPECIFICATIONS

Engines: **1953-55** ohv I-6, 235.5 cid (3.56 × 3.94), 150 bhp **1955** ohv V-8, 265 cid (3.75 × 3.00), 195 bhp

Transmissions:	**1953-55** 2-speed Powerglide automatic **1955** 3-speed manual
Suspension, front:	unequal-length A-arms, coil springs, anti-roll bar
Suspension, rear:	live axle, semi-elliptic leaf springs
Brakes:	front/rear drums
Wheelbase (in.):	102.0
Weight (lbs):	2840-2850
Top speed (mph):	**Six** 107 **V-8** 119
0-60 mph (sec):	**Six** 11.0 **V-8** 8.7
Production:	**1953** 315 **1954** 3640 **1955** 674

1955-56 Chevrolet

The 1955 Chevrolet was one of those happy cars whose whole exceeded the sum of its parts. Completely redesigned, with pretty styling and a potent new V-8 option, it was not just the most changed Chevy since the war but the most exciting ever. Overnight it transformed the image of General Motors' volume make from "old fogy's" car to hot performer. Today, the 1955 and its '56 successor remain as much a phenomenon as they were more than 30 years ago.

GM knew full well the sales value of styling, and company design chief Harley Earl put his best staffers to work on shaping Chevy's '55 passenger cars. Clare MacKichan, Chuck Stebbins, Bob Veryzer, and Carl Renner followed his dictum of "Go all the way, then back off." Though the result wasn't as radical as renderings implied, it was still a knockout. It looked longer, lower, wider, and altogether sleeker, with no ties to the upright 1953-54 models despite retaining their 115-inch wheelbase. Overall, the '55 Chevy was attractively trendy yet free of the excesses that marred many of its contemporaries.

This handsome styling clothed a completely new tubular chassis, far lighter than the previous frame, yet stronger and more rigid. A new weight-saving ball-joint front suspension appeared. Out back, Hotchkiss drive and a banjo-type axle replaced the heavy old torque-tube drive and Salisbury axle—and leaf springs were lengthened a full nine inches. It all added up to greatly improved ride and handling in a lighter, more nimble package.

But the real excitement came from Chevy's first production V-8 in 35 years. It was largely the work of division chief engineer Edward N. Cole, with light weight and high rpm capability the major design objectives. "We knew a certain bore/stroke relationship was most compact," Cole said. "We knew we'd like a displacement of 265 cubic inches, and that automatically established the bore and stroke. And we never changed any of this." Among a slew of innovations were individual rocker

"New Look! New Life! New Everything!" That's what Chevy advertising touted for 1955, but for once the hype was accurate. Among the wide array of models offered for '55 were the $2067 Bel Air Sport Coupe (below)*, the $2206 Bel Air convertible* (opposite, top)*, and the $1835 Two-Ten Delray* (bottom)*, which sported a classy vinyl interior.*

SPECIFICATIONS

Engines: 1955 ohv I-6, 235.5 cid (3.56 × 3.94), 123/136 bhp (manual/Powerglide); ohv V-8, 265 cid (3.75 × 3.00), 162 bhp (180 bhp with Power Pack option) **1956** ohv I-6, 235.5 cid (3.56 × 3.94), 140 bhp; ohv V-8, 265 cid (3.75 × 3.00), 162/170 bhp (manual/Powerglide), 205 bhp (Power Pack), 225 bhp (Corvette option)

Transmissions:	3-speed manual; overdrive or 2-speed Powerglide automatic optional
Suspension, front:	upper and lower A-arms, coil springs
Suspension, rear:	live axle, longitudinal semi-elliptic leaf springs
Brakes:	front/rear drums
Wheelbase (in.):	115.0
Weight (lbs):	**1955** 3070-3300 **1956** 3117-3330
Top speed (mph):	85-110
0-60 mph (sec):	9.0-11.4 (V-8)

Production: 1955 One-Fifty 2d sdn 66,416 **4d sdn** 29,898 **2d utility sdn** 11,196 **Handyman 4d wgn** 17,936 **Two-Ten 2d sdn** 249,105 **4d sdn** 317,724 **Townsman 4d wgn** 82,303 **Delray 2d sdn** 115,584 **Handyman 2d wgn** 28,918 **Sport Coupe 2d htp** 11,675 **Bel Air 2d sdn** 168,313 **4d sdn** 345,372 **Beauville 4d wgn** 24,313 **cvt** 41,292 **Sport Coupe 2d htp** 185,562 **1956 One-Fifty 2d sdn** 82,384 **4d sdn** 51,544 **2d utility sdn** 9879 **Handyman 2d wgn** 13,487 **Two-Ten 2d sdn** 205,545 **4d sdn** 283,125 **Townsman 4d wgn** 113,656 **Sport Sedan 4d htp** 20,021 **Beauville 4d wgn** 17,988 **Delray 2d sdn** 56,382 **Handyman 2d wgn** 22,038 **Sport Coupe 2d htp** 18,616 **Bel Air 2d sdn** 104,849 **4d sdn** 269,798 **Sport Sedan 4d htp** 103,602 **Beauville 4d wgn** 13,279 **cvt** 41,268 **Sport Coupe 2d htp** 128,382

ILLINOIS
PZG 397

arms, hollow pushrods providing splash lubrication, and interchangeable die-cast heads with a common water inlet from the intake manifold.

Remarkably, this new "Turbo-Fire" V-8 weighed 40 pounds less than Chevy's old "Stovebolt Six." And it produced some 32 percent more horsepower from only 13 percent more displacement. Both engines teamed with standard three-speed manual transmission, newly optional overdrive, or extra-cost two-speed Powerglide automatic. Even more V-8 sizzle was on tap with the optional Power Pack—dual exhausts and four-barrel carburetor. Even without that, ad writers could fairly describe the '55 Chevy as "The Hot One."

Hot it was, on the road and in the showroom. Some 1.7 million were sold, nearly a quarter of Detroit's total 1955 output of 7.1 million-plus, giving Chevy a stunning 44 percent of the low-price market.

Retaining its now-customary three-series line of economy-priced One-Ten, value-packed Two-Ten, and top-shelf Bel Air, Chevy made "The Hot One Even Hotter" for '56. A $40 million facelift brought bolder, brighter styling. Higher compression made for a hotter six and V-8. A specific intake manifold, higher-lift camshaft, and Chevy's tightest squeeze yet (9.25:1) were included with this year's Power Pack, which turned the Turbo-Fire into a Super Turbo-Fire. Icing the performance cake was the mid-season arrival of the top V-8 from the Corvette sports car as an option for any passenger model, with mechanical instead of hydraulic lifters, plus twin four-barrel carbs, lightweight valves, and larger intake and exhaust passages.

Responding to a popular trend, Chevy added Sport Sedan four-door hardtops to the '56 Bel Air and Two-Ten lines. (The unique hardtop-style Bel Air Nomad wagon was still around, and would be through '57. It deserves a separate entry, which you'll find elsewhere in this book.) Longer, softer front springs and more widely separated rear springs reduced nosedive in hard braking and improved cornering stability.

In short, the '56 was not only a hotter "Hot One," but a smoother and more comfortable one. It didn't sell as well as the '55, but that's because the market took a breather in '56. Still, Chevy managed to increase its market share from 23 to nearly 28 percent on just 88 percent of its '55 volume—no mean feat.

The '55 had been planned for a three-year design cycle, so 1957 would see the last of the cars long since revered as the "Classic Chevys." Some say Chevy saved the best for last, but you'll have to read on a little ways to find out why.

Ads for the '56 Chevrolet proclaimed that "The Hot One's Even Hotter." And indeed it was, with up to 225 bhp on tap. A heavy facelift highlighted a new full-width grille, restyled taillights (the left one hid the fuel filler cap), and revised two-toning. The $2344 Bel Air convertible (below) *was the most glamorous model in the lineup.* Opposite page: *Other Bel Air offerings included the $2176 Sport Coupe* (top)*, the $2025 two-door sedan, and the new-for-1956 Sport Sedan at $2230* (center left)*. As in 1955, the dashboard featured twin-cowl, fan-shaped nacelles.*

CALIFORNIA
1HWG056

RW 7511

1955-57 Chevrolet Nomad

Although not enough people realized it at the time, Chevy had created a masterpiece with the 1955-57 Nomad. Applying hardtop styling to a station wagon looked like a million bucks, but buyers were turned off in 1955 (top) by the high $2571 price, $266 more than the Bel Air convertible. The '56 (above and below) and the '57 (opposite) saw most of the same styling changes as the rest of the passenger-car line.

Where there's a choice, collectors invariably covet the convertible and hardtop coupe over other body styles in a given car line. One of the few exceptions is Chevrolet's 1955-57 Bel Air Nomad, perhaps the prettiest wagon ever built and a car with immense, longtime appeal simply because it's a "classic Chevy."

The 1955-57 Chevys are highlighted elsewhere in this book, but the Nomad is a story in itself. Though generally credited to General Motors design domo Harley Earl, its actual creators were Chevy studio head Clare MacKichan and stylist Carl Renner. MacKichan's group had suggested a "sport wagon" as one addition to Chevy's all-new '55 line. "The Corvette theme was a popular one," he recalled, and "Renner...had come up with a sketch for a station wagon roof that caught Earl's eye. Bringing this idea to the Chevrolet studio, Earl asked that it be incorporated into a station wagon version as one of [three] Corvette idea cars for the 1954 Motorama."

The result was the Corvette Nomad, a non-running prototype with fiberglass bodywork on a '53 Chevy wagon chassis. Renner's roof nicely suited the lower body lines of Chevy's recently announced sports car and the name was perfect. Unveiled in January 1954, the Corvette Nomad was such a hit that an Earl assistant hurriedly ordered MacKichan to adapt its roofline to Chevy's forthcoming '55 passenger-car styling—in just two days.

Renner hustled. "The [show car's] roof was taken from a full-size drawing, cut apart, stretched out, and mated to the...1955 Chevrolet lower body," said MacKichan. "The hardtop front-door glass framing, forward-sloping rear quarters, wide B-pillar, fluted roof, wraparound rear side glass, the rear wheel housing cutout, and the seven vertical accent strips on the tailgate were all retained in a remarkably good translation from the dream car."

Aside from all-steel bodywork, the production Bel Air Nomad differed in using a conventional liftgate—a heavy, chrome-plated affair—instead of the show car's drop-down tailgate window. The "fluted roof" refers to the nine transverse grooves at the rear, a visual remnant of Earl's plan for a retracting stainless-steel section that was quickly nixed by leak worries and high cost.

Alas, the marriage of hardtop flair and wagon utility wasn't bliss. Though it looked like other '55s, the Nomad shared little with them aft of the cowl and was thus the most expensive Chevy ever: $2571 with V-8—$265 more than a similarly equipped Bel Air convertible. The lack of four doors limited its appeal among wagon buyers, its glassy interior could get uncomfortably warm, the liftgate sucked in exhaust fumes when open, and the slanted rear was prone to water leaks. With all this the nifty Nomad was Chevy's least popular '55.

Nevertheless, it returned for '56, this time bowing with the rest of the line (the '55 had arrived in February). *Motor Trend* named it one of the year's most beautiful cars, but admitted that "its distinct personal-car feel forces certain limiting features..." One GM stylist disputed that, pointing out that the Nomad had more cargo capacity than some conventional contemporaries.

But price was still a problem and it prompted some economizing for the '56. Seat inserts were now standard Bel Air hardtop (instead of the '55's unique "waffle" material). So was all exterior trim save for the "bananas" and, exclusive to the '56, a small chrome "V" below each tail lamp (other Chevys signified a V-8 with one large "V" on trunklid or tailgate). A nice detail touch was reversing the Bel Air's short rear-quarter "slash" moldings to match B-pillar angle. Chevy hoped that a full year's production would push Nomad sales past the 10,000 mark, but it still had to raise price more than $130 despite the cost-cutting measures, and production declined.

With that, Chevy decided not to do a Nomad version of its all-new '58 design. The valedictory '57, like its predecessors, offered most of the same good qualities as other Chevy passenger models—it wore that year's heavy facelift particularly well—but cost another $150 more and thus saw the lowest production for the three-year run. Trim was again stock Bel Air except for Nomad script and a small gold "V" on V-8 tailgates.

Though the name has since been used on conventional wagons and, lately, on vans, the first Nomad is the only one Chevy fans care to remember. And why not? To paraphrase a well-worn cliché, the first shall sometimes be best.

SPECIFICATIONS

Engines: **1955** ohv I-6, 235.5 cid (3.56 × 3.94), 123/136 bhp (manual/Powerglide); ohv V-8, 265 cid (3.75 × 3.00), 162 bhp (180 bhp with Power Pack option) **1956** ohv I-6, 235.5 cid (3.56 × 3.94), 140 bhp; ohv V-8, 265 cid (3.75 × 3.00), 162/170 bhp **1957** ohv I-6, 235.5 cid (3.56 × 3.94), 140 bhp; ohv-8, 265 cid (3.75 × 3.00), 162 bhp; 283 cid (3.88 × 3.00), 185/245/270 bhp (carbureted), 250/283 bhp (fuel injection)

Transmissions:	3-speed manual; overdrive, 2-speed Powerglide and Turboglide (1957) automatics optional
Suspension, front:	upper and lower A-arms, coil springs
Suspension, rear:	live axle, semi-elliptic leaf springs
Brakes:	front/rear drums
Wheelbase (in.):	115.0
Weight (lbs):	3285-3465
Top speed (mph):	90-120
0-60 mph (sec):	8.0-11.0
Production:	**1955** 8386 **1956** 7886 **1957** 6103

1956-57 Chevrolet Corvette

Had it not been for the Ford Thunderbird, we might not have a Corvette today. In early 1955, profit-minded General Motors executives were ready to kill off Chevrolet's fiberglass-bodied two-seater, which since its 1953 debut had not made the hoped-for impression on America's admittedly minuscule sports-car market. But Dearborn's posh "personal" car was a challenge GM could not let go unanswered, so Corvette was granted a stay of execution.

Enthusiasts have been grateful ever since, for the reprieve brought a renaissance. With the all-new second-generation design of 1956-57, Chevy could at last rightfully proclaim Corvette as "America's only true sports car"—as indeed it did.

Compared to its slab-sided predecessor, the '56 was stunning. GM design director Harley Earl came up with fresh new styling that was tasteful in an age of garishness, yet sexy, low-slung, and distinctly American. Its only questionable elements were phony air scoops atop the front fenders, dummy knock-off hubs on the wheel covers (carried over from 1953-55), and a dash that was more flash than function. Still, the '56 looked more like the serious sports car it was, and it was also more civilized, with new seats, roll-up door glass (no more clumsy side curtains), and an optional lift-off hardtop (previewed on a 1954 Motorama Corvette) for sedan-like weather protection.

Beneath this finery was a chassis heavily reworked by engineering wizard Zora Arkus-Duntov. Without upsetting the '55's near-equal front/rear weight distribution (52/48 percent), he tightened up both steering response and handling. Though understeer was still a tad excessive and the cast-iron all-drum brakes "faded into oblivion" in hard stops, as one magazine stated, the Vette was now as quick through turns as it was on straights.

And quick it was. Chevy's superb 265-cubic-inch V-8, designed by Harry Barr and Edward N. Cole, had been an option fitted to all but six of the '55 models. Now it came standard—and with up to 210 horsepower in normal tune or 225 bhp with high-lift cam, twin four-barrel carburetors, and dual exhausts. The close-ratio three-speed manual gearbox, introduced late in the '55 run, was standard now too, replacing Powerglide, which shifted to the options sheet. The most potent '56 could hit 60 mph from rest in a swift 7.5 seconds and top 120 mph.

There was no need to change the handsome styling for '57, but Chevy upped performance by boring out its V-8. The result was 283 cubic inches in five engines offering 220 bhp up to an amazing 283 bhp, the latter courtesy of new "Ramjet" fuel injection. A four-speed Borg-Warner manual transmission arrived in May at $188 extra, and combined with axle ratios as low as 4.11:1 to make the "fuelie" '57 thunderingly fast. Published road tests showed 0-60 in 5.7 seconds, 0-100 mph in 16.8, the standing quarter-mile in 14.3 seconds at 96 mph, and a maximum of 132 mph. Alas, mechanical bugs and a $500 price limited injection installations to only 240 units.

Chevy also offered a $725 "heavy-duty racing suspension" package for '57, comprising high-rate springs and shocks, front anti-roll bar, quick steering, and ceramic-metallic brake linings with finned ventilated drums. Add one of the high-power engines and you had a Corvette virtually ready to race right off the showroom floor.

Indeed, these were the years when Corvette began to make its mark in international competition. Dr. Richard Thompson won the Sports Car Club of America C-Production national championship in 1956, then took the '57 crown in B-Production, where the Vette qualified by dint of its larger engine. John Fitch's '56 was the fastest modified car at that year's Daytona Speed Weeks, a Corvette finished ninth in the grueling 12 Hours of Sebring in '56, and another came home second (behind a Mercedes 300SL) at Pebble Beach that same year. Chevy's 1957 Sebring assault saw production Corvettes finish first and second in the GT class and 12th and 15th overall.

It was all symbolic of a dramatic metamorphosis. Said one European writer: "Before Sebring...the Corvette was regarded as a plastic toy. After Sebring, even the most biased were forced to admit that [it was one] of the world's finest sports cars...."

That included buyers. Encouraged by attractively stable prices ($3149/$3465), they happily took 3467 of the '56s and 6339 of the '57s, a far cry from 1955's 674-unit low. The Corvette's future was assured.

The fuel-injected Corvette engine of 1957 (above) carried the code designation EL. Reportedly, it actually delivered about 290 horsepower—more than advertised! Unfortunately, reliability problems and high cost limited FI's appeal, but the badges (top) added snob appeal. The '57 Corvette design (opposite) was remarkably free of excess chrome and trickery, except for the fake vents atop the front fenders.

SPECIFICATIONS

Engines: ohv V-8 **1956** 265 cid (3.75 × 3.00), 210/225 bhp **1957** 283 cid (3.88 × 3.00), 220/245/250/270/283 bhp

Transmissions:	3/4-speed manual, 2-speed Powerglide automatic
Suspension, front:	unequal-length A-arms, coil springs, anti-roll bar
Suspension, rear:	live axle, semi-elliptic leaf springs
Brakes:	front/rear drums
Wheelbase (in.):	102.0
Weight (lbs):	2880
Top speed (mph):	**1956** 121-129 **1957** 115-130
0-60 mph (sec):	**1956** 7.3-8.9 **1957** 5.7-8.0
Production:	**1956** 3467 **1957** 6339

1957 Chevrolet

In *The Hot One,* author Pat Chappell summed up the 1957 Chevrolet as "a nice way to end a three-year era of superlative accomplishments in design, engineering, and competition." That's putting it mildly. The '57 Chevy was nothing less than terrific. Many still judge it the best of the "classic" mid-Fifties models, and it's long been one of the most widely coveted collector cars.

Even so, it was not an unqualified success when new. While its Big Three rivals fielded all-new and discernibly larger passenger models for 1957, Chevy had to make do with a heavy rework of its 1955-56 platform. Despite an extensive and expensive facelift, the '57 Chevy seemed unfashionably tall, narrow, and dated next to that year's jazzy Ford and ultra-sleek Plymouth—and both offered bigger V-8s. Plymouth could boast the most available horsepower and, said contemporary motor-noters, the best handling. Adding injury to insult, Ford nipped Chevy in model year production—by a scant 131 units.

Yet it's the Chevy that enthusiasts have come to desire most, and we can think of at least four reasons. First, Chevy retained the trim proportions its competitors abandoned (as Chevy itself would do for 1958) to the benefit of maneuverability and performance. Second, Chevy had a big edge in workmanship. The new Fords and Plymouths were notorious for early rust-out, which partly explains why they're proportionally scarcer today.

Third, the '57 was pleasingly different from the 1955-56 Chevys, and if not the last word in style, it was quite attractive. Moreover, as designer Carl Renner later observed, "I think it was our objective to make [the '57] look like a 'little Cadillac'....I think that is one reason why [it] sold so well." Finally, the '57 Chevy was a better car than its immediate predecessors in many ways. The chassis was beefed up to handle the extra weight of the longer, restyled bodies; front suspension was revised;

After the four-door sedan, the Sport Coupe two-door hardtop (below) was the most popular '57 Bel Air. It sold for $2299, compared to $2364 for the Sport Sedan (top) and $2511 for the convertible (opposite). The base 283-cid V-8 added about $100 to the price, and a wide array of power and appearance options was available.

the rear leaf springs were moved still further outboard to improve roadholding; 14-inch wheels and tires replaced 15-inchers for a lower stance; and gearing was altered to enhance off-the-line acceleration.

Chevy didn't change its lineup for '57—no need for that—but there were two major engineering developments: a bigger version of the already-famous small-block V-8 and the first fuel-injection system ever offered by a mass-market domestic nameplate. Bored to 283 cubic inches, the livelier new Turbo-Fire V-8 packed 185 horsepower in base two-barrel trim and 245/270 bhp with four-barrel carburetor. The numbers read 250/283 bhp with "Ramjet" fuel injection, but high price ($500) and several sticky service problems held passenger-car installations to a mere 1503. A mechanical system, Ramjet was what we'd now call a continuous-flow multi-point setup, with a separate injector for each cylinder, plus a special fuel meter, manifold assembly, and air meter (the last replacing the normal carburetor and intake manifold).

Interestingly, the top 283-bhp "fuelie" 283 was not the first U.S. production engine to achieve the magic "1 hp per cu. in." ideal extolled in Chevy advertising. The 354 hemi in the Chrysler 300B had performed that trick the previous year, and without fuel injection.

Equally problematic was Turboglide, a new two-speed automatic introduced during the year to answer Hydra-Matic. A $231 option for any V-8 save the 270- and 283-bhp versions, it weighed 82 pounds less than the familiar Powerglide but was far more complex, with three drive turbines and two planetary gearsets, plus a variable-pitch stator and a conventional torque-converter pump. Predictably, Turboglide turned out to be far less reliable, and quickly proved a nightmare for customers and dealers alike. By 1961 it was gone.

But if not exactly perfect, the '57s were surely the fastest Chevys yet. The typical four-door sedan with automatic and the 270-bhp engine could run 0-60 mph in 10 seconds flat and the standing quarter-mile in 17.5 seconds at about 80 mph—more than enough to keep pace with the opposition.

Alas, June 1957 brought the Automobile Manufacturers Association's "anti-racing" edict, which brought a temporary end to truly hot Chevys that could carry more than two passengers. And that's probably the main reason the '57s are still so fondly remembered. They were the last of a truly special breed.

SPECIFICATIONS

Engines: ohv I-6, 235.5 cid (3.56 × 3.94), 140 bhp; ohv V-8, 265 cid (3.75 × 3.00), 162 bhp; 283 cid (3.88 × 3.00), 185/245/270 bhp (carbureted), 250/283 bhp (fuel injection)

Transmissions:	3-speed manual; overdrive, 2-speed Powerglide/Turboglide optional
Suspension, front:	upper and lower A-arms, coil springs
Suspension, rear:	live axle, semi-elliptic leaf springs
Brakes:	front/rear drums
Wheelbase (in.):	115.0
Weight (lbs):	3163-3561
Top speed (mph):	90-120
0-60 mph (sec):	8.0-12.0

Production: **One-Fifty 2d sdn** 70,774 **4d sdn** 52,266 **2d utility sdn** 8300 **Handyman 2d wgn** 14,740 **Two-Ten 2d sdn** 160,090 **4d sdn** 260,401 **Townsman 4d wgn** 127,803 **Sport Sedan 4d htp** 16,178 **Beauville 4d wgn** 21,083 **Delray 2d sdn** 25,644 **Handyman 2d wgn** 17,528 **Sport Coupe 2d htp** 22,631 **Bel Air 2d sdn** 62,757 **4d sdn** 254,331 **Townsman 4d wgn** 27,375 **Sport Sedan 4d htp** 137,672 **cvt** 47,652 **Sport Coupe 2d htp** 166,426

1958-59 Chevrolet Corvette

It's easy to dismiss the 1958-60 Corvette as a hokier, heftier version of the memorable second generation—mainly because it was. And indeed, even Corvette enthusiasts overlooked it for years. But lately these cars have come to be appreciated, and for very sound reasons—not least because this Corvette assured a permanent place in the Chevrolet line for "America's only true sports car."

Nineteen fifty-eight was hardly a vintage year for Detroit styling, but Harley Earl's valedictory Corvette could have fared much worse. Wheelbase was unchanged on the mostly new '58 model but, in the spirit of the times, overall length went up 10 inches, width more than two inches, and curb weight 200 pounds. The basic shape remained broadly the same as 1956-57 but busier and shinier, with quad headlamps (all the rage that year), a dummy air scoop ahead of each concave bodyside "cove" (decorated with chrome windsplits no less), simulated louvers on the hood, and equally silly longitudinal chrome strips on the trunklid.

Yet beneath all the glitz were some genuine improvements. Bumpers, for example, were newly mounted on long brackets instead of directly to the body, thus giving better protection. And a redesigned cockpit grouped all instruments directly ahead of the driver for the first time. Also featured were a new passenger grab bar, locking glove box, and self-seeking "Wonder Bar" radio.

Bigger and plusher it may have been, but the '58 was still a vivid performer—no surprise, since the '57 engine lineup returned with few changes. The top fuel-injected 283 V-8 actually gained seven horsepower for a total of 290, thus exceeding the hallowed "1 hp per cubic inch" benchmark achieved the previous year. Also carried over were a wide array of performance options, many bargain-priced: Positraction limited-slip differential ($48.45), metallic brake linings ($26.90), four-speed manual transmission ($188.30), and heavy-duty suspension and brakes ($425.05). Inflation plagued the national economy in '58, yet base price was still reasonable at $3631.

Perhaps surprisingly, critics generally liked the '58. Buyers certainly did. Model year production gained 2829 units over the '57 tally as the Corvette actually turned a profit for the first time.

Volume rose another 500 units for '59, when Chevy smoothed the washboard hood, deleted the chrome backstraps, and added trailing radius rods to counteract rear axle windup in hard acceleration, the year's only noteworthy mechanical change. Despite rumors of a smaller all-new model with independent rear suspension, this basic package continued for 1960 as Corvette production broke the magic 10,000-unit barrier for the first time.

Though Corvette was moving away from *pur sang* sports car toward plush GT, the third generation proved no less a track competitor than the second-generation cars. Highlights included a GT-class win and 12th overall at Sebring '58, national SCCA B-Production championships in 1958-59, fastest in the sports-car division at the 1958 Pikes Peak Hill Climb, and a slew of victories by privateers. Thanks to the Auto Manufacturers Association mid-1957 edict, Chevy was officially "out of racing" now, though not above lending under-the-table support to those campaigning its cars. Among them was sportsman Briggs Cunningham, who gave the Corvette its finest racing hour yet when one of his three team cars (driven by John Fitch and Bob Grossman) finished eighth overall in the 1960 running of the prestigious 24 Hours of Le Mans.

With achievements like that, not to mention great style and flashing performance, the 1958-60 Corvette surely deserves the enthusiast recognition it has belatedly come to enjoy. It may not be "first among equals," but it is a Corvette. For many car lovers, that's all that counts.

The 1958 Corvette (opposite, top) *featured quad headlights, glitzier styling, and five versions of the 283-cid V-8. The '59* (bottom) *lost the washboard ridges on the hood and chrome strips on the trunk. The 1958 base price of $3631 increased to $3875 the following year.*

SPECIFICATIONS

Engines: ohv V-8, 283 cid (3.88 × 3.00), 230/245/270 bhp (carbureted), 250/290 bhp (fuel injected)

Transmissions:	3/4-speed manual; 2-speed Powerglide automatic optional
Suspension, front:	unequal-length A-arms, coil springs, anti-roll bar
Suspension, rear:	live axle, semi-elliptic leaf springs
Brakes:	front/rear drums
Wheelbase (in.):	102.0
Weight (lbs):	3085
Top speed (mph):	103-128
0-60 mph (sec):	6.6-9.2
Production:	**1958** 9168 **1959** 9670 **1960** 10,261

Y2ND58

1958 Chevrolet Impala

Mention "Impala" and most people immediately think "Chevrolet." For the better part of 25 years the names were virtually synonymous: the most popular model line from America's perennial best-seller—the nation's favorite family car. But in the beginning, Impala meant something very special.

The Impala debuted as the flagship of a 1958 Chevrolet fleet virtually all-new from the ground up. Conceived as a "Bel Air Executive Coupe," it was intended to stretch the make's coverage from the low-price field into the lower reaches of the medium segment, which product planners had concluded would be the biggest growth market of the late '50s.

Reflecting that view, the '58s were deliberately bigger and heavier than the agile, spirited 1955-57 Chevys. This is one reason collectors once ignored the '58s, including Impala, but Chevy was only playing catch-up with Ford and Plymouth, which had moved to their "mid-size" platforms the year before.

And in retrospect, the '58 Chevy was generally much improved, with a lot of what buyers wanted. Its new X-member chassis was not only heftier, but delivered a smoother ride, thanks to a 2.5-inch-longer wheelbase and a new four-link rear suspension with coil springs instead of leaf springs. The latter was designed to facilitate installation of "Level Air," but the air bag springs were prone to leaks and the option found few takers at $124.

Of greater interest was a larger V-8 option: the new 348-cubic-inch "Turbo-Thrust" V-8 offering 250 standard horsepower or 280 bhp with optional 9.5:1 compression and three dual-throat carbs, and 315 bhp with 11.0:1 compression, special cam shaft, and high-speed valve train. Although originally designed for Chevy trucks, the 348 made any '58 Chevy more lively than it was usually given credit for—perhaps not as fast as a "fuelie" '57 but quick enough to qualify as a "Hot One" nonetheless. A 250-bhp Bel Air hardtop sedan could run 0-60 mph in a respectable 9.9 seconds; *Motor Trend* timed a 280-bhp Impala Sport Coupe at 9.1 seconds, with 16.5 seconds in the standing quarter-mile. These figures were achieved with Turboglide, the new two-speed Chevy automatic that had bowed during 1957 as an extra-cost alternative to Powerglide. Veteran tester Tom McCahill said it was "as smooth as velvet underpants" when working properly—which it didn't do very often.

Chevy styling had been moving closer to Cadillac's since 1955, and the '58 was the closest yet. Not everyone applauded the new look, but it was at least distinctive—especially the tasteful "gullwing" rear fenders—and far less shiny than this year's Buick and Oldsmobile. Both the Impala convertible—the only one in the line—and Sport Coupe two-door hardtop were set apart from their Bel Air sisters by stainless-steel rocker moldings, special emblems and wheel covers, and dummy "pitchfork" trim (suggesting air scoops) ahead of the rear wheels.

Yet contrary to popular opinion, the first Impala was more than just fancy trim. Both models had longer rear decks than other '58s (though overall length was the same) and a somewhat different lower body. Interior exclusives ran to brushed-aluminum door-panel appliqués, color-keyed horizontal-stripe upholstery, and a pull-down rear armrest below a central radio speaker grille.

With all this, the Impala was a timely hit, enabling Chevy to weather the dulling 1958 recession far better than most Detroit makes. Despite just two body styles, close to 181,500 were sold—fully 15 percent of the division's model year volume—helping Chevy capture a record 30 percent of the U.S. auto market. By contrast, total industry production dropped to 4.5 million from six million the year before.

Encouraged by this success, Chevy expanded Impala offerings to create a new top-line series for 1959. But in doing so it watered down the concept and, except for the high-performance Super Sports of the '60s, future Impalas would be nowhere near as unique or memorable.

But collectors have since come to recognize the '58 as the "Hot One" it is. Today these cars are being gathered in and restored with the same enthusiasm once reserved for the 1955-57s. If not quite as capable, the first Impala is certainly just as nostalgic as the "classic" Chevys—one of the more pleasant symbols of an unforgettable automotive age.

The '58 Chevrolet was longer, lower, wider, and heavier. Nothing showed off the new-found size better than the Impala, a new Bel Air subseries available in two body styles: a $2841 convertible (opposite, top)*, or a striking hardtop* (bottom) *priced at $2693. Both could be had with the 145-bhp six, but most got the 283- or 348-cid V-8.*

SPECIFICATIONS

Engines: ohv I-6, 235.5 cid (3.56 × 3.94), 145 bhp; ohv V-8, 283 cid (3.88 × 3.00), 185/230 bhp (250/290 with fuel injection); 348 cid (4.13 × 3.25), 250/280/315 bhp

Transmission:	3-speed manual; overdrive and 2-speed Powerglide/ Turboglide automatic optional
Suspension, front:	upper and lower A-arms, coil springs
Suspension, rear:	4-link live axle, coil springs
Brakes:	front/rear drums
Wheelbase (in.):	117.5
Weight (lbs):	2586-2841
Top speed (mph):	95-105
0-60 mph (sec):	9.1-12.0
Production:	**Sport Coupe 2d htp** 125,480 **cvt** 55,989

Impala

AMU 636

1959 Chevrolet

No doubt about it: the "batwing" 1959 Chevy couldn't be mistaken for anything else. It was, to quote an old Studebaker slogan, "different by design," and a '59 can still be spotted a block away—especially from the rear. Which was, of course, the whole point of making Chevrolet "All New, All Over Again." If the result seemed bizarre, well...it could have been worse.

Despite what some former executives say, General Motors had been sharing bodyshells among its various car lines for at least two decades before the 1959 program rendered the '58 Chevy a one-year-only design. Nevertheless, the '59 effort gave GM stylists a chance to let their imaginations roam. Boy, did they ever. "We were encouraged to do the wildest things," said former Chevy studio chief Clare MacKichan. "One design had the headlights above the other in the center and the headlights on the outside for markers. Fortunately, that didn't go too far, especially considering the Edsel."

Things went far enough, though. If the stylists had used a trowel to ladle chrome on GM's '58s, as former design chief Bill Mitchell once said, they must have used one to sculpt the '59 Chevy's weird rear end, which looked "big enough to land a Piper Cub," according to the ever-quotable road tester Tom McCahill. Still, that titanic tail afforded a cavernous 32-cubic-foot trunk; the rest of the package was really quite conventional.

Larger, too, in the spirit of times: two inches longer, 2.4-inches lower, and two inches wider than the '58 on a wheelbase stretched 1.5 inches. Weight increased as well, but the new styling somehow managed to look lighter—especially from inside, thanks to 50-percent more glass—and structural revisions added useful extra inches to head, hip, and elbow room.

Reflecting its 1958 success, the luxurious Impala expanded its top-of-the-line spot into a full-blown series. It listed eight models in four body styles, the convertible and Sport Coupe hardtop being joined by a four-door sedan and Sport Sedan hardtop. Bel Air and Biscayne, with six models apiece, moved down a notch to make room. A separate station wagon series returned in 10 versions, up one from '58. As before, V-8-engined cars were considered separate models. Prices ranged from $2160 for a

SPECIFICATIONS

Engines: ohv I-6, 235.5 cid (3.56 × 3.94), 135 bhp; ohv V-8, 283 cid (3.88 × 3.00), 275/300 bhp (carburetor), 290/305 bhp (fuel injection); 348 cid (4.13 × 3.25), 250/280/300/305/315/320/335 bhp

Transmissions:	3-speed manual; overdrive, 4-speed floorshift manual, and 2-speed Powerglide and Turboglide optional
Suspension, front:	upper and lower A-arms, coil springs
Suspension, rear:	4-link live axle, coil springs
Brakes:	front/rear drums
Wheelbase (in.):	119.0
Weight (lbs):	3490-4020
Top speed (mph):	90-135
0-60 mph (sec):	9.0-13.0

Production: **Biscayne** 311,800* **Bel Air** 447,100* **Impala** 473,000* **Station Wagons** 214,583*
*Figures approximate; model breakdowns not available

six-cylinder Biscayne utility sedan to $3009 for a four-door Nomad V-8 wagon. The sporty $2967 Impala V-8 ragtop saw 65,800 copies built, but four-door sedans predominated with more than 525,000 built out of a total production run of 1,462,140 units.

Mechanically, the '59s mimicked the '58s, but engine choices numbered a dozen now, including four small-block 283 V-8s (two with fuel injection) and seven big-block 348s. The base 283 and the trusty "Blue Flame" six were detuned slightly as a sop to the public's new-found economy consciousness brought on by the '58 recession. Braking improved across the board via 17-percent-larger drums and slotted wheel rims to dissipate heat.

A surprising new option came in the form of Corvette's four-speed floorshift transmission. Not many found their way into the passenger models, to be sure, but already Chevy was hinting at the big Super Sport Chevys that would come in the Sixties. Automatics remained a more popular choice: Powerglide and a more reliable Turboglide. Overdrive was optional (at $108) for the basic "three-on-the-tree" manual. "Level Air" suspension still hung on, too, but its previous, well-publicized troubles and the public's growing annoyance with complicated gimmickry resulted in few orders despite a reasonable $135 price tag.

The mid-priced Bel Airs and the expanded Impala lineup ran neck and neck in popularity in 1959, both easily beating out the low-cost Biscayne. Bel Air managed 447,000 units with only three body styles (two- and four-door sedans and a Sport Sedan hardtop), while Biscayne managed 311,800. Nearly 215,000 station wagons found buyers. But Impala, thrusting upward, saw output of about 473,000 units and would go on to cement its position as the most popular of the toned-down '60 Chevys—and remain on top until ousted by Caprice a decade later. In the production race with Ford, whose '59s were heavily but conservatively facelifted, Chevy emerged the victor by just over 11,000 units, though Dearborn finished about 100,000 ahead for the calendar year.

The '59 (and '58) Chevys have been criticized for starting the trend toward the overblown, overweight "standard" cars that Detroit would peddle through the late Seventies. In retrospect, they were right on the money, paving the way for the full-size Sixties Chevys that sold by the boxcar-load year after year.

As for the '59 styling, time heals more than wounds. Surprising though it may seem, these Chevys—and the Impala two-doors in particular—are being appreciated anew, often by those too young to remember them firsthand. Because of this new following, along with long-standing '59 partisans, the batwing Chevy is at last having its day. Call it the "Revenge of the Weird."

Love it or hate it, most everyone remembers the 1959 Chevrolet. Who could miss it, with its wild "batwing" rear fins and flaring "nostrils" above the wide, low grille? To move the dazzle down the street, buyers could choose any one of 12 engines, ranging from 135 to 335 horsepower.

1959 Chevrolet El Camino

Car-based utility vehicles are an idea as old as the Model T. Even in the Lizzie's earliest days you could buy a commercial roadster with a rumble seat that could be left off for cargo-carrying. This later gave way to the roadster pickup, again the basic two-seat T with an open cargo box behind.

By the mid '30s, the advent of closed all-steel bodywork and integral trunks had led to the coupe-pickup (or coupe-delivery) at companies like Studebaker, Hudson, and Chevrolet. All were essentially plain-Jane business coupes with a cargo box instead of a trunk; on a few, the trunklid was removable and the box could be slid in or out so the vehicle could be used as either car or "truck." Yet another variation was the panel delivery, essentially a station wagon with blanked-off rear side windows.

But "real" trucks, especially pickups, had been evolving almost as rapidly as cars, becoming more civilized, stylish, and easier to drive—in short, more car-like. With that, the car/pickup became pretty much a dead duck, and none were revived after World War II. Chevy and Ford, among others, continued offering business coupes and utility sedans into the mid-'50s, but recorded diminishing sales, especially once all-steel station wagons arrived.

Nevertheless, Ford was ultimately moved to revive the car/pickup, figuring that a market still existed for a vehicle that looked like a car and worked like a truck. The result appeared for 1957 as the Ranchero, essentially the two-door Ranch Wagon with the roofline terminated at the B-pillars and an open cargo box instead of an enclosed load deck. Otherwise, more or less identical with the wagon, it offered much the same features, options, and even powertrain choices.

Never one to leave any market to Ford, no matter how limited, Chevy took a look and issued a reply for 1959. Immodestly called "the brightest new idea of the year," the El Camino ("the road" in Spanish) debuted as the Ranchero idea wrapped up in

The El Camino was Chevrolet's response to the Ford Ranchero, which had come out in 1957. It was basically a two-door station wagon with the rearmost two-thirds of the roof chopped off. As with other Chevys, a wide variety of engines, transmissions, and options was offered.

the division's startling new "batwing" styling. Chevy seemed pleased, its ads boasting, "It's Terrifico!...It's Magnifico!" Trim and standard equipment were roughly as for Chevy's low-end Brookwood wagon, which in turn was outfitted like a Biscyane sedan. Base price came in at a reasonable $2470, about the same as that year's Ranchero. An interesting appearance feature was the lipped roofline with an overhanging trailing edge above a huge wraparound rear window, an abbreviated version of the new '59 GM style used on Chevy hardtop sedans.

El Camino rode the same rangy new wheelbase as Chevy's '59 passenger cars and offered most of their drivetrain choices. The base engine for model 1180 was naturally the workhorse "Stovebolt" six, dubbed "Hi-Thrift." Model 1280 came with the 283 V-8 in 185-bhp form, but 230- and 285-bhp versions were on tap. The new 348-cid V-8, which was actually based on a truck engine, could be had in ratings of 250, 280, 300, and 315 bhp. Transmission choices comprised standard "three-on-the-tree" manual, the same with optional overdrive, and extra-cost Powerglide and Turboglide automatics.

Because Chevy hardly needed two high-style pickups, the El Camino displaced the fancy-pants, truck-based Cameo Carrier of 1957-58. "Good looks never carried so much weight" (1150-pound payload), boasted Chevy. Alas, the El Camino carried about as much sales weight as the Cameo Carrier, which wasn't much. Production figures are hard to come by, but one source quotes a figure of 22,246 units built for 1959—low enough to disappoint division managers because El Camino was abruptly dropped after 1960. It resurfaced for 1964 as a derivative of the new 115-inch-wheelbase intermediate Chevelle, but that's another story.

It's interesting to wonder how the El Camino might have fared had it arrived as a derivative of the "classic" 1955-57 Chevy. While the idea certainly appeals in retrospect, it's likely that the outcome would have been the same. Even in those days, the needs of truck buyers and car buyers had become specialized enough that neither group was likely to be satisfied by a compromise vehicle, which was what the El Camino was. Indeed, this is probably the reason it failed in 1959-60, though it was somewhat more successful in its later "downsized" form. For that matter, so was the Ranchero.

In short, the first El Camino proves that not even Chevy can please all of the people all of the time. Then again, pleasing most of the people most of the time is how Chevy got to be "USA-1," and you can't expect much more than that.

SPECIFICATIONS

Engines: ohv I-6, 235.5 cid (3.56 × 3.94), 135 bhp; ohv V-8, 283 cid (3.88 × 3.00), 185/230 bhp; 348 cid (4.13 × 3.25), 250/280/300/315 bhp

Transmissions:	3-speed manual; overdrive, 2-speed Powerglide/Turboglide automatics optional
Suspension, front:	upper and lower A-arms, coil springs
Suspension, rear:	4-link live axle, coil springs
Brakes:	front/rear drums
Wheelbase (in.):	119.0
Weight (lbs):	est. 3500
Top speed (mph):	90-110
0-60 mph (sec):	8.0-14.5
Production:	22,246

1950 Chrysler Town & Country

The 1950 Town & Country Newport, with its pillarless beltline, "Clearbac" rear window, white ash embellishments, four-wheel disc brakes, and deluxe interior stood as the most impressive Chrysler in the 1950 line, and the last of the luxury Town & Country models; after 1950, the name was applied strictly to Chrysler station wagons.

The series had begun back in 1941, when the general manager of Chrysler Division, David Wallace, got the idea of a "civilized" station wagon: wood-bodied, of course, but with smoother, more aerodynamic styling than the huge boxes-on-wheels which had comprised wagons up to that point. Under Wallace, Chrysler built a handful of Town & Country wagons for 1941 and '42: nicely rounded shapes with distinctive "clamshell" rear doors.

After the war, Chrysler needed something new to light up showrooms replete with warmed-over prewar bodies. Wallace hit upon the idea of non-wagon woodies: the Town & Country sedan and convertible. Built from 1946 to 1948, these were the best known and most luxurious examples of the T&C breed, the convertible priced as high as $3400. They were beloved by moneyed classes, especially Hollywood society. Leo Carillo, slapstick "Pancho" in the *Cisco Kid* TV western, drove a T&C convertible with a huge steer's head on the hood, the eyes wired to blink for left and right turns!

With its 1949 restyle, Chrysler continued the Town & Country as a convertible on the 131.5-inch New Yorker wheelbase. Then in 1950 the Town & Country nameplate went on Chrysler's newest body style, the Newport hardtop. (A convertible '50 model was considered but dropped in favor of the Newport, which was thought a better sales prospect. However, the 1950 version accounted for only 700 sales, 300 fewer than the year before and well short of the 1946-48 annual rate.)

Chrysler promoted the "low-swept, road-hugging lines of a convertible with a permanent solid steel top that gives the comfort and convenience of a sedan," and the Clearbac rear window with its broad glass area. T&C interiors were beautifully tailored and designed, available in green or tan leather and nylon cord, or black leather with silver-gray nylon cord. The four-wheel disc brakes (a feature shared that year with Chrysler Imperials) were a "first" for the industry, although Crosley's Hot Shot/Super Sport roadster, which also appeared about this time, had them too. The discs were Ausco-Lamberts, with twin expanding discs that rubbed against the inner surface of a cast iron brake drum/housing. They remained standard on Chrysler Imperials through 1954 and a $400 option on other models.

Through 1948, Town & Country models had used mahogany (or mahogany decal) inserts between the white ash wooden trim, but this was abandoned and the inserts on 1950 (and 1949) T&Cs were painted the body color. The white ash itself was largely decorative rather than structural, as it had been in earlier T&Cs. Still, it was of uniformly excellent quality, beautifully finished, and mitered at the corners and joints with the precision of fine furniture.

Applying all this extra trim cost a great deal of money, of course, and the 1950 Town & Country was base-priced at $4003, almost $900 more than a New Yorker Newport. Even the Imperial Newport, when it debuted in 1951, cost only a few dollars more. In fact, the Town & Country took honors as the most expensive closed car in the 1950 Detroit lineup, excepting limousines and corporation sedans. It cost about $500 more than the Cadillac Coupe de Ville and over $1000 more than the four-door hardtop Kaiser Virginian.

Chrysler didn't expect a car of this class to sell in large numbers, but it certainly anticipated building more than 700. At that level the Town & Country simply didn't justify the extra labor it took to manufacture (from New Yorker Newport shells). The decision to drop it in favor of an Imperial Newport for 1951 was obvious. "Imperial" had a better name, and "Town & Country" was now also being applied to workaday Chrysler wagons, which confused and diluted the image. Unfortunately, the 1951 Imperial Newport sold only about 750 copies in 1951, so the change didn't make much difference—and the Imperials never had the sheer class of the Town & Country hardtop.

At $4003, the 1950 Chrysler Town & Country cost a bundle and was built in limited numbers, only 700 units. It was powered by a 323.5-cubic-inch straight eight that cranked out 135 horsepower. Despite the low production, the T&C did accomplish its mission of adding a bit of glamor to a basically dull Chrysler lineup.

SPECIFICATIONS

Engine:	sidevalve I-8, 323.5 cid (3.25 × 4.88), 135 bhp
Transmission:	Prestomatic Fluid Drive
Suspension, front:	independent, coil springs, tube shocks
Suspension, rear:	live axle, leaf springs, tube shocks
Brakes:	front/rear discs
Wheelbase (in.):	131.5
Weight (lbs):	4670
Top speed (mph):	95
0-60 mph (sec):	22.0
Production:	700

F·778 P
OHIO-1950

DJ 64

1951-54 Chrysler Imperial

Through 1954, Imperial was always a Chrysler model—the highest class of Chrysler, a car competing with the likes of Cadillac, Packard, and Lincoln. Imperials received the best material and componentry Chrysler had in the 1951-54 period (Ausco-Lambert disc brakes, the biggest hemi V-8, and Fluid-Torque Drive or Powerflite transmission all standard) and naturally offered the best grades of upholstery. Like Cadillac and Lincoln, Imperial never offered a station wagon.

The 1951 hemi-head V-8 was as notable for Imperial as the lesser Chrysler models, though arguably more important in the Imp's luxury market. Imperial's price range ($3661-4402) put it farther up the scale than Cadillac ($2810-4142), Lincoln ($2529-3950), and the senior Packard ($3234-3662), and it certainly needed the hemi power. But Imperial regularly trailed all these in sales (even the senior Packard outsold it two-to-one in '51)—partly because of its image as a Chrysler rather than an Imperial; partly because of its dowdy styling.

Farther up the scale in extra-long-wheelbase territory resided the Crown Imperial—also a Chrysler in these years, but built on a 145.5-inch wheelbase to rival the Cadillac Seventy-Five and, in 1953-54, the Packard Executive sedan and Corporation limousine. Again, the Crown Imp scored only a fraction of Cadillac's sales, and barely kept pace with Packard's. Its obvious image problem tells why Chrysler decided to run Imperial as a separate make for 1955.

Least common of the 1951-54 Imperials (and conversely most desirable today) was the convertible model, which saw only 650 sales in 1951, was dropped, and appeared only as a solitary prototype in 1954. Mounted on the longest standard wheelbase, it was quite similar to the New Yorker convertible except in price—it cost $4402, about $500 more. This moved it ahead of the former champion, Packard's Custom Eight Victoria, as the single most expensive non-limo production car on the American market. It also explains why so few found buyers.

Imperial also offered a club coupe during 1951 and '52, a relatively trim looking model, but another slow seller (about 3500 in two years). Another two-door, the Imperial Newport hardtop, was always in the lineup, touting convertible-like airiness, a part-leather interior, and an expansive (for Chrysler) glass area.

Virgil Exner, who had been hired away from Studebaker to join Chrysler styling in 1949, effected improvements in the look of Chryslers from 1953 on. They evolved into a more shapely form—but most any form felt soothing to the eye after the upright-oblongs of 1949-52. There was more glass; windshields became curved, one-piece units; and all sense of dark caverns inside the car disappeared, helped by a large, wraparound rear window. While the Imperial's grille duplicated that of 1951-52, the near-vertical eagle hood ornament stood out as a unique touch.

Though lesser Chrysler models had been reduced in bulk, Imperial—striving for a greater visual difference—was enlarged to a 133.5-inch wheelbase for four-door models. An interesting new model debuted as the Town Limousine, fitted with a division window and riding this standard wheelbase. Unfortunately, the idea of providing a "compact" limousine for chauffeur-driven city work had little appeal. Production of Town Limousines amounted to 243 units in 1953 and only 85 in 1954. All standard cars in these two model years were referred to as "Custom Imperials," though there was nothing custom about them.

The Crown Imperial on its long wheelbase continued as before in these years, but production made it rare even then: a mere 48 long sedans and 111 limousines in 1953; another 23 sedans and 77 limousines for 1954. Unlike the Cadillac Seventy-Five, Chrysler did not cater to the commercial body builders with this model: only one bare chassis is listed in company records, and that for a special parade model.

The Chrysler Imperials of 1951-54 were the match of any American car in terms of engineering and luxury, but suffered because of conservative upright styling. Nonetheless, collectors find them attractive today. The 1953 Imperial (opposite, bottom) *featured a heavily chromed grille and a 180-horsepower hemi V-8. The 1954 model* (above) *sported a revised grille. The '54 Custom Imperial Newport hardtop* (opposite, top) *listed at $4560 and 1249 were built.*

SPECIFICATIONS

Engine: ohv V-8, 331.1 cid (3.81 × 3.63) **1951-53** 180 bhp **1954** 235 bhp

Transmissions:	**1951-53** Fluid-Torque Drive **1954** Powerflite automatic
Suspension, front:	independent, coil springs, tube shocks
Suspension, rear:	live axle, leaf springs, tube shocks
Brakes:	front/rear drums; discs optional (standard on Crown Imperial)
Wheelbase (in.):	**1951-52, 1953-54 Newport** 131.5 **1953-54 sedan & Town limo** 133.5 **Crown Imperial** 145.5
Weight (lbs):	4230-4570 **Crown Imperial** 5220-5450
Top speed (mph):	100-105
0-60 mph (sec):	11.0-13.0

Production: Imperial 1951 17,303* **1952** 9780* **1953** 8859 **1954** 5661 **Crown Imperial 1951** 442* **1952** 258* **1953** 160 **1954** 100

*Estimated breakdown from combined 1951-52 figures.

1951-54 Chrysler New Yorker

During the early Fifties the Chrysler New Yorker was either the most popular (1953-54) model in the line or a close second (1951-52) to the ubiquitous, lower priced Chrysler Windsor. Its popularity had certainly as much to do with its engineering as its styling, maybe more so considering its boxy lines. At the heart of that engineering was the new Chrysler 331 V-8 with hemispherical-head combustion chambers: the fabled "Hemi."

The purpose of the hemi heads was to achieve exceptional volumetric efficiency and truly outstanding performance, while relying on a lower compression ratio that could allow the use of lower-octane fuels than comparably sized non-hemis—or, conversely, producing a lot more power than comparably sized non-hemis of the same or even higher compression. This the hemi proved, in competition as wide-ranging as the Mexican Road Race and at National Hot Rod Association dragstrips, Le Mans, and the stock car oval tracks. It was expensive to build, and Chrysler several times abandoned it. In the early Fifties, though, the hemi reigned supreme among V-8s.

Also new in 1951 were two further permutations of Chrysler's old Fluid Drive: Fluid-Matic (standard on New Yorker) and Fluid-Torque ($167 option). Fluid-Matic was simply the original, fluid-coupling four-speed Fluid Drive; Fluid-Torque adopted a torque converter mounted ahead of the clutch. The clutch pedal was used to select high or low shift ranges; within the ranges you "shifted" by lifting your foot from the accelerator pedal.

The 1949-52 "new" Chrysler products were boxy and practical—but not svelte. And although much was done to improve them in 1953, their looks cost Chrysler a lot of sales. In 1954, Buick, Olds, and Pontiac all rushed past Plymouth in the production race, while Chrysler output skidded from 170,000 units to barely 100,000. Later on, Chrysler would ask the man-in-the-street, "What do you think about when you think about Chrysler?" The answers the pollsters bothered to record almost always were, "Engineering." As far as the public was concerned, that was all Chrysler

SPECIFICATIONS

Engine: ohv V-8, 331.1 cid (3.81 × 3.63) **1951-53** 180 bhp **1954 New Yorker** 195 bhp **New Yorker Deluxe** 235 bhp

Transmissions:	**1951-53** Fluid-Matic; Fluid-Torque optional **1954** Powerflite automatic
Suspension, front:	independent, coil springs, tube shocks
Suspension, rear:	live axle, leaf springs, tube shocks
Brakes:	front/rear drums (Ausco-Lambert discs optional, $400)
Wheelbase (in.):	**1951-52** 131.5 **1953-54** 125.5 **1953-54** 139.5 8-passenger sedans
Weight (lbs):	3950-4500
Top speed (mph):	110-115
0-60 mph (sec):	10.0-12.0

Production: **1951** 34,286* **1952** 17,914* **1953** 76,518 **1954** 54,742

*Estimated breakdown from combined 1951-52 figures

had going for it in this period. Relatively few buyers realized that Chryslers of 1951-54 were also beautifully built, almost impervious to rust, and would last a couple hundred thousand miles with minimal maintenance. But these qualities did not seem very important until the 1960s (by which time Chrysler had lost them).

The broad chromium smiles of the 1949-50 models were cleaned away with a neat, three-bar grille for 1951-52. There were no significant changes between the 1951 and 1952 models (the only obvious difference was the incorporation of backup lights into the tail lamp assembly of the '52s), and Chrysler didn't even keep separate production records for those two years. The reason was the Korean conflict, which many feared would stop civilian car production dead, but didn't.

The 1951-52 Saratoga, hemi-powered on the shorter Windsor chassis, was the hottest Chrysler and a notable stock-car racer, but for young upwardly-mobile professional people (you didn't abbreviate that in those days), the posh New Yorker was the favored choice. Chrysler realized this, offering the hemi V-8 New Yorker for not that much more than the six-cylinder Windsor; in 1953 the difference between the (ex-Saratoga) Windsor Deluxe and New Yorker sedans was only $550.

Chrysler tried different body mixes each year. For 1951 the New Yorker could be ordered as a sedan, club coupe, Newport hardtop, convertible, or Town & Country wagon. For 1952, with Korean caused production cutbacks, all but the sedan, Newport, and convertible were scrubbed. During 1953-54 the line split into a standard and Deluxe series, with a full ration of sedans, coupes, and Newports, but the wagon and long sedans came only in the standard series and the convertible only as a Deluxe. Of course, the lion's share of sales each year went to four-door sedans, and some of the production figures for other models were astonishingly low:

1951 convertible 1386*	1953 convertible 950
1951 T&C wagon 251	1954 std Newport 1312
1952 convertible 814*	1954 8-pass sedan 140
1953 8-pass sedan 100	1954 convertible 724

*estimated from combined 1951-52 factory figures

You can bet that Chrysler collectors are on the watch for New Yorker convertibles, though the scarcity of eight-passenger long-wheelbase sedans, wagons, and the standard '54 Newport is worth bearing in mind if you hanker to own one of these big, hefty highway cruisers.

Many new-car buyers considered the styling of the 1949-54 Chryslers too conservative, but modern-day collectors don't. The 1952 New Yorker Newport (opposite) *sparkled with all its chrome, but only about 2146 were built. The 1954 New Yorker DeLuxe* (this page) *featured somewhat smoother styling and a 195-horsepower hemi V-8.*

1955-56 Chrysler New Yorker

Despite its fine craftsmanship and the brilliant "Firepower" hemi-head V-8, Chrysler Division suffered steadily declining sales in 1951-54. Dull styling was the culprit, but Virgil Exner had come aboard from the distinguished Loewy team at Studebaker, and he had plans to thrust Chrysler Corporation into the forefront of Detroit design. Remarkably, he managed it in just 18 months, beginning in the winter of 1952-53.

The result appeared for 1955 in what Chrysler Division called "The 100-Million-Dollar Look," a veiled reference to the cost of the corporate-wide "Forward Look" restyle. Shared with DeSoto and a newly separate Imperial line, its handsome basic shape had evolved from Exner's early-Fifties Parade Phaeton show cars. Rear fenders kicked up slightly, ending on Chryslers in prominent "Twin Tower" tail lamps. A fashionably wrapped windshield lightened up the greenhouse, and the divided eggcrate grille looked like a cut-down version of Imperial's handsome design. Though wheelbase snuck up a mere half-inch over 1951-54, the '55 Chryslers were obviously longer, lower, wider—and altogether more contemporary.

Change was just as evident on the model chart. The low-end Windsor had vanished after 1953. Now, besides Imperials and all long sedans, the lineup forsook the standard New Yorker, leaving two series to garner the bulk of sales: Windsor Deluxe and New Yorker Deluxe (names that seemed pretty silly without any base series). Each offered a four-door sedan, Town & Country wagon convertible, and Newport hardtop coupes. Listed also were a slightly detrimmed Windsor Deluxe Nassau hardtop selling for $115 below the Newport, and a two-toned New Yorker St. Regis at $42 above its Newport counterpart ($3690).

Windsor got the lion's share of mechanical attention. Company president L.L. "Tex" Colbert had decreed the old six-cylinder series "dead as a dodo," so the '55 came with V-8 only. It wasn't a hemi, though, but rather a 301-cubic-inch polyspherical unit, cheaper to make and almost as efficient. Similar to Plymouth's new 1955 "Hy-Fire" design, this "Spitfire" V-8 delivered 188 horsepower. New

Chrysler called its 1955 styling "The 100-Million-Dollar Look." And indeed, the 1955-56 Chrysler New Yorkers did look like a million bucks. As in the past, the four-door sedan was the most popular body style in 1956. It sold for $4173 and saw a production run of 12,369 units. The '56 sported a new grille and modest fins.

Yorkers retained the original 331-cid hemi, with one-point higher compression adding 15 horsepower. Powerflite, the two-speed fully automatic transmission that Chrysler had introduced in '54, cost $189 extra on a Windsor but came standard on the New Yorker. As on all '55 Chrysler makes, it was controlled by a wand jutting from the dash to the right of the steering wheel, a one-year-only device that wasn't nearly as spindly as it looked.

As the finest Chryslers—as opposed to Chrysler's finest, which remained Imperial—the '55 New Yorkers exuded luxury. Upholstery was a lush leather/nylon combination except on the T&C and sedan, the latter using cloth. Besides Powerflite, standards included power brakes, electric clock, backup and brake-warning lamps, and full courtesy lighting, all extras on a Windsor. Mid-model year brought a "Summer Special" sedan and Newport with St. Regis-style two-toning for just $8.60 additional. Windsor offered the more elaborate Green Falcon and Blue Herron, sedans and Newports in those colors plus white.

If not as fast as the mighty new C-300 (see entry), the '55 New Yorker was still a fine performer. At that year's Daytona Speed Weeks it scored a class win in the flying mile at 114.6 mph and in the standing-start mile at 73.3 mph.

Sales were almost as impressive. Despite fewer models, Chrysler Division built some 47,000 more '55s than '54s, though it remained ninth in the industry. The make dropped to 10th in the market's retreat of 1956 with 128,322 units, down from 152,777.

The '56 "Powerstyle" Chryslers changed in an evolutionary way. A bolder Forward Look gave uplifted rear fenders and extra length to all but wagon models, and both series—now shorn of Deluxe badges—added Newport four-door hardtops, following GM's mid-1955 lead. All models wore large new trapezoidal grilles, but inserts and front bumpers differed. Windsors displayed three horizontal bars and a plain bumper; New Yorkers had much finer bars with five vertical dividers, plus a more sculptured bumper with flared ends. Keeping pace with the horsepower race, New Yorker carried a newly bored 354-cid hemi with 280 bhp. Windsor switched to the 331, with 225 bhp in detuned standard form or 250 bhp with optional "Power-Pak" (dual exhausts and four-barrel carburetor, for the '55 New Yorker). Rounding out mechanical developments were improved floating-shoe "Center Plane" brakes and pushbutton Powerflite, now standard across the board.

Swift, smooth, good-looking, and well appointed, these Chryslers have long had a small but enthusiastic collector following. They were arguably the best-built Chryslers until the mid-Sixties, but the significant '57s have their own loyal fans—as you'll find out a little further on.

SPECIFICATIONS

Engines: ohv V-8, **1955** 331 cid (3.81 × 3.63), 250 bhp **1956** 354 cid (3.94 × 3.63), 280 bhp

Transmission:	2-speed Powerflite automatic
Suspension, front:	upper and lower A-arms, coil springs
Suspension, rear:	live axle, semi-elliptic leaf springs
Brakes:	front/rear drums
Wheelbase (in.):	126.0
Weight (lbs):	4125-4360
Top speed (mph):	111-120
0-60 mph (sec):	10.0-10.5

Production: **1955 4d sdn** 33,342 **Newport 2d htp** 5777 **St. Regis 2d htp** 11,076 **cvt** 946 **1956 4d sdn** 24,749 **Newport 4d htp** 3599 **Newport 2d htp** 4115 **St. Regis 2d htp** 6686 **cvt** 921

1955-56 Chrysler 300

Almost as an afterthought to 1955's "The 100-Million- Dollar Look," Chrysler announced the 300 (officially C-300) on February 8, 1955. It was greeted by a cacophony of praise from buff books and stock-car racers and more than a few Chrysler fans who had never, and would never, own one. A lot of those who *could* plunk down the $4110 it took to own one test drove a 300 and bought a New Yorker or Imperial instead. They soon found that what Karl Ludvigsen later called the "Beautiful Brute" was pretty brutish to drive as an everyday Chrysler. But that wasn't why it was invented.

There is no doubt that the legendary 300 rates as one of the great performance cars of all time. As Tom McCahill of *Mechanix Illustrated* put it, in his own unmatched style, it was "the most powerful sedan in the world, and the fastest, teamed up with rock-crushing suspension and a competition engine capable of yanking Bob Fulton's steamboat *over* the George Washington Bridge....This is definitely not the car for Henrietta Blushbottom, your maiden schoolmarm aunt, to use for hustling up popsicles. In fact, the 300 is not a car for the typical puddling male to use. This is a hardboiled, magnificent piece of semi-competition transportation, built for the real automotive connoisseur."

In fact, a connoisseur conceived the 300: Robert MacGregor Rodger, chief engineer of Chrysler Division. Then 38 years old, he was a veteran of the hemi engine project. It was he who looked at early competition efforts with the hemi by privateers and decided that the engine deserved factory backing. Bob Rodger may have been the godfather of the "works" teams which now dominate the sport, although similar thoughts were occurring to several European companies about the same time.

Stylist Virgil Exner, who came to dominate Chrysler design with the successful '55s, encouraged Roger to engineer a super-stock Chrysler, but division general manager Ed Quinn told them both that its styling could not deviate too much from

the '55 norm. Exner hit upon a combination of Imperial and Chrysler: a New Yorker hardtop body; Windsor rear quarter panels; an Imperial grille, parking lights, front bumper, and wheel covers. Later, Exner substituted less bulky Chrysler bumpers and parking lights, with Imperial bumper guards set far apart. The Imperial dashboard Exner chose had no space for a tachometer, but this wasn't too serious since the 300 came only with Powerflite automatic in '55. Few extras found their way into those first 300s, radio, heater, and power steering being typical. Less often specified were power seats/brakes/windows, clock, tinted glass, and wire wheels. Air conditioning was not available. Only red, white, and black paint jobs were offered, all combined with tan leather upholstery.

The 300 proved unbeatable in 1955 competition. It won its first NASCAR Grand National at a 92-mph average, sped through the Daytona flying mile at 127, set a standing-start mile record for its class (76.84 mph), and took the checkered flag at 37 NASCAR and AAA races of more than 100 miles. It underscored Chrysler's already-prominent engineering reputation, sparked sales of more mundane Chryslers, and itself notched up 1725 sales in 1955—very good indeed for such a specialized model.

The 1956 Chrysler 300B boasted a logical refinement of the original '55, again combining a Chrysler hardtop body with an Imperial grille and special identification. Introduced late again, at the Chicago Automobile Show in January 1956, it featured a bored-out 354 hemi with 340 horsepower stock, 355 bhp optional via higher compression heads. It was the first (and last) 300 to exceed one horsepower per cubic inch. It also surpassed Packard's 310-bhp Caribbean as the horsepower champion of '56—as its predecessor had in 1955.

Axle ratios spanned an enormous range, from 3.08:1 to a stump-pulling 6.17:1. No test of the latter is on record, but it must have done 0-60 in something like four seconds! Again, the 300 dominated NASCAR; Kiekhafer Racing's Tim Flock winning the Grand National race at a 90.836 mph average, closely followed by Vicki Wood, who set a new women's lap record of 136.081 mph.

Chrysler offered more options on the 300B, including "factory air" and Mopar's new "Highway Hi-Fi" record player. But 1956 was a regressive year sales-wise, and production reached only 1102 units. Be it a '55 or '56, the 300 owner of today is fortunate and widely envied. Notwithstanding the abuses to which the word is subject today, these cars are true classics.

SPECIFICATIONS

Engines: ohv V-8 **1955** 331.1 cid (3.81 × 3.63), 300 bhp **1956** 354.0 cid (3.94 × 3.63), 340 bhp; 355 bhp optional

Transmission:	Powerflite 2-speed automatic
Suspension, front:	independent, coil springs, tube shocks
Suspension, rear:	live axle, leaf springs, tube shocks
Brakes:	front/rear drums
Wheelbase (in.):	126.0
Weight (lbs):	**1955** 4005 **1956** 4145
Top speed (mph):	130 (with normal axle ratio)
0-60 mph (sec):	9.0-10.0 (with normal axle ratio)

Production: **1955** 1725 **1956** 1102 (includes CKD export models)

Although officially known as the C-300, everybody called the '55 model (below) the 300. This Chrysler was a no-compromise high-performance car built for the true automotive connoisseur, according to tester Tom McCahill. The 1956 model, the 300B (opposite)*, added modest fins and 40 horsepower (55 with higher compression), for a total of 340 or 355 bhp.*

1957-59 Chrysler New Yorker

Not content with its 1955-56 sales comeback, Chrysler Corporation spent another $300 million to restyle and reengineer its entire line for 1957. The results were as unbelievable as they were unexpected. With these radically changed cars, Highland Park decisively wrested industry design leadership from General Motors and, in so doing, forever banished its staid image.

Though all the firm's '57s looked good, Chrysler arguably wore this second-generation "Forward Look" best of all. From a clean, horizontal-bar grille to gracefully upswept rear fenders, it flaunted the sort of unified design that could only have come from one mind, not several. A wedge profile, dramatically lower beltline, vast new expanses of glass, and striking height reductions—three inches on sedans, five on hardtops—combined to suggest greater overall length, yet the '57s were actually a bit shorter than the '56s (on unchanged wheelbases). In all, this "New Look of Motion" was distinctive and exciting, yet commendably restrained for the period. It made the '57 exactly what Chrysler claimed: its "most glamorous car in a generation."

Along with its corporate cousins, the '57 Chrysler introduced two major mechanical innovations. One was "Torsion-Aire Ride," a new front suspension comprising longitudinal torsion bars acting on lower transverse arms, plus upper A-arms and an anti-roll bar. Its design goals called for improved handling with no penalty in ride comfort, and it succeeded admirably. Torsion-Aire made Chrysler Corporation cars America's most roadable '57s, aided by a new box-rail chassis with wider tracks and a reduced center of gravity.

Highland Park's other technical triumph that year was TorqueFlite, a new three-speed automatic transmission offered throughout the corporate stable as an alternative to two-speed Powerflite. Standard for all '57 Chryslers save Windsors, where it cost $220 extra, and also featuring pushbutton control, TorqueFlite received plaudits for its quick response and smooth shift action.

As another path to higher '57 sales, Chrysler revived the Saratoga series, a sedan and two hardtops slotted between Windsor and New Yorker. All other offerings returned from '56 save the New Yorker St. Regis and Windsor convertible and Nassau. Windsor moved up to the previous year's 354-cubic-inch hemi V-8, with 285 standard horsepower or 295 optional; the latter was included on Saratogas. New Yorker, befitting its top-line status (not counting this year's equally new 300C) received an even larger 392 hemi packing 325 bhp.

For all their worthy changes, the '57s did nothing for Chrysler's model year production and industry rank, both of which held steady from '56. This must have been a disappointment, but nothing compared to what 1958 would bring. Thanks to that year's deep recession, plus the '57s' growing reputation for indifferent workmanship and early body rust, Chrysler slipped from 10th to 11th.

Predictably, the '58 Chryslers were much like the '57s. Higher compression boosted horsepower across the board (to 290/310/345 for Windsor/Saratoga/New Yorker), and a minor facelift typical of an all-new design in its sophomore year involved mainly grilles (more DeSoto-like, oddly enough), smaller taillights, and revised trim.

The market began a modest recovery for 1959 and so did Chrysler volume, though the model year total was up less than 6300 units to just 30 shy of 70,000—still pretty dismal. A more substantial facelift that year brought rather duller-looking front and rear ends, and the Windsor convertible reappeared (actually, two had been built in 1958) in what was called the "Lion-Hearted" line. That name referred to a crop of new wedgehead V-8s that cost much less to build than the hemis, yet offered more horsepower. New Yorker carried a big-bore 413-cid version (shared with this year's 300E) tuned for 350 bhp; Windsor and Saratoga ran a 383 rated respectively at 305 and 325 bhp. New Yorker convertible sales slowed down to a trickle and, except for the Windsor sedan, no '59 Chrysler model saw more than 10,000 copies.

Unfortunately, matters would get worse before they got better for Chrysler Division, with product miscues and inept marketing policies taking a big sales toll in the first half of the '60s. Some—but far from all—of these troubles began with the 1957-59s, which are significant not only as the last hemi-powered Chryslers but the last with body-on-frame construction and distinctive styling free of outrageousness. Fine all-round performance and the aforementioned rarity of certain New Yorkers have only enhanced their appeal as some of the more collectible cars from this decade.

Chrysler Corporation stunned the automotive world with its daring, exciting, finned designs of 1957. The top-of-the-line Chrysler was the New Yorker (opposite), which sold for $4202 as a two-door hardtop and $4259 as a four-door hardtop.

SPECIFICATIONS

Engines: ohv V-8 **1957** 392 cid (4.00 × 3.90), 325 bhp **1958** 345 bhp **1959** 413 cid (4.00 × 3.90), 350 bhp

Transmissions:	3-speed TorqueFlite automatic
Suspension, front:	upper A-arms, lower transverse arms, longitudinal torsion bars, anti-roll bar
Suspension, rear:	live axle, semi-elliptic leaf springs
Brakes:	front/rear drums
Wheelbase (in.):	126.0
Weight (lbs):	4220-4445
Top speed (mph):	110-115
0-60 mph (sec):	10.0-11.0

Production: **1957 4d sdn** 12,369 **4d htp** 10,948 **2d htp** 8863 **cvt** 1049 **Town & Country 4d wgn** 1391 **1958 4d sdn** 7110 **4d htp** 5227 **2d htp** 3205 **cvt** 666 **Town & Country 4d wgn** 1203* **1959 4d sdn** 7792 **4d htp** 4805 **2d htp** 2434 **cvt** 286 **Town & Country 4d wgn** 1008*
*includes 6- and 9-passenger models

CHRYSLER

1957-58 Chrysler 300

With the arrival of Virgil Exner's tailfinned cruisers, torsion bar front suspension, and TorqueFlite automatic in 1957, Bob Rodger and Chrysler Division stayed with their now-established Chrysler 300 formula: an all-out performance car, "semi-competition" as roadtester Tom McCahill called it, within the framework of Chrysler production line components. The '57 wore a 300C badge designating its place as third in the 300 series—though this caused confusion with the original 1955 C-300.

This time the 300's distinctive grille was borrowed from nothing else: a big, trapezoidal structure, honeycombed with vertical and horizontal bars, designed to emphasize the wideness of the car. Small intakes on either side channeled air directly to the front brake drums, which benefited from increased lining area, now 251 square inches. The new front end design took its inspiration from a prototype, number 613, which incidentally prefigured the enormous tailfins of the 1959 production Mopar models to come. In 1957, though, the tailfins were elegantly done, Chrysler's particularly well integrated with the dart-shaped lines of the car, and certainly not gawky. That was to come later—at Ford and General Motors, as well as Chrysler.

Mechanical refinements to the 300C included SilentFlite fan drive, which automatically stopped the radiator fan at 2500 rpm, boosting power. The 300's torsion bars were 40 percent stiffer than those of the New Yorker (it rode as hard as ever). Power steering cost extra, but proved useful since it required only 3.3 turns lock-to-lock; most 300C's had it.

Like the Windsor (but unlike any other 1957 Chrysler), the 300 could be ordered with a three-speed manual shift instead of TorqueFlite. And in addition to its base 375 horsepower, a buyer could specify a high-lift cam, which increased power to a whopping 390. Most of the 390-bhp cars had the stick shift, and must have been awesome to behold on dragstrips and traffic light Grands Prix.

The 1957-58 Chrysler 300 wore an aggressive-looking grille all its own. The 300C (this page) *boasted 375 horsepower, or 390 via an optional high-lift cam. It was priced at $4929 for the hardtop, $5359 for the ragtop. The 1958 300D sported a modified grille and taillights, and saw the prices bumped to $5173 and $5603, respectively. Production dipped from 2402 units in 1957 to only 809 in recession-wracked '58.*

New for the 300 this year was a convertible, representing about a third of production. As with past 300s, however, 300C trim options remained limited: tan leather again for all interiors, with a choice of Copper Brown, Parade Green, Cloud White, Gauguin Red, and Jet Black for the exterior. Like other 1957 Chryslers, 300Cs came with dual or quad headlamps. Not all states had legalized quads yet, so the front fenders had been designed to accept either treatment. (Only Nash and the Cadillac Eldorado Brougham offered standard quads in 1957; one wonders whether they had to offer a clumsy dual headlamp adaptation where quads were banned, or just didn't sell cars in those states.) Prices started at $5000 for the hardtop, about $5400 for the convertible.

Anyone who read Tom McCahill's road tests in *Mechanix Illustrated* would know that the Chrysler 300 was right up his alley. He described the '57 as "the most hairy-chested, fire-eating land bomb ever conceived in Detroit." Uncle Tom reported 0-60 mph in 8.4 seconds with TorqueFlite, and a top speed of 150 with a high (low numerical) rear axle ratio. Unfortunately, the 300's dominance of racing was ending through no fault of its own—this was the year the Auto Manufacturers Association instituted its simplistic ban on racing promotion, responding to a safety lobby which insisted advertising race results caused dangerous driving on public roads. Within a few years, the car companies were all cheating on the "ban," and it was soon forgotten, but it effectively squelched factory support of stock car racing. In any case, the 300C did take the national standing- and flying-mile championships at Daytona, privateer Brewster Shaw exceeding 130 mph.

Changes were slight on the 1958 300D: a simpler eggcrate grille; queer, truncated taillights that no longer filled the space designed for them in the tailfins; a small boost in compression and horsepower; Bendix Electrojector fuel injection as a $400 option. The last, ordered on only 16 cars, proved unreliable, and most of them were converted to dual four-barrel carbs. Power brakes came standard, the hemi had a new valve timing lift, heavier pistons, and a new cam. In one of its few competitive outings, the 300D set a new speed record: 156.387 mph in Class E at Bonneville, with Norm Thatcher driving. Brewster Shaw showed up again at Daytona, turning a quarter-mile in 16 seconds at 94 mph. There was no doubt that the 1958 300D was still a brute, and still beautiful.

SPECIFICATIONS

Engine: ohv V-8, 392.0 cid (4.00 × 3.90) **1957** 375 bhp; 390 bhp optional **1958** 380 bhp; 390 bhp optional

Transmissions:	3-speed manual; TorqueFlite 3-speed automatic
Suspension, front:	independent, torsion bars, tube shocks
Suspension, rear:	live axle, leaf springs, tube shocks
Brakes:	front/rear drums
Wheelbase (in.):	126.0
Weights (lbs):	**Hardtop** 4235-4305 **Convertible** 4390-4475
Top speed (mph):	130-150 (depending on gearing)
0-60 mph (sec):	7.7 to 8.7 (range of reported results)

Production: 1957 Hardtop 1918 **Convertible** 484 **1958 Hardtop** 618 **Convertible** 191

1959 Chrysler 300E

The fifth generation Chrysler muscle-car retained its distinctive trapezoid grille and clean flanks bearing the traditional 300 emblem and spear, but wore 1959-style taillights, rear bumper, and deck. These didn't help its styling, and worse, a rumor surfaced that the 300 had lost its fangs. Reason? The hemi engine had given way to a wedge-head V-8, 101 pounds lighter, without the wild cam, hydraulic lifters, and optional Bendix fuel injection.

Chrysler promotion didn't help. The company (or at least its ad agency) had apparently decided that with the racing ban in effect they might as well tout the 300E as a kind of fast luxury car. A full range of New Yorker-like equipment joined the options list, including a new Chrysler invention that seemed like a better idea than it was: swivel seats. Mounted on a pivot, both the driver's and passenger's large individual seats swiveled outward when the doors were opened. It sounded sensible, but its main accomplishment was to snag dresses under the steering wheel—with mixed results, depending on whether you were driving or just observing.

Other accessories included auto pilot (cruise control), air conditioning, comprehensive radio and heater units, power windows, power seats, power antenna, tinted glass, Highway Hi-Fi, and other assorted tinsel. An attractive but impractical 300E wheel cover was introduced with a black-painted center disc and a gear-shaped dummy hub surrounding the red, white, and blue 300 emblem (which also appeared on the rear seat). Leather still covered the interior—an interesting woven porous texture designed to breathe better on hot days. Exterior colors remained limited: black, red, copper, turquoise-gray, and tan. But all the fluff, and the concentration of such non-functional ephemera as unventilated wheel covers with phoney hubs, naturally made many people wonder if the 300E had become a paper tiger.

It wasn't.

Take for example Bill Callahan, writing in *Motor Trend* in March 1959: "Performance of the 300E tops its predecessor by a good margin. The 300E this year weighs a little over 4300 pounds at the curb. The big 380-bhp engine (with 10.1:1 compression, improved TorqueFlite transmission, and 3.31 to 1 rear end) handles this poundage with no difficulty at all." Chrysler's own engineering figures virtually duplicate Callahan's data. Both show the 300E doing 0-60 in a little over eight seconds, and Chrysler reported a 0-90 mph blast in 17.6 seconds versus 20.6 seconds for the 300D.

Unfortunately, the mixed message Chrysler was sending about this new 300 apparently turned off the traditional customer while failing to turn on the luxury buyer, who chose instead the New Yorker or Saratoga. Money was a factor too: Model for model the New Yorker cost $900 less than the 300E, the Saratoga hardtop $1300 less than the 300E hardtop. In a year of improving sales generally, the "E" had the lowest production to date, and the lowest of any 300 letter series Chrysler until 1963; even the tail-enders to the series, the much-tamed 300K and 300L of 1964 and '65, sold in far greater quantities.

The letter series made a major comeback the following year with the 300F, all bucket seats and muscle, a ram-induction version of the 413 wedge head belting out a claimed 400 gross horsepower. The 300G of 1961 dished up more of the same, and helped to bring letter-series sales up to 1600-plus, the best year since the beginning.

By that time, the 300's reputation was so well established that the bean counters took over, and in 1962 Chrysler fielded a new series of standard "300" production cars, including four-door models, in place of the Windsor. These lacked all the individuality and hairy-chested performance of the letter series, and immediately watered down the latter's image. A 1962 300H was also offered that year, with even more power than the 300F and 300G, but sales hit rock bottom again, and didn't improve with the 300J in 1963. So the bean counters began taming even the letter series 300, dropping standard power to 360 for the 1964 300K. The final 300L in 1965 hardly differed in appearance or performance from a New Yorker, which weighed the same and could be ordered with the 360-bhp engine. The song had ended, but the memory lingered on.

Revised rear deck styling marked the 1959 Chrysler 300E; up front, the grille texture took on a horizontal motif, although the 300E's face looked much the same otherwise. Horsepower actually declined by 10, to 380, although the engine was enlarged from 392.0 to 413.0 cubic inches. Production slipped, however, to only 140 units for the convertible, 550 for the hardtop (opposite page). *Output would improve to 1212 units for the restyled 1960 300F.*

SPECIFICATIONS

Engine:	ohv V-8, 413.0 cid (4.18 × 3.75), 380 bhp
Transmissions:	3-speed manual; 3-speed Torque-Flite automatic
Suspension, front:	independent, torsion bars, tube shocks
Suspension, rear:	live axle, leaf springs, tube shocks
Brakes:	front/rear drums
Wheelbase (in.):	126.0
Weight (lbs):	**Hardtop** 4290 **Convertible** 4350
Top speed (mph):	130
0-60 mph (sec):	8.0-9.0
Production:	**Hardtop** 550 **Convertible** 140

300
ILLINOIS
59300

1956-57 Continental Mark II

In 1953, the Ford Motor Company decided to produce an ultimate luxury car that would in one swoop eclipse everything else in the industry. Its name, ipso facto, would be "Continental," reviving the famous line of *grand luxe* Lincolns conceived by Edsel Ford back in the late Thirties. Since the last Continental was sold in 1948, dealers and the public had been demanding its return. Ford determined that their wish should come true.

The resulting 1956-57 Continental Mark II differed from the "Mark I" (never officially so-called) in one crucial respect: it was not a Lincoln. Rather, it debuted as a product of the "Continental Division," headed by Bill Ford, Henry Ford II's younger brother. This new arm of the Ford Motor Company had the responsibility of launching not only the Mark II coupe but a whole line of ultra-luxurious cars aimed at a market sector higher even than Lincoln and Cadillac. The Continental's target was none other than Rolls-Royce, and for a time it appeared to have succeeded admirably. But not for long.

What became Continental Division started in 1953 as Special Product Operations, staffed by a star-studded array of designers and engineers: Gordon Buehrig, John Reinhart, Bill Ford, Harley Copp. The last, as chief engineer, designed a unique chassis that dipped low between the front and rear axles. This "cow belly frame," as they called it, allowed chair-high seats without requiring a high roofline. Power came from Lincoln V-8s, specially selected from the assembly line and individually hand balanced, connected to Multi-Drive three-speed automatic transmissions.

Although the in-house team of Ford designers confidently expected to be the final arbiters of Mark II styling, Special Products called in four outside consultants to compete for the final assignment by top management: A. B. "Buzz" Grisinger/Rees Miller, Walter Buell Ford, Vince Gardner, and George Walker. Each competitor

The Continental Mark II became a "classic" in its own time because its design was universally admired and because of the quality that went into the car. Although initial sales looked promising, the market for a $10,000 car in 1956 wasn't large enough to sustain production at a reasonable level for long. The Mark II thus died during its second year. The interior (above) *boasted top grain leathers and expensive fabrics.*

worked from the same exact measurements and submitted two or three designs in front, rear, side, and three-quarter front/rear views. The final renderings were scaled to a single size and colored identically: deep blue with tan interiors.

Ultimately, proposal number two from Special Products' own design team was selected—and little changed for production. But some of the also-rans were quite ingenious. Walter Buell Ford proposed a retractable hardtop, which was later tried but not produced for the Mark II (though successfully executed on the 1957-59 Ford Skyliner). One of George Walker's designs was closely patterned after the original 1940 Lincoln Continental: a long, clean hood flowing into the famous split radiator grille, each segment curving delicately back to the line of the front end and back out again to culminate in the headlamps. "Building dies to handle that one would have been tricky," John Reinhart remembered, "and probably very expensive." But Reinhart greatly admired the Walker concept.

Later, rumors circulated that the "competition" story was a wild PR concoction—that there never was any doubt about Ford's in-house team winning the contest. But Reinhart said, "There was no plot. We won the contest with unlabeled presentations."

The winning design was quite deserving: a sleek, clean coupe measuring 218.5 inches overall, with a simple die cast grille, a "kick-up" at the rear fender, the traditional Continental closed rear roofline and spare tire outline on the trunk, elegant bumpers, and neatly inset taillights. The simple, almost stark cockpit took inspiration from aircraft and locomotive designs, and the richly furnished interior featured top grain leathers and expensive fabrics. The Mark II debuted at a list price of $10,000, then the highest priced car in America, and was universally admired on both sides of the Atlantic. Continental Division was well into plans for a convertible and four-door berline when the roof fell in.

For whatever reason—the tall price and conservative styling must be considered factors—the Mark II did not sell well enough to satisfy the accountants. "A Mercury cost analyst was brought in to downgrade future products," Gordon Buehrig remembered. "It was a shame. What we had going for us in the Mark II was literally a revival of the Duesenberg concept. What we ended up with was something much less—and even that didn't last long....It was a project that for a time broke Bill Ford's heart, and I guess you could say that in many ways it broke ours, too."

SPECIFICATIONS

Engine: ohv V-8, 368.0 cid (4.00 × 3.66) **1956** 285 bhp **1957** 300 bhp

Transmission:	Turbo-Drive 3-speed automatic
Suspension, front:	independent, coil springs, tube shocks
Suspension, rear:	live axle, leaf springs, tube shocks
Brakes:	front/rear drums
Wheelbase (in.):	126.0
Weight (lbs):	4800
Top speed (mph):	115
0-60 mph (sec):	12.0
Production:	**1956** 1325 **1957** 444

1958-59 Continental Mark III/IV

When the Ford Motor Company decided to downgrade the Continental by $4000, expand the line, and try to make it profitable, it simultaneously gave up on the idea of an American Rolls-Royce, or modern Duesenberg. A Mercury production manager was called in to advise Ford how the deed might be done. Not surprisingly, the resulting 1958 Continental Mark III ended up based on Lincoln's huge new unit body. Thus, the Mark III wore the same elongated fenders, large chrome appliqués, tailfins, and canted quad headlamps as Lincoln. There was also a change in powerplant, Lincoln having now adopted a mammoth 430-cubic-inch V-8 developing 375 horsepower. The Mark III got that, too.

The line expanded from the previous Mark II coupe to encompass Lincoln's four 1958 body styles: four-door sedan, hardtop, convertible, and Landau four-door hardtop sedan. The Mark III ranged in price from $5825 for the hardtop coupe to $6283 for the convertible—obviously they had been "built to a price," slotted-in at about $700 more than the corresponding Lincoln Premiere. The game plan worked to the extent that each sold reasonably well, despite an off year for the industry at large. The most popular model was the four-door hardtop Landau, which accounted for close to 6000 units.

Elsewhere at Ford Motor Company, success was more proving elusive. The Edsel, which also started off as the product of a separate, new division, flopped after an initial burst of sales, scoring only about a third the production Ford had planned for it. Management moved hastily to compensate, deciding to fold the Edsel and

Continental output increased dramatically for 1958, when the Lincoln-based '58 Mark III replaced the ill-starred Mark II. Price and the availability of four body styles helped. The '58 convertible (opposite, top) *listed at $6283 (almost $4000 less than a Mark II); it single-handedly exceeded the total output of the 1956-57 Mark II. The '59 Mark IV, here a $6845 Landau hardtop sedan* (this page)*, featured a cleaner grille and an extended side sculpture. A '59 Lincoln* (opposite, bottom right) *shows just how closely the 1958-60 Continentals were related to it.*

Continental Divisions back into Lincoln-Mercury. James J. Nance, late president of Studebaker-Packard, came in as president of the Edsel Division to handle this transition, while Continental was summarily absorbed by Lincoln-Mercury in mid-1958. Accordingly, the "Continental Mark IV" for 1959 became a Lincoln model, as would all Continentals in the future.

The Mark IV was again priced upmarket from the Premiere—but by $1300 model for model. In addition to the previous four models, two new pricey executive-class Continentals appeared: a division window limousine and a similar formal sedan. These were in essence the kinds of cars that Continental Division had planned to spin off from the Mark II. They cost a great deal more than the other body styles, the formal starting at $9208 and the limousine at $10,230, but they offered nothing extra in the way of length or interior space, so sales were predictably light. Volume also fell off for the more conventional body styles, except for the four-door hardtops, which increased slightly. Horsepower rating for the 430 V-8 fell back by about 10 percent also, a result of America's new-found interest in fuel economy.

The downgraded Continental would have one more year of this approach in 1960, when the Mark V appeared, offering an unchanged lineup of six body styles, a still-further-detuned V-8, and unchanged sales. Then in 1961, Lincoln-Mercury recast the entire formula and produced the brilliant and highly successful line of Lincoln Continental four-door sedans and four-door convertibles. This new series did not include any limousine models, so limo work was farmed out to Lehmann-Peterson, who produced special bodies on lengthened wheelbases.

The new Continental hadn't worked out as Ford had anticipated back in 1953. But it did lead to a wholly new interpretation of the theme in 1961—and in due course to another "personal luxury" Continental Mark series in 1968. This '68 was confusingly again called "Mark III" (instead of Mark VI, which was the next number in line). However, it lasted longer than the 1958 Mark III, and bit deeply into Cadillac's domination of the luxury car field.

SPECIFICATIONS

Engine: ohv V-8, 430 cid (4.30 × 3.70) **1958** 375 bhp **1959** 350 bhp

Transmission:	Turbo-Drive 3-speed automatic
Suspension, front:	independent, coil springs, tube shocks; air suspension optional, rarely fitted
Suspension, rear:	live axle, coil springs, trailing arms, tube shocks; air suspension optional
Brakes:	front/rear drums
Wheelbase (in.):	131.0
Weight (lbs):	5000-5200
Top speed (mph):	110-115
0-60 mph (sec):	12.0

Production: **1958 4d sdn** 1,283 **htp cpe** 2,328 **cvt cpe** 3,048 **Landau htp sdn** 5,891 **1959 limo** 49 **formal sdn** 78 **4d sdn** 955 **htp cpe** 1,703 **cvt cpe** 2,195 **htp sdn** 6,146

1950-52 Crosley Hot Shot/ Super Sports

Cincinnati radio-and-refrigerator magnate Powel Crosley, Jr., entered the car business in 1939 with dreams of an American *Volkswagen:* a small, cheap economy model that would make every family a two-car family. Prewar Crosleys were cute but crude little boxes with two-cylinder engines, mechanical brakes, very basic equipment, and prices as low as $299. Powel even sold them in his appliance stores as well as through auto dealerships.

Postwar Crosleys tried to be more like "real" cars: 28 inches longer, more impressively styled, somewhat better equipped—but not much—and more powerful, with an overhead-cam four derived from the copper-brazed "CoBra" unit that had been developed for wartime helicopters and was made of sheetmetal. Despite this engine's near-predictable durability problems, Crosley did relatively well in the postwar seller's market, building some 5000 cars for 1946 and over 19,000 for '47. In a burst of optimism, Crosley predicted annual sales would soon reach 80,000. Production did climb for 1948—to 28,374—but would go no higher. The very next year, Crosley volume plunged nearly 75 percent in the face of a sated market and new models from larger, more prosperous rivals.

Seeking salvation, Crosley turned to more specialized products in 1949. First came the versatile "FarmORoad" utility vehicle, followed by, of all things, a sports car. Aptly named Hot Shot, this bare-bones two-seat roadster spanned a four-inch-longer wheelbase than other Crosley cars but shared their drivetrain and chassis. What made it interesting was a racy, uniquely styled body with cut away sides, a bulbous nose flanked by freestanding headlamps, and a spare tire perched jauntily on a stubby, trunkless tail.

Though blessed with only 26 horses, the Hot Shot lived up to its name with surprisingly good performance due largely to its bantam build and sparse equipment. It was no race car in stock tune, but all things considered it was a good goer. The typical example could do 0-60 mph in 20 seconds, the standing quarter-mile in 25 seconds at 66 mph, and reach 77 mph tops. Being a Crosley, it was dirt cheap: just $849. The scarcely quicker MG-TC sold for twice as much.

By this time, Crosley had abandoned the trouble-prone CoBra engine for a sturdier CIBA (Cast-Iron Block Assembly) version. With five main bearings, full-pressure lubrication, and a safe 10,000-rpm limit, it looked a natural for souping up. Accessory houses soon obliged with a slew of low-cost bolt-ons that halved the stock model's 0-60 time and upped top speed to a genuine 100 mph. Braje, for instance, offered a full-race cam for $25, headers for $28, and dual manifolds with Amal motorcycle carburetors for $60. Vertex and H&C sold high-performance ignition systems, and S.CO.T listed a Roots-type supercharger that more than doubled horsepower. Happily, the CIBA engine could easily handle such muscle-building goodies.

So could the Hot Shot chassis, which delivered nimble handling and leech-like roadholding despite a primitive suspension. Brakes were another story. All 1949-50 Crosleys used aircraft-derived Goodyear-Hawley "spot" discs in front. They resisted fade but lacked proper sealing, and thus often froze when exposed to salt or road grime. A switch to all-round Bendix drums for 1951-52 solved the problem and were more than a match for even a modified Hot Shot's performance.

Which could be formidable. The Crosley's finest hour came in 1950 when one of that year's new Super Sports, basically a Hot Shot with accessory doors, won the Index of Performance at the inaugural Sebring 12-hour race. A similar car entered by American sportsman Briggs Cunningham might have repeated the feat at the prestigious Le Mans 24 Hours in '51 but retired with electrical problems.

Crosley itself retired at the end of 1952, a victim of plummeting sales in a "bigger is better" market. The Hot Shot listed at $952 by then, while the Super Sports had risen from an initial $925 to $1029. Still, these were astonishingly low prices considering the cars' performance potential and high "fun quotient." They should have sold like hotcakes, and they might have had they been built by one of the Big Three.

But they weren't and they didn't, which probably explains why they remain America's "forgotten" early-postwar sports cars. Too bad. They were appealing little giant-killers fully worthy of the term. Come to that, they still are.

Back in 1949, America's sports car was the Crosley Hot Shot. A mini by anyone's standards, it rode an 85.0-inch wheelbase and was powered by a tiny 44-cubic-inch four. No matter, a curb weight of around 1000 pounds and a wide selection of aftermarket performance parts meant that a Hot Shot, or the Super Sports (with doors), could embarrass many larger cars. In point of fact, a Super Sports won the index of performance at the prestigious 1950 Sebring 12-hour race.

SPECIFICATIONS

Engine:	ohv I-4, 44 cid (2.50 × 2.25), 26.5 bhp
Transmission:	3-speed manual
Suspension, front:	I-beam axle, semi-elliptic leaf springs
Suspension, rear:	live axle, quarter-elliptic leaf springs
Brakes:	**1950** front/rear discs **1951-52** front/rear drums
Wheelbase (in.):	85.0
Weight (lbs):	1180-1240
Top speed (mph):	80
0-60 mph (sec):	20.0
Production:	**1950** 742 **1951** 646 **1952** 358

HISTORICAL
OHIO 3658 H
VEHICLE

Hotshot

3658H

1952-55 Cunningham

Hollywood could make a movie about Briggs Swift Cunningham and should. The son of a Cincinnati banker and godson of the Proctor half of Proctor & Gamble, he cut a dashing figure in high society. He knew all the "right" people (many as rich as himself) and had a passion for sports: golfing, flying, yachting especially—and sports cars. After joining the infant Sports Car Club of America in the early postwar years, Briggs drove to second at Watkins Glen in 1948 in his unique "Bumerc," a rebuilt Mercedes SSK with Buick power.

Then Briggs got serious. Having met Phil Walters and Bill Frick at the Glen, he acquired their services as drivers and engineers by buying their small company, hoping to enter their hybrid "Fordillac" in the 1950 running of the Le Mans 24 Hours, the world's premier endurance race. But the Fordillac didn't qualify, so Briggs fielded two cars powered by Cadillac's new overhead-valve V-8. One was a big special-bodied streamliner (nicknamed Le Monstre by appreciative French racegoers), the other a stock 1950 Coupe de Ville. The latter finished 10th overall, the special 11th.

Buoyed by this success, Briggs turned to crafting his own sports/racing cars, setting up a company in West Palm Beach, Florida that same year. "We don't intend to build two types of car, one for racing and the other for touring," he said. "Our policy is to concentrate on one model readily adaptable for both purposes."

The first, logically tagged C-1, was a smooth, low-slung roadster that looked like a cross between the early Ferrari Barchettas and some of the later Ghia-bodied Chrysler specials. Power was supplied by Chrysler's 331-cubic-inch hemi-head V-8, mounted in a strong tubular-steel chassis with independent coil-spring front suspension, De Dion rear end, generous 105-inch wheelbase, and broad 58-inch front and rear tracks. Only one C-1 was completed, equipped for road use, rather lavishly so by European standards.

Next came the evolutionary C-2. Only three were built; all racers designated C-2R. Walters and Fitch drove one at Le Mans in 1951 but had to settle for 18th overall.

Late that year, Briggs decided to make the C-2 more of a road car and sell it in limited numbers. The resulting C-3 would be offered as a coupe in addition to the usual roadster at respective base prices of $9000 and $8000. Also planned was a $2915 racing package comprising four-carburetor manifold, ported and polished heads, oil cooler, competition brakes, and racing bumperettes and grille screen. But by the time the prototype coupe saw completion, someone had figured out that each C-3 would cost $15,000 just to build.

SPECIFICATIONS

Engine: Chrysler ohv V-8, 331 cid (3.81 × 3.63) **1952-53** 220 bhp **1953-55** 235 bhp

Transmissions:	Cadillac 3-speed manual; Chrysler semi-automatic
Suspension, front:	upper and lower A-arms, coil springs (Ford)
Suspension, rear:	Chrysler live axle, parallel trailing arms, coil springs
Brakes:	front/rear drums (Mercury)
Wheelbase (in.):	105.0; 107.0
Weight (lbs):	approximately 3500
Top speed (mph):	120
0-60 mph (sec):	6.9-8.5
Production:	**Coupe** 18 **Cabriolet** 9

Briggs Cunningham loved sports cars, and in the early Fifties he set about to build one that would be appropriate for racing or touring. The C-3 was designed by Giovanni Michelotti, built by Vignale of Italy on a chassis out of Cunningham's Palm Beach, Florida, works, and powered by a Chrysler hemi V-8. It emerged as an American gran turismo that was as elegant and exciting as anything from Europe, but "production" difficulties kept output low. Ultimately, only 18 coupes and nine cabriolets were built.

That was no way to run things, so in early 1952 Cunningham contracted with Vignale of Italy to build C-3 bodies to a new design by Giovanni Michelotti. With this, the projected base price dropped back to $9000.

What emerged was an American gran turismo as elegant and exciting as any from Europe. The C-3's ladder-type tube chassis (with modified Ford front suspension) was almost identical with the C-2's, but the De Dion rear end gave way to a coil-sprung Chrysler live axle located by parallel trailing arms. Brakes consisted of a combination of 11-inch-diameter Mercury drums and Delco actuating mechanisms. Wheelbase remained at 105 inches initially but was later stretched two inches for more proper 2+2 seating. The V-8 used was basically as supplied by Chrysler Industrial except for Cunningham's own log-type manifolds with four Zenith downdraft carburetors.

Inside and out, the C-3 bore more than a passing resemblance to other Michelotti/Vignale designs of the period, particularly some early Ferraris. The bodywork was distinctively Vignale, though one of the coachbuilder's better efforts in these years. Pleated-leather seats graced the cockpit, while a large speedometer and matching combination gauge with clock dominated the dash; a small tachometer nestled between and slightly above the main dials. Luggage had to be carried inside because the spare tire and fuel tank occupied most of the normal trunk.

The first C-3 coupe, named Continental, was finished in time for the Cunningham team to drive to the Glen in September 1952. It then toured U.S. auto shows while a second car went on display at the Paris Salon that October.

"Production" got underway by early 1953. Unfortunately, while the Palm Beach works could build a chassis a week, Vignale needed almost two months to complete the rest of the car. A planned cabriolet derivative was shown at Geneva in March while assembly continued at this snail's pace. Ultimately, just nine cabrios and 18 coupes would be built, the former carrying a delivered price of exactly $11,422.50.

Nevertheless, the C-3 looked svelte and compact next to most contemporary American cars—a styling tour de force. Arthur Drexler, then director of New York's Museum of Modern Art, put the coupe on his list of the world's 10 best designs. For a discerning, monied few, the C-3 was a terrific buy, and it sold as quickly as the Cunningham company could build it.

Still, it might have made real money with a lower price or more sophisticated running gear. A Cadillac, Lincoln, or Chrysler could carry twice the people for half the money, while some of those able to pay the lofty price doubtless shunned the Cunningham as just a bunch of Yankee parts in a fancy foreign wrapper. The C-3 was probably every bit as good as a contemporary Ferrari—maybe better in some respects—but it wasn't Italian. And while the Chrysler hemi was likely the best engine of its day, it had pushrods, rocker arms, and only one camshaft. Anyone spending $12,000 for a car in the early '50s wanted something exotic, even if it wasn't reliable.

A pity. They missed a wonderful car.

1950-52 DeSoto

Hernando de Soto, born around 1500, ranks as an historical also-ran, lacking the fabled brutish qualities of Indian-bashing Cortez and Pizarro, as well as the romanticism of Columbus or Ponce de Leon. What would have been the car's fate had Walter Chrysler named it the Ponce de Leon? Happily, he chose Hernando's moniker, hoping to create an image of "travel, pioneering, and adventure."

That was what the press notices said back in 1928 when the DeSoto made its entrance. As onetime Chrysler sales wizard Joseph W. Frazer told this writer, the choice was somewhat more haphazard: "I'd come up with 'Plymouth' for the new small car, but I had nothing to do with DeSoto. W.P. thought Plymouth was such a good old American name that he just grabbed a history book and picked out another one that had a nice ring to it."

DeSoto's traditional role at Chrysler slotted in much like Mercury's at Ford and Oldsmobile's at GM: to fill a market gap between a lower-priced corporate make (Dodge, Ford, and Pontiac, respectively), and a higher-priced make whose image could not be watered down by a cheaper model (Chrysler, Lincoln, Buick). Usually, it worked well. DeSoto never outsold Dodge or Chrysler, but in good years it accounted for more than 100,000 cars, helping to keep Chrysler Corporation number two in the industry through 1951.

Unlike Mercury or Oldsmobile, however, DeSoto had never been a corporate style-setter. The most distinctive model was probably the '42, with its novel hidden headlights—but these were deemed costly and unnecessary after the war, when anything on wheels could be sold, so the prewar "waterfall grille" was rejiggered slightly, the illuminated maiden hood ornament kept on salary, and conventional sealed beam headlamps put back on the fenders. This basic approach continued with the boxy new '49s, except that Hernando's head replaced the maiden-form on the hood, a definite step backward.

Production in 1950 reached an all-time record 133,854 units. DeSoto capitalized on

DeSoto's best-seller was always the four-door sedan, often taking up to two-thirds of production. The '51 Custom four door seen here listed at $2438, about $200 more than the DeLuxe. It ran the faithful 250.6-cubic-inch L-head six, which developed 116 bhp. Performance was leisurely considering the 3685 pound curb weight.

the seller's market with a very lightly facelifted, but attractively priced and expanded range of models in two series, DeLuxe and Custom. Included were no fewer than five "specialty" models. The top-line Custom range on the standard 125.5-inch wheelbase listed two huge wagons (wood- and steel-bodied); then, on a wheelbase 14 inches longer, DeSoto offered an eight-passenger sedan and the novel Suburban utility car. The latter, like Kaiser's Traveler and Vagabond, featured a folding rear seat for added cargo capacity (but, unlike Kaiser, no hatchback). Two folding jump seats gave the Suburban true nine-passenger capacity. The DeLuxe series offered a Carry-All, similar to the Suburban but on the standard wheelbase. Excepting the Carry-All, which sold 3900 copies, the long-wheelbase models were peripheral, and only about 1500 were sold in total. DeSoto's big sellers were its sedans and coupes, which started under $2000 in the DeLuxe series. All cars used a flathead six, midway between Dodge and Chrysler in size and power.

The 1951 facelift helped DeSoto look a bit longer and lower, and marked the first appearance of its well-known grille teeth; also, the wood-bodied wagon was dropped and horsepower raised slightly. Aside from a minor trim shuffle, including a handsome new cockpit, with instruments grouped in big dials under the steering wheel on a mahogany-finish dashboard, the '52s looked the same. But an additional series, the Firedome, made its debut packing DeSoto's version of the Chrysler hemi-head V-8.

In some ways the FireDome was rather better than Chrysler's Firepower hemi. Despite a low 7.1:1 compression ratio, it led the industry in horsepower per cubic inch (.58). Its "surging delivery of power throughout the speed range is impressive," said *Motor Trend*. "Torque is so good during hill-climbing that it's hard to believe you're not in third gear, when you're actually in fourth [DeSotos were still using Fluid Drive]...We heard no pinging, in spite of Regular Mobilgas being used as fuel."

In those horsepower-conscious years the Firedome was a useful shot in the arm. About 45,000 were sold—50 percent of DeSoto output for 1952, and by the end of 1953 the Firedome dominated the sixes by a ratio of two to one. Against the competition, though, DeSoto's position was falling: only 88,000 cars were built during 1952, partly because of restrictions brought on by the Korean conflict. Like its sister makes, DeSoto was seen by many as high, wide, and *un*handsome, not keeping up with the smooth, sleek new offerings from Ford and GM. Chrysler Corporation lost its position as number-two manufacturer to Ford this year, partly for styling reasons.

SPECIFICATIONS

Engines: sidevalve six **1950** 236.6 cid (3.44 × 4.25), 112 bhp **1951-52** 250.6 cid (3.44 × 4.50), 116 bhp **1952 FireDome** ohv V-8, 276.1 cid (3.63 × 3.34), 160 bhp

Transmissions:	**DeLuxe** 3-speed manual **Custom** overdrive or Fluid Drive optional **Firedome** Tiptoe Shift Fluid Drive
Suspension, front:	independent, coil springs, tube shocks
Suspension, rear:	live axle, leaf springs, tube shocks
Brakes:	front/rear drums
Wheelbase (in.):	125.5 **8-pass & Suburban** 139.5
Weight (lbs):	3450-4400
Top speed (mph):	**Six** 90 **V-8** 100
0-60 mph (sec):	**Six** 22.0 **V-8** 16.0

Production: **1950 DeLuxe clb cpe** 10,704 **4d sdn** 18,489 **Carry-All** 3900 **4d sdn 8P** 235 **chassis** 1 **1950 Custom clb cpe** 18,302 **Sportsman htp cpe** 4600 **cvt cpe** 2900 **4d sdn** 72,664 **4d wgn (wood)** 600 **4d wgn (steel)** 100 **4d sdn 8P** 734 **4d Suburban 9P** 623 **chassis** 2 **1951-52 DeLuxe clb cpe** 6100 **4d sdn** 13,506 **Carry-All** 1700 **4d sdn 8P** 343 **1951-52 Custom clb cpe** 19,000 **Sportsman htp cpe** 8750 **cvt cpe** 3950 **4d sdn** 88,491 **4d wgn** 1440 **4d sdn 8P** 769 **4d Suburban 9P** 600 **1952 Firedome clb cpe** 5699 **Sportsman htp cpe** 3000 **cvt cpe** 850 **4d sdn** 35,651 **4d wgn** 550 **4d sdn 8P** 50

1950-52 DeSoto Sportsman

There is no dearth of stories about how some inspired genius stumbled onto the "hardtop convertible." A Chrysler man speaks of Mopar's pioneering 1946 Town & Country (production 7) as a vision bestowed from Olympus. Then there's the one about how Sarah Ragsdale, wife of Buick's general manufacturing manager, suggested the Riviera because she liked convertibles but not the buffeting that went with them. Buick said the Riviera "looks like a convertible, except that it doesn't convert"—which ranks right up there alongside Calvin Coolidge's ageless, "The future lies before us."

So it goes. The most logical theory is that the hardtop, a postwar phenomenon of the first magnitude, was simply an experiment that caught on. It certainly stood as the most significant body engineering breakthrough since the closed coach had arrived during the early 1920s. Combined with the later air conditioner, the hardtop caused the near-demise of the convertible, and for a time hardtop sales rivaled those of conventional four-door sedans. By 1956, hardtop volume had soared to 1.7 million units (against just 223,000 convertibles), representing a one-fifth slice of industry output. Yet in 1950, when DeSoto joined hardtop ranks with its aptly named Sportsman, this body style had thus far taken but a tiny fraction of industry production.

The order in which the first hardtops arrived is educational, for it shows bluntly where the styling action was and who the heavy hitters were. General Motors, expectedly, sat on top of the heap, offering a hardtop in three lines in 1949 and in all of its five model lines by 1950. Ford, recovering from the financial chaos left by the elder Henry, was in those days slow on the draw; and Chrysler Corporation took its usual cautious steps under conservative president K.T. Keller, not realizing that it had "invented" the hardtop with the semi-experimental Town & Country sport coupes of 1946 (but remembering the bath it had taken with the advanced Airflow in the Thirties).

In terms of actual production, then, Chrysler entered the hardtop race a year after General Motors and just ahead of Ford. Like other Mopar hardtops, the DeSoto Sportsman was a hasty cobbling job using a convertible shell equipped with a convertible-like interior and a solid steel roof, along with an attractively airy, wraparound rear window.

DeSoto did not promote the Sportsman the way Chrysler pushed its corresponding Newport, and Dodge its Diplomat. Brochures illustrated it along with all the other styles but showed no special features like the pillarless windowline or broad backlight or deluxe interior. Perhaps this was because the Sportsman was a fairly unimportant part of the line. Output amounted to only 4600 units in 1950, and in 1951-52 (when Chrysler combined its production figures), the total reached only 8750.

The Firedome model, which arrived in 1952, added another 3000 Sportsman hardtops to the total—and provided performance to go with the rakish (for DeSoto) styling. Zero to 60 time was cut by almost a third, and top speed nudged 100 for the first time in DeSoto's history. The FireDome V-8 was not, however, very good on gas, averaging around 15 miles per gallon—and the Fluid Drive was obsolete and unequal to the V-8's performance.

"Low range was virtually useless for any really meaningful acceleration," wrote Walt Woron in *Motor Trend*. "You'd step on it in first gear and the engine would peak out within a few seconds. To get into second you had to take your foot all the way off the throttle and wait a *very* long time for the shifting mechanism to put you into second gear, thereby losing any advantage gained from the lightning responsiveness of the FireDome engine. [In second you] wound the engine up again, and shifted to the high range. The DeSoto clutch has a huge assist spring which, on our test car, was probably out of adjustment. The result was that, shifting to High, removing foot from clutch and hitting the throttle simultaneously, the clutch pedal stayed on the floor-board of its own accord! Naturally the engine screamed in protest and nothing happened. You let off on the throttle, things slowed down a bit, and all of a sudden, 'SNAP!'—the clutch flipped out automatically, the drivetrain protested audibly, and power hit the driving wheels without warning. Now you were in third gear, but getting there wasn't easy."

DeSoto would have an answer to all this in 1954. It was called Powerflite, Chrysler's first fully automatic transmission.

SPECIFICATIONS

Engines: sidevalve six **1950** 236.6 cid (3.44 × 4.25), 112 bhp **1951-52** 250.6 cid (3.44 × 4.50), 116 bhp **1952 FireDome** ohv V-8, 276.1 cid (3.63 × 3.34), 160 bhp

Transmission:	Tiptoe Shift Fluid Drive
Suspension, front:	independent, coil springs, tube shocks
Suspension, rear:	live axle, leaf springs, tube shocks
Brakes:	front/rear drums
Wheelbase (in.):	125.5
Weight (lbs):	3720-3850
Top speed (mph):	**Six** 90 **V-8** 100
0-60 mph (sec):	**Six** 20.0 **V-8** 16.0

Production: **1950** 4,600 **1951-52 Custom** 8,750 **1952 Firedome** 3,000

Except for the aberration of hidden headlights in 1942, DeSoto remained a rock-solid conservative of the automotive world well into the Fifties. It might seem surprising, then, that DeSoto debuted its first hardtop (as seen here) in mid-1950, ahead of those from Ford Motor Company and most of the independents. It was called the Sportsman, and it sported a large three-piece wraparound rear window, a redesigned likeness of explorer Hernando DeSoto riding the hood, and an inviting interior. The rest was pure DeSoto: solid, durable, and—in retrospect—delightful.

1953-54 DeSoto

For DeSoto Division, the years 1953 and 1954 represented a giant game of snakes and ladders. In 1953, DeSoto came close to breaking its all-time 1950 volume record, churning out 130,000 cars, rising from 13th to 11th in the production race, and recording a record profit. But in 1954—ironically with a much improved product—DeSoto sank to 76,580 and 12th place. This downturn was due at least partly to an outside factor: the infamous sales battle between Ford Motor Company and General Motors, who shipped unordered cars to dealers in order to achieve quotas in the process of trying to outproduce each other. Much of this production blitz was between Chevrolet and Ford, but some of it rubbed off on the middle-priced GM divisions and Lincoln-Mercury. The battle did little harm to GM or Ford but hurt Chrysler and the independents, whose dealers could not afford to discount cars like the high-volume dealerships, who were often selling at a loss just to reduce bulging inventories.

The '53 DeSoto received a handsome facelift, rendering it lower and longer looking, though little changed in actual measurements. Wheelbases went unchanged, though the cars measured five inches longer and an inch wider. But designer Virgil Exner had lowered the hood and integrated the toothy grille more smoothly with the front end, installing wide parking lights on either side and adding a "V"-type hood ornament to symbolize the now-dominant V-8. These '53s were the first DeSotos with a curved one-piece windshield instead of the old-fashioned two-piece flat types—which shows how far behind Chrysler styling had really fallen.

The days of the DeSoto six were positively numbered now, dealers reporting that at least three out of four customers demanded V-8 power. The supply of FireDome hemis actually fell short of demand, and in fact the proportion of Firedome (small

The 1953 DeSoto lineup consisted of Powermaster sixes and Firedome V-8s. The latter included DeSoto's only convertible (below), *a $3114 offering that could be optioned with real wire wheels. Only 1700 were built. The '54 DeSoto sported rearranged trim and, at midyear, a luxurious Firedome Coronado four-door sedan* (opposite).

"d") models to six-cylinder Powermasters ended up around two to one. Indications are that DeSoto could have sold even more cars in 1953, had it had enough engines to go round.

The V-8 was unchanged from its 1952 specification, still developing 160 bhp (compared to 180 for the larger Chrysler hemi). The flathead six also went unaltered, but the Powermaster series had now replaced both the old DeLuxe and Custom six-cylinder ranges. The Powermaster was a smooth, quiet performer delivering excellent fuel economy, upwards of 20 mpg in this heavy automobile, but sixes had fallen out of favor.

Both 1953 series included a coupe, sedan, wagon, Sportsman hardtop, and long-wheelbase sedan, the last built in small numbers—225 Powermasters, 200 Firedomes. The Firedome line included DeSoto's only convertible, base priced at $3114, the most expensive standard-wheelbase car in the line. Top-seller honors, as always, went to the four-door sedan, accounting for 100,000 units in the '53 model year.

For 1954, styling remained much the same but could be quickly distinguished by round parking lights and side chrome carrying the model name. Brighter interiors highlighted new fabrics, leathers, and vinyls, all available in a variety of light pastel colors, while a handsome new dashboard sported big, round, legible instruments.

Most important by far, though, was Powerflite, Chrysler Corporation's new two-speed automatic. Arriving at last to replace the clunky Fluid Drive, it sold for a modest $189 extra on both the Powermaster six and Firedome V-8 (semi-automatic Fluid Drive had cost $237). Throughout the year, all DeSotos came standard with three-speed column-mounted stickshift, with overdrive listing at $96. An increasing proportion of cars were fitted with Powerflite, however, and by 1955 it rolled out of the factory on 95 percent of production.

But a good new automatic wasn't the crutch DeSoto or any other Chrysler product needed in 1954, and neither was performance, which was already excellent in the V-8 lines anyway. A spring model, the luxurious Coronado Firedome four-door sedan, didn't help either. The problem was styling, which still looked old, and the aforementioned GM-Ford sales wars which were beyond Chrysler's control. Calendar year production fell by almost half, but model year production, which is more indicative of the strength of any one model, skidded a stunning 46 percent.

SPECIFICATIONS

Engines: **Powermaster** sidevalve six, 250.6 cid (3.44 × 4.50), 116 bhp **1953 FireDome** ohv V-8, 276.1 cid (3.63 × 3.34), 160 bhp **1954** 170 bhp

Transmission:	**1953** 3-speed manual; overdrive, Tip Toe Shift with Fluid Drive, Fluid Torque Drive (V-8 only) optional **1954** 3-speed manual; overdrive and Powerflite optional
Suspension, front:	independent, coil springs, tube shocks
Suspension, rear:	live axle, leaf springs, tube shocks
Brakes:	front/rear drums
Wheelbase (in.):	125.5 **8-pass** 139.5
Weight (lbs):	3480-4305
Top speed (mph):	**Powermaster** 90 **Firedome** 100
0-60 mph (sec):	**Powermaster** 20.0 **Firedome** 13.0-14.0

Production: 1953 Powermaster clb cpe 8063 **Sportsman htp cpe** 1470 **4d sdn** 33,644 **4d wgn** 500, **4d sdn 8P** 225 **Firedome clb cpe** 14,591 **Sportsman htp cpe** 4700 **cvt** 1700 **4d sdn** 64,211 **4d wgn** 1100 **4d sdn 8P** 200 **1954 Powermaster clb cpe** 3499 **Sportsman htp cpe** 250 **4d sdn** 14,967 **4d wgn** 225 **4d sdn 8P** 263 **Firedome clb cpe** 5762 **Sportsman htp cpe** 4382 **cvt** 1025 **4d sdn, incl Coronado** 45,095 **4d wgn** 946 **4d sdn 8P** 165 **chassis** 1

1955-56 DeSoto Fireflite

"And tonight, Groucho, our first guest is a pig farmer from Secaucus who raises orchids in his spare time and has patented a recipe for a dish called Ham and Flowers."

It seems like yesterday. There we were, glued to the ten-inch Dumont, watching George Fenneman take another beating as Groucho Marx's straight man on *You Bet Your Life,* the comedy quiz show brought to us by our friendly neighborhood DeSoto-Plymouth dealer. It was 1955, archetypal year of the Fabulous Fifties, and Detroit was poised to sell a record eight million cars, while Volkswagen was still just a funny import owned by a few nutballs.

To Americans of "a certain age," Groucho's famous program instantly recalls a two-toned, toothy-grilled, hemi-headed charger like the ones on these pages. Marx's was the best show DeSoto ever sponsored; 1955, when DeSoto built a near-record 130,000 cars, was one of its best years. DeSoto played a key role in the Mopar game plan, anchored square in the middle of the medium-price field, about $500 more expensive than a comparable Dodge and $500 to $1000 cheaper than a Chrysler.

The Powermaster six had passed into history, DeSoto's standard-bearer now being the FireDome V-8 bored out to 291 cubic inches. And the new top-of-the-line series was the more heroically decorated Fireflite, distinguished immediately by the large chrome moldings tapering back from the headlamp rims along the tops of its fenders. There were only three Fireflite models: Sportsman hardtop, four-door sedan, and convertible. The last is one of the postwar world's rarities—only 775 were built and, incidentally, DeSoto produced only 625 copies of the lower-line Firedome ragtop.

DeSoto styling was directed by Virgil Exner, but the man who had the most to do with it was Maury Baldwin. Retaining the identifying toothy grille, Baldwin added an ornate hood emblem but kept the sides and rear relatively clean. Fireflites could be bought in monotone with a simple, bright metal side molding, but in two-tone-crazy '55 most customers opted for the huge color-sweep, which carried the contrasting roof color along the body sides and down around the rear wheel wells. Color schemes were bright Paper Mate pen combinations. (If you were really with it, you got a Paper Mate to match your car.)

If two-tones were still not enough, DeSoto introduced a "Spring special" Fireflite four door, the "Coronado" (another Spanish explorer out of history). This model, with Dodge and Packard, pioneered the three-tone paint job. Coronados all had a black roof, turquoise body, and white sweepspear, with a matching interior—they represented the essence of their era.

Fireflite horsepower was up 30 from 1954, thanks to more displacement, larger valves, cam modifications, and a four-barrel carburetor. Nineteen fifty-five was also the year when Powerflite's gear selector moved to the dashboard, where a mean-looking prong took aim at the occupants—surely a device that would give the National Highway Traffic Safety Administration apoplexy today. Chrysler made it of SAE 1010 steel, which bends easily, and said it would snap off, dontcha know, if hit with more than 10 pounds per square inch of force. It was also angled slightly, so it would bend properly. Nobody was much convinced by these measures, but Chrysler had something much more intriguing in the works for 1956: pushbuttons! These were mounted left of the steering wheel and worked well.

The 1956 Fireflite wore a curious facelift involving a mesh grille which replaced the long-running dentures. The first of Exner's tailfins also appeared, modestly grafted onto the rear fenders, notched at the rear for a trio of taillight lenses. The new rear bumper ends contained dummy exhaust ports, in fact exhaust was ducted out underneath in normal fashion. The instrument panel changed little, except for the instruments, which sported gold-on-white lettering so you didn't have to read them. The enlarged engine cranked out a rollicking 255 horses.

Two new Fireflites this year were a four-door hardtop Sportsman, which sold in small quantities, and the Pacesetter replica of the 1956 Indy 500 pace car, of which only 100 were built. Model year 1956 was a bit less profitable; still, DeSoto built over 100,000 cars and looked like a permanent part of the American automotive scene.

Like its other corporate stablemates, the 1955 DeSoto was all-new. Previously it had been competent—but dull. Now it literally sparkled with up-to-the-minute styling and flashy two-toning. The '55 Fireflite came as a $3151 convertible (above), *a $2939 Sportsman hardtop* (opposite, top), *and a four-door sedan. The '56 model* (bottom) *sported modest fins.*

SPECIFICATIONS

Engine: ohv V-8 **1955** 291.0 cid (3.72 × 3.34), 200 bhp **1956** 330.4 cid (3.72 × 3.80), 255 bhp

Transmissions:	**1955** 3-speed manual; Powerflite optional **1956** Powerflite standard
Suspension, front:	independent, coil springs, tube shocks
Suspension, rear:	live axle, leaf springs, tube shocks
Brakes:	front/rear drums
Wheelbase (in.):	126.0
Weight (lbs):	3890-4115
Top speed (mph):	**1955** 105 **1956** 115
0-60 mph (sec):	**1955** 12.0-13.0 **1956** 10.0-11.0

Production: **1955 Sportsman htp cpe** 10,313 **cvt** 775 **4d sdn, incl Coronado** 26,637 **1956 Sportsman htp cpe** 8475 **Sportsman htp sdn** 3350 **cvt** 1385 **Pacesetter cvt** 100 **4d sdn** 18,207

21395A

1956 DeSoto Adventurer

The impact of the Chrysler 300 on sales of more ordinary, "civilian" Chryslers was not lost on the Highland Park corporation. It was a relatively simple business to apply the same kind of factory hot-rodding to other makes in the Chrysler stable, producing a limited edition performance model for each Chrysler division. This occurred in 1956 when Plymouth announced the Fury, Dodge the D-500 performance package across-the-board for all models, and DeSoto wheeled out the $3728 Adventurer hardtop—one of the highest priced DeSotos to date. Few were built, but this wildly decorated, mighty road machine brought many a soul into DeSoto-Plymouth showrooms, to emerge clutching an order slip for more conventional models. Today, the Adventurer rates highly among collectors as well as enthusiasts.

The Adventurer name had been coined by Virgil Exner in 1954 for one of his Ghia-bodied show cars built in Turin to Exner specifications, using DeSoto componentry. Cast in the image of the K-310, the '51 show car that had helped transform Chrysler's stodgy image, the compact Adventurer measured only 190 inches long and rode a 111-inch, shortened DeSoto chassis. It was by far the smallest Exner showmobile—the K-310 stretched out over two feet longer. Since most of its length rested between the wheels, the Adventurer could accommodate four passengers comfortably. Painted off-white, the handsome coupe sported a black leather interior, full instrumentation and, of course, the 276.1-cid DeSoto hemi V-8. "It was my favorite," Exner told this writer. "I owned it for three years and kept it at home."

Later the same year, Ghia built the Adventurer II, which lacked bumpers, giving it what stylists joked was an "Andy Gump" appearance at the front end. Designed almost wholly by Ghia, the Adventurer II's most novel feature was a retracting rear window that slid away into the trunk, following the rakish lines of the sleek roof. Despite a standard wheelbase, its styling handled the length well, with graceful, rounded lines. It recently surfaced in Massachusetts, in good original condition.

DeSoto announced the "production" Adventurer in time for the spring 1956 selling season, and the entire production run of 996 units sold out within six weeks of introduction. There was no mistaking the few that were built, with their eggshell white paint job, contrasting gold roof and sweepspear, and special anodized gold, pseudo-spoked wheelcovers. But what most distinguished the Adventurer lurked under the hood.

DeSoto still offered its three-speed manual gearbox on the '56 Firedome, but this was not a performance transmission. Thus, the Adventurer, like the Fireflite, came with standard Powerflite automatic. The engine, a slightly bored out version of the 1956 hemi with a ¾-race camshaft, produced 320 horsepower: 65 more than the Fireflite, 90 more than the Firedome. Following the formula of the other Chrysler performance specials, the Adventurer received stiffer-than-stock springs and shocks, producing a taut ride—not every DeSoto customer's cup of tea. But it certainly resulted in excellent handling for so heavy a car—the Adventurer weighed only 100 pounds less than the Chrysler 300B and measured just two inches shorter overall.

Test driver Don MacDonald borrowed the last Adventurer not already in private hands, a brand new car that had not been broken in. At Daytona Beach, he flew through the clocks on the sand at 137 mph, but the same car later did 144 around the Chrysler proving ground track at Chelsea, Michigan. Surprisingly, the Adventurer was only marginally quicker than the '56 Fireflite, but MacDonald attributed this to his car's newness: "The small difference in low-speed acceleration between the '56 Fireflite and the Adventurer is attributable to the ¾-race cam which favors high-end performance. Actually, give or take the spread between production cars of the same make, a '56 Fireflite will get ahead of an Adventurer between 0-40 mph, but don't carry the same race on up to 90 mph or you will lose." The figures are revealing:

	'55 Fireflite*	'56 Fireflite	'56 Adventurer
bhp	200	255	320
0-30	4.3 sec	4.0 sec	4.0 sec
0-60	12.1 sec	10.9 sec	10.5 sec
¼-mile	18.9, 77 mph	17.8, 78.5 mph	17.5, 81 mph
30-50	4.7 sec	3.9 sec	3.9 sec
50-80	13.2 sec	11.2 sec	10.4 sec
Top speed	118 mph	108.7 mph	144 mph

*Manual transmission, "Hi-Tork" differential

Driving the Adventurer was obviously an adventure. Like the Chrysler 300, it was too much car for the average driver, but proved how fast and agile a big Detroiter could be.

The '56 DeSoto Adventurer featured eggshell white paint, with contrasting gold hubcaps, roof, and side sweepspear. The main point of interest, however, was the 341.4-cubic-inch, 320 horsepower V-8 that lurked under the hood.

SPECIFICATIONS

Engine:	ohv V-8, 341.4 cid (3.78 × 3.80), 320 bhp
Transmission:	Powerflite automatic
Suspension, front:	independent, coil springs, tube shocks
Suspension, rear:	live axle, leaf springs, tube shocks
Brakes:	front/rear drums
Wheelbase (in.):	126.0
Weight (lbs):	3870
Top speed (mph):	140-145
0-60 mph (sec):	10.0-11.0
Production:	996

YRM 476

YRM 476

1957-59 DeSoto Fireflite

The DeSoto Adventurer carried on as a very limited production specialty car after its introduction in 1956, and through 1959 the Fireflite remained DeSoto's top-of-the-line series. Ironically, DeSoto was expanding its model lineup just as its market began to shrink; it added the low-priced Firesweep series on a shorter wheelbase in 1957, and ended 1959 with 18 different models sharing only 45,000 sales. To this extent some of DeSoto's problems in the late Fifties were of its own making; but one could also argue that division general manager John Wagstaff *had* to move downward, what with inflation in general and Chrysler's steady push toward lower priced models of its own. And, of course, nobody expected the recession of 1958 when the '58 DeSoto line was being finalized in late 1955.

In 1957, Chrysler Corporation reached its styling apogee, pacing the field by a country mile as General Motors struggled to re-orient its divisions around shared bodies, and tried to get by with clumsy facelifts of aging designs. The '57 DeSoto perhaps typified the Exner era at its peak, with a broad, three-model line of fully restyled, rakishly tailfinned cruisers on the traditional 126-inch wheelbase, with the new Firesweep riding 122 inches. The Firesweep had been designed to bring DeSoto prices back down under $3000, and the four-door sedan started at only $2777. Firesweeps were lighter than senior DeSotos, and also had a smaller engine.

Shifting through Chrysler's new improved TorqueFlite automatic, '57 Fireflites used a 341-cubic-inch engine developing 290 horsepower. Body styles continued as before with Sportsman hardtop coupes and sedans, a convertible, and a four-door sedan, but for the first time Fireflite wagons were added: the six-passenger Shopper, and the three-seat, nine-passenger Explorer. Handsome, airy wagons with rear-facing back

The 1957 DeSoto Fireflite (bottom right) *boasted all-new styling, DeSoto's all-time best according to some observers. A mild facelift followed for 1958* (top right), *highlighted by a fussier grille and pinched exhaust outlets. A more extensive restyling was seen on the '59 models* (below), *the main elements being a much heavier grille and revised side trim and two-toning. Horsepower escalated from 290 in 1957 to 305 in 1958, and topped out at 325 for 1959.*

seats and novel spare tire housings built into the right rear fender, they set a new price record: Explorers started at $4124 and typically sold for close to $5000. Their production figure of 934 shows exactly how popular this price tag was with DeSoto buyers.

DeSoto's last great year turned out to be 1957 with 117,000 cars built for the model year. This was good enough for an 11th place finish, only 7000 short of Chrysler, and about as close as DeSoto ever came. But the recession murdered the largely unchanged line in 1958. The luxury Fireflite, which had alone accounted for 28,000 DeSotos in 1957, barely edged past 12,000.

On paper, the '58 Fireflite couldn't have been better. It wore essentially the same swoopy styling that had been so popular the year previous; its new 361-cid "Turboflash" V-8 would dash from 0-60 in under eight seconds, 0-80 in 13.5, and reach a top speed of 115 mph. Torsion bar front suspension, a '57 development, gave it handling unmatched by any rivals except other Chrysler products. It was the recession and the too-optimistic assortment of models and body styles that were causing the trouble.

Decisions in Detroit cannot be turned around all at once and DeSoto went into 1959 with the same broad line as in 1958, including six Fireflites with larger and still more powerful engines. Though 1959 was an improving year for just about everybody in the industry, DeSoto actually built fewer cars, and its fate was now sealed. Ironically, rumors of DeSoto's demise began circulating just as the division was celebrating its 30th Anniversary and two-millionth car.

General manager Wagstaff said the '59 could "do everything a motorist can possibly ask of it," and said it was "only the beginning of a very promising future." The '60s wore a handsome facelift, but the line was chopped to only Fireflite and Adventurer models with short 122-inch Chrysler Windsor wheelbases and low powered engines. The '61s, which bore no model name at all and consisted solely of a sedan and hardtop, had scarcely been announced when Chrysler took DeSoto out of the auto business. The fleet, good looking Fireflites of 1957-59 (and the handful of limited edition Adventurers) were the last of the great DeSotos.

SPECIFICATIONS

Engines: ohv V-8 **1957** 341.0 cid (3.78 × 3.80), 290 bhp **1958** 361.0 cid (4.13 × 3.38), 305 bhp **1959** 383.0 cid (4.25 × 3.38), 325 bhp; 350 bhp optional

Transmission:	3-speed TorqueFlite automatic
Suspension, front:	independent, torsion bars, tube shocks
Suspension, rear:	live axle, leaf springs, tube shocks
Brakes:	front/rear drums
Wheelbase (in.):	126.0
Weight (lbs):	3910-4295
Top speed (mph):	110-120
0-60 mph (sec):	7.0-9.0

Production: **1957 Sportsman htp cpe** 7217 **Sportsman htp sdn** 6726 **cvt** 1151 **4d sdn** 11,565 **Shopper 4d wgn 6P** 837 **Explorer 4d wgn 9P** 934 **1958 Sportsman htp cpe** 3284 **Sportsman htp sdn** 3243 **cvt** 474 **4d sdn** 4192 **Shopper 4d wgn 6P** 318 **Explorer 4d wgn 9P** 609 **1959 Sportsman htp cpe** 1393 **Sportsman htp sdn** 2364 **cvt** 186 **4d sdn** 4480 **Shopper 4d wgn 6P** 271 **Explorer 4d wgn 9P** 433

1950-51 Dodge Wayfarer Sportabout

Dodge underwent a dramatic change in the '50s, switching from dull dependability to potent pizzazz within a mere four years. But you'd never have guessed it as the decade opened.

Ever devoted to practical cars, Chrysler Corporation president K.T. Keller had decreed that his company's all-new postwar '49s would be exactly that—newer and shinier than the 1946-48 models but resolutely utilitarian and firmly un-faddish. Chrysler thus fielded Detroit's dullest '49s: roomy and solid but upright and boxy. Though it made little difference at first, buyers were more style-conscious than ever, and sales slumped once the postwar seller's market became a buyer's market—so much so that Ford displaced Chrysler as the industry's number two producer in 1952.

Keller's staunch conservatism largely reflected the reactionary cautiousness that had pervaded Chrysler ever since its radical Airflow laid a giant egg in the Thirties. Yet there had been attempts at flash, all under the Chrysler badge: the smooth, wood-sided 1941-42 Town & Country wagon with its unique clamshell tail; the posh, early-postwar T&C sedan and convertible; the new-for-1950 T&C Newport hardtop. These, of course, were all pricey glamor items that sold in small numbers. But where was an affordable car with a touch of sport to offset plodding mechanicals and stodgy styling?

At Dodge Division, that's where. It didn't arrive until the all-new '49s did, but there it was: a reincarnation of the romantic roadster. Dodge called it Wayfarer.

Though Dodge had long catered to the market just above Plymouth's, the division wanted to maintain a toehold in the low-price field. The Wayfarer was it—or rather, Wayfarers, as the new line also included a business coupe and semi-fastback two-door sedan. All rode on the shortest of three Dodge wheelbases, 115 inches, four inches longer than that of Plymouth's corresponding junior DeLuxe models. Dodge's mainstay '49s, the new Meadowbrook and Coronet, rode a 123.5-inch span, five inches longer than their Plymouth counterparts.

Deliberately "built down to a price," the Wayfarers looked plainer than other '49 Dodges, with less exterior brightwork and rather spartan interiors. This also explains why the $1727 roadster came with a manual top and snap-on Plexiglas side windows. At least the former was a lightweight aluminum-framed affair and easy to operate. The latter, however, must have prompted second thoughts about saleability, because they gave way to conventional roll-up windows with separate door ventwings very late in the model run—meaning that some of the 5420 roadsters built for '49 were technically convertibles. Oh well...

Mechanically, the '49s weren't all that different from early postwar Dodges; ditto the 1950-52s. Their chassis was orthodox, their engine the tough-but-tepid 230.2-cubic-inch L-head six that had been around for years—albeit uprated to 103 horsepower, a gain of one. Chrysler's equally familiar Fluid Drive semi-automatic transmission came standard. A new option was Gyro Matic, basically the same thing with a torque converter instead of a fluid coupling; working the clutch pedal "shifted" between high and low ranges. With all this, performance could hardly be called Dodge's strong suit in these years. Other changes included Chrysler's new rivetless "Cyclebond" brake linings and a key-actuated starter/ignition switch.

Chrysler Corporation's 1950 models wore rather substantial facelifts, surprising for all-new designs in their second year. This, too, may have been prompted by second thoughts, but it provided more visual interest. Like its divisional sisters, Dodge gained sleeker rear-end styling and a wider-looking front (via a pleasingly simplified two-bar horizontal grille). The winsome open Wayfarer came back as the Sportabout, but not even unchanged prices seemed to help the bargain-basement series, and convertible production dropped by almost half.

A still-bolder face showed up as the main change for '51, though prices went up across the board, the Sportabout to $1924. Neither did anything for sales, the convertible sliding to just 1002 units. Predictably, the Sportabout didn't return for '52, a year when Chrysler Corporation cars were all but unchanged, followed by other Wayfarers a year later.

In retrospect, the open Wayfarer stood out as a novel aberration in a corporate line predicated mostly on common sense, but at a time when buyers were feeling anything but sensible. Collectors have since recognized it as one of the few bright spots in an otherwise very gray group. A faint sign of the more exciting Dodges to come? Not likely, but it's a charming thought.

SPECIFICATIONS

Engine: L-head I-6, 230.2 cid (3.25 × 4.63), 103 bhp

Transmission:	Fluid Drive; Gyro Matic 2-speed semi-automatic optional
Suspension, front:	upper and lower A-arms, coil springs
Suspension, rear:	live axle, semi-elliptic leaf springs
Brakes:	front/rear drums
Wheelbase (in.):	115.0
Weight (lbs):	3145-3175
Top speed (mph):	85
0-60 mph (sec):	24.5
Production:	**1950** 2903 **1951** 1002

The Wayfarer roadster made its debut on Dodge's short-wheelbase series in 1949, but it wasn't long before Dodge replaced the snap-on Plexiglass side windows with proper roll-up units. This made it a true convertible, which Dodge called the Sportabout; a few were built in late '49. The 1950 model (below) received a simpler, more attractive grille and neat flush-mounted taillights. The trusty old 230.2-cid L-head six (opposite) plodded along with 103 horsepower; the dashboard (top) featured three square gauges set side by side in front of the driver.

1953-54 Dodge V-8

Chevrolet's mid-'50s transformation from dull to dynamite in 1955 is well known, but it's often forgotten that Dodge underwent a similar metamorphosis two years before. The year was 1953 and it was largely accomplished with the fabled hemi V-8.

Named for its "half-a-dome" combustion-chamber shape, the hemi had set Detroit performance on its ear when introduced with the 1951 Chrysler line. That it would spread to the corporation's less costly cars was almost a foregone conclusion, and it did. DeSoto got a smaller hemi for '52. Dodge's turn came the following year.

Though much costlier to build, the hemi offered a number of advantages over conventional V-8s with wedge-shape or "pent-roof" combustion chambers. Chief among them was that the spark plug could be positioned in the center of the chamber, rather than off to one side, for more complete combustion and higher thermal efficiency. This in turn allowed larger valves spaced further apart, which meant faster, fuller cylinder "filling" of the air/fuel mixture. Other pluses included smoother porting and manifolding, larger water passages for superior cooling, and less heat loss to coolant, which permitted a smaller, lighter radiator. It all added up to an engine packing more punch per cubic inch.

And punch was something Dodge definitely needed by 1953. Though ever admired for rugged dependability, Dodge had little else to offer a postwar public gone crazy for glitter, gadgets, and go. A downward-trending sales curve suggested a change was needed yesterday. Company planners woke up, put the rush on flashy all-new '55 designs, and did what they could to give the 1953-54 models a little pizzazz.

Work on the '53 corporate line began at about the time K.T. Keller became Chrysler chairman and L.L. "Tex" Colbert replaced him as president. Keller thought buyers would go for an even smaller, more practical Dodge and Plymouth, but the savvy Colbert knew better. The '53s thus ended up a compromise: more stylish than the Keller "boxes" of 1949-52, but still primly upright next to most competitors. Greater

Dodge paced the Indy 500 in 1954. To commemorate the event, 701 Royal 500 convertible pacecar replicas (opposite) were built. Like the ragtop, the '54 hardtop, seen here (below) as a midyear special edition, shared Plymouth's 114-inch wheelbase. The '53 Coronet four-door sedan cost $2220 and was that year's most popular model.

market distinction seemed desirable, so it was decided to give Dodge a small hemi and leave Plymouth with nothing but sixes until '55.

This ploy wasn't entirely successful. Both makes scored higher 1953 volume, but only because the Korean conflict wound down and, with it, government restrictions on civilian auto production. The following year, Dodge dropped a notch to eighth in the industry as sales plunged by more than half.

Nevertheless, the '53 took a big step in the right direction. Dubbed "Red Ram," the hemi arrived with 241.3 cubic inches and 140 horsepower for a new Coronet Eight series: club coupe and four-door sedan on a 119-inch wheelbase; convertible, Diplomat hardtop coupe, and two-door Sierra wagon on a five-inch shorter span shared with Plymouth. If not 1953's most exciting design, Dodge styling—by the recently hired Virgil Exner—was neat and trim, with a new one-piece windshield and straight-through fenderlines, an evolution of the 1951-52 grille, and a lower hood (with a small air slot on V-8s). Dodge also boasted wider-opening "Space-Saver" doors and a new double-channel "Road Action" chassis with revised front suspension. Transmissions included a pair of semi-automatic options: Gyro-Drive and Gyro-Torque. The latter "changed" gears by lifting off the accelerator rather than depressing a clutch pedal.

Nineteen fifty-four brought attractive detail styling changes and a more complicated lineup headed by a quartet of posh Royal V-8s. A fifth Royal arrived at mid-season: the hot 500 convertible, a replica of the Dodge that paced that year's Indy 500. Included were a tuned 150-bhp hemi, Kelsey-Hayes chrome wire wheels, outside "continental" spare tire, and special ornamentation. Dodge also offered a dealer-installed Offenhauser manifold with four-barrel carburetor; output was never revealed but it must have been a screamer. In addition to the Royals, the 150-bhp hemi came standard on two Coronet sedans, the 140-bhp unit on two Meadowbrooks.

Dodge sold only a handful of Royal 500s, but the Red Ram had already shown its prowess. Danny Eames drove a '53 to a record 102.6 mph at El Mirage dry lake in California, and a factory team set 196 new AAA stock-car speed records at Bonneville in September 1953. Just as impressive, Dodge V-8s finished 1-2-3-4-6-9 in the Medium Stock class at the '54 running of the grueling Mexican Road Race, yet also won their class in the 1953 and '54 Mobilgas Economy Runs.

With all this, Dodge had become a performance power to be reckoned with. But literally bigger and better things awaited over the horizon.

SPECIFICATIONS

Engine: ohv V-8, 241.3 cid (3.44 × 3.25) **1953** 140 bhp **1954 Royal/Coronet** 150 bhp **Meadowbrook** 140 bhp

Transmissions:	3-speed manual; overdrive optional **1953-54** Gyro-Torque/ Gyro-Drive semi-automatics optional **1954** 2-speed Powerflite automatic optional
Suspension, front:	upper and lower A-arms, coil springs, anti-roll bar
Suspension, rear:	live axle, semi-elliptic leaf springs
Brakes:	front/rear drums
Wheelbase (in.):	114.0; 119.0
Weight (lbs):	3325-3660
Top speed (mph):	105+
0-60 mph (sec):	16.2

Production: **1953 Coronet Eight clb cpe** 32,439 **4d sdn** 124,059 **cvt** 4100 **Diplomat htp cpe** 17,334 **Sierra 2d wgn** 5400 **1954 Coronet V-8 clb cpe** 7998 **4d sdn** 36,063 **Sport htp cpe** 100 **cvt** 50 **Suburban 2d wgn** 3100 **Sierra 4d wgn** 988 **Royal V-8 clb cpe** 8900 **4d sdn** 50,050 **Sport htp cpe** 3852 **cvt** 1299 **chassis** 1 **Royal 500 cvt** 701

1955-56 Dodge D-500

Having made its performance point for 1953-54, Dodge emphasized styling for 1955. Not that it stood pat on performance—no make could afford to, what with the horsepower race tighter than ever—so the '55s became not only the most potent Dodges ever, but among the fastest cars in all Detroit.

If not totally new, they were unquestionably different from any Dodges than had gone before—part of the sudden, dramatic swing to high power and high style evident throughout the '55 Chrysler Corporation line. This meant bolder, brighter cars with bigger engines and mostly longer wheelbases—in Dodge's case a new 120-inch span across the board, up 1-5 inches from 1953-54. Offerings were blissfully simplified into Coronet sixes and V-8s, and V-8-only Royal and new Custom Royal models. Hardtop coupes were subtitled Lancer along with the Custom Royal convertible, which topped the line at $2748.

Though Virgil Exner oversaw the styling of Chrysler Corporation's '55s, Dodge and Plymouth received the attention of his assistant, Maury Baldwin. All the firm's cars embodied the "Forward Look," Dodge calling its version "Flair-Fashion." Announcing it was an aggressive snout with two large horizontal bars wrapped around from the sides into a divided grille cavity. A dummy scoop appeared at the front of the hood and flared outward and back toward the cowl. On some models this ran to the rear fenders as an upper body molding, dipped near the C-pillars; in a contrasting color, the area thus defined made what was still a rather high-sided body look lower. Cars conventionally two-toned at the beltline looked a lot chunkier. Other features included "New Horizon" wraparound windshield and, for Custom Royal Lancers, embryonic chrome tailfins. Wild three-tone paint jobs could be had on Custom Royals, with different colors on roof, body sides, and the hood/deck area.

Dodge's famed "Red Ram" V-8 expanded to 270 cubic inches for '55—but wasn't necessarily a true hemi. It was if you bought a Custom Royal, where you got a Super Red Ram with an ample 183 horsepower. Otherwise you got what Chrysler termed a "polyspherical" engine. Its key difference was intake and exhaust valves placed

Dodge shed its "old maid" image in 1955 with all-new "Flair-Fashion" styling. The luxurious Custom Royal Lancer (this page) *stood at the top of the lineup, and looked best as a convertible. Only 3302 were built. The 1956 model* (opposite) *sported modest fins and revised two-toning. The D-500 option meant that a potent hemi V-8 lurked under the hood.*

diagonally across from one another rather than directly opposite, which permitted a single rocker shaft for each cylinder bank instead of two and improved plug accessibility. With lighter rocker arms and this simpler valvetrain, the poly weighed less and cost less to make than the hemi, yet retained most of its desirable breathing qualities. Most of its power, too: 175 bhp.

Dodge also offered an extra-cost "Power Pack" for the hemi— four-barrel carb and dual exhausts adding 10 horses. With it, the hemi was officially (and clumsily) called the "super-powered Super Red Ram," but soon became known simply as the "D-500" option.

The D-500 returned for '56 on a hemi stroked out to 315 cubic inches. Larger valves, mechanical lifters, reprofiled camshaft, and higher compression (9.25:1) gave it a mighty 260 horses, close to double the maximum power Dodge had offered just two years before. A two-barrel, 218-bhp version came standard on Royal and Custom Royal. Coronets retained the poly at a slightly more muscular 189 bhp.

Dodge's mild '56 facelift brought higher, finned rear fenders to all models, which now included V-8 Lancer four-door hardtops in each series. As on other Chrysler makes, control of the optional Powerflite automatic changed from the chromed corporate dashboard wand of 1955 to the soon-to-be-infamous pushbuttons.

Highland Park went more heavily into high-performance limited editions for '56, issuing the new Plymouth Fury and DeSoto Adventurer to supplement the follow-up version of the hairy Chrysler 300. Little appreciated is the fact that Dodge had a similar special, the Golden Lancer. This was basically a D-500-equipped Custom Royal hardtop coupe with Sapphire White and Gold Gallant Saddle paint; gold-colored dash, windshield, and door moldings; and patterned white/gray/black upholstery. Production is unknown, even to Chrysler, but was doubtless minuscule.

Equally rare was "La Femme," a new-for-'55 trim package offering umbrella holder, makeup case, and a dazzling pink-and-white exterior in a patronizing nod to women buyers typical of the age. The '56 La Femme kept most of milady's accessories, but the colors changed to Regal Orchid over Misty Orchid. Limited to the Custom Royal hardtop coupe—and available with the D-500 option—it sold fewer than 1500 copies through '56 (estimates range from 300 to 1100), after which it was tastefully withdrawn.

But you can't say Dodge wasn't trying, and for 1957 it would try even harder by offering D-500 performance on every model in the line. For that exciting story, just turn the page.

SPECIFICATIONS

Engines: ohv V-8 **1955** 270.1 cid (3.63 × 3.25), 193 bhp **1956** 315.0 cid (3.63 × 3.80), 260 bhp

Transmissions:	3-speed manual; overdrive and 2-speed PowerFlite automatic optional
Suspension, front:	upper and lower A-arms, coil springs
Suspension, rear:	live axle, semi-elliptic leaf springs
Brakes:	front/rear drums
Wheelbase (in.):	120.0
Weight (lbs):	average 3550
Top speed (mph):	115-120
0-60 mph (sec):	9.5-10.0
Production:	NA

1957-59 Dodge

Glitter, gadgets, and go were usually the keys to sales success in Detroit in the Fifties, and the last three Dodges of that decade went all out in each category. For reasons explained below, the '58s and '59s were less than successful, but the '57 ranked as the most popular Dodge yet. No wonder. Longer, lower, and wider, chromier and more colorful, it was faster and flashier than anything the division had ever offered. Nearly 288,000 people bought one, 37,000 more than in 1956—a new Dodge record that lifted it from eighth to seventh in industry standings.

Like its corporate siblings, Dodge was virtually all-new for '57. Even the engines, the only holdovers, saw plenty of changes. But not all automotive children are treated equally. Most critics agree that Dodge got the short end of Highland Park's 1957 styling stick, emerging as certainly the busiest-looking member of the family. Dodge described the styling as "Swept-Wing," but surely no aircraft had ever been so contrived.

Few argued with the dramatically altered silhouette, though. Dodge naturally came in for Chrysler Corporation's new 1957 torsion-bar front suspension, which necessitated a completely different and much lower box-rail frame with a recessed rear floor—shades of the Step-down Hudson—that allowed greatly reduced overall height with hardly any loss of interior space. Stylists thus lowered rooflines by three inches on sedans and wagons and a whopping five inches on hardtops (the last standing a mere 56.8 inches tall), aided by 14-inch-diameter wheels and tires (an inch smaller than before). Though wheelbase crept up two inches, overall length remained at 212.2 inches. Width, however, bulged 3.3 inches, to 77.9.

Dodge's '57 engine lineup solidified its role as Chrysler's performance outfit. A bore stretch added 10 cubic inches to the poly-head V-8, which also received higher 8.5:1 compression, larger intake valves, and a camshaft reprofiled for faster valve opening. A two-barrel, 245-bhp version powered the low-line Coronets and mid-range Royals. The top-shelf Custom Royals ran a four-barrel carb, upping the ante to 285 bhp.

For flat-out flying the hemi-head D-500 option reigned supreme. Newly available in any model, it turned even plain-Jane Coronet two-doors into screamers. And this year there were two D-500s: a four-pot high-compression (9.25:1) 325 boasting 310 bhp, and a new 354-cid Super D-500 engine with twin four barrels cranking out 340 horsepower. Both came with stiffened shocks, front torsion bars, and rear leaf springs for what one magazine termed "close liaison with the road."

Though larger than any previous Dodge, the '57s were still fairly light and thus real chargers with the more powerful engines. The typical base V-8 could do 0-60 mph in less than 10 seconds, while the D-500s were simply astounding. This year's newly optional TorqueFlite three-speed automatic also aided performance: quick and positive, yet very smooth. It proved rugged and trouble-free from the first, leading even drag racers to favor it—along with most Dodge buyers.

Unhappily for Dodge, the '58s attracted far fewer buyers, thanks to a deep national recession and a growing reputation for early body rust and indifferent workmanship on the '57s. Performance fans mourned the hemi's dismissal for a new generation of lighter, cheaper-to-make wedgehead V-8s, but there was still power aplenty. This year's D-500 boasted 361 cubes and packed 320 horses with four-barrel carb, a rousing 333 with optional Bendix fuel injection. A mild facelift brought quad headlights and the usual trim shuffles to a carryover lineup. Bolstering it at mid-season was a lush Custom Royal Regal Lancer hardtop coupe (whew). For all that, Dodge slid to ninth place on less than half its 1957 volume, a decade low 137,861 units.

Output improved for 1959 by about 18,500 cars, but styling didn't: heavier-looking and a bit odd in places, especially the droopy headlamp "brows," scalloped fins, and rather vulgar taillights. Dodge's long-running "Get-Away" L-head six put in its last appearance, down three bhp from 1957-58. The 361 wedgehead V-8 returned with a pair of bored-out 383 D-500 companions: 320-bhp "standard" and 345-bhp Super, the latter still fuel-injected. This year's base V-8 was a slightly more potent 326-cid wedge with 255 bhp (versus 1958's 325-cid 252-horse poly). Swivel front seats and a self-dimming rearview mirror were among several new optional gimmicks shared with other '59 Chrysler cars.

It would be several years before Dodge styling and workmanship again became sales assets. The 1957-59 models thus stand as Dodge's high and low points of the decade—and proof that success in the auto industry is a fickle friend at best.

Of the three convertibles Dodge offered in 1957, the $2842 Coronet (opposite, top) *cost the least. It came with a 245-bhp, 325-cid V-8. A mild facelift attended to the '58s. The Coronet V-8 series listed four body styles, including the $2679 Lancer two door seen here* (center). *A more extensive facelift followed in 1959. The top-of-the-line Custom Royal four-door sedan* (bottom) *featured three windows per side and stickered at $3145.*

SPECIFICATIONS

Engines: 1957 L-head I-6, 230.2 cid (3.25 × 4.63), 138 bhp; ohv V-8, 325 cid (3.69 × 3.80), 245/285/310/340 bhp (2-/4-barrel/D-500/Super D-500) **1958** L-head I-6, 230.2 cid (3.25 × 4.63), 138 bhp; ohv V-8, 325 cid (3.69 × 3.80), 252 bhp; 361 cid (4.12 × 3.38), 305/320/333 bhp (base/D-500/fuel-injected Super D-500) **1959** L-head I-6, 230.2 cid (3.25 × 4.63), 135 bhp; ohv V-8, 326 cid (3.95 × 3.31), 255 bhp; 361 cid (4.12 × 3.38), 295/305 bhp; 383 cid (4.25 × 3.38), 320/345 bhp (2-/4-barrel)

Transmission:	3-speed manual; overdrive, 2-speed Powerflite, 3-speed TorqueFlite optional
Suspension, front:	upper A-arms, lower transverse arms, longitudinal torsion bars, anti-roll bar
Suspension, rear:	live axle, semi-elliptic leaf springs
Brakes:	front/rear drums
Wheelbase (in.):	122.0
Weight (lbs):	3360-4035
Top speed (mph):	90-120
0-60 mph (sec):	8.0-14.5

Production: 1957 Coronet Six, V-8 160,979 **Royal V-8** 40,999 **Custom Royal V-8** 55,149 **Station Wagon V-8** 30,481 **1958 Coronet Six, V-8** 77,388 **Royal V-8** 15,165 **Custom Royal V-8** 25,112 (including 1163 Regal Lancer 2d htp) **Station Wagon V-8** 20,196 **1959 Coronet Six, V-8** 96,782 **Royal V-8** 14,807 **Custom Royal V-8** 21,206 **Station Wagon V-8** 23,590

Coronet
IOWA

DODGE

1956-58 Dual-Ghia

As fools are apt to venture where wiser souls don't, so do car enthusiasts sometimes dare what major manufacturers won't. The '50s was full of such attempts. Among the most notable had to be the Dual-Ghia, the offspring of Eugene Casaroll and Chrysler Corporation, by way of Italy's Carrozzeria Ghia.

Casaroll had formed Dual Motors, Inc. during the war to build twin-engine military trucks and generators. He also owned Auto Shippers, a car-transport firm under contract to Chrysler and other Detroit producers. Casaroll was wealthy and also a genuine car nut (he'd sponsored several "Auto Shippers Specials" in the Indy 500) who dreamed of a sporty four-place touring car combining reliable American mechanicals with European styling and craftsmanship. He thus naturally found himself attracted to the early-'50s Ghia-built show cars that Virgil Exner designed to perk up Chrysler's staid styling image.

Among them was the 1953-54 Firearrow, a quartet of Dodge-based two-seaters that included a coupe and convertible. The first, a low-slung roadster, proved so popular on the auto-show circuit that Chrysler asked Ghia to build a second. Betty Skelton, well-known aviatrix and race-car pilot, demonstrated Firearrow number two at the dedication of Chrysler's new Chelsea, Michigan proving grounds in 1954, circling the high-speed oval at 144 mph. It was this car that most tickled Casaroll's fancy.

All the Ghia-built Exner specials were mere pipe dreams to Chrysler, but when company president William Newberg said that the Firearrow would never be built for sale, Casaroll saw a chance to realize his dream. After buying production rights to the design, he teamed with engineer Paul Farago to make it a practical road car. Farago, a whiz at combining parts from Chrysler's various bins, worked up several prototypes in 1955, and Casaroll announced late in the year that his new "Firebomb" would soon be available at about $5500. Further development postponed introduction to late '56, by which time components from that year's Dodge had been adopted, rear-end styling revised to incorporate modest fins, and the name changed to Dual-Ghia.

Casaroll called on Ghia to construct most of his car, not only because of Ghia's reputation as a master coachbuilder, but also to minimize costs and maximize snob appeal. Ghia's Giovanni Savonuzzi worked out the chassis design. Stock '56 Dodge frames were sectioned five inches in Turin, reinforced, then welded back together. Welded to this was a convertible body hand-formed of steel instead of the aluminum

SPECIFICATIONS

Engine: Dodge ohv V-8, 315 cid (3.63 × 3.80), 230/260/285 bhp

Transmission:	Chrysler 2-speed Powerflite automatic
Suspension, front:	upper and lower A-arms, coil springs, anti-roll bar
Suspension, rear:	live axle, semi-elliptic leaf springs
Brakes:	Imperial front/rear drums
Wheelbase (in.):	115.0
Weight (lbs):	est. 4000
Top speed (mph):	120+
0-60 mph (sec):	8.6

Production: 117 (102 convertibles, 2 special hardtops, and 13 assorted prototypes)

Eugene Casaroll liked the Virgil Exner-designed 1953-54 Dodge Firearrow show cars so much that he bought the production rights from Chrysler Corporation. Expensive and fast, they became an instant favorite with movie stars and the rich and famous. Casaroll lost about $4000 on each car built, however, so he reluctantly gave up after 117 had been delivered.

Ghia traditionally used. This resulted in an uncommonly strong unit structure for a soft top. When Ghia finished its part, Dual Motors installed the drivetrain and completed assembly in Detroit.

Custom touches abounded. Grille, wheel covers, windshield frame, door handles, even side-trim clips were made of brass. Seats mimicked fine furniture, including coil springs and English Connolly leather upholstery. Even out-of-the-way places were covered—literally. The inside of the hood was blanketed with fiberglass insulation overlaid with quilted leather; the trunk was lined in black felt. The manual top was, according to one writer, "so carefully counterbalanced that one person can raise or lower it in less than a minute." Power windows replaced the slow (11 turns) manual winders shortly after production began.

Other interior and exterior hardware came from various production Chrysler cars. The drivetrain was essentially that of the hot '56 Dodge D-500: a 315-cubic-inch hemi V-8 and two-speed Powerflite automatic (with floorshift instead of Chrysler's pushbuttons). Standard horsepower started at 230 with four-barrel carb. Solid lifters, long-duration cam, twin rocker-arm shafts, and double valve springs added another 30, and a twin-four-barrel version yielded 285. Standard equipment included Chrysler's "Coaxial" power steering, Imperial power brakes, heavy-duty springs and shocks, and performance-oriented 3.54:1 axle.

With all this, the Dual-Ghia was the proverbial iron fist in a velvet glove: fast on the straights, beautifully controllable in corners, and surprisingly frugal (13-16 mpg in town, a bit over 20 mpg on the highway). Yet, it oozed luxury and was built with obvious care. Ghia lavished 1300 man-hours on each body, Dual another 200 hours on final assembly.

Price was predictably stiff: $7741 base, another $100 for either high-power engine. Shrewdly, Casaroll planned to build only 150 a year and sell to whomever he pleased, mostly Social Register and Hollywood types. Among the favored few: singers Frank Sinatra, Sammy Davis, Jr., and Eddie Fisher; composers Hoagy Carmichael and David Rose; and film stars Lucille Ball and Peter Lawford. (Lawford's Dual-Ghia graced the opening credits of the "Thin Man" TV series in 1957-58). Some rich-and-famous luminaries were turned down, enhancing the car's aura, causing leading columnist Dorothy Kilgallen to quip that a "Rolls-Royce is the status symbol for those who can't get a Dual-Ghia."

But the phenomenon didn't last. Ghia's long build time limited sales, and Casaroll—not so shrewdly—underpriced his car, losing at least $4000 on each one. Worse, Chrysler's planned switch to unibody construction would end his chassis supply after 1959. The only alternative was to try a different design, so the Dual-Ghia convertible was discontinued after 1958 in favor of a sleek 2+2 coupe. Called L6.4, this bowed in August 1960, but proved even less successful. A third-generation car went into the planning stage, but got no further, prompting Casaroll to leave the car business for good.

1958 Edsel

A lot of hoary myths surround the Edsel, named in memory of Henry Ford's son, today a word equated with "blunder." The Edsel project did cost Ford some money, but it was hardly a crippling experience, and Ford learned a lot in the process.

It bears mentioning that the Edsel sold 63,100 copies in its first model year, which was not so bad for a brand new make, and certainly respectable. Chrysler, for example, also sold 63,000 of its '58 model; Edsel sales outnumbered those for DeSoto (50,000), Studebaker (45,000), Lincoln/Continental (30,000), and Imperial (16,000). What the Edsel failed to do was to meet expectations: Ford had hoped to sell 100,000 the first year.

Partly as a result of that expectation (conceived in 1955, when a car like the Edsel would have easily acquitted itself), there were too many variations spread around to be viable at the 60,000 level. There were two basic chassis/drivetrains for four separate series—Ranger, Pacer, Corsair, and Citation—spread over no fewer than 18 different models. This was far too ambitious a spread in a year which (unexpectedly, of course) saw a severe recession and a sales plunge for almost every domestic make.

Another factor which has never been mentioned in accounts of the Edsel's decline was the failure to make it distinctly cheaper or more expensive than Mercury. The short-wheelbase Ranger and Pacer (where Edsel Division hoped to garner two-thirds of its sales) were priced between $2375 and $3247; the more luxurious, longer-wheelbase Corsair and Citation hardtops and convertible ran between $3346 and $3801. These were base prices: actual delivered prices were therefore around $2750 to $4500.

But Mercury's prices were quite comparable. The standard-bearer Monterey and Montclair, on a wheelbase just shorter than the senior Edsels, sold for $2721 to $3536 base; the Park Lane on a longer wheelbase started at $3944 to $4118. And Mercury cut into the Edsel market by introducing a new low-priced Medalist series ($2547-2617). Withal, Mercury delivered prices almost identical to Edsel's. (Nor was direct rivalry peculiar to Mercury-Edsel; the same kind of overlaps were beginning to occur between Buick-Olds-Pontiac and Chrysler-DeSoto-Dodge.)

The distinguishing (and to many disqualifying) mark of the Edsel was its enormous vertical "horsecollar" grille—some critics called it many worse things—so prominent that it required separate, flanking front bumpers. The rest of the design was conventional, though a curious feature of automatic Edsels was the placement of the gear selector ("Tele-Touch") pushbuttons in the center of the steering wheel hub. Notably, the Edsel didn't carry faddish tailfins, although by 1958 this was likely an advantage. The engines chosen were big, powerful V-8s: 361 cubic inches for Ranger and Pacer, a mighty 410 for Corsair and Citation. The latter were lavishly equipped and trimmed, with the top-of-the-line Citation convertible selling for what had been, two or three years before, a Lincoln price.

Only at the last minute did the Edsel receive its name. The advertising agency had prepared a list of 6000 possibilities (of which Ranger, Pacer, Corsair, and Citation were the top selections). But Ford chairman Ernest Breech didn't like any of them. In desperation, Ford's PR people turned to poet Marianne Moore to help them come up with some ideas. Moore suggested a handful of stunners, including "Mongoose Civique," "Turcotinga," and "Utopian Turtletop," none of which were quite what they had in mind. They sent her a bouquet of roses and a card of thanks.

In the hour of final decision, the name Edsel inexorably took precedence. When told that Henry Ford II was against naming the car after his father, Ernie Breech told the board of directors, "I'll take care of Henry." He placed a phone call, telling Henry everyone wanted Edsel, so Henry finally agreed.

On the whole, the Edsel wasn't such a bad car in that year of so many really dreadful automobiles. Its styling, if not everyone's cup of tea, was at least different, and all Edsels performed well. The worst thing we can say about it in retrospect is that it was a car designed for the best of times, with the misfortune to be offered in the worst of times.

The 1958 Edsel bowed in the middle of a severe recession, which helped to seal its fate. The top-of-the-line Citation convertible (opposite) *saw production of only 930 units, while the less expensive Pacer ragtop* (above) *didn't fare much better: 1876 units. They are remembered for their controversial "horse collar" grille and electric "Tele-Touch" gear selector pushbuttons in the middle of the steering wheel* (top).

SPECIFICATIONS

Engines: ohv V-8 **Ranger/Pacer** 361.0 cid (4.05 × 3.50), 303 bhp **Corsair/Citation** 410.0 cid (4.20 × 3.70), 345 bhp

Transmission:	**Ranger/Pacer** 3-speed manual with optional overdrive; Tele-Touch 3-speed automatic **Corsair/Citation** Tele-Touch automatic
Suspension, front:	independent, coil springs, tube shocks
Suspension, rear:	live axle, leaf springs, tube shocks
Brakes:	front/rear drums
Wheelbase (in.):	**Wagons** 116.0 **Ranger/Pacer** 118.0 **Corsair/Citation** 124.0
Weight (lbs):	3729-4311
Top speed (mph):	105-115
0-60 mph (sec):	9.0-11.0

Production: **Ranger 2d sdn** 4615 **4d sdn** 6576 **htp cpe** 5546 **htp sdn** 3077 **Roundup 2d wgn** 963 **Villager 4d wgn 6P** 2294 **9P** 978 **Pacer 4d sdn** 6083 **htp cpe** 6139 **htp sdn** 4959 **cvt** 1876 **Bermuda 4d wgn 6P** 1456 **9P** 779 **Corsair htp cpe** 3312 **htp sdn** 5880 **Citation htp cpe** 2535 **htp sdn** 5112 **cvt** 930

EDSEL
1958

20A1958
INDIANA

1959 Edsel

Ford moved rapidly to locate the Edsel in a distinct market niche for 1959. Management adopted an across-the-board 120-inch wheelbase, dropped Pacer and Citation to thin-out the model range, and held base prices to a narrow field: $2700 to $3100. This put the Edsel distinctly below Mercury (which had increased commensurately in size and price), while keeping it some $500 above the comparable Fords. Had they pitched its price so precisely in its initial year, the Edsel might have done well enough to establish its own market, and to survive.

The narrowness of the '59 price bracket was itself indicative of the encroachments being made by the Ford-Chevy-Plymouth trio into the medium-price field. The top-of-the-line 1959 Fairlane 500s, Chevy Impalas, and Plymouth Sport Furys were all priced alongside comparable Edsels. All Edsel could offer was a "fourth choice," as *Motor Trend* put it: "a car much different in outer appearance from the luxury models of Ford, Chevy, and Plymouth (all of which bear a close resemblance to their less expensive lines)."

The baseline Ranger included two- and four-door hardtops and sedans, while the Corsair offered a four-door sedan and hardtop, a hardtop coupe, and a convertible. The wagons were broken out in a separate Villager series, comprising a single four-door body style, with six- or nine-passenger capacity.

Underlining Ford's attempt to target Edsel at a sub-Mercury buyer, standard V-8s were much smaller: 292 cubic inches for the Ranger, 332 for the Corsair. The previous 410 was scrubbed, but the 361 could be ordered at extra cost. For the first time, a six-cylinder engine would be offered, for the Ranger or Villager. Ford said these changes came in response to customer preferences: only five percent of 1958 Edsel buyers had opted for high-compression engines and high-performance equipment. However, the engines featured high-lift cams for improved low-speed torque, less valve overlap, and better carburetion. Only the 361 required premium fuel.

To this expanse of engine options Edsel added a choice of transmissions and rear axle ratios. New for '59 was Mile-O-Matic two-speed automatic ($41 cheaper than Dual-Range), which used 25 percent fewer parts and weighed 50 pounds less, thanks to its aluminum converter housing and gear case. The three-speed Dual Power Drive transmission was available only with the 361 engine. A conventional shift lever replaced 1958's steering wheel pushbuttons.

In 1958, many road testers had found the Ford-based Ranger/Pacer chassis taut and competent, but the Mercury-based Corsair/Citation chassis sloppy and ill-handling. For 1959, the Edsel line uniformly rode a Ford-based chassis with modified crossmembers to suit Edsel bodies and side members bowed out to the full track width. The Corsair convertible had an additional X-braced frame, but Ford did not have to make many of these, since only 1343 soft tops were built—the scarcest '59 Edsel.

On paper at least, these were sensible changes. Indeed, two models—the Ranger sedans—became the best-selling Edsels ever; the Ranger four door being the only Edsel model to sell over 10,000 examples. Though five inches shorter than the '58 senior Edsels, there was more interior space; the controversial "horse collar" was integrated into a full-width grille and one-piece front bumper. The garishness of 1958 had melted away.

But it was all in vain: the formula may have been right this year, but for Edsel it arrived too late. People who had rejected it in 1958 were unlikely to buy the '59 model; customers for something in Edsel's price range preferred to pay the same or a little more money for an established make like Pontiac or Dodge.

Ford seriously considered perpetuating Edsel by applying the name to a new Mercury compact, eventually known as the Comet. Enthusiasts point to the Comet's taillights and flared rear fenders as proof of intent to carry the Edsel name and "look" forward. In the end, though, the marque was too crippled to be worth keeping. After a handful of Ford-based 1960 models were run off in late 1959, the Edsel quietly bowed out.

The 1959 Edsel carried more conservative styling and came in only two series, Ranger and the more expensive Corsair. Just one convertible was offered this year, the $3072 Corsair, of which only 1343 were built. It came with a 225-bhp, 332-cid V-8; a 303-bhp, 361-cid motor cost extra.

SPECIFICATIONS

Engines: **Ranger/Villager** ohv V-8, 292.0 cid (3.75 × 3.30), 200 bhp; ohv I-6, 223.0 cid (3.62 × 3.60) 145 bhp optional **Corsair** 332.0 cid (4.00 × 3.30), 225 bhp (optional others); 361 cid (4.05 × 3.50), 303 bhp (optional all models)

Transmissions:	3-speed manual; overdrive, 2-speed Mile-O-Matic, 3-speed Dual-Range Mile-O-Matic optional
Suspension, front:	independent, coil springs, tube shocks
Suspension, rear:	live axle, leaf springs, tube shocks
Brakes:	front/rear drums
Wheelbase (in.):	120.0
Weight (lbs):	3547-3790
Top speed (mph):	95-105
0-60 mph (sec):	11.0-16.0

Production: **Ranger htp sdn** 2352 **4d sdn** 12,814 **htp cpe** 5474 **2d sdn** 7778 **Corsair htp sdn** 1694 **4d sdn** 3301 **htp cpe** 2315 **cvt** 1343 **Villager 4d wgn 6P** 5687 **9P** 2133

EDSEL
1959

1953-55 Edwards America

While Eugene Casaroll dreamed in Detroit (see Dual-Ghia), Sterling H. Edwards dreamed in San Francisco. Both had the same vision: an exclusive, low-production personal-luxury car. Casaroll had considerable clout with Chrysler and able engineering assistance and cooperation from one of Italy's premier coachbuilders. Edwards could rely only on home-grown design talent and whatever parts he could lay his hands on. Casaroll managed 143 Dual-Ghias in all; Edwards built only six of his Americas.

Edwards first car was the 1949 Special, a four-seat convertible with a hardtop and windshield removable for racing. The Special did race, mainly in West Coast Sports Car Club of America events, and with some success.

Weighing just 2500 pounds for the road or 2000 pounds race-ready, the Special rode a sophisticated chassis built of chrome-molybdenum tubing with all-round independent suspension and disc brakes. Power was supplied by the inevitable Ford flathead V-8, downsized to 122 cubic inches to stay within the 2.0-liter displacement limit for racing. To make up for lost size, Edwards fitted dual Stromberg carburetors, a hot cam, and a special overhead-valve cylinder head with ultra-high 11.0:1 compression. With 115 horsepower available at 5300 rpm, the Special could run about 155 mph flat out.

SPECIFICATIONS

Engines: all ohv V-8, Oldsmobile 303.7 cid (3.75 × 3.44), 185 bhp; Lincoln 317.5 cid (3.80 × 3.50), 205 bhp; Cadillac 331 cid (3.81 × 3.63), 210 bhp

Transmission:	GM 4-speed Hydra-Matic
Suspension, front:	upper and lower A-arms, coil springs
Suspension, rear:	live axle, semi-elliptic leaf springs
Brakes:	front/rear drums
Wheelbase (in.):	107.0
Weight (lbs):	approx. 3000
Top speed (mph):	est. 115
0-60 mph (sec):	est. 10.0
Production:	6

The Edwards America was the dream of San Franciscan Sterling H. Edwards, who wanted to build an all-American personal-luxury sports car. The "production" model rode a Mercury station wagon chassis sectioned to a 107-inch wheelbase and used either a 205-bhp Lincoln V-8 or a 210-bhp Cadillac mill. The planned $4995 price (a fortune then) ballooned to $7800 by 1955, when Edwards gave up the effort after building only six cars.

Edwards followed up in 1951 with a second experimental that made greater use of stock components. Among them were the rugged, 100-inch-wheelbase chassis from Kaiser-Frazer's compact Henry J and Chrysler's potent new 180-bhp, 331-cid hemi V-8. A lightweight, carefully assembled fiberglass body made up for the heavier Henry J chassis, and this plus the hemi combined for an excellent power-to-weight ratio. But though it had plenty of muscle, this Edwards oversteered merrily, and chassis flex reared its ugly head. Sterling went back to his drawing board.

What ultimately emerged from it was his "production" model, the America. Announced in late 1953, this was another four-seat convertible but with good-looking, rather Italianate lines. Highlights included a large, rectangular eggcrate grille; slab sides relieved by a pronounced character line ahead of the rear wheel openings; and a boxy back wearing stock 1952 Mercury tail lamps. The instrument panel and steering wheel were contemporary Oldsmobile items, the upholstery leather.

Edwards retained the Henry J chassis for the first America but exchanged the hemi for a 185-bhp, 303.7-cid Oldsmobile Rocket V-8. Series production was definitely contemplated, though on a very limited basis, with an as-delivered target price of $4995. But Edwards' tiny facilities and time-consuming hand-construction methods precluded reaching even this modest goal, and only five more cars would be completed. Two received Lincoln's 205-bhp, 317.5-cid V-8; the other three ran with 210-bhp 1953-spec Cadillac 331s. All rode a Mercury station wagon chassis sectioned to a 107-inch wheelbase, providing greater rigidity.

By 1955, Edwards was forced to charge over $7800 for an America, though that included such niceties as electric window lifts, GM's Hydra-Matic transmission, and Kelsey-Hayes wire wheels. But the entire effort amounted to little more than a hobby—and on a shoestring at that. After developing a pretty lift-off hardtop, Edwards threw in the towel and turned to other pursuits.

1956-57
El Morocco

Custom cars were a big '50s craze, and it occurred to one Ruben Allender, a millionaire Detroit industrialist and confirmed auto enthusiast, that there might be a market for a Chevy with a ready-made restyle in the image of the Cadillac Eldorado, a car at the top of most everyone's "dream" list. Allender not only had lots of money to pursue this idea but a big war-surplus warehouse filled with suitable hardware. It also had space to carry out the conversions. Even General Motors cooperated, making the '56 Chevy look even more like a baby Cadillac than the '55 he'd planned to start with.

For a prototype design, Allender called on Creative Industries, an independent Detroit styling and fabrication house that had built the recent Ford Atmos and Packard Panther show cars under contract. The result was a handsomely restyled '56 Bel Air convertible resembling a scaled-down Eldorado Biarritz. Allender found the production engineer and shop manager he needed in one 28-year-old Cyril Olbrich, who'd been experimenting with tools designed for that new wonder material, fiberglass. Once a nearby Chevy dealer agreed to supply ragtop Bel Airs at about $50 over cost, the third floor of Allender's warehouse was cleared for small-scale production of his cut-price imitation Caddy.

Allender called it El Morocco, a name close to "Eldorado" but not so close as to invite legal hassles from Cadillac. He even managed to register it as a make (which perturbed some Chevy officials, including division chief Ed Cole). The conversion involved no mechanical or interior changes, but the revised exterior was as much a "junkyard jumble" as any '50s custom, though it was professionally executed to Olbrich's design.

Many of the parts came from Allender's stock. The "Dagmar" front bumper guards were fiberglass-reinforced headlamp shells from a '37 Dodge truck, the hood medallion a modified Kaiser-Frazer horn button, the "saddle top" door trim made from '55 Willys dashboard pieces. Olbrich castings mimicked 1955-56 Eldo side trim,

SPECIFICATIONS

Engines: **1956** ohv I-6, 235.5 cid (3.56 × 3.94), 140 bhp; ohv V-8, 265 cid (3.75 × 3.00), 162/170 bhp **1957** 283 cid (3.88 × 3.00), 245 bhp

Transmissions:	3-speed manual; overdrive and 2-speed Powerglide/Turboglide automatic optional
Suspension, front:	upper and lower A-arms, coil springs
Suspension, rear:	live axle, semi-elliptic leaf springs
Brakes:	front/rear drums
Wheelbase (in.):	115.0
Weight (lbs):	3260-3330
Top speed:	90-120
0-60 mph (sec):	8.0-11.0
Production:	**1956 cvt** 18 **2d htp** 2 **1957** approx. 16

In the mid-Fifties, most every American dreamed of someday owning a Cadillac. Most couldn't, of course, but Ruben Allender figured he could offer them something that at least looked similar to the real thing—for about $10,000 less than the 1957 Eldorado Brougham. Taking a stock 1956-57 Chevy, he grafted on Cadillac-style fins, grille, and trim, which really made the '57 (above) *look like a "baby" Eldo. Even the name was chosen so it would have a Cadillac "ring" to it.*

and there were aftermarket wheel covers resembling the Caddy's "Sabre Spoke" wheels. Of course, the major changes were at the rear. A portion of the Chevy fenders was cut away and Eldo-style fiberglass fins bolted on, then finished with epoxy resin for a smooth seam that was invisible under paint.

Priced at $3250 (around $3400 with the optional "continental kit" fitted to most '56s), the El Morocco made quite a splash. But that's about all. Though it cost only half as much as the Eldo, it sold for $1000 more than the stock Bel Air ragtop—a lot in those days. Then too, many of those who could afford the ersatz styling could just as easily afford the real thing. As a result, only 20 of the '56 El Moroccos were called for: two hardtops and 18 convertibles.

Only about 16 more would be built, all based on the restyled '57 Chevy and equipped with four-barrel 283 V-8, Powerglide automatic, radio, and heater. Again the styling mods were beautifully executed and involved mainly the rear, but were now rendered in metal on Two-Ten two- and four-door hardtops as well as Bel Air convertibles. Though still patterned on the Eldo Biarritz/Seville, the '57 El Morocco looked much like Cadillac's new $13,000 Eldorado Brougham from behind, with similarly styled fins, bumper, and side trim. As you might expect, the transformation was most effective on the four-door hardtop. The add-on fins were now welded to the Chevy body, and the stock hood and front bumper were slightly altered. Small "El Morocco" badges appeared on hood and trunklid above the Chevy "V's" and on a leather pad in the steering wheel hub, which also bore the words "Custom Built For..." and the appropriate owner's name.

Remarkably, the price difference between Chevy and El Morocco was much lower in '57. The hardtops retailed for $2750-$2800, about $500 above the stock Two-Tens, and the convertible was actually reduced to $2950, less than $500 more than the equivalent Bel Air.

But it was too late. Though Allender had hoped to sell El Morocco through selected Chevy dealers, the plan fizzled, perhaps due to lack of GM backing. Moreover, his warehouse facilities offered no hope of increasing volume to a profitable level, and demand for medium-priced cars was on the wane anyway.

Fortunately, a few El Moroccos survive today—and still prompt double-takes, just as Allender intended. They're perhaps the most distinctive artifacts of the "Classic Chevy" era—certainly the rarest. They're also a reminder that, Xerox and the Japanese excepted, making copies is no way to make it big in business.

1950-51 Ford Crestliner

The clean-lined, slightly boxy Fords of 1949-51 were the cars that saved Ford Motor Company. Henry Ford, Sr., who had resumed managing his company after his son Edsel's untimely death in 1943, was wedded to ideas once great, now grown obsolete. His company staggered under the pressure. Ford in those days was still a family-owned corporation, and in 1945 the Ford family finally insisted on a change in command. Control passed to a grandson, Henry Ford II. Even before the first Henry passed away in 1947, the recovery effort was underway.

"HF2", whose reign would last 33 years, hired talented, bright new managers, engineers, stylists, and the "Whiz Kids." Notable among the new faces were Robert S. McNamara and Ernest R. Breech. The new management team encouraged ground-up rethinks of the Ford product line. The results emerged in 1949: a handsome new Lincoln, a Mercury cast in its image, and the all-new Ford.

Styling for the '49 Ford was a competitive exercise between Ford's own designers and several outsiders, including George Walker, later destined to head Dearborn's styling department. One of Walker's employees was young Dick Caleal, a stylist who worked so hard selling his cars that his colleagues nicknamed him "the Persian rug salesman." Asked to "finalize" a pre-set Walker "package" based on given dimensions, Caleal ran into trouble with the front and rear styling. So he appealed to a friend, Robert E. Bourke. At the time, Bourke was running the Loewy Studios team at Studebaker, which had just finished the famous "bullet-nose" Stude. But he liked the "rug salesman" and wanted to help him.

Late night sessions at the Caleal home in Mishawaka, Indiana, found Caleal, Bourke, and Bourke's assistant Bob Koto concocting a smooth clay model with a bullet-nose, not unlike that of the Studebaker. The small scale clay model was actually baked in the kitchen—so you might affectionately refer to the '49 Ford as "the car from Dick Caleal's wife's oven." However one wishes to think of it, the recipe worked. Walker presented the Caleal model to a delighted Ford management team and saw it accepted almost verbatim. And for the 1949 model year, Ford built a whopping 1.1 million vehicles (the most since 1930), out-producing Chevrolet for the first time since 1937 in the process.

All was not roses, however. One spot of trouble ahead was General Motors' new "hardtop convertible," a ragtop-like body with pillarless side windows and steel top. Nobody knew in 1949 whether it would prove a winner or a fluke, but to be on the safe side Ford styling conceived sporty two-door models using existing bodyshells that would come as close as possible to the hardtop idea. Enter the Crestliner.

This limited-edition tudor sedan was distinguished by a vivid contrasting "color sweep" along the body sides, not unlike the pattern on classic-era LeBaron custom bodies. (Bob Gregorie, who claimed some credit for it, said once that LeBaron's famous color sweep had inspired him.) Crestliners came with standard fender skirts, and the two-tone color was repeated on the padded vinyl top, replicating the look of a convertible. Like the convertible, the Crestliner came only with a V-8.

Crestliners were distinguished by wild two-tone combinations that were ahead of their time in 1950; chartreuse and black was one memorable example. Interiors were color keyed to exteriors, with lush materials. Full wheel covers, and the "Crestliner" script in anodized gold on the front fenders, were part of the package. Whereas the Custom Ford Tudor started at $1511, the Crestliner cost $200 extra, which was not much for the distinction it offered (and $250 less than the convertible). Ford sold over 17,000 Crestliners in 1950, more than management had expected.

Although a hardtop appeared for 1951, the Crestliner was left in the line to use up remaining special trim. Production of the '51 model was much smaller as a result. The '51 facelift (double-spinner grille, handsome new dash with instruments and controls set asymmetrically) combined with scarcity of numbers make the '51 Crestliner a very desirable collector's item. But try to find one for sale!

Ford didn't have a hardtop in 1950. Chevy did. Something had to be done, so Ford did about the only thing it could do on quick notice—give the regular two-door sedan as many hardtop cues as possible. The result was called the Crestliner, and it bowed with a vinyl roof, special colorful two-toning, gold badging, and a very deluxe interior. It didn't fool anyone, of course, but it's a hit with collectors today, whether it's a 1950 model (bottom) *or a '51* (top).

SPECIFICATIONS

Engine: sidevalve V-8, 239.4 cid (3.19 × 3.75), 100 bhp

Transmissions:	**1950-51** 3-speed manual; overdrive optional **1951** 3-speed Ford-O-Matic optional
Suspension, front:	independent, coil springs, tube shocks
Suspension, rear:	live axle, leaf springs, tube shocks
Brakes:	front/rear drums
Wheelbase (in.):	114.0
Weight (lbs):	3050-3065
Top speed (mph):	100
0-60 mph (sec):	14.0-16.0
Production:	**1950** 17,601 **1951** 8703

1321 693

1951 Ford Victoria

Ford lagged behind Chevrolet in two major areas in 1950—it lacked a hardtop and an automatic transmission. Those deficiencies were neatly solved in 1951 with the appearance of the hardtop Victoria, which could be equipped with Ford-0-Matic if desired. Customers approved; the Victoria outsold Chevy's Bel Air that year.

Had the 1949 Ford not been a hit, Ford Motor Company might not have survived to celebrate its 50th anniversary in 1953. But the '49 *was* a hit, and the main reason Dearborn came back from the brink to again rank as Detroit's number-two producer by 1952, ousting a fumbling Chrysler Corporation.

That year brought the second and final update of the winning '49 design, which had been notable not only for its neat, slab-sided styling but for Ford's first truly modern chassis: a box-section ladder-type frame mounting independent front suspension— at last!—and a lighter rear end with Hotchkiss drive (replacing torque-tube) and parallel, longitudinal semi-elliptic leaf springs. Though wheelbase and engines largely carried over from 1946-48, the '49 arrived lower, wider, and much roomier, although actually an inch shorter. But it wasn't built nearly as well, and an engine shoved forward some eight inches produced handling problems that couldn't be solved immediately. Both reflected the last-minute change in postwar plans and ensuing crash development program ordained by Ernest R. Breech, who had told the Dearborn board that "this company will be judged on the next Ford it produces." Breech was right, and Ford hustled to get the '49 from drawing board to assembly line in record time—a mere 19 months.

And to Ford's credit, most of the '49's flaws were quickly dealt with, enabling the firm to claim with some justification that the 1950 models were "50 Ways New, 50 Ways Finer." Among their improvements: stronger, better-fitting body panels; more durable upholstery; further internal refinements to the venerable flathead V-8; a standard front anti-roll bar. Gilbert Spear provided subtle but effective styling changes.

This "debugging" process continued for '51: "Automatic Posture Control" seats with non-sag springs; even more durable upholstery (though colors remained rather drab); waterproof ignition system; high-capacity fuel pump; variable-rate rear springs

SPECIFICATIONS

Engine: L-head V-8, 239.4 cid (3.19 × 3.75), 100 bhp

Transmission:	3-speed manual; overdrive and 3-speed Ford-O-Matic automatic optional
Suspension, front:	upper and lower A-arms, coil springs, anti-roll bar
Suspension, rear:	live axle, semi-elliptic leaf springs
Brakes:	front/rear drums
Wheelbase (in.):	114.0
Weight (lbs):	3188
Top speed (mph):	95
0-60 mph (sec):	17.8 (Ford-O-Matic)
Production:	110,286

and "Viscous Control" shock absorbers all-round; and another Spear facelift, marked by a handsome "twin-spinner" grille. But the two most important developments came as responses to 1949-50 General Motors initiatives. One was Ford-O-Matic, Dearborn's first fully automatic transmission, arriving as a $159 option for all models. Although a year behind Chevrolet's Powerglide, it offered three speeds instead of its rival's two, though first had to be selected manually. It did nothing for performance, of course (no automatic really did in those days save GM's Hydra-Matic), but earned critical plaudits from the press and public alike.

Ford also came in a year behind Chevy with its other 1951 development: a hardtop coupe. But it didn't matter, because the new Victoria, announced on January 28th of that year, was a smash. Reviving the name of Ford's close-coupled early-'30s coupes, it predictably fell into the upper-level Custom V-8 series. Price started at $1925, a whopping $330 above the gap-filling Crestliner sedan (see entry) and only $44 below the Custom convertible.

With its airy roofline, developed by the renowned Gordon Buehrig, and a lush, convertible-like interior, Ford aptly billed the Victoria the "Belle of the Boulevard...smart as a convertible, snug as a sedan." And of course Ford pointed out that the Victoria was the only such car in its class with a standard V-8. That was true. Plymouth, which introduced its new Cranbrook Belvedere that year, and Chevy, which began the battle of the low-priced hardtops with its 1950 Bel Air (see entries), were both still tied to sixes.

Though as much a rush job as the '49, the Victoria sold like the proverbial hotcakes, partly because it was new, partly because it was a Ford. At 110,286 units despite the late introduction, it bested that year's Bel Air by nearly 7000 units and the new Belvedere by some 80,000. The Victoria also put paid to the Crestliner, outselling it by more than 10 to 1.

Another rush job? Yes, because Ford had already planned hardtops for its fully redesigned 1952 line, yet didn't want to let a whole year pass without a more direct reply to Chevy than the Crestliner. The '51 Victoria thus stands as a unique one-year-only Ford, reflecting the aggressive new Dearborn management team led by Breech, company president Henry Ford II, and the talented "Whiz Kids." That group would take Ford to even greater heights beginning with the 1952 models, which are the subject of our next installment.

1952-54 Ford

If the '49 Ford had saved Dearborn's hide, the 1952-54 line solidified its dramatic postwar resurgence. As before, much of this success was due to Ford alone, Mercury and Lincoln being far less significant in their respective markets.

Proclaimed as the "big" '52, the second new Ford in only three years rode an inch-longer wheelbase and stood lower, wider, and a tad longer than the 1949-51 models. Yet, the boxy new styling somehow made for a smaller look. At least the new look was clean and trim—and fresh in a year when Chevy and Plymouth had to make do with peddling rehashed '49 models. Highlights included a return to the center-bullet grille and discreet bulges around the rear wheel openings, with thrust-forward leading edges (decorated with moldings suggestive of air scoops), imparting a sense of motion. Round taillights, soon to be a Ford hallmark, flanked a squared-up rear deck. The fuel filler was newly hidden behind a pull-down license plate holder. Inside, the driver peered through the first one-piece windshield on a postwar Ford and operated brake and clutch pedals with suspended—instead of floor-mounted—pivots. The restyled dash managed to remain pleasingly simple.

Three series instead of two now encompassed 11 models. Mainline and Customline replaced the previous DeLuxe and Custom but offered the same choices. Most were powered by Ford's first overhead-valve six, a lively unit rated a 101 bhp (and which some claimed was faster than the V-8 up to 60 mph). The Victoria hardtop coupe, a newly named Sunliner convertible, and a new four-door Country Squire wagon sat atop the line in the new Crestline series. They came with the time-honored flathead V-8, mechanically unchanged but packing 10 more horsepower, probably a paper increase. The new four-door Customline Country Sedan, with all-steel construction as on all '52 Ford wagons (covered separately), also used the V-8.

Ford boasted about its equally new '52 chassis. Called a "K-bar" frame, with five crossmembers welded to box-section side rails, it was claimed to be more rigid than the previous ladder chassis. At the rear rode longer, stronger "Para-Flex" multi-leaf springs, assisted by shocks resited to reduce side way in turns. Redesigned brake seals provided better protection against dust and water. And at the front, "Hydra-coil" springs allegedly allowed for easier steering and more precise handling. All this resulted in what Ford described as "automatic ride control," aided by a lower center of gravity and wider track front and rear. Extra weight may have helped, too: up by about 100 pounds on the Victoria hardtop, for example, and 70 pounds on the convertible.

The continuing Korean conflict led to further industry-wide, government-mandated production declines for 1952. Ford's total fell from slightly over a million units to about 672,000. Front-running Chevy dropped by about the same amount.

Ford observed its 50th anniversary in 1953 but made no major changes to its cars, though it made far more of them. A production "blitz" forced dealers to sell cars they hadn't ordered at less than cost, an attempt to outgun Chevrolet that was somewhat successful. Ford's 1953 volume was up nearly 50 percent from '52—and less than 100,000 units behind Chevy. The effort peaked in 1954, but Ford and Chevy suffered far less than Chrysler and the independents.

For 1954, Ford retired its 22-year-old flathead V-8 for a modern overhead-valve unit, the last of three such engines that originated in a late-'40s project begun under chief engineer Harold Youngren (the '52 Ford six and ohv Lincoln V-8 were the others). Though displacement didn't change, the new design allowed for room to grow (the flathead had reached its limit), was far more efficient, and offered greater reliability and smoothness via a five-main-bearing crankshaft. Hard tappets, pressure-lubricated rocker arms, umbrella-type valve guides, and dampening coils on valve-spring ends contributed to quiet running and low oil consumption. A deep crankcase suggested the "Y-block" moniker featured in Ford ads.

Significantly, Chevrolet and Plymouth wouldn't have high-compression V-8s until 1955. And as the "Low-Price Three" were mostly carryovers for '54, the Y-block undoubtedly proved to be a key factor in lifting Ford to the top in industry production. Its margin over Chevy was slim to be sure—less than 23,000 units—but an important moral victory nonetheless and a sign of how far the Ford Motor Company had come in just five years.

The all-new 1952 Ford Crestline Sunliner (opposite, bottom) *listed at $2027; buyers snapped up 22,534 of them. A new grille and more side chrome marked the '53 models, the last to use the old flathead V-8. The Crestline Victoria* (top) *cost $1941 and found 128,302 customers.*

SPECIFICATIONS

Engines: **1952-53** ohv I-6, 215.3 cid (3.56 × 3.60), 101 bhp; L-head V-8, 239.4 cid (3.19 × 3.75), 110 bhp **1954** ohv I-6, 223 cid (3.62 × 3.60), 115 bhp; ohv V-8, 239.4 cid (3.50 × 3.10), 130 bhp

Transmissions:	3-speed manual; overdrive and 3-speed Ford-O-Matic optional
Suspension, front:	upper and lower A-arms, coil springs
Suspension, rear:	live axle, semi-elliptic leaf springs
Brakes:	front/rear drums
Wheelbase (in.):	**1952-53** 115.5 **1954** 115.5
Weight (lbs):	3034-3339
Top speed (mph):	90-100
0-60 mph (sec):	14.5-16.5

Production*: **1952 Mainline 2d sdn** 79,931 **business cpe** 10,137 **4d sdn** 41,227 **Customline 2d sdn** 175,762 **club cpe** 26,550 **4d sdn** 188,303 **Crestline Victoria 2d htp** 77,320 **Sunliner cvt** 22,534 **1953 Mainline 2d sdn** 152,995 **business cpe** 16,280 **4d sdn** 69,463 **Customline 2d sdn** 305,433 **club cpe** 43,999 **4d sdn** 374,743 **Crestline Victoria 2d htp** 128,302 **Sunliner cvt** 40,861 **1954 Mainline 2d sdn** 123,329 **business cpe** 10,665 **4d sdn** 55,371 **Customline 2d sdn** 293,375 **club cpe** 33,951 **4d sdn** 262,499 **Crestline Victoria 2d htp** 95,464 **4d sdn** 99,677 **Sunliner cvt** 36,685

*For wagon production, see 1952-59 Ford Wagons; 1954 Crestline does not include Skyliner 2d htp (see entry).

PMJ 181
J.R. DALL

1952-59 Ford Station Wagons

Ford Division has long proclaimed itself "America's Wagonmaster," and not without reason. The firm pioneered the factory-built station wagon with its 1929 Model A "woodie," breaking from the standard practice of an automaker furnishing the chassis for its wagons, but not the coachwork. Ford even set up its own timber forests to supply the raw materials and a plant in Iron Mountain, in Michigan's rugged Upper Peninsula, to supply the wagon bodies. No surprise, then, that Ford sold more wagons than most anyone else through World War II, and that it's usually been America's top wagon producer since.

What is surprising is that Ford was the last of the "Low Price Three" to abandon structural-wood wagons. Its first all-steel models didn't arrive until 1952—three years behind Chevy and Plymouth. That year, however, Ford got a leg-up on its rivals with an all-new wagon design, its second since the war.

Ford offered more wagon choices that year than Chevy and Plymouth, expanding from the single two-door woodie of 1949-51 to a trio of more practical "steelers." There was one for each series, trimmed and equipped like corresponding non-wagons. The most affordable was the two-door Ranch Wagon, an $1832 entry in the bottom-end Mainline series. Next came the $2060 Country Sedan four door in the mid-range Customline group. Both were six-seaters. The top-shelf Crestline offered a new eight-passenger Country Squire at $2816.

The last parted company with its 1950-51 forebear in having four doors and bodyside trim that strived to look like the real wood of old. Ford was just following other makes in this, substituting a simulated wood framework with decal inserts. But while Chevy and Plymouth gave up on pseudo-wood trim by 1954, Ford persisted with it for the Squire. Though nobody mistook it for genuine tree wood, this traditional touch proved so perennially popular that both rivals would revive it in the '60s.

Though not generally known, Ford's first all-steel wagons were partly the work of Gordon M. Buehrig, who'd joined the Dearborn design staff in 1949. They were, of course, a far cry from the legendary Auburn Speedster, Duesenberg Model J, and Cord 810 he'd created in the '30s, let alone other Ford assignments that included the '50 Crestliner, '51 Victoria, and the matchless '56 Continental Mark II (see entries). But Buehrig was a professional and he did a professional job, making the wagons as neat and trim as other Fords—and arguably better-looking than their Chevy and Plymouth contemporaries.

Benefiting from the basic changes applied to other 1952-54 Fords (see entry) and reflecting the growing popularity of all-steel wagons generally, Ford's 1952 models garnered unprecedented sales—up over 40 percent from '51. The upward trend continued, prompting the division to make wagons a separate series for 1955 and add a spiffy new Custom Ranch Wagon and eight-seat Country Sedan. Like other '55 Fords, the wagons bore rakish new styling and hotter engines. The following year, Ford nodded in the direction of Chevy's hardtop-styled Nomad (see entry) with yet a third two-door, the posh Parklane, carrying top-line Fairlane trim and often two-toned, but otherwise little different from the Ranch Wagons.

Five wagons returned in Ford's all-new '57 line, but not the same five. The Parklane exited due to meager sales, the Custom Ranch became the Del Rio, and the six-seat Country Sedan returned after a year's absence. All rode the 116-inch Custom/Custom 300 wheelbase. New features included single-latch liftgate/tailgate release, modestly wrapped rear windows, and a distinctive transverse roof groove about a third of the way back from the windshield.

As the basic Country Sedan had been Ford's most popular wagon since 1954, the division logically decided to offer a lower-priced version in a four-door six-seat Ranch Wagon for 1958. It sold well at $2451, just $53 upstream of the cheapest two-door, but the $100-dearer Country Sedan remained the best-seller. The same lineup returned for 1959 with a two-inch longer wheelbase.

As utility vehicles that weren't necessarily utilitarian, Ford's '50s wagons probably did more than any other to popularize a body style that remains an American staple to this day. Like most wagons, they're not hot collector's items, but there's no more nostalgic or practical car for carting bargains home from a flea market—or carrying a few extra souls on a Saturday night cruise.

SPECIFICATIONS

Engines: **1952-53** ohv I-6, 215.3 cid (3.56 × 3.60), 101 bhp; L-head V-8, 239.4 cid (3.19 × 3.75), 110 bhp **1954** ohv I-6, 223 cid (3.62 × 3.60), 115 bhp; ohv V-8, 239.4 cid (3.50 × 3.10), 130 bhp **1955** ohv I-6, 223 cid, 120 bhp; ohv V-8, 272 cid (3.62 × 3.30), 162/182 bhp (2-/4-barrel) **1956** ohv I-6, 223 cid, 137 bhp; ohv V-8, 272 cid, 173 bhp; 292 cid (3.75 × 3.30), 200/202 bhp (manual/automatic); 312 cid (3.80 × 3.44), 215/225 bhp (manual/automatic) **1957** ohv I-6, 223 cid, 144 bhp; ohv V-8, 272 cid, 190 bhp; 292 cid, 212 bhp; 312 cid, 245/270/285 bhp **1958** ohv I-6, 223 cid, 145 bhp; ohv V-8, 292 cid, 205 bhp; 332 cid (4.00 × 3.30), 240/265 bhp; 352 cid (4.00 × 3.50), 300 bhp **1959** 223 cid, 145 bhp; 292 cid, 200 bhp; 332 cid, 225 bhp; 352 cid, 300 bhp

Transmissions:	3-speed manual **1952-57** overdrive; 3-speed Ford-O-Matic optional **1959** 2-speed Ford-O-Matic optional **1958-59** 3-speed dual-range Cruise-O-Matic optional
Suspension, front:	upper and lower A-arms, coil springs
Suspension, rear:	live axle, semi-elliptic leaf springs
Brakes:	front/rear drums
Wheelbase (in.):	**1952-53** 115.0 **1954-56** 115.5 **1957-58** 116.0 **1959** 118.0
Weight (lbs):	3212-3808
Top speed (mph):	90-105
0-60 mph (sec):	10.5-18.0

Production*: **1952 Mainline 2d Ranch Wagon** 32,566 **Customline 4d Country Sedan** 11,927 **Crestline 4d Country Squire 8P** 5426 **1953 Mainline 2d Ranch Wagon** 66,976 **Customline 4d Country Sedan** 37,743 **Crestline 4d Country Squire 8P** 11,001 **1954 Mainline 2d Ranch Wagon** 44,315 **Customline 2d Ranch Wagon** 36,086 **Customline 4d Country Sedan** 48,384 **Crestline 4d Country Squire 8P** 12,797 **1955 2d Ranch Wagon** 40,493 **2d Custom Ranch Wagon** 43,671 **4d Country Sedan** 53,075 **4d Country Sedan 8P** 53,209 **4d Country Squire 8P** 19,011 **1956 2d Ranch Wagon** 48,348 **2d Custom Ranch Wagon** 42,317 **2d Parklane** 15,186 **4d Country Sedan 8P** 85,374 **4d Country Squire 8P** 23,221 **1957 2d Ranch Wagon** 60,486 **2d Del Rio Ranch Wagon** 46,105 **4d Country Sedan** 137,251 **4d Country Sedan 9P** 49,638 **4d Country Squire 9P** 27,690 **1958 2d Ranch Wagon** 34,578 **2d Del Rio Ranch Wagon** 12,687 **4d Ranch Wagon** 32,854 **4d Country Sedan** 68,772 **4d Country Sedan 9P** 20,702 **4d Country Squire 9P** 15,020 **1959 2d Ranch Wagon** 45,588 **2d Del Rio Ranch Wagon** 8663 **4d Ranch Wagon** 67,339 **4d Country Sedan** 94,601 **4d Country Sedan 9P** 28,811 **4d Country Squire 9P** 24,336

*6-passenger unless otherwise noted

Ford has long been known as America's station wagon king. The all-new '52 Country Sedan (opposite, bottom) *boasted all-steel construction. The '55* (opposite, top and center) *was essentially a heavily revised '52, but now had an overhead-valve V-8. The 1957 lineup included a Country Sedan* (this page, top) *at $2451 and a fancier Country Squire at $2684.*

1954 Ford Skyliner

It wasn't at all unusual in the '50s for features from some dazzling Detroit "dream car" to appear on a manufacturer's showroom model a few years later. Indeed, show cars have always been used to test public reaction to new ideas as a prelude to production.

Rooflines were an obvious area for innovation, and way-out treatments on show cars were *de rigueur* in the '50s. And nobody in Detroit offered more of them for sale than Ford, which seemed to have a particular fascination for novelty roofs at the time, whether for their own sake or, as Packard's Jim Nance put it, "a difference to sell." But sell them Ford did—or tried to—beginning with the 1954 Crestline Skyliner, together with that year's new Mercury Sun Valley—the first production cars with a see-through top.

Designers had been thinking about "bubbletops" since the late '30s, when technical advances in the infant plastics industry began yielding stronger materials that could be used structurally, not just decoratively. The first such application was executed by John Tjaarda for Briggs, a one-piece plastic top for a 1939 Plymouth convertible sedan. By the end of World War II, the public had been titillated with promises of radical "see-through" cars from various companies, but nobody actually built one for sale to the public until Ford.

The Skyliner (and Sun Valley) likely gained impetus with the arrival of Gordon M. Buehrig, who'd come to Dearborn in 1949 to design Ford's Crestliner and '51 Victoria. He also helped develop the all-steel '52 Ford/Mercury wagons, and would handle body engineering for the beautiful 1956 Continental Mark II. Buehrig had previously worked at Studebaker with Raymond Loewy, a leading proponent of the see-through top, then became a freelance designer and created the stillborn TASCO sports car, which had hinged roof sections of transparent plastic, an idea he patented.

A more direct forecast was Ford's own fiberglass-bodied XL-500 show car of 1953, with a clear plastic top and B-posts raked forward to form a "basket handle" roof band. The idea resurfaced two years later on the experimental Mystere, where the up-and-over pillars served as the only structural roof members.

Ford's production bubbletoppers were, as might be expected, considerably less radical: just the ordinary pillarless coupes with Plexiglas inserts ahead of the B-pillars, tinted deep green to ward off heat and glare. The Skyliner listed at $2164 with standard six, $109 more than the normal Crestline Victoria. Aside from the half-plastic roof and minor identifying trim, it was virtually identical with the steel-top model.

Ford rather floridly claimed that the Skyliner offered "a freshness of view, a new gaiety and glamor, vast new areas of visibility, a whole new concept of light and luxury....You're comfortably 'out of doors' all year long...with that wonderful feeling of being fashionably first." This happy puffery, while partly true, wasn't entirely accurate either. The green tinting made for a kind of bilious, slightly weird interior ambience. As *Motor Trend* magazine's Walt Woron quipped: "It may cause many a young lady to check her makeup."

A more serious problem involved perspiring passengers. Though desert tests showed that the regular steel-roof hardtop was only about five degrees cooler inside, the bubbletopper undoubtedly *felt* much warmer on sunny days than that difference implied. And as air conditioning wasn't common in those days, costing upwards of $600, very few cars had it. What the Skyliner *did* have, however, was an interior sunshade that snapped onto the headliner around the transparent section's perimeter, but it provided only partial relief.

An interesting car with all the good qualities of other '54 Fords (see separate entry), the Skyliner was nonetheless a relatively poor seller, attracting just 13,344 orders versus nearly 95,500 for that year's standard Victoria. Though Mercury gave up on the concept after 1955, Ford persisted with it—with decreasing success—as an option for the jazzy hardtop-style Fairlane Crown Victoria coupe of 1955-56 (see entry).

At least Dearborn was trying to give buyers something they couldn't get anywhere else, and it tried again with an even wilder Skyliner for 1957. Ah, but that's another story, one you'll find a few pages further on.

Although the '54 Ford was only modestly facelifted, new features like an overhead-valve V-8 and ball-joint front suspension made it a much improved automobile. The top-line Crestline series listed five models, among them the novel Skyliner seen here, basically a regular Crestline Victoria hardtop with a Plexiglass roof over the front passengers. It cost $109 extra and found 13,344 buyers.

SPECIFICATIONS

Engines: ohv I-6, 223 cid (3.62 × 3.60), 115 bhp; ohv V-8, 239.4 cid (3.50 × 3.10), 130 bhp

Transmission:	3-speed manual; overdrive and 3-speed Ford-O-Matic optional
Suspension, front:	upper and lower A-arms, coil springs
Suspension, rear:	live axle, semi-elliptic leaf springs
Brakes:	front/rear drums
Wheelbase (in.):	115.5
Weight (lbs):	3265
Top speed (mph):	100
0-60 mph (sec):	14.5
Production:	13,344

MK·362
COLORADO

1955-56 Ford Crown Victoria

The Crown Victoria was a curious model: a hardtop convertible with a thick bar that wrapped over the roof and down to the beltline, thus canceling out the open-air feeling of a hardtop. But it was stylish, and costly for a Ford—$107 more than the regular Victoria, plus another $70 for the glass-top version. The '55 (below and top) started at $2202; the '56 (above and opposite) sold for $2337.

The '55 Chevy commands a vast enthusiast following. The '55 Ford garners far less attention. That's curious, because in many ways Ford more than matched Chevy that year. Though admittedly not "ground-up" fresh, it offered colorful new styling and the most powerful engines in Ford history. And it was a solid hit, helping Ford to unprecedented postwar model year production of over 1.4 million units—less than Chevy's, but impressive nonetheless. Of course, high volume alone doesn't make for a great car of the Fifties or any other era, but it does reflect just how much the '55 Ford had going for it.

What Ford mainly had going for it in '55 was a thoroughly reworked rendition of its successful 1952-54 platform, so heavily revised, in fact, that it almost qualified as all-new—and most people thought it was. Designer Frank Hershey modified the existing bodyshell to impart a rakish new look of motion. Highlights included a trendy wrapped windshield, full-width concave grille, hooded headlamps, artfully angled "speedlines" in the sheetmetal around the wheel openings, modestly finned rear fenders, and large round taillights. The lineup now comprised four series, with wagons a separate group and Mainline and Customline sedans as before. Replacing Crestline at the top of the heap was the new Fairlane (named after the Ford family estate in Dearborn), identified by bold chrome moldings that started above the headlamps, then dipped saucily at the A-posts to run back to the tail lamps at mid-body.

Besides two sedans, Sunliner convertible, and Victoria hardtop coupe, the '55 Fairlane line included the new Crown Victoria, a two-door hardtop with its own flatter roof panel that the regular Victoria would have in 1956. The work of Hershey protégé L. David Ash, it featured a wide, raked-forward band wrapped up and over to conceal the (non-existent) B-pillars. This looked like a rollover bar, although it didn't function like one, and company chief engineer Harold T. Youngren thought body flex sufficient

(as on other hardtops) to specify the convertible's stiffer X-member frame. As a result, the "Crown Vicky" ended up tight and solid-feeling. For an extra $70 a buyer could step into a glass-top Crown Vic, which sported a quarter-inch-thick Plexiglas roof panel ahead of the band. It afforded front seaters the same bilious green view above that the '54 Skyliner did. This time, though, the idea garnered far fewer buyers.

Ford bested Chevy in 1955's "horsepower race" with a pair of larger V-8s derived from its new-for-'54 Y-block design. The basic 272 cubic-inch unit produced 162 horsepower with two-barrel carb, 182 with four-barrel and dual exhausts. A 292, at first reserved for Mercury, delivered 198 bhp, and a 205-bhp "Interceptor" police special was offered on a limited basis late in the year. At the other end of the spectrum, the 223-cid Ford six moved up to 120 bhp, a gain of five.

Ford moved in two different directions for '56: safety and performance. Passenger models wore a conservative—and handsome—rehash of their '55 styling, with a grated grille and larger parking lamps the main differences. Providing new intramural competition for the Crown Vic was a Fairlane Town Victoria four-door hardtop (most everybody else had one in '56, too).

Ford horsepower kept climbing, again an industry given in 1956. The 272 edged up to 173 bhp as the Mainline/Customline option, Fairlane's 292 to 200 bhp. A new '56 choice was a 312-cid enlargement with 215 bhp in base two-barrel form or 225 bhp in four-barrel trim, the latter offered only with Ford-O-Matic. A 245-bhp twin-four-barrel version arrived at mid-year as a Thunderbird option, but a few of the passenger Fords may have been built with it. At the same time, Ford hawked "Lifeguard Design" safety features: standard impact-absorbing dished steering wheel, breakaway rearview mirror, and crashproof door locks, plus extra-cost front seatbelts and padded dash and visors. The public took to them in a modest way, but performance still sold cars in those days.

Gimmicky roof treatments didn't, however, and Crown Victoria demand fell, more than for any other '56 Ford. The '55 had garnered 35,164 sales, of which only 1999 were see-through units; the '56 skidded to 9811, including just 603 "bubbletoppers." The Crown Victoria thus bid adieu, but only because Ford had something even more fantastic for '57: a new Skyliner retractable hardtop. That tale is told a little further on.

Today, the distinctively styled Crown Victoria remains the focus of most 1955-56 Ford fans and, obviously, there aren't nearly enough to go around. If you want one in your garage, you'll have to be ready (with plenty of cash) the next time one comes up for sale. As the proverb reminds us, opportunity seldom knocks twice.

SPECIFICATIONS

Engines: 1955 ohv I-6, 223 cid (3.62 × 3.60), 120 bhp; ohv V-8, 272 cid (3.62 × 3.30), 162/182 bhp (2-/4-barrel); 292 cid (3.75 × 3.30), 198/205 bhp **1956** ohv I-6, 223 cid (3.62 x 3.60), 137 bhp; ohv V-8, 292 cid (3.75 × 3.30), 200/205 bhp (manual/automatic); 312 cid (3.80 × 3.44), 215/225 bhp (2-/4-barrel)

Transmission:	3-speed manual; overdrive and 3-speed Ford-O-Matic optional
Suspension, front:	upper and lower A-arms, coil springs
Suspension, rear:	live axle, semi-elliptic leaf springs
Brakes:	front/rear drums
Wheelbase (in.):	115.5
Weight (lbs):	3289-3321
Top speed (mph):	95-110
0-60 mph (sec):	9.5-13.0

Production: 1955 steel-top 33,165 **glass-top** 1999 **1956 steel-top** 9209 **glass-top** 603

1955-57 Ford Thunderbird

Legend says the Thunderbird was born in October 1951, when Ford Division general manager Louis Crusoe visited the Paris Auto Show with styling consultant George Walker. America had fallen in love with European sports cars in the early postwar years, and both men were taken by the ones they saw there: the curvy Jaguar XK-120 and the new Anglo-American Nash-Healey, for example. "Why don't we have something like that?" Crusoe asked. Walker replied, "Oh, but we do!"—then hurried to phone Dearborn to get his crew cracking.

Like many apocryphal stories, this one isn't true. Ford stylists had been conjuring two-seaters before this, of course, but never rushed to build one because sports-car sales then accounted for a minuscule 0.27 percent of the total U.S. market. But in January 1953, General Motors threw down a gauntlet Ford couldn't ignore: the Chevrolet Corvette. Barely a month later, Ford was hard at work on the car that would ultimately be named for the god worshipped by America's Southwest Indians as the bringer of rain and prosperity.

First displayed as a wood mock-up at the Detroit Auto Show in early 1954, the Thunderbird debuted as a "personal" car, *not* a pure sports car. It rode the same wheelbase as the first-generation Corvette, to be sure, but emphasized luxury and practicality. In place of creaking fiberglass and clumsy side curtains stood a sturdy steel body with convenient roll-up windows. Instead of an ill-fitting soft top came a snug power top, lift-off hard top, or both. And in place of a plodding six, the T-Bird's engine bay packed a burly Mercury V-8.

Nobody really knew how much demand there was for two-seater sports cars in mid-Fifties America. But Chevy had its Corvette, so Ford would have its Thunderbird. The '55 (below and opposite, top) *had a "Ford look" to it and was billed as a "personal" car—and it beat the stuffing out of the Vette sales-wise. The '56* (bottom) *featured a continental spare tire out back and more horsepower.*

Thunderbird
1955
THUNDERBIRD

Thunderbird
AL 1956

Bill Burnett supervised the engineering, which relied heavily on standard Ford components. Styling, chiefly the work of young Bill Boyer directed by Walker's lieutenant, Frank Hershey, couldn't have been better: simple and smooth, yet clearly Ford. To many, the T-Bird's rakish long-hood/short-deck proportions recalled the classic early-Forties Lincoln Continental.

With European style and American comfort, convenience, and go, Thunderbird proved well-nigh irresistible. It whipped the rival Chevy in 1955 model-year production by nearly 24 to 1!

You don't mess with success in Detroit, and Ford didn't with the '56 Thunderbird. The few changes included a larger 312-cubic-inch V-8 option, exterior-mount spare (for more trunk space), softer suspension (for a smoother ride), and optional portholes for the hardtop. Production eased slightly, but still beat out Corvette by five to one. Trouble was, Ford wanted much higher volume, and had already settled on four-seaters for 1958 and beyond.

So the '57 ended up being the last two-seat Bird—and arguably the best. A handsome facelift brought a prominent bumper/grille and a longer deck (again enclosing the spare) wearing modest blade-like tailfins. Power soared upward again, too, with 285 bhp available on the top twin-four-barrel 312 with 10.0:1 compression. Ford even built 208 supercharged "F-Birds" with 300/340 horsepower courtesy of Paxton-McCulloch blowers, mainly for racing.

And race the early T-Birds did, albeit with limited success. A '55 sponsored by *Mechanix Illustrated* magazine's Tom McCahill swept the production sports car class at that year's Daytona Speed Weeks, with Joe Ferguson's two-way average of 124.633 mph besting every Austin-Healey, Porsche, and all but one Jaguar XK-120. Chuck Daigh did even better in '56 with a Pete DePaolo-prepped car, running 88.779 mph in the standing mile, though Zora Arkus-Duntov's modified Vette proved a bit faster at 89.735 mph. In 1957, Daigh scored 93.312 mph, and a privately entered T-Bird ran the flying mile at 146.282 mph one way, 138.775 mph both ways. Then the Automobile Manufacturers Association issued its infamous racing "ban"—and development stopped.

But the Thunderbird had proved its point. If not a true sports car, it could be a high-performance car. That it also exuded style and luxury made it all the more remarkable—and memorable. An extra-long model year made the '57 the most numerous of the flock, the first American two-seaters to sell in really high numbers.

Which was, of course, the most important point. By proving that two-seaters could be a commercial success, the T-Bird paved the way for the many sports cars that followed it in the U.S., domestic and foreign. For that alone it deserves our respect. For what they were, the early T-Birds will always have our affection.

SPECIFICATIONS

Engines: ohv V-8 **1955** 292 cid (3.75 × 3.30), 193/198 bhp **1956** 292 cid (3.74 × 3.30), 202 bhp; 312 cid (3.80 × 3.44), 215/225 bhp (overdrive/automatic) **1957** 292 cid (3.75 × 3.30), 212 bhp; 312 cid (3.80 × 3.44), 245/270/285 bhp (300/340 bhp supercharged)

Transmission:	3-speed manual; overdrive and 3-speed Ford-O-Matic optional
Suspension, front:	upper and lower A-arms, coil springs
Suspension, rear:	live axle, semi-elliptic leaf springs
Brakes:	front/rear drums
Wheelbase (in.):	102.0
Weight (lbs):	2980-3145
Top speed (mph):	105-125
0-60 mph (sec):	7.0-11.5
Production:	**1955** 16,155 **1956** 15,631 **1957** 21,380

Thunderbird was extensively restyled for 1957 (both pages): new grille and front bumper, larger taillights, modest fins, new rear bumper, larger trunk (which again held the spare tire), and a new dashboard. And whereas the highest horsepower rating in 1956 had been 225, buyers could now choose from engines with 212/245/270/285/300 horses, the last via supercharging. Ford built 21,380 T-Birds for '57, the best yet, but the two-seater's fate was sealed as Ford busily readied a four-seater for 1958.

1957-59 Ford Ranchero

Ford Motor Company celebrated its 50th anniversary in an atmosphere of feisty optimism. The '49 Ford had saved the firm from oblivion, and the mostly new '52 corporate line had enabled it to reclaim second place in industry production from Chrysler Corporation. Now, in 1953, Ford was determined to beat General Motors by matching the perennial league-leader model for model. Thus, when GM announced the two-seat Chevy Corvette that year, Ford began conjuring the Thunderbird to meet it. Even the ill-timed Edsel, planned in 1955 but released in recession '58, fit into Ford's ambitious expansion program.

Despite its more limited resources, Ford also tried to outflank GM by offering cars the public couldn't get elsewhere—what we now call "niche marketing." Hence the innovative "see-through top" of the 1954 Ford Skyliner/Mercury Sun Valley, and an ultra-luxury challenge to Cadillac in the handsome 1956 Continental Mark II.

Rising station wagon sales and the growing popularity of pickup trucks with car-like styling and features suggested another niche vehicle: a revival of the prewar car/pickup. The idea likely gained impetus when Robert S. McNamara became Ford Division general manager in early 1955. An all-new '57 Ford was in the works, partly in preparation for the forthcoming Edsel line, and a pickup was the sort of practical product that appealed to the profit-minded McNamara, especially since it could be built at low cost with tooling from the new station wagons.

The resultant newcomer to Ford showrooms surprised most buyers as much as the "retrac" '57 Skyliner did. Called Ranchero, reflecting the division's brief flirtation with Spanish-sounding names, it was exactly what it looked like: the two-door Ranch Wagon with a three-seater cab and open pickup box instead of an enclosed rear cargo deck. The Ranchero shared the same 116-inch wheelbase used for all '57 wagons.

Sheetmetal and Ford's new '57 styling were naturally shared too. The one obvious difference was the Ranchero roof's slightly extended trailing edge. Interior appointments and even the optional two-toning took their cues from the Ranch Wagon and Custom/Custom 300 sedans. It all made for America's most stylish pickup ever. Ford called it "America's first work or play truck."

Because it was built like Ford's '57 passenger cars, the Ranchero also shared their technical changes. Chief among them were a new wide-rail "cow-belly" frame, longer rear leaf springs with inboard forward mountings, swept-back lower front-suspension control arms, redesigned hypoid final drive, improved recirculating-ball steering, and 14-inch wheels and tires.

Ranchero arrived in standard and Custom models carrying the more potent 144-horsepower version of Ford's familiar 223-cubic-inch "Mileage Maker" six. A 190-bhp 272-cid V-8 cost extra on the base model, while the Custom could be ordered with a 212-bhp 292. Each engine teamed with standard three-speed manual, the same with optional overdrive, or extra-cost Ford-O-Matic. Also like passenger models, Rancheros could be had with power steering and brakes, and even electric seat and windows.

For all its car-like civility, the Ranchero was technically a half-ton pickup and a product of Ford Truck Division. And with prices starting at a low $1920, it was a tempting alternative to the basic F-100 for those who wanted a car but needed a truck. A good many buyers—21,705 according to Robert C. Ackerson in *Ranchero: A Source Book*—gave in to that temptation. Thus, the Ranchero returned for 1958, again with the major changes applied to that year's passenger models, including revised front-end styling and somewhat more power. Rear-end styling remained as in 1957. The '59 story changed a bit, because the standard model was axed. The remaining Custom model adopted the 118-inch wheelbase used on all '59 Ford cars and featured a longer 83-inch cargo bed. Not only that, but a copy-cat rival appeared: Chevy's El Camino.

Perhaps reflecting McNamara's push for even higher profits, the 1960 Ranchero switched from Ford's standard chassis to become a version of that year's new Falcon compact. It would remain as such through 1965, after which it moved to the intermediate Fairlane platform. By the early '70s, as a relative of the successor Torino line, it had become larger and heavier than the late-Fifties original. Sales, previously steady but modest, began tapering off and the Ranchero vanished after 1979—ironically leaving the car/pickup field entirely to Chevrolet's El Camino and GMC Caballero (which in turn disappeared after 1987). Ford, of course, had other niches to try, but that's another story.

The Ranchero was basically a two-door station with the rear part of the roof removed. The '57 (opposite) and '58 (this page, top) had side trim similar to the Custom 300 cars. The '59 seen here (bottom), a daily driver, has been upgraded to Galaxie side trim and has non-stock seats.

SPECIFICATIONS

Engines: **1957** ohv I-6, 223 cid (3.62 × 3.60), 144 bhp; ohv V-8, 272 cid, (3.62 × 3.30), 190 bhp; 292 cid (3.75 × 3.30), 206/212 bhp **1958** ohv I-6, 223 cid, 145 bhp; ohv V-8, 292 cid, 205 bhp; 352 cid (4.00 × 3.50), 300 bhp **1959** ohv I-6, 223 cid, 145 bhp; ohv V-8, 292 cid, 200 bhp; 332 cid (4.00 × 3.30), 225 bhp; 352 cid, 300 bhp

Transmissions:	3-speed manual; overdrive, Ford-O-Matic, 3-speed Cruise-O-Matic (1958-59) optional
Suspension, front:	upper and lower A-arms, coil springs
Suspension, rear:	live axle, semi-elliptic leaf springs
Brakes:	front/rear drums
Wheelbase (in.):	**1957-58** 116.0 **1959** 118.0
Weight (lbs):	approx. 3500
Top speed (mph):	90-105
0-60 mph (sec):	9.5-12.5
Production:	**1957** 21,705 **1958** 9950 **1959** 14,169

GARVER
FEED & SUPPLY CO., INC.

1957-59 Ford Skyliner

Ford went all out for 1957, fielding its biggest, brightest cars ever, with longer wheelbases and more power and in five separate series. At the very top of the line, in that year's new Fairlane 500 group, debuted a revived Skyliner—only it wasn't a "bubbletopper" like the '54 model, but the world's first mass-produced retractable hardtop.

The concept was first broached in Dearborn by stylist Gilbert Spear, whose designs convinced William Clay Ford, head of Special Projects Division, to earmark $2.2 million to develop it for the 1956 Continental Mark II (see entry). But cost escalation precluded it there, so it went to the Ford Division in 1955, but only after another $18 million commitment for testing. As Ford's all-new '57 line was then less than two years away, a crash program was instituted to get the Skyliner out in time.

The Skyliner arrived slightly behind the rest of the line looking little different from the soft-top Sunliner, apart from three-inch-longer and somewhat higher rear fenders. This "bustle," of course, had to be there to provide enough room for the roof—shorter and squarer than that on standard hardtops, but still plenty big—and its hardware. The decklid was hinged in the only possible way, at the back; the top was hinged 10 inches from the front to create a space-saving flap that folded under as it slid back. Even the convertible chassis had to be modified with closer-set side rails to leave room for the top's control linkage. Remarkably, little rear legroom was lost. The gas tank took up valuable space under the trunk floor, however, so it moved aft of the back seat—an "accidental" safety benefit for rear-end collisions—with the spare taking its place.

The Skyliner's "nervous system" comprised 600 feet of wiring and no fewer than 10 power relays, eight circuit breakers, 10 limit switches, three drive motors, and a safety interlock that prevented anything from happening without the transmission in Neutral. It was complicated, but more reliable than generally believed.

Here's how it worked. Pressing a steering-column switch with the ignition on (and, preferably, the engine running, to minimize battery drain) activated two (1957-58) or three (1959) switches to start a deck motor that lifted the long lid via twin shafts at each edge. When the deck locked open, it tripped another motor (behind the rear seat) that raised the package shelf to deck level. This started yet another motor that unlocked the top, after which two more motors (one on the '59) hoisted the roof and sent it back into the yawning cavity. A separate servo folded the flap as the roof eased its way down. A dashboard warning light glowed throughout, and the sequence could be reversed at any point

Skyliner advertising made a legitimate point by asking, "How can it be a 'hardtop convertible' if the top doesn't go down?" Enough buyers agreed to make the '57 a fair success for a novelty item priced at $2942, the costliest passenger Ford by far. Trouble was, the soft-top Sunliner offered open-air driving for a whopping $437 less, and was more practical besides. The Skyliner had no luggage space with the top down, just 6.5 cubic feet with it up, and it could be accessed only from the high sides. Worse, its price premium grew each year; other Fords went up too, but not as much.

Ultimately, the Skyliner was doomed by division chief Robert S. McNamara, who deplored costly "gimmick engineering" and turned Ford toward more profitable, no-nonsense products. With a major design change and the new Falcon compact already scheduled for 1960, he allowed the Skyliner to run two more years, but no longer. The '58 and '59 models naturally shared all the styling and engineering changes made to other Fords in those years, but garnered fewer sales: 14,713 and 12,915 respectively. Throughout, the Skyliner was the only Ford with a standard V-8: a 190-horsepower 272 for '57, a 292 of 200-205 bhp for 1958-59.

Collectors have since come to covet the "retrac" as a unique reminder of an age when merchandizing strove to make us believe that the "good life" equated with material wonders like the Hula Hoop, two-tone ballpoint pens, and refrigerator doors that opened from the left *and* right. Today it's microwave ovens, overpriced gym shoes, and video recorders, so for all society's changes in the intervening 30 years, perhaps we haven't come so far after all.

The Skyliner was a technological marvel: a "hardtop convertible" that really converted. It was complicated, and expensive, so sales were modest. The '57 (opposite, top) *gives an idea of how the all-steel top retracted. The '58* (this page, bottom) *received the same styling changes as the rest of the line, as did the '59* (opposite, bottom).

SPECIFICATIONS

Engines: ohv V-8 **1957** 272 cid (3.62 × 3.30), 190 bhp; 292 cid (3.75 × 3.30), 212 bhp; 312 cid (3.80 × 3.44), 245 bhp **1958** 292 cid, 205 bhp; 332 cid (4.00 × 3.30), 265 bhp; 352 cid (4.00 x 3.50), 300 bhp **1959** 292 cid, 200 bhp; 332 cid, 225 bhp; 352 cid, 300 bhp

Transmission:	3-speed manual; overdrive, Ford-O-Matic optional **1958-59** 3-speed Cruise-O-Matic optional
Suspension, front:	upper and lower A-arms, coil springs
Suspension, rear:	live axle, semi-elliptic leaf springs
Brakes:	front/rear drums
Wheelbase (in.):	118.0
Weight (lbs):	3916/4069
Top speed (mph):	100-105
0-60 mph (sec):	9.5-12.0
Production:	**1957** 20,766 **1958** 14,713 **1959** 12,915

1958-59 Ford Thunderbird

Perspective changes with time, and the 1958-60 Thunderbird proves it. A generation of enthusiasts once condemned the "Squarebird" as a crass business move that led to the premature demise of the classic two-seater—and to the vastly more overblown Birds of the '60s and '70s. Happily, the pioneer of the personal-luxury car is now recognized as the great car it is. As co-author Richard M. Langworth observed in his book *The Thunderbird Story:* "...All that stuff about forsaking the sports car [and] adding the hated back seat...misses the point...The 1958 Thunderbird was [perhaps] the outstanding automotive breakthrough of the decade."

Doubts about the sales prospects for Ford's two-seat "personal" car surfaced as early as December 1954, just as production was getting underway. That was enough for Robert S. McNamara, who became chief of Ford Division early the next year. As veteran company stylist Bill Boyer recalled for *Collectible Automobile®* magazine: "The success of that vehicle wasn't guaranteed at all...The reason they wanted to drop it was because...it wasn't a money-maker—you couldn't prove it [would yield a return] within the financial guidelines of the company." But McNamara knew a four-seater would make money, and he fought hard for it. "[He] simply recognized that the Thunderbird image...had an immense rub-off value that you couldn't put a dollar amount on," says Boyer, "which was unusual for Bob McNamara, known best as a tightfisted financial kind of guy. The fact that he came to the defense of the Bird...astounded everybody." But he carried the day.

Reversing normal practice, Boyer's styling studio—and not engineering—laid down the new four-seater package. Wheelbase was pegged at 113 inches (versus the two-seater's 102), and unit construction returned to Dearborn for the first time since the war to suit the ground-hugging stance styling wanted. The lower 5.8-inch ground clearance that resulted left a high transmission tunnel, but it served as the structure's main stiffening member. And Boyer cleverly turned a vice into a virtue by making

SPECIFICATIONS

Engines: ohv V-8 **1958-59** 352 cid (4.00 × 3.50), 300 bhp; 430 cid (4.30 × 3.70), 350 bhp (1958 production questionable)

Transmissions:	3-speed manual; overdrive and 3-speed dual-range Cruise-O-Matic optional
Suspension, front:	upper and lower A-arms, coil springs
Suspension, rear:	**1958** live axle, trailing arms, coil springs **1959** live axle, semi-elliptic leaf springs
Brakes:	front/rear drums
Wheelbase (in.):	113.0
Weight (lbs):	3681-3979
Top speed (mph):	110
0-60 mph (sec):	9.9

Production: **1958 2d htp** 35,758 **cvt** 2134 **1959 2d htp** 57,195 **cvt** 10,261

The two-seater Thunderbird easily outsold the Corvette in 1955-57, but Ford management figured they could sell even more T-Birds as four-seaters. The '58 (left) pioneered a new market, the "personal-luxury" segment. Despite higher prices, it easily outsold the two-seater T-Bird, so it was little changed for 1959 (top row). In fact, the '59 by itself outsold all the 1955-57 Ford and Chevy two-seaters combined—much to the delight of Ford's bean counters.

it a console carrying power window switches, heater/defroster controls, and a radio speaker. A massive cowl provided further rigidity, as did reinforced rear deck and quarter panels, and six-inch-deep chassis side rails that created a recessed cabin floor.

The all-coil suspension was also new. The front used conventional geometry, but the rear carried a complex trailing-arm arrangement intended to accommodate optional Ford-Aire suspension, which ended up being scratched at the 11th hour (a wise decision as air suspensions proved to be undependable). The 1959-60 models reverted to ordinary leaf springs.

Power came from a 352-cubic-inch version of Ford's new-for-'58 FE-series V-8 with a rated 300 horsepower. The standard transmission, a three-speed column-shift manual, could be ordered with optional overdrive, but most buyers opted for the new three-speed dual-range Cruise-O-Matic.

Offered as a convertible and hardtop coupe, the latter a first for T-Bird, the '58 turned out to be a smashing success. Famed car tester Tom McCahill curiously termed it a "sedan with fairly live characteristics, capable of turning 0-60 mph in 9.9 seconds." Buyers also loved the sporty luxury and the hardtop's air of jaunty formality. Ford couldn't build them fast enough, but still ended up building more than twice as many '58s as it had the last of the two-seaters. McNamara had been vindicated.

Despite the four-seat T-Bird's fairly revolutionary nature, Ford Division allotted only $5 million for design and body/chassis engineering, plus another $2 million for model changes through 1960. Cost overruns on convertible development more than ate up the last, however, so the '59 appeared almost unchanged. Besides minor styling revisions and the aforementioned rear-suspension alterations, the main differences were optional availability of the Lincoln 430 V-8 with 350 bhp and, late in the season, a standard fully automatic top for the convertible. The '60 would finish out this design series, marked by triple rear lamps, a busier grille, more standard equipment, and a new extra-cost sliding steel sunroof for the hardtop, the first in U.S. postwar production.

Despite the minimal mods, the T-Bird continued to sell like gangbusters: over 67,000 of the '59s and nearly 91,000 of the '60s. The latter turned out to be a T-Bird record that wouldn't be surpassed until 1977.

With all this, the "Squarebird" clearly ranks as a great American car of the '50s. The mystery is why it took us so long to recognize it.

1959 Ford Galaxie

It was fashionable in the '50s to chide Detroit for passing off style as substance, and some critics still do. To be sure, the decade produced more than its fair share of "all-new" cars that weren't, "major innovations" that really boiled down to superficial gimmicks, and styling sizzle masquerading as design steak. Yet it must be asked whether this was really so bad when we happily bought most everything the industry put before us. If we were sometimes duped, as the critics said, some of us were at least willing victims.

As the best-known practitioner of "design by opinion research," Ford Motor Company came in for much of this criticism, especially once the Edsel bombed. Yet the approach gave Ford at least as many successes. The 1955 Ford and Mercury, the '56 Lincoln, the '57 Ford, and especially the four-seat '58 Thunderbird (see entry) came about as considered responses to what buyers said they wanted—and who promptly put their money where their mouths were.

Ford would score even greater marketing triumphs in the '60s (like the phenomenally successful Mustang, to name the biggest), but we shouldn't forget a popular 1959 development: the first Galaxie. It came as a hasty effort to cash in on the success of the "Squarebird" hardtop, whose semi-formal wide-quarter roofline met with overwhelming acceptance. Of course, it had been too late to change 1959 standard-Ford styling by the time buyers rendered their verdict on the T-Bird, but company planners figured a similar roofline might boost the appeal of Fairlane 500 sedans and hardtops. It did.

As the final Ford in the design cycle began with the all-new '57, the '59 received far more changes than most end-of-the-line evolutions, probably because Ford knew an all-new '59 Chevy was coming. The previous 116-inch-wheelbase models moved over to the 118-inch Fairlane/Fairlane 500 span. New outer panels covered a much-changed 1957-58 inner structure, resulting in bigger, brighter, blockier cars. Ford rather immodestly hyped them as "The World's Most Beautifully Proportioned Cars."

SPECIFICATIONS

Engines: I-6, 223 cid (3.62 × 3.60), 145 bhp; ohv V-8, 292 cid (3.75 × 3.30), 200 bhp; 332 cid (4.00 × 3.30), 225 bhp; 352 cid (4.00 × 3.50), 300 bhp

Transmissions:	3-speed manual; overdrive, 2-speed Ford-O-Matic, 3-speed dual-range Cruise-O-Matic optional
Suspension, front:	upper and lower A-arms, coil springs
Suspension, rear:	live axle, semi-elliptic leaf springs
Brakes:	front/rear drums
Wheelbase (in.):	118.0
Weight (lbs):	3388-4064
Top speed (mph):	95-110
0-60 mph (sec):	10.0-18.0

Production: 4d Town Sedan 183,108 **2d Club Sedan** 52,848 **Club Victoria 2d htp** 121,869 **Town Victoria 4d htp** 47,728 **Sunliner cvt** 45,868 **Skyliner retractable 2d htp** 12,915

The Galaxie arrived later than other '59 Ford models, but it quickly became very popular. The award-winning styling looked conservative next to the "batwing" '59 Chevy's, but Ford sold nose to nose with Chevy that year, turning out 464,000 Galaxies—45,868 of them Sunliner convertibles.

However dubious that claim, the '59 Ford looked downright conservative next to the radical new "bat-fin" Chevy, but it went on to win a Gold Medal for exceptional styling at the 1959 Brussels World Fair. It could have been otherwise. Some '59 proposals were ugly, heavily sculptured affairs with enormous round tail lamps, reverse-slant rear windows *à la* '57 Mercury Turnpike Cruiser and—amazingly enough—"batwing" tails, though more subdued than Chevy's. Fortunately, Ford had the good sense to reject those nightmares.

Ford's '59 engineering showed good sense, too: a stronger frame with more widely spaced side rails for extra interior room; engines slightly detuned for better economy (a definite selling point after the '58 recession); a lighter, redesigned two-speed Ford-O-Matic with 105 fewer parts; and a new link-type front stabilizer bar and variable-rate rear springs that did nothing for handling, but softened the ride. Of greater long-term importance were the adoption of more durable aluminized mufflers, full-flow filters providing 4000-mile oil-change intervals, and "Diamond Lustre" enamel paint that wasn't supposed to need waxing.

The wisdom of introducing a new top-line standard series with T-Bird roof styling caused little debate, but there was debate about its name. Ford considered variations on its more popular recent monikers, including Townliner, Crown 500, and even Thunderstar, then chose Galaxie—incorrectly spelled, but perhaps inspired by the belated success of the U.S. space program.

No matter. The big Fords with "the Thunderbird look" sold strongly despite a late, mid-model-year start: better than 464,000 units. That figure is a bit misleading, however, in that the Fairlane 500 Sunliner and Skyliner became Galaxies at the same time through a simple change of rear fender script, though all '59 Galaxies retained Fairlane 500 rear-deck identification. Yet even if the two drop-tops are added to the Fairlane 500's total, Galaxie still comes out ahead by almost three to one. At over 405,000 units, its four closed models accounted for better than 27 percent of Ford's total 1959 volume.

With this, plus vastly better quality than in 1957-58, Ford nipped Chevy in calendar 1959 sales, though Chevy won the model year production race by a bit less than 12,000 units. But the Galaxie had made its point, and would remain the top standard Ford for the next decade, always a strong seller. It also prompted a similar roof graft for the '62 Falcon compact, which proved just as popular. Which only goes to show that even the best steak seems to taste better with the right sizzle.

1950 Frazer Manhattan Convertible

Kaiser-Frazer was the only American automaker to build a postwar convertible sedan until Lincoln fielded one in 1961. The 1949-50 Frazer Manhattan four-door ragtop (here a '49) was flawed in that the window frames didn't retract, but its rarity makes it a hot collectible now.

Joseph Washington Frazer, scion of the Virginia Washingtons and Clan Fraser of Scotland, was born with a silver spoon in his mouth, but spit it out early and joined the auto industry. Honing his sales skills at Packard and General Motors dealerships, he joined Walter P. Chrysler's fledgling company in 1924 and, in 1928, named the Plymouth, Chrysler's new economy model. Later, Frazer revived Willys-Overland with the Americar and the Jeep. Then, during the war, he and some associates gained control of moribund Graham-Paige Motors, which he teamed with Henry Kaiser and then folded into the Kaiser-Frazer Corporation.

Kaiser-Frazer hit the postwar seller's market like a mini-tornado, outproducing all the other independents. By 1948, K-F stood eighth in the industry, producing over 180,000 cars (about 50,000 of them Frazers), and looking like a sure thing to become a fourth member of the auto world's "big four." But things went sour in 1949, when Kaiser went into debt to finance his compact Henry J and a new full-size car design. Frazer departed as an active management official that spring, and K-F discontinued the Frazer car as soon as it could decently do so.

The most opulent Frazer was the Manhattan convertible, carved out of a four-door sedan bodyshell (because it was the only shell K-F had), and heroically reinforced "all over hell" by engineers John Widman and Ralph Isbrandt. "We had instructions to do no reinforcing of the sedan shell—no X-frame," Isbrandt told this writer. "Even the pillars and headers were sedan parts....[The first prototype] was like a bowl of jelly. I finally convinced [K-F president Edgar] Kaiser that GM, Ford, Chrysler, etc.

SPECIFICATIONS

Engine: sidevalve I-6, 226.2 cid (3.31 × 4.38), 112 bhp

Transmission:	3-speed manual; overdrive optional
Suspension, front:	independent, coil springs, tube shocks
Suspension, rear:	live axle, leaf springs, tube shocks
Brakes:	front/rear drums
Wheelbase (in.):	123.5
Weight (lbs):	3726
Top speed (mph):	90
0-60 mph (sec):	22.0
Production:	70 (estimate 1949-50)

weren't putting X-member frames and special pillars on convertibles for the fun of it, and then we began to get results." Isbrandt even went so far as to purchase a prewar Packard convertible "to use as a benchmark....I wanted to know what they did, and apply it to ours." In production form, after extensive reengineering, the convertible proved quite solid.

Another engineering problem that gave the designers pause was how to tie the door pillars to the roof. Prewar four-door convertibles had used steel pillars, but stylist A.B. "Buzz" Grisinger had a more elegant solution: a metal-framed glass panel between the front and rear side windows. This remained in place (along with the side window frames) with the top up or down, providing good visibility.

K-F's ingenious interior designer Carleton Spencer coordinated the Manhattan's glorious array of fabrics and colors—probably the most deluxe materials that went into any cars of this period, maybe any period: top grain, color-back leather, fabrics suitable for fine furniture, handcrafted and installed with care, combined with vivid paint jobs to make the Frazer an eye-catching car. An impressive eggcrate grille and jumbo taillights added to its look of luxury.

Unfortunately, under the hood lurked a low-powered flathead six that had originated as an industrial engine, powering stationery machinery or vehicles like forklifts. The six was never up to the looks and glamor (and high price—$3295) of the Manhattan convertible.

Although Joe Frazer had given the ragtop his blessing before he departed as an active manager ("We thought it would sell because it didn't have the four-door competition"), he looked upon it in later life as a good idea gone wrong. His nephew, Hickman Price, Jr., snorted at the convertible project as a colossal waste of money, believing that the funds expended might have better gone into the 288-cubic-inch V-8 that K-F developed but did not build. When reminded that the Manhattan convertibles were very rare, Price was wont to reply, "I have no doubt—so is the ossified egg of a dodo bird."

Rare it is, though—and a striking car for its time. Total production of four-door convertibles by K-F was 253. Of these, 124 were 1949 models, an estimated 70 being Frazers and the rest Kaisers. Some of these were reserialed as 1950 models. The balance were fitted with facelift trim and marketed as 1951 Frazers.

1951 Frazer

The 1950 "model year" at Kaiser-Frazer lasted only from November 1949 through March 1950, when the new '51 models bowed. Frazers bearing 1950 titles were merely reserialed '49s, left over from the huge overproduction budgeted but not amortized. But the 1951 Frazer—last of the marque—was a clever job, inspired by Dutch Darrin, finalized by a talented K-F stylist named Herb Weissinger. Herb had lots of models to work with: sedans, convertibles, leftover Kaiser Virginian hardtops, and Kaiser Vagabond and Traveler utility vehicles—some 10,000 bodyshells, all of which were decked out as 1951 Frazers.

The standard Frazer series consisted of the sedans and utility cars, the latter all known as Frazer Vagabonds. Upmarket were the Frazer Manhattan convertibles and hardtops, very few of which were built. Serial number spans indicate 152 hardtops and 131 convertibles, but K-F club researchers believe these figures may be slightly optimistic. Of the 10,000 standard models, about a third were Vagabonds and the rest sedans.

Making the '51 Frazer look completely new despite its leftover bodyshell took ingenuity, and some of the alternatives were shocking. One idea was to use old-style front fenders, hood, and deck bolted to the new 1951 Kaiser bodyshell, which made a Sherman tank look svelte by comparison. But since it was more important to use up bodyshells than fenders and hoods, the reverse was decided upon.

Dutch Darrin, K-F's styling consultant, wanted them to restyle the rear doors too, using his traditional "Darrin dip" in the creaseline, but this would have required 20,000 new doors and was therefore much too expensive. So Weissinger fashioned a facelift of the fenders only (plus a slightly wider back window). Herb did manage to put in the Darrin "dip" just behind the rear doors. Up front was a ponderous grille, bearing a lucite Frazer badge in its center; the hood ornament was the most elegant feature of the car: a stylized jousting knight. The knight's spear was originally lucite—Herb thought of wiring it to light up in the dark—but when gas pump jockeys began breaking these off, the parts department offered a chrome plated metal spear replacement part.

The 1951 Manhattan, "Pride of Willow Run," offered its hardtop with or without a padded top, though only one has been found with the padding intact. As before, its interior was beautifully upholstered in a wide variety of cloth or leather/cloth upholstery, "woven to K-F specifications from special yarns" like Bedford cord and African cape wool; top grain color-back leather and heavy-duty vinyls were also used.

Retaining the old bodyshell did give the '51 Frazers certain advantages over the new Kaisers: quality Marshall coil seat springs instead of zig-zag wires, a long wheelbase versus Kaiser's shorter one, a huge 27-cubic-foot trunk (versus Kaiser's 19). "While Frazers are not built to a price standard, they are definitely engineered to a revolutionary value standard," said press releases. Frazer's sales targets in this field were Cadillac, Chrysler, and Lincoln buyers who wanted distinction and didn't worry about the marque going out of production (which was widely expected). Prices were not quite at the Cadillac level, but close to it: the Manhattans started at $3075. The sedans and Vagabonds began around $2400. Optional at $115 was Frazer's first automatic transmission, a Hydra-Matic purchased from General Motors. The six-cylinder powerplant was unchanged except in detail, putting out three more horsepower, which was still not nearly enough for such a heavy car.

Curiously enough—and probably much to the embarrassment of Kaiser managers who knew it was finished—the 1951 Frazer experienced a boomlet of demand. Dealers placed over 55,000 orders for it—over five times the number available. It was an irony, rendered more so by the fact that the 1951 Kaiser, not the Frazer, would be a "leftover" by the end of the year—having been produced in too great a quantity again!

Joseph W. Frazer was but an onlooker as the last Frazers rolled into history. He was, however, granted another 20 years to live—long enough for his cars to take on the status of collector's items, which pleased him greatly. Interviewed toward the end of his life, he never failed to mention that he was the only man left alive "whose name is on 100,000 cars."

In 1950, they couldn't give Frazers away. In 1951, when only 10,000 would be built, dealers ordered 55,000! Seventy percent of 1951 production went to the four-door sedan (above), *which listed at $2359. More interesting was the lavishly fitted Manhattan hardtop sedan* (opposite, top). *It sold for $3075, but only 152 left the Willow Run factory. The $2399 Vagabond four-door utility sedan, a forerunner of the hatchback, fared better with 3000 built.*

SPECIFICATIONS

Engine: sidevalve I-6, 226.2 cid (3.31 × 4.38), 115 bhp

Transmission:	3-speed manual; overdrive and Hydra-Matic optional
Suspension, front:	independent, coil springs, tube shocks
Suspension, rear:	live axle, leaf springs, tube shocks
Brakes:	front/rear drums
Wheelbase (in.):	123.5
Weight (lbs):	3456-3941
Top speed (mph):	90
0-60 (sec):	22.0

Production: 4d sdn 6,900* **Vagabond 4d utility sdn** 3000* **Manhattan htp sdn** 152 **Manhattan cvt sdn** 131
*estimated breakdown from exact total of 9,931 four-door sedans and Vagabonds

1955-57 Gaylord

Jim and Ed Gaylord were heirs to a fortune: their father had invented the bobby pin, an inoffensive little piece of metal that proved to be worth a couple dozen oil wells on the world market. Growing up in the late Thirties, the brothers Gaylord could have anything they wanted. Most often this turned out to be a fast car, anything from the 1949 V-8 Cadillac which Ed claimed would lose a Jaguar on Chicago's Lake Shore Drive, to the cream of European exotica. But Jim and Ed were not your run-of-the-mill rich kids; they were natural engineers, who made it their business to learn everything they could about cars. When in 1954 they decided to build the ultimate production sports car, those who knew them actually thought they might succeed.

The concept of the Gaylord was world-class performance combined with luxury-car refinement: total isolation from noise and vibration. To achieve these seeming self-canceling goals, the Gaylords decided to spend whatever it took, hence the car's estimated retail price of $10,000. (Jim soon decided this was not enough to cover costs, so he blithely raised the tab to $17,500.)

The frame was constructed of chrome-moly tubing, to which were attached channel steel perimeters and a strong steel platform. The insides of the tubes were rustproofed and all were sealed, making condensation impossible. The suspension looked conventional, but wasn't. The independent front wishbones used oversized rubber bushings and had "maximum triangulation," in Jim Gaylord's words. This gave enormous wheel travel, but relatively little movement at the mounting points. The suspension was lubed with permanent molybdenum disulfide; ten years before the no-grease chassis, the Gaylords put one on the street.

Detail features included variable-ratio power steering (controlled manually with a dashboard knob); modified Hydra-Matic (no shift occurred until peak rpm was reached in any gear, unless it was shifted manually); a "no-creep" feature; double-safe

SPECIFICATIONS

Engine:	ohv V-8, 365.0 cid (4.00 × 3.63), 305 bhp
Transmission:	modified 4-speed Hydra-Matic with anti-creep feature
Suspension, front:	independent, coil springs, tube shocks
Suspension, rear:	live axle, leaf springs, tube shocks
Brakes:	front/rear drums
Wheelbase (in.):	100.0
Weight (lbs):	3985
Top speed (mph):	125
0-60 mph (sec):	9.0
Production:	2, plus one prototype

The Gaylord was conceived with world-class performance and luxury-car refinement in mind. The styling, by Brooks Stevens Associates, had a contradictory goal: "a modern car with classic overtones." One of the more novel features was a retractable hardtop that disappeared into the deck (right) *and a spare tire that slid out from a rear panel and flopped upright onto the road. Unfortunately, only three cars were built, including one prototype.*

instruments featuring both needle gauges and warning lights. The engine was initially a 331 Chrysler hemi, but Ed Cole convinced the brothers that the '56 Cadillac 365 was lighter and quieter.

The styling, by Brooks Stevens Associates, wasn't up to the engineering, mainly because of a contradictory goal: "a modern car with classic overtones." For example, the Gaylords had wanted P-100 headlamps—but they made the car look like a malevolent four-foot owl, and had to be scrubbed. They also wanted to revive the classic "open wheel" look. This was tried on the prototype, but proved impractical—it allowed road grit to pepper the bodywork. Conventional wheel wells were then used, the wheels decorated with Eldorado Sabre Spoke wheel covers bearing special "double G" emblems. The door design, which Stevens called the "Washington coach door," looked terrific—a sleek upward cut, opening along the line of the ivory two-tone color panel, itself inspired by the classics.

Final touches of novelty were a retractable hardtop which disappeared into the deck, and a spare tire that slid out from a rear panel and flopped upright on the road, where it could easily be rolled into position. The retractable top—much simpler than the later Ford Skyliner's—required only one motor for the whole operation, and the sequence could be reversed at any point. When GM's chairman saw the Gaylord top retract at the Paris Auto Salon in 1955, he remarked to his cadre of engineers, "You bastards told me this couldn't be done. So how did these idiots do it?"

Shown widely in America and Europe during 1955-56, the Gaylord was ordered by everybody from Dick Powell to King Farouk, but the project lingered, withered, and fell apart—in the end only a show chassis and three complete cars were built. Tremendous problems of fit and finish occurred with the bodies, built by Spohn (prototype) and Luftschiffbau Zeppelin (later models). In the midst of a lawsuit against Zeppelin for failing to perform, the strain got to Jim Gaylord and he had a nervous breakdown. His family prevailed on him to let the project die.

The prototype with open wheel wells was broken up, and one "production" car disappeared in Europe—it may still exist. The third car, along with a magnificently crafted show chassis, is on display at the Early American Museum in Silver Springs, Florida, to which it was donated by the Gaylords. It remains a monument to two bright guys, a benchmark in automotive history.

1951-54 Henry J

The crux of the Kaiser-Frazer story came in 1949, after two years of success. The Big Three were about to spring their all-new postwar designs on the marketplace, but Kaiser had nothing new for '49. So the question was this: Would the postwar wonder company now retrench—or would it plunge ahead and damn the torpedoes? By then, the board of directors was controlled by Kaiser people, and Henry Kaiser had the answer: "The Kaisers never retrench."

The company thus borrowed $44 million from the Reconstruction Finance Corporation to maintain inventories, build the 1951 Kaiser, and—this is what swung the loan—to produce a "people's car." Henry Kaiser told the RFC's Jesse Jones, "It'll be another Model T—a car for the common man: something people who've always had to buy used cars can afford to buy new!" You might surmise, reading all this, what the little wonder would be called. After a nationwide "contest," in which the winner was the first person to come up with the name already chosen, the new Car for the Common Man was christened the Henry J. It was very common indeed.

Howard A. "Dutch" Darrin, evergreen styling consultant to K-F (likewise the bane of the in-house stylists) had already concocted the basic lines of the stunning 1951 Kaiser. The Henry J, he suggested, should have a compact body related to it. In his California studios, Dutch had actually built a prototype, deftly borrowing the Kaiser's smoothly rounded lines. But Henry Kaiser, wanting something new, chose a proposal from American Metal Products, a supplier of frames and springs for car seats.

Stunned, Darrin tried to improve the styling of the AMP car, but in the end he just went away mad. Two '51 Kaiser touches that survived were a "dip" behind the doors, and a "sweetheart curve" in the rear window. Henry J detail styling came from Herb Weissinger, who gave it pert little tailfins and a "floating" grille. When Weissinger got through, the little car looked fairly good. In retrospect, he deserves a lot more credit for it than Darrin. (We may be sure Darrin wouldn't object.)

The Henry J used Willys engines, L-head fours and sixes that were quite good for the purpose. The four delivered mind-blowing economy—40 mpg was not extraordinary under ideal conditions—while the six turned the car into a mini-hot rod delivering 0-60 mph times around 14 seconds. Despite its short wheelbase, the Henry J could accommodate four passengers and a lot of luggage. But early models were very spartan, some lacking trunklids, sun visors, even glove box doors. Even then, most examples cost as much as a Chevrolet, although the bare-bones, stripped four-cylinder model initially came in about $200 below Chevy's lowest price.

The Henry J sold well briefly—but very briefly. The production run for the initial 1951 model came to 82,000 units, and that seemed to quench the public thirst. Sales fell sharply for 1952. Some '51s were left over at the end of the model year; true to K-F practice, these were reserialed. They became 1952 Henry J "Vagabonds," identified by Vagabond script (taken from Kaiser parts bins), black plastic and chrome hood ornaments, and a "continental" spare tire.

The "true" '52 Henry J sported a more massive grille and taillights fitted into its rear fender tailfins. It also had a model name: Corsair. (Edsel would unsuccessfully resurrect the name for one of its series in 1958.) Corsairs came with a standard four-cylinder engine, DeLuxes got the six. Interiors were always bright, though of cheap materials—save for a few Henry Js handsomely finished in leather or exotic patterned vinyl by K-F's interior expert Carleton Spencer. The '53s and '54s were identical, the latter being reserialed again to use up what was left of the failed attempt.

Some motoring pundits have written that America wasn't ready for a "compact" in 1950. Partly true, perhaps, but they forget the history of the Nash Rambler, which sold in increasing numbers from that year on, and eventually displaced Nash itself at American Motors. But the Rambler was offered "dressed up," as a snazzy wagon or a convertible. The Henry J, by comparison, was a poor relation. Nash knew that it couldn't compete at the lowest price level with the Big Three, so it brought out a "luxury" job which won its own little niche in the marketplace. Kaiser fell victim to a recurrent impossible dream: beating the big guys.

The 1951 Henry J made an initial splash, and then sunk quickly into oblivion. Almost 82,000 units were built the first year, far more than Rambler. But even at that, some 7,000 surplus '51s became '52s by the simple expedient of giving them a continental spare tire, a black plastic and chrome hood ornament, and a Vagabond nameplate. Like other Henry Js, the standard Vagabond used a four-cylinder engine, the DeLuxe a six. They were priced at $1407 and $1552, respectively.

SPECIFICATIONS

Engines: Standard models sidevalve I-4, 134.2 cid (3.13 × 4.38), 68 bhp **DeLuxe/Corsair DeLuxe** sidevalve I-6, 161.0 cid (3.13 x 3.50), 80 bhp

Transmission:	3-speed manual; overdrive optional
Suspension, front:	independent, coil springs, tube shocks
Suspension, rear:	live axle, leaf springs, tube shocks
Brakes:	front/rear drums
Wheelbase (in.):	100.0
Weight (lbs):	2293-2455
Top speed (mph):	**Four** 75 **Six** 85
0-60 mph (sec):	**Four** 25.0 **Six** 14.0-15.0

Production: 1951 81,942 **1952 Vagabond** 7,017 **1952 Corsair** 16,500 approx. **1953** 16,672 **1954** 1,123

44 231
ILL. 1952

10 752

1950 Hudson Commodore

In 1950, the Commodore stood at the top of the Hudson lineup. It rode the longest wheelbase, boasted a big six *or* a smooth straight eight, received more luxurious trim than the concurrent Supers, and was by far the most popular of big Hudsons. Commodores outsold Supers by more than two to one, despite their rather higher prices. The range began with the Commodore Six club coupe at $2257, and ended with the Commodore Eight Brougham (convertible) at $2893. With accessories, options, and dealer prep, the typical Brougham cost about $3300, roughly on par with that year's Buick Roadmaster. An estimated 1100 of Hudson's 3,322 convertibles built in the 1950 model year were Commodores.

The Commodore's unit body-chassis ranked as one of the cleverest early postwar designs. Low and sleek, it hugged the ground and handled well, thanks to its radically low center of gravity. The design, which had begun as early as 1940, was directed by the brilliant Frank Spring, a fixture at Hudson and one of the most talented stylists of the Forties. The "Step-down" body evolved from wartime doodling—sleek, aerodynamic forms modeled in quarter- and eighth-scale clay and plaster. As Bob Andrews, a member of Spring's team, commented later, "It was the Ivory Soap school of design: you'd take a bar of Ivory and start carving the fenders, hood and deck, and presto!"

Like all Hudsons since 1932, the unit body-chassis was extremely strong, rigid, and rattle-free. The nickname "Step-down" referred to the dropped floorpan, which was completely surrounded by frame girders. It was probably the safest automotive package of the time, perhaps any time. Also, in its own way, it radiated its own understated beauty. The "fuselage" was clean, with a neat mid-height creaseline to eliminate any tendency toward slab sides. The grille sat low and wide; the taillights were functional rather than decorative. The dashboard was flat and positioned upright in front of the driver. It contained a big clock and speedometer (with 10-mph increments marked off in single digit numbers), warning lights for amperes and oil pressure, and gauges for fuel and water temperature.

While the Commodore Eight's engine dated back to the 1932 "Greater Eight," it had been improved through the years, going from 101 to its final 128 horsepower. By the time it made its last appearance, in 1952, it had achieved a reputation for smoothness and reliability, running through five main bearings and ample water jackets. It was as good an inline eight as the industry ever developed. The alternative six, which cost $84 less on comparable Commodore bodies, was perhaps more interesting. Violating an old Detroit rule about restyling and reengineering the same year, Hudson had brought this 262-cubic-inch L-head out in 1948 with the new Step-down body. By 1950, the six developed 123 horsepower, only five less than the eight (some say it was deliberately under-rated so as not to embarrass the eight). Although it had only four main bearings, it was also a smooth and durable engine. In 1951 it evolved into the memorable Hornet engine.

In these pre-automatic days, Hudson offered three transmission options for its basic three-speed stickshift: mechanical overdrive, priced at $95; Drive-Master ($105); and Supermatic ($199). Drive-Master was a semi-automatic that eliminated both clutch and gear lever motion: the driver would place the shift lever into "High" and accelerate in a low gear, lifting his or her foot when the shift to High was desired (or at a preset 22 mph when a dashboard button was pressed). Supermatic added a high cruising gear.

Also, there was one flaw in the Hudson formula, and in the end it would prove crucial: the handsome Step-down was difficult to facelift for the then-mandatory annual model change, and almost impossible to seriously restyle. Also, Hudson lacked the financial resources to construct variant bodies—the lack of a station wagon was an increasing problem to Hudson dealers in the early Fifties. All Hudson had were closed two-doors and four-doors—and the convertible, itself carved out of a coupe. Thus the ragtop's characteristic huge steel header, really the chopped-off coupe roof, was left there to save tooling money. Hudson made a virtue of this necessity by claiming, correctly, that it offered more protection in the event of a rollover—although the low-slung Step-down was almost impossible to roll anyway! In this respect it was doubly safe.

Hudson received its first postwar restyling for 1948, its famed "Step-down" design. For 1950, there were six top-line Commodores (three sixes, three eights), priced from $2257 to $2893, here the $2257 Six two-door club coupe.

SPECIFICATIONS

Engines: Six sidevalve I-6, 262.0 cid (3.56 × 4.38), 123 bhp **Eight** sidevalve I-8, 254.0 cid (3.00 × 4.50), 128 bhp

Transmission:	3-speed manual; overdrive, Drive-Master, and Supermatic semi-automatic optional
Suspension, front:	independent, coil springs, tube shocks
Suspension, rear:	live axle, leaf springs, tube shocks
Brakes:	front/rear drums
Wheelbase (in.):	124.0
Weight (lbs):	3640-3865
Top speed (mph):	85-90
0-60 mph (sec):	15.0-18.0, depending on transmission

Production: Commodore Six 24,605 **Eight** 16,731 (Hudson production figures by individual body style have not survived, but the author estimates about 700 Six and 425 Eight Commodore convertibles of the known 3,322 total 1950 Hudson convertibles. Four-door sedans made up at least 75 percent of Commodore production.)

CALIFORNIA
DIXS 50

1951-53 Hudson Hornet

Working late one night at Hudson Motor Company, a PR man was approached by a factory guard who said, "There's a man named Marshall Teague. He's been trying all day to get into Engineering. He's waited and waited." The PR man decided to help this then-unknown person: "I took Marshall to dinner. The next day I phoned Engineering and got him some manifolds. Hudson's advertising director, Bob Roberts, was scratching around for some excuse for publicity then, and Marshall's ideas appealed to him. Suddenly Advertising was really interested, and I was traveling around the country to these stock-car races. And then we started winning..."

Hudson had never been known as a racing car, though in the past Hudsons proved themselves in various incidental competitions. But for four straight years, 1951-54, the "Fabulous Hudson Hornet" was a *force majeure* in American stock-car racing: 11 wins in 1951 (second to Oldsmobile because of Hudson's late start); 27 wins in 1952-53, an unbeatable record which made it National Association of Stock Car Auto Racing (NASCAR) Champion, despite a sea of V-8 rivals. All this was accomplished, to the outright amazement of hot-rodders and car fans nationwide, with a sidevalve six which everybody in Detroit said was obsolete.

In an age of rapid transition to overhead-valve V-8s, the Hornet engine seemed an anomaly. At 308 cubic inches and the only "big six" in the country, it bespoke Hudson's engineering conservatism—and Marshall Teague's optimism. The six did have certain attributes in its favor. In its understressed, easy-revving form, with proven durability, it was not unlike Hudson's Super and Special Sixes of 30 or 40 years before. Introduced at 262 cubic inches in 1948, it quickly proved as reliable as anything on the road. Thanks to its thick wall construction, blowing it out to 308 cubes was not difficult. But why not a V-8? "Hudson had six-cylinder manufacturing equipment," former chief engineer Stuart Baits told this writer. "The V-8 was not yet so dominant at the time and cost certainly was a factor."

The Hornet made its fame in NASCAR racing because of its powerful, though outdated, 308-cid six and low center of gravity. The '51 Hollywood hardtop (below) *sold for $2869, but most buyers chose the $2568 four-door sedan* (above). *The '52 model received a minor facelift, but the four-door sedan* (opposite, top) *now cost $2769. The '53 sported a cleaner grille; the club coupe* (bottom) *listed at $2466. When equipped with Twin-H-Power, the Hornet engine was good for 160 horsepower.*

Torque was the big plus on what Hudson called the H-145 Hornet engine, 30 percent more of it than on the 262-inch Super Six. There was also 18 percent more horsepower on tap, a 10 mph increase in top speed, a second or two less elapsed time from rest to 50. The Hornet reduced Hudson's pounds/horsepower ratio from an already good 28.0:1 to just 24.8:1. Combined with the immensely strong Step-down unit body, it gave tremendous roadability if not off-the-line neck-snapping acceleration—and it was this roadability, plus the skill of drivers like Teague, Herb Thomas, Dick Rathmann, Al Keller, and Frank Mundy that won races for Hudson.

The Hornet effectively replaced the Super Eight, leaving the Commodore as Hudson's only eight-cylinder '51 model. Style for style (both came as sedans, coupes, Hollywood hardtops, and convertibles), Hornet matched Commodore Eight prices exactly, ranging from $2543 base for the coupe to $3099 for the convertible, or "brougham" as Hudson preferred to call it. The hardtop Hollywood, offered also in the Commodore Six and Super Six lines, appeared as Hudson's major styling innovation that year—a rather late response to the competition, perhaps, but a year ahead of Nash and Studebaker.

The Step-down cried for a restyle in 1952-53, but Hudson couldn't afford more than a minor trim shuffle, having sunk most of its spare cash into its new compact, the Jet. What did improve was the Hornet engine. The H-145 claimed only 145 bhp at 3800 rpm in stock form, but tuning experts like Teague could get 112 mph from a Hornet certified as stock by AAA or NASCAR. The factory helped by developing "severe usage" options that were an advance form of "factory race equipment" common a decade later. Twin H-Power, offered in 1953, comprised twin carbs and dual manifold induction (the first on a six) for greatly improved breathing and a solid 160 horsepower. The 7-X racing engine, which arrived late the same year, used .020 overbored cylinders, special cam and head, larger valves, higher compression, Twin H-Power, and headers. Output estimates ran from 170 to 210 horsepower, the latter seemingly quite possible.

Marshall Teague finished his 1952 AAA racing season 1000 points ahead of his nearest rival, winning 12 of the 13 AAA stock-car events. The Hornet also scored well on long-distance enduros. In November 1951, Teague finished sixth overall in the car-killing, 2000-mile *Carrera Panamericana* (Mexican Road Race), running mostly dirt roads from Guatemala to Texas. The Hornet actually held the Ferraris on the fast bends, to the "Carambas!" of spectators.

SPECIFICATIONS

Engines: sidevalve I-6 **1951-53** 308.0 cid (3.81 × 4.50), 145 bhp **1953** 160 bhp with Twin-H-Power option **7-X racing engine** 341.0 cid (4.01 × 4.50), approximately 200 bhp

Transmission:	3-speed manual; overdrive and Hydra-Matic optional **1951** Drive-Master semi-automatic optional
Suspension, front:	independent, coil springs, tube shocks
Suspension, rear:	live axle, leaf springs, tube shocks
Brakes:	front/rear drums
Wheelbase (in.):	124.0
Weight (lbs):	3530-3780
Top speed (mph):	100-105; 110-115 (modified)
0-60 mph (sec):	14.0; 11.0-12.0 (modified)

Production: . **1951** 43,656 **1952** 35,921 **1953** 27,208 (Breakdowns not available. Estimates: Hollywood htp cpe 2,100, 2200, 900 (1951-52-53); cvt cpe 500, 350, and 100.)

1953-54 Hudson Jet

There are few generalities in the car business—few rules by which one can solidly predict a product's success or failure. In the ideal world, car sales would be directly proportional to engineering and design quality. But this has never been an ideal world, and its most unpredictable determinant is the customer. Those who say the industry "dictates" taste were not keeping the books at Ford when the Edsel arrived, or at Chrysler in the 1970s, or at General Motors in the later Eighties—or at Hudson during the short, sad flight of the Jet.

"This should have been a successful small automobile," American Motors president Roy Chapin, former Hudson sales manager, recalled in 1976. "The dealers were just crying for a car of that type. In preliminary drawings it wasn't a bad-looking car [but] the finished product didn't look like the drawing. It was high and narrow and bulged in the wrong places. [Yet] conceptually the car was excellent."

Hudson president Ed Barit's go-ahead for the Jet was predicated on dealer demand for an "economy car," and a careless look at the Rambler and Henry J. But the Henry J tailed off very rapidly after its 1951 introduction, and Rambler's line consisted of fringe models—convertibles, wagons, and hardtops—making it more a luxury second or "personal" car. As to imports, the best-selling economy model, the British Austin, managed only 4490 units in 1952. There was a lot of talk about "compacts," but Barit should have noticed that the Big Three had no plans to build any. It would have been hard (in fact it proved impossible) to undercut Ford-Chevy-Plymouth prices with a small Hudson.

The evidence is that Barit overruled Frank Spring's initial prototype—a handsome, smooth-lined car—to build something like the '52 Ford, which had just come out and which he admired. Barit also wanted the interior dimensions of the Fiat 1400, an

SPECIFICATIONS

Engine: sidevalve I-6, 202.0 cid (3.00 × 4.75), 104 bhp; 106 bhp (optional high compression head); 114 bhp (Twin H-Power)

Transmission:	3-speed manual; overdrive and Hydra-Matic optional
Suspension, front:	independent, coil springs, tube shocks
Suspension, rear:	live axle, leaf springs, tube shocks
Brakes:	front/rear drums
Wheelbase (in.):	105.0
Weight (lbs):	2650-2760
Top speed (mph):	85-95
0-60 mph (sec):	14.0-20.0
Production:	**1953** 21,143 **1954** 14,224

Italian compact with unit construction much like Hudson's. But Barit specified chair-high seats, and so the Jet emerged with a beltline actually higher than that of the full-size Hudson. This, combined with its narrow width, gave it an ungainly appearance that ended up anathema to mid-Fifties car buyers.

The design problems were magnified when Millard Toncray engineered the Jet to traditional Hudson standards, building it like an armored truck. It weighed 2700 pounds, much more than the Rambler, Henry J, or Aero Willys. This did not affect performance because Hudson equipped it with a 202-cid six (using old Commodore Eight tooling, minus two cylinders). The long-stroke L-head that resulted produced 114 bhp with high-compression aluminum head and Twin H-Power. This delivered 0-60 times in the 14-second range, much better than the aforementioned rivals. But this over-engineering came at high cost, so even the most spartan, stripped-down Hudson Jet ended up with a base price of $1858—$250 *more* than a Chevy.

This sort of pricing (the more deluxe Super Jet started around $2000) quickly proved disastrous: over the course of 1953, the Jet barely topped 20,000 sales. While overall Hudson volume that year held steady compared to 1952, the company lost $10.4 million on sales of $193 million. It ranked as the largest loss in Hudson's history. Roy Chapin viewed the Jet as "the thing that really caused the downfall, or accelerated it at least." The following year Ed Barit accepted a merger as a junior partner with Nash, and by 1955 Hudson had become a badge-engineered Nash. One of Nash president George W. Mason's demands during merger negotiations was that the Jet had to go; it duly disappeared as soon as the supply of body parts ran out in 1954.

The basic Jet was available as a four-door sedan, while the up market Super Jet came as a four-door or a club sedan. Supers were distinguished by better upholstery and a colorful if chromey dashboard. Hudson called the combination of two-tone worsted and broadcloth upholstery (with thoughtful touches like a robe rail and tailored pocket built into the back of the front seat) the "Salon Lounge Interior," and compared to, say, the Henry J, it indeed exuded luxury. In 1954, the line expanded top and bottom with a pricier Jet-Liner series ($2050) and a rock-bottom "Family Club" two-door ($1621), but even the latter cost more than the cheapest models of the traditional "low-priced-three."

Designer Frank Spring penned a handsome, smooth-lined compact for Hudson, but president Ed Barit wanted chair-height seats. The result was a car that stood much higher than originally intended. But it was a good performer with up to 114 bhp via Twin H-Power and a high-compression head.

1954
Hudson Hornet

With the Ford-General Motors sales wars in full pitch during late 1953, the introduction of the 1954 Hudsons seemed almost anticlimactic. Nobody bothered to notice that once again, for the seventh straight year, Hudson had trotted out its original 1948 body design. The attention of the auto world was drawn elsewhere, even though the Hornet would again (just barely now) capture the NASCAR racing championship. But the '54 really represented a heroic effort to update the fast-aging body.

The front end received a dramatic cleanup. In place of the vast chromium bars of the past rode a simple, pleasing grille partly composed of stainless steel; a single center bar bore the Hudson emblem. Overall, the frontal design gave an impression of low build and wide stance. The sides were cleaner, too, and if not really different, improved by careful ornamentation. Huge triangular taillights, visible from the sides as well as the rear, sat high up on the rear fenders, the most obvious alteration on the new Hornet. These had been raised and squared off, and for the first time in a Step-down, the driver could see the tail end of his car when backing up.

New fabrics and vinyls adorned the interior, highlighted by a more modern and attractive instrument panel, which nevertheless preserved Hudson's distinctive single-digit speedometer markings. Gauges and controls were conveniently grouped close to the driver. Elongated rear quarter windows improved visibility, and the windshield at long last adopted a one-piece configuration. As one magazine remarked, "the 'antique shop' look is gone."

Mechanically, this final version of the "Fabulous Hornet" ranked as the best yet—and, because it also ended up being the last Step-down, the best ever. Some 7-X engine features became standard, with a hotter camshaft and a 7.5:1 compression

aluminum cylinder head giving the stock Hornet 160 horsepower, or 170 with Twin-H-Power. Power brakes and power steering were optional.

The Commodore series had vanished after 1952, but in mid-model-year 1954 a new Hornet Special took its place. Priced about $150 below the Hornet, it borrowed the same wheelbase and engine but weighed a bit less. With Twin-H-Power, the Special thus became the hottest Hudson Hornet yet. Offered as a four-door, two-door, or club coupe, Specials featured luxury interiors with worsted fabrics and Plastic-Hide trim.

But the V-8 age was now upon us, and buyer reluctance was even more pronounced in Hudson showrooms than before. Wilbur Shaw made a few good cases for the old sidevalve six in *Popular Science,* pointing out that in brake horsepower per cubic inch, the Hornet still ranked third in the industry—only the Lincoln and Cadillac V-8s bettered it, while the Chrysler hemi scored worse.

Such facts did not weigh with buyers, however. Through April 30, 1954, when Hudson closed the books as an independent corporation, it had lost over $6 million on sales of only $28.7 million since January 1. By April, it became official that Hudson would merge with Nash-Kelvinator Corporation.

Word of merger talks between Hudson's Barit and Nash's George Mason had leaked some months earlier (which couldn't have helped sales either, since the rumor had it that Hudson might be "orphaned" by the deal). On May 1, 1954, the Hudson Motor Car Company ceased to exist. Henceforth, the destiny of a marque that had been on the American scene since 1909 would rest on the corporate decisions of American Motors Corporation.

The Hudson Hornet was the product of noble spirits and the highest-performance six of its era. It is recognized now as a Milestone car and beyond any serious question proved itself one of the best American cars of the Fifties. More perhaps than any other independent, Hudson showed how much development could be wrung out of old designs on limited budgets. Certainly its engineers managed to give both the Step-down body and the Hornet six—both of which went back to 1948—a remarkably long run. As Don Vorderman wrote, those who drive Hudson Hornets today "have the pleasure of knowing they're behind the wheel of a retired champ, with all the respect due a Jack Dempsey or a Joe Louis."

SPECIFICATIONS

Engine: sidevalve six, 308.0 cid (3.81 × 4.50), 160 bhp; 170 bhp with optional Twin-H-Power

Transmission:	3-speed manual; overdrive or Hydra-Matic optional
Suspension, front:	independent, coil springs, tube shocks
Suspension, rear:	live axle, leaf springs, tube shocks
Brakes:	front/rear drums
Wheelbase (in.):	124.0
Weight (lbs):	3505-3800
Top speed (mph):	105-110
0-60 mph (sec):	12.0
Production:	24,833

Hudson was in deep trouble by 1954. The compact Hudson Jet had bowed for '53—and bombed. The big Hudson hadn't seen a major restyling since 1948. With little money, the best Hudson could do for '54 was to give it a modest facelift that included a simple new grille, modified hood, and uplifted rear fenders with triangular taillights. The Hornet convertible listed at $3288, the Hollywood hardtop at $2988. They would be the last "real" Hudsons.

1954-55 Hudson Italia

In the Fifties, anybody who was anybody in the automobile business needed a limited edition "sports" model. For Chevy it was the Corvette, for Ford the Thunderbird, for Kaiser the Darrin, for Nash the Nash-Healey—and for Hudson the Italia. There were, however, these differences: the Italia held four rather than two passengers and, more than just a sports car, it was intended to spark a new generation of Hudsons.

Like the other sports models mentioned above, Italia's underparts came "off-the-shelf," in this case mainly from the Hudson Jet, in order to keep its costs down. In the end, it didn't matter, because Hudson merged with Nash and the combined American Motors put its faith in Nash designs for the future. Hudson sold only 26 Italias, including the prototype.

The man who had to sell them was Roy D. Chapin, Jr., later board chairman of AMC, who told this writer: "Well, I got rid of them!" When told that the 26 Italias allegedly paid for themselves, Chapin chuckled: "Shows what a good salesman I was, but I don't believe it. The research and development figure for the Italia [sources had quoted $28,000] sounds like our racing budget in those days."

The Italia was the dream of Hudson's respected chief stylist Frank Spring. Writer Michael Lamm once suggested that it came as a "reprieve" for Spring, who "had been terribly disappointed with the Jet." Added Chapin: "Another reason is that somebody got to [Hudson president Edward] Barit and convinced him that we had to have a more modern image. The old Step-down was in production too long; we had to do something to dramatize Hudson."

The Italia was indeed dramatic, standing 10 inches shorter than the big Hudsons but retaining their low center of gravity and granitic durability. Notable features included a stylishly wrapped windshield; functional, brake-cooling fender scoops; doors cut into the roof for easy entry; scads of interior space; and the industry's first flow-through ventilation system (obviating vent windows). The interior sported the most anatomically correct car seats thus far designed, adjustable fore/aft and for rake, with two separate leather covered seat cushions of varying density for the back and seat.

And of course the Italia was Italian—a good thing to be in those days of fascination with Pinin Farina and his ilk. Built out of sheet aluminum by Carrozzeria Touring, the Italia took shape in what Ed Barit's son remembered as "a hole-in-the-wall operation down a narrow Torino side street, with a sort of production line snaking through a series of old dilapidated buildings." Now *that's* Italian!

Announced in August 1953, the Italia prototype toured car shows and dealerships and received a warm reception along the way. With the exception of its trick taillights, built into triple sets of external dummy exhaust pipes, and the "praying mantis" front bumper, it was a good, clean design, bristling with interesting features: esoteric, unexpected, aircraft-inspired, and unlike anything else on the market. Hudson commissioned a run of 25 "production" cars and priced them at $4350 POE New York. At this price (a '54 Cadillac started at $3838), initial enthusiasm waned, and factory sources state that only 19 orders were received. Some Hudson collectors say this was actually a figure for initial deliveries, since many potential buyers tried to order Italias at the time and were turned away by dealers, who thought of it as a one-off pipe dream.

High price combined with lackluster performance (despite the aluminum body, it weighed over 2700 pounds) to severely hamper the Italia's appeal. But Hudson never put much faith in it as a sales weapon; its real purpose was to act as an advance product for future Hudson passenger cars. One of these, called X-161 (Spring's 161st experimental prototype) was a four-door derivation with the Hornet engine; it delivered good if not blinding performance. Hindsight is cheap, but many now believe that Hudson should have launched the X-161 instead of the Jet in 1953—that it would have sold much better than the Jet did.

Roy Chapin sums up the Italia and X-161 project this way: "Of course, today it is dated—but it's still a terrific exercise in automotive design. Again, the problem was much the same with the other Hudsons. It was a very costly car to make and couldn't command the price you had to get for it—coupled with the fact that the decision was made to put nothing but a six-cylinder engine in it."

The Italia came along too late to save Hudson, but it was certainly an interesting design. It was penned by Hudson chief stylist Frank Spring and built by Carrozzeria Touring in Italy over Jet mechanicals. Only 26 were produced.

SPECIFICATIONS

Engine: sidevalve I-6, 202.0 cid (3.00 × 4.75), 106 bhp; 114 bhp optional

Transmission:	3-speed manual
Suspension, front:	independent, coil springs, tube shocks
Suspension, rear:	live axle, leaf springs, tube shocks
Brakes:	front/rear drums
Wheelbase (in.):	105.0
Weight (lbs):	2710
Top speed (mph):	90
0-60 mph (sec):	14.0-15.0

Production: **1954** 20 titled **1955** 5 titled (plus one prototype and a prototype X-161 four-door, which still exists)

HUDSON

1955 Hudson Hornet

After Hudson joined Nash-Kelvinator to form American Motors, the Hudson plant on Jefferson Avenue in Detroit closed, sealing the fate of the Step-down Hudson. With it came the final eclipse of the Hudson Jet, and Hudson's independent advance plan as symbolized by the Italia and the X-161. One of the stipulations by Nash's George Mason, in fact, had been that the Jet had to go—aside from its limited appeal, he considered it an unnecessary duplication and sales rival to the Nash Rambler, which was finding a much more viable market. From 1955 through '57, to compensate for the loss of the Jet, Hudson dealers sold Hudson-badged Ramblers (and the subcompact Metropolitan); after 1957 the Nash and Hudson names disappeared forever, leaving the Rambler and Met to fend for themselves under their own names.

In 1955, however, the Rambler had not yet earned the total confidence of management that it would soon enjoy, so the initial AMC product plan called for a continuation of both the Nash and Hudson full-size cars. With Jefferson Avenue out of the picture, that meant a badge-engineered Hudson, based on the then-current Nash bodyshell. In its first form, for 1955, this curious amalgam emerged as an attractive automobile, while retaining a number of traditional Hudson features.

Design work for the 1955 Hudson was done by Nash's Edmund E. Anderson. He gave it an expensive looking eggcrate grille and an ultra-wide wraparound windshield, creating an up-to-date look—something Hudson had long needed. With conventional, fender-mounted headlights and full front wheel cutouts, it appeared more orthodox and correct than the counterpart 1955 Nash with its inboard-mounted headlights and skirted front wheels.

After merging with Nash in 1954 to form American Motors, a rush job was undertaken to convert the full-size Nash bodyshell into a 1955 Hudson. Although the final result fooled no one, Hudson cues (especially up front) did *make the Nash identifiably a Hudson, and the 308-cid Hornet six was still around (along with a Packard-built V-8). Four-door sedans came as Supers or Customs, Hollywood hardtops as Customs only. Detractors called them "Hashes."*

Anderson and AMC wanted to retain certain Hudson hallmarks, hoping to keep former Hudson buyers interested in the car. The famous white triangle Hudson badges stood out prominently, and the instrument panel looked similar to that of the independently built 1954 Hudson. Also offered was an array of Hudson six-cylinder engines, including the 308-cid Hornet unit that belted out 170 bhp with Twin H-Power.

Hudsons for 1955 comprised the short-wheelbase underpowered Wasp and the 121-inch wheelbase Hornet. The latter corresponded to the big Nash Ambassador and could be ordered with a 320-cubic-inch Packard-built V-8, as well as the Hornet six that had previously seen Hudson to so many stock-car championships during 1952-54. The Hornet six and V-8 were available as a four-door sedan in two states of trim, Super and Custom, and as a Hollywood two-door hardtop.

Among the many ironies of the Nash-Hudson merger, this one must have particularly irked the old Hudson hands: here at last was the new body that Hudson had needed so badly since about 1951 or 1952—but supplied to Hudson by those other unit-body people in Kenosha, whose products Hudsonfolk had oft criticized as too light, too high, and too clumsy. Longtime followers of the marque soon came up with a name for this strange combination of Nash and Hudson componentry: they called it the "Hash." Odds are that the play on words was intentional. It was certainly accurate.

The Hash was no "stock car champion," as its advertisements pronounced. There is a well-known story about Marshall Teague, the great Hudson stock-car racing driver, trying one lap in a 1955 Hudson and pulling into the pits, vowing never to enter a new Hudson again. On the other hand, car for car against other 1955 products, it stacked up quite well indeed. The Hornet had an excellent combination of handling, ride, and performance; it was well built and offered good value for money (most copies sold for around $3000-3200 delivered). From Nash it inherited twin reclining front seats, dual-speaker radio, a V-8 option, the unsurpassed Weather-Eye heating/ventilation system, and the widest windshield in the industry. The public responded. Counting its badge-engineered Ramblers, Hudson enjoyed over 45,000 model year sales for 1955 (13,130 of them Hornets), against only 32,000 in 1954.

SPECIFICATIONS

Engines: sidevalve I-6, 308.0 cid (3.81 × 4.50), 160 bhp, 170 bhp with Twin H-Power; ohv V-8, 320.0 cid (2.81 × 3.50), 208 bhp

Transmission:	3-speed manual; overdrive and Hydra-Matic optional
Suspension, front:	independent, coil springs, tube shocks
Suspension, rear:	live axle, coil springs, tube shocks
Brakes:	front/rear drums
Wheelbase (in.):	121.3
Weight (lbs):	3495-3878
Top speed (mph):	100-110
0-60 mph (sec):	11.0-13.0

Production: Hornet Six 4d sdn 5357 **htp cpe** 1640 **V-8 4d sdn** 4449 **htp cpe** 1770

1956-57 Hudson

The initial sales spurt of the "Nashified" Hudson didn't last beyond 1955. The following year, sales of Hornets and Wasps dropped by about 50 percent to the 10,000-unit level. In part, styling had to shoulder the responsibility; even for the mid-Fifties, it was too garish for many potential buyers—as good as the cars underneath remained.

Stylist Ed Anderson comes in for the blame here, of course, but like Duncan McRae's 1958 Packards and Clare MacKichan's 1959 Chevrolets, the final product was affected by many influences beyond the designers' control: sales executives, among others. When the '56 Hudson was finalized late in 1954, virtually everyone in Detroit *knew* that chrome sold cars, that anodized gold sold even more cars, and that tailfins and "dollar grins" and radical two- or three-tone paint jobs opened the door to untold prosperity.

Anderson faced other hurdles, too, such as a minuscule styling budget. So he tooled the simplest decorations he could come up with and slapped them on: tiny scoops over the headlamps, a less costly stamped grille to replace the heavy '55 eggcrate, and a motif called "V-line styling," reportedly to emphasize the V-8 engines. "V" patterns dominated the front end and even the side molding. Overall, the '56 Hudsons simply looked too busy. AMC also adopted the craze for multi-colored pastel paint jobs, and the 1956 Hudson was among the first three-toned cars. (Dodge, Packard, and DeSoto started this curious practice in 1955.)

The short-wheelbase Wasp remained in the 1956 Hudson line, but just barely: a single four-door sedan base priced at $2214. The big Hornet lineup was left mainly alone, except that a Hornet Special replaced the Packard-engined V-8s in March. Because of its late introduction, the Special is among the scarcest of the "Hashes."

The '56s had hardly hit the showrooms before George Romney, inheritor of command after the death of George Mason in late 1954, made the decision to dump all big cars and stake AMC's future on the Rambler. (Trying to pin Romney down about automotive history is as difficult as comprehending his Vietnam position when he was running for president. Asked recently when exactly the big Hudsons passed the point of no return, Romney replied, "Just as soon as I made the decision.")

It does seem certain, however, that the 1957 Hudsons, last of the breed, were foredoomed even before they arrived in dealer showrooms. They were certainly few in number. Rambler, its sales soaring, had been broken out as a separate make, and old Hudson dealerships were fast becoming "AMC" showrooms. The Wasp was dropped out of hand, and the Hornet came only as a Super or Custom in sedan or hardtop body styles. "V-line Styling" was reshuffled: the cars sprouted fins front *and* rear, and a big gold "V" emblem was plastered on the grille. All were powered by the new AMC 327-cid V-8 designed by Dave Potter, who had earlier tried to come up with a V-8 for Kaiser-Frazer. In his K-F days, Potter's engine had the earmarks of a winner, but the 327's 255 horsepower wasn't enough for the 3700-pound 1957 Hudsons. Zero to 60 took longer than the former Hornet six and was inferior to most competitive makes.

Further, the "Hash" can't really be called a totally honest car. There is something contrived about any badge-engineering job, be it Hudson or Bentley. But neither was it the total disaster it is sometimes made out to be—nor was it "AMC's Edsel," as one Hudson nut thoughtfully put it.

The 1955 Hudson, conceived while AMC chairman George Mason still lived, was a genuine attempt to perpetuate the Hudson marque. The '57 was an ungenuine attempt to amortize tooling before throwing Hudson (and Nash) onto the scrap heap of history. The '56 ended up being a cross between the two.

In a way, we might look upon what happened to the proud old name of Hudson as a portent of General Motors' plight today: foolish management trying to palm off the same cars as different makes to a public far wiser than they give it credit for being. To this extent we could call the last Hudsons what Churchill called the India Bill in 1935: "a gigantic quilt of jumbled crochet work...no theme, no conviction, no simplicity, no courage...a monstrous monument of shame built by pygmies."

Hudson entered 1956 using the Nash body it had adopted in '55, but a facelift gave it what the ads called "V-line styling." Some models had V-8s, but the Hornet Custom four door (opposite) *still used the hoary 308-cid Hornet six, good for 175-bhp with Twin-H Power. The '57s* (this page) *received a final trim shuffle and came only with AMC's 327-cid, 255-bhp V-8. After 1957, Hudson was gone.*

SPECIFICATIONS

Engines: sidevalve I-6 **1956 Wasp** 202.0 cid (3.00 × 4.75), 120 bhp, 130 bhp optional **1956 Hornet** 308.0 cid (3.81 × 4.50), 165 bhp, 175 bhp optional; ohv V-8, 320 cid (3.81 × 3.50), 208 bhp (through 3/56); 250 cid (3.50 × 3.25), 190 bhp (after 3/56) **1957** 327.0 cid (4.00 × 3.25), 255 bhp

Transmission:	3-speed manual; overdrive and Hydra-Matic optional
Suspension, front:	independent, coil springs, tube shocks
Suspension, rear:	live axle, coil springs, tube shocks
Brakes:	front/rear drums
Wheelbase (in.):	**Wasp** 114.3 **Hornet** 121.3
Weight (lbs):	**Wasp** 3264 **Hornet** 3467-3826
Top speed (mph):	**Wasp** 95 **Hornet** 100-110
0-60 mph (sec):	**Wasp** 18.0 **1956 Hornet** 12.0-14.0 **1957 Hornet** 15.0

Production: **1956 Wasp** 2519 **Hornet Special sdn** 1528 **Hollywood htp** 229 **Hornet Six sdn** 3022 **Hollywood htp** 358 **Hornet V-8 sdn** 1962 **Hollywood htp** 1053 **1957** 3876*
*no model breakdowns survive in AMC archives

1955-56 Imperial

Virgil Exner's handsome Imperials of 1955-56 remain among the more timeless examples of Fifties styling since they lacked (or almost lacked, in the case of the '56) tailfins. Today, tailfins are held to be products of that time and date as much as they made a car appear up-to-date when new.

Imperial became a separate and distinct make in 1955, as Chrysler began reaching for a product with which to challenge Cadillac and Lincoln. It remained separate through 1975, when Imperial production was halted; it reappeared in the 1980s for a couple of years, and rumors are that it is to appear again very shortly. Throughout its time as a separate make, however, Imperial could not shake its image as a Chrysler. Though many of its cars were beautiful and luxurious, they retained that middle-class aura which cost them important sales points in the luxury-car field.

The 1955 Imperial took its cues from the 1951 K-310 show car and Exner's Parade Phaetons, the first of which appeared on a 1952 Crown Imperial chassis with a stretched 147.5-inch wheelbase. Three Phaetons were built, assigned to parade use in New York, Detroit, and Los Angeles. They later received an updating, and in turn helped inspire the production '55 Imperial. According to Virgil Exner, Jr., his father and the Chrysler design team "swiped ideas off the parade cars and put the 1955 line together." The '55 Imperial had the same side treatment and hopped-up rear fender as the Phaetons, and wore prominent hallmarks of Exner's hand: big open wheel wells and divided eggcrate grilles. The K-310 contributed Imperial's bombsight tail lamps and gaudy bird hood ornament, as well as the eggcrate grille theme.

Imperials rode a 130-inch wheelbase and did not offer a convertible model, though a running prototype was built for evaluation. A 15-bhp increase over 1954 for the Firepower hemi engine was obtained through a one-ratio rise in compression and a redesigned four-barrel carburetor with vacuum-controlled secondary throttles. These came into operation when the primaries were more than half open. Dual exhausts, routed out through the rear bumper extremities, came as standard equipment, along with Powerflite automatic transmission, the latter controlled by a dashboard-mounted stick. In addition to Imperial sedans and Newport hardtops, a long-wheelbase version, the Crown Imperial, was offered as a sedan or limousine (with divider window). But Cadillac had a stranglehold on the limo business, and fewer than 200 Crown Imperials left the factory.

The only significant styling change for 1956 was the advent of tailfins—modest ones, sweeping up from the "dip" at midpoint in the body line. Like Chrysler, the '56 Imperial line contained a new four-door hardtop model but, along with the two-door hardtop, it was called the "Southampton" to distance it from Chrysler's Newport hardtop.

Imperial interiors were spacious and trimmed in fine leather and a special fabric called Imperial Eagle faille. All were color-keyed to match the exterior. Powerflite transmission abandoned 1955's dashboard stick control and went to an array of mechanical pushbuttons, mounted to the left of the steering wheel on an extension of the dashboard. Gunsight taillights reappeared on the '56, though the fuel filler now hid behind the corner of the right fender instead of under the taillight mount as in '55. "Imperial is, by our firm intent, conservative," said its maker. "But in this reserved refinement is a modern new note of design that gives Imperial its own unique distinction that immediately identifies it and separates it from other cars, both here and abroad...In the Imperial [we] have striven to create a style, a design that is, first of all, in impeccable taste, a perfect complement to the other fine possessions of those for whom this car was expressly designed and created."

The 1956 Crown Imperial soldiered on at the top of the line; its manufacture would be taken up by Ghia in Italy the following year. As before, the Crown was offered as either an eight-passenger sedan or limo, with air conditioning the only significant option. In a curious move for design-conscious Exner, the Crown retained its 1955 fenders but attempted to present a new look by adding tacked-on fins. Again only a handful of Crown Imperials were built.

Chrysler spun off the Imperial as a separate make for 1955. Although it shared its basic body with Chrysler, it rode a four-inch-longer wheelbase and much of its sheetmetal was exclusive. The Newport two-door hardtop (above) *listed at $4720, the four-door sedan* (opposite, top)*, $4483. For 1956, Imperial rode a longer 133-inch wheelbase and sprouted modest fins. An enlarged 354-cid hemi V-8 upped horsepower to 280. The $4832 four-door sedan* (bottom) *was easily the most popular model in the line, accounting for two-thirds of production that year.*

SPECIFICATIONS

Engines: ohv V-8 **1955** 331.0 cid (3.81 × 3.63), 250 bhp **1956** 354.0 cid (3.94 × 3.63), 280 bhp

Transmission:	Powerflite
Suspension, front:	independent, coil springs, tube shocks
Suspension, rear:	live axle, leaf springs, tube shocks
Brakes:	front/rear drums
Wheelbase (in.):	130.0 **Crown Imperial** 149.5
Weight (lbs):	4555-4680 **Crown Imperial** 5145-5205
Top speed (mph):	115
0-60 mph (sec):	11.0-12.0

Production: 1955 4d sdn 7840 **Newport 2d htp** 3418 **chassis** 1 **prototype cvt** 1 **4d sdn 8P** 45 **limo** 127 **1956 4d sdn** 6821 **Southampton htp sdn** 1543 **Southampton 2d htp** 2094 **4d sdn 8P** 51 **limo** 175

3413H

1957-59 Imperial

Like all other Chrysler products, the 1957 Imperials wore Virgil Exner's "Forward Look," which temporarily wrested the styling initiative from General Motors. Imperials sprouted huge tailfins and a full-width, complicated grille. The Imperial body now shared no outer panels with Chrysler—it was unique unto itself but far "busier" looking than the Chrysler, which was probably Exner's best design that year.

In an effort to surpass Lincoln in production and finish second to Cadillac in the luxury field, Imperial added two new series, the Crown and LeBaron, the latter named for the famous coachbuilding firm whose name had come into Chrysler's possession during the 1930s. More elaborately trimmed than standard Imperials, the Crown came as a sedan, two- and four-door hardtop, and a new convertible—the first Imperial soft top since 1953. The LeBaron series arrived in January, comprised of a pillared sedan and a four-door Southampton hardtop. Both new series cost considerably more than the baseline models; conceptually, the LeBaron rivaled Cadillac's Sixty Special (though its wheelbase was not lengthened compared to lesser models).

From 1957 onward, Ghia built the Crown Imperial limousines in Turin, Italy. Based on potential sales, Chrysler could no longer justify the time and space necessary to build such cars in Detroit. Against a potential $3.3 million tooling bill at home, Ghia offered to tool Crown Imperials for only $15,000, provided Chrysler shipped the basic "kit" to Italy. Ghia limos began as an unfinished two-door hardtop body mounted on a rigid convertible chassis, which was shipped with all body panels intact. Ghia cut them apart, added 20.5 inches of wheelbase, reworked the structure above the beltline, fitted and trimmed the luxurious interior, and finished off the exterior using 150 pounds of lead filler. Construction of each car took a month, and initial delays resulted in a late 1957 introduction. Prices started at a stratospheric $15,075 for the Crown Imperial—the highest price for a "production" American car for many years to come.

To the vast restyling program were added some notable mechanical improvements. A pushbutton-controlled TorqueFlite three-speed automatic transmission replaced the two-speed Powerflite; torsion bar front suspension made these huge cars the most roadable in their class; the V-8, blown out now to 392 cubic inches, developed more power and torque than ever. All the changes and model expansion worked: output soared to 37,593 units for 1957, and Imperial just edged out Lincoln in sales. Never again would Imperial sell in such large numbers, and this would be the only time in history that Imperial outsold Lincoln (although Cadillac outsold both by a four-to-one margin that year).

Styling changes were minimal for 1958, a year that started with good sales prospects but quickly went sour as a recession moved in. New fabrics and trims arrived, among them the Imperial's Diamond-glow jacquard and vinyl on its baseline series (which still bore no model name), crown pattern jacquard and vinyl on the Crown, and wool broadcloth on the LeBaron.

Except for a mild shuffle of regalia, a change to a more crosshatched grille pattern, and the replacement of square parking lights with round ones, the "Triumphant 1958 Imperial" looked like the '57 models. But it did feature two Chrysler firsts—the first cruise control and the first integrated electro-mechanical door locking system on an American car. New also were Captive-Air tires, 9.50×14s standard, 11.00 × 14s optional—the latter the fattest passenger car tires in the world. The Imperial also boasted more power than ever, the 392 V-8 being goosed to 345 horsepower, except on Crown Imperials (Ghia still had a big supply of 325-bhp engines!)

Imperial received a new, toothy, DeSoto-like grille for 1959, but was generally little altered. What *was* new was the engine, with less expensive-to-build, wedge-shaped combustion chambers replacing the hemispherical chambers: 392 cubic inches, 350 horsepower. Optional on the Imperial, in response to competitive developments, was an automatic self-leveling rear suspension: a compressor acting on nylon-reinforced, flexible rubber air springs controlled the action.

Sales in the dim model year of 1958 came to only about 16,000 units, fewer than half 1957's total; for 1959 they rose to over 17,000. Alas, the Imperial was a much finer car than the sales figures would suggest.

Imperial became a separate make in 1955 but didn't receive its own body until 1957 (above). *Like other Chrysler cars that year, it flaunted big fins. In 1959 it still used the same sheetmetal but faced the world with a toothy grille that looked like it had been stolen from a '54 Chevy. The Crown Southampton hardtop coupe* (opposite) *listed at $5388.*

SPECIFICATIONS

Engines: ohv V-8 **1957 1957-59 Crown Imperial** 392.0 cid (4.00 × 3.90), 325 bhp **1958** 345 bhp **1959** 413.0 cid (4.18 × 3.75), 350 bhp

Transmission:	TorqueFlite three-speed automatic
Suspension, front:	independent, torsion bars, tube shocks
Suspension, rear:	live axle, leaf springs, tube shocks **1959** automatic self-leveling rear suspension optional
Brakes:	front/rear drums
Wheelbase (in.):	129.0 **Crown Imperial** 149.5
Weight (lbs):	4640-4900
Top speed (mph):	115
0-60 mph (sec):	12.0

Production: 1957 4d sdn 5654 **htp sdn** 7527 **htp cpe** 4885 **Crown 4d sdn** 3642 **htp sdn** 7843 **htp cpe** 4199 **cvt** 1167 **LeBaron 4d sdn** 1729 **htp sdn** 911 **Crown Imperial limo** 36 **1958 4d sdn** 1926 **htp sdn** 3336 **htp cpe** 1801 **Crown 4d sdn** 1240 **htp sdn** 4146 **htp cpe** 1939 **cvt** 675 **LeBaron 4d sdn** 501 **htp sdn** 538 **Crown Imperial limo** 31 **1958 4d sdn** 2071 **htp sdn** 3984 **htp cpe** 1743 **Crown 4d sdn** 1335 **htp sdn** 4714 **htp cpe** 1728 **cvt** 555 **LeBaron 4d sdn** 510 **htp sdn** 622 **Crown Imperial limo** 7

OHIO
750-MFS

1950 Kaiser Virginian

One of Kaiser-Frazer's legacies to the industry was its novel hardtop, the Kaiser Virginian, patterned after the unique K-F convertibles and personifying "The Southern Spirit of Pride and Importance," according to sales brochures. (Incidentally, Kaiser's beautiful, oversize parchment broadsides won an advertising design award and are highly valued today.)

"Hardtop convertibles" were not new—the first attachment of a solid top to an open body dates at least back to the Kissel "All Year Top" of 1915-21, though the first hardtop in the modern sense was built experimentally by Chrysler in 1946. Seven production Town & Country convertibles received steel roofs skinned from Chrysler club coupes, bolted on for "evaluation." By 1948, General Motors was putting the finishing touches on the Cadillac Coupe de Ville, Olds Holiday, and Buick Riviera. But the Chrysler version never made it into production, and the GM hardtops weren't offered until mid-1949, whereas the Virginian made its entrance on February 23rd of the same year. And—salesmen thought this most important—the Virginian had four doors.

The Virginian was simple in concept, though semanticists dispute the hardtop claim, since the side window frames were fixed and the little vertical pane of glass between them prevented an unobstructed, all-windows-down effect. Like the Town & Country, the Virginian carried a steel top coupled to a convertible body, lighter than that of the ordinary sedans and strengthened by crease lines designed to resemble convertible top bows. Padded nylon or cotton was applied over the roof to complete the convertible look—a painted top was listed as a reverse option, but no such Virginians have been found. The car actually bore "Hardtop" script on its flanks before the name was settled.

This "blueblood of all cars" was the subject of fascination to Kaiser-Frazer fabric expert Carleton Spencer, who created a variety of special color combinations and upholstery materials—at least 54, according to factory records. Spencer even produced a "Custom Virginian" in low quantity for the first several months, with interior combinations of Stockholm and Volta cloth and mouton-like Imperial Crush floor and lower door panel carpeting. The Custom Virginian sold for $200 more than the standard model. Spencer put the production of this variant at fewer than 100 units.

Salesmen's facts books told promoters to trumpet the Virginian's exceptionally fine visibility, achieved through an extra-large backlight divided into three sections, curving around the sides—17 inches high and 73 inches wide. From the side, the car appeared to have "a single wide window extending from cowl to deck. The Virginian has the full rigidity of a conventional sedan. The support provided by the steel roof is augmented by special bracing in back of the front seat and by special construction in the rear." From the beltline down it was the same as other Kaisers, except that the windowsills were covered with chrome panels and a wide chrome rocker panel molding extended the length of the car and met the bumpers at each end. Chrome-plated exterior trunk hinges were a final touch.

At a base price of $2995, give or take a few dollars with price fluctuations (and $3195 for the Custom Virginian), this car faced very rough competition in the Cadillac-Packard-Lincoln market sector, where its anemic six-cylinder, formerly industrial engine was handily outclassed by big, powerful eights. Leather upholstery added $400 to its price, overdrive close to $100, and power windows $75. As a result, the promise of this intriguing new body style, soon to become so indispensable to the Big Three manufacturers, was squandered by Kaiser-Frazer. Production of Virginians came to just over 900 for the combined 1949-50 model year. Leftover 1949s were simply reserialed as 1950 models; the breakdown is probably six or seven to one, 1949 to 1950. Since about 1200 Virginian bodies were built, even the reserialed '50s were not enough to move them all out; an additional 152 were thus turned into 1951 Frazer Manhattan hardtops (see that chapter).

The Kaiser Virginian could lay claim to being the first production convertible hardtop, but it wasn't quite a true hardtop because the glass "post" between the doors was fixed. The hardtops that were sold in 1950 were actually reserialed '49s. The car shown here can be seen at the Kissel Car Museum in Hartford, Wisconsin.

SPECIFICATIONS

Engine:	sidevalve I-6, 226.2 cid (3.31 × 4.38), 112 bhp
Transmission:	3-speed manual; overdrive optional
Suspension, front:	independent, coil springs, tube shocks
Suspension, rear:	live axle, leaf springs, tube shocks
Brakes:	front/rear drums
Wheelbase (in.):	123.5
Weight (lbs):	3541
Top speed (mph):	90
0-60 mph (sec):	20.0
Production:	approximately 950, including 1949-serialed models

KAISER-FRAZER
178A

1951-53 Kaiser Dragon

The Kaiser Dragon was the work of Carleton Spencer, the ingenious designer who revolutionized the auto industry by bringing home fabrics into the automobile, erasing forever the dull pinstripes and monotonous grays and browns of the past. The first Dragons, announced in November 1950, were strictly trim options, using the same "Dragon" vinyl Spencer had developed for the Traveler.

Although offered in eight different single- and two-tone color combinations, all were called "Golden Dragons," probably because the most common variety was painted Arena yellow, and spread over a two-page color advertisement in national magazines. Spencer's vinyl, pleated in 2½-inch ribs, covered seat cushions, package shelf, and instrument panel. Stretched smooth, it went on seat risers, front seatbacks, and door panels, and was complemented by thick-weave carpeting. All this, plus Hydra-Matic (apparently standard on Dragons), brought the price to $2400, which was very costly (the price of a Buick Super Riviera or Packard 200), but not so bad for a publicity gimmick.

In February 1951, a new series of Dragons arrived with a new upholstery pattern, "Dinosaur" vinyl, a matching padded top, and two removable armrests, which were basically upholstered blocks. These three models (plus a fourth added in April) bore individual names based on their color/trim combination: the Silver (grey paint/scarlet upholstery), Emerald (Cape Verde green paint and upholstery), Golden (Arena yellow paint/black upholstery) and Jade (Tropical green paint/straw upholstery). The Jade Dragon, rarest of all, was done up in straw-colored "Tropical" vinyl, embossed to resemble woven straw.

No Dragons were officially offered in the 1952 model year, though Spencer did pull a few 1952 Manhattans off the line to fit with various Dragon trim items, as

The 1953 Kaiser "Hardtop" Dragon sold for $3924, only $71 less than a Cadillac Coupe de Ville. The Dragon pictured here was first displayed at the 1953 Chicago Auto Show and then toured the show circuit; 30 years later, in 1983, it again made an appearance at the Chicago Auto Show, but alas not on the Kaiser stand this time.

experiments or for VIP use. These led to the most exotic of them all, the 1953 Kaiser "Hardtop" Dragon, a four-door sedan with a padded "Bambu vinyl" top and Carleton Spencer's most exotic interior.

An entirely separate series for the first time, the '53 Dragon was all-Spencer, except for the "Laguna" pattern cloth seat inserts, which had been designed for Spencer by fashion consultant Marie Nichols. Its price was very close to $4000, and one can gather from this (it had the same underpowered six as the rest of the Kaiser line) that it did not sell: only 1277, at the outside, rolled off the assembly line.

But the Dragon was spectacular to look at. Bambu vinyl was applied everywhere, even to the trunk walls, package shelf, and glove box liner. It contrasted nicely with Nichols' Laguna cloth seat inserts. Carpeting was a special long-filament shag called "Calpoint" (also used on the Kaiser-Darrin). Dragons featured 200 pounds of extra insulation, giving them a much quieter, heavier feel than other Kaisers, which were hardly noisy. A final touch was 14 carat gold trim for the hood ornament, hood and deck "V" medallions, deck and fender script, even the trunklid keyhole cover. The price included as standard power steering, Hydra-Matic Drive, tinted glass with darker-banded upper windshield, oversize whitewall tires, radio with rear speaker, heater/defroster, windshield washer, and folding center armrests.

The Dragon's color/trim combinations were tasteful and good: onyx (black) or Stardust ivory, with black-on-beige Laguna and black Bambu vinyl; Jade Tint with green-on-beige Laguna and green Bambu vinyl; Maroon Velvet metallic with maroon on beige Laguna and maroon vinyl inside, "bleached" vinyl on the roof. One other Dragon came with a white canvas (instead of vinyl) top; painted Frosted Holly green, this car had green Bambu vinyl upholstery with white vinyl inserts in a "Boucle" pattern.

A number of show Dragons were built with fancier and gaudier trim, including a dozen with gold anodized wire wheels (chrome wires were a $270 option on all '53 Kaisers) and turquoise paint with rust-colored Boucle vinyl tops and upholstery. Finally, an occasional Dragon order was met by pulling a low-priced Deluxe off the line and trimming it to match the Dragon in K-F's sales brochure (ivory with green vinyl upholstery, a type not actually offered in production).

SPECIFICATIONS

Engine: sidevalve I-6, 226.2 cid (3.31 × 4.38) **1951** 115 bhp **1953** 118 bhp

Transmission:	4-speed Hydra-Matic
Suspension, front:	independent, coil springs, tube shocks
Suspension, rear:	live axle, leaf springs, tube shocks
Brakes:	front/rear drums
Wheelbase (in.):	118.5
Weight (lbs):	3320
Top speed (mph):	90
0-60 mph (sec):	15.0

Production: 1277 (because some serial numbers may have been skipped, this is the maximum number)

1951-53 Kaiser Traveler

Henry J. Kaiser averaged about 100 ideas an hour and about one of them was good. The good ones, however, were worth pausing over. During World War II, one of these was Kaiser's "cookie cutter" production line of Liberty and Victory ships, which broke the U-boat threat by sheer numbers; after the war, another idea emerged as the Kaiser Traveler: the first hatchback.

Improbable as it seems, the story really *is* true. Henry Kaiser conceived the Traveler by tracing the outlines of its double-opening hatches with his finger in the dust on a sedan in the Kaiser garage in Oakland. At that point, the idea was simplistic: cut out the entire deck and rear window area, hinge half of it to lift up and half to flop down, let them meet about halfway on the deck, and presto: a new kind of utility car. It wasn't quite so easy; 200 changes had to be made to the basic sedan before the Traveler could be built. It required stronger springs and shocks to handle the increased payload, new floor pan wiring, a method to display the license plate, and reinforcement "all over hell" (according to engineer Ralph Isbrandt) to replace lost stiffness.

The detail execution was clever. Harvey Anscheutz, Kaiser-Frazer's head of body development, spent three weeks with the laws of 48 states on his desk, devising a lighted license plate holder that would flop down when the deck was lowered without violating any position or visibility laws. A big, T-shaped handle was devised to ease the operation of the hatches, and a strong piano hinge strengthened the lower hatch. When open, this member was suspended by strong chains, bagged in vinyl to prevent rattles. Anscheutz also created a folding rear seat by tilting the cushion forward against the front seats and lowering the backrest to extend the cargo platform to its seven-foot length. The seat folding method is still used in wagons today.

The Kaiser Traveler, first seen in 1949, could be thought of as the granddaddy of the modern hatchback. The '51 Traveler received the same handsome all-new styling as the rest of the line. It came as a four-door sedan (below) *priced at $2317 for the Special, $2433 for the DeLuxe. The two door* (opposite) *sold for $2265 and $2380.*

SPECIFICATIONS

Engine: sidevalve I-6, 226.2 cid (3.31 × 4.38) **1951-52** 115 bhp **1953** 118 bhp

Transmission:	three-speed manual; overdrive and Hydra-Matic optional
Suspension, front:	independent, coil springs, tube shocks
Suspension, rear:	live axle, leaf springs, tube shocks
Brakes:	front/rear drums
Wheelbase (in.):	118.5
Weight (lbs):	3210-3370
Top speed (mph):	90
0-60 mph (sec):	15.0-16.0

Production: (all estimates) **1951 Special 2d sdn** 1500 **4d sdn** 2000 **Deluxe 2d sdn** 1000 **4d sdn** 1000 **1952 Virginian Traveler** included with above **Deluxe 2d sdn** probably a few hundred **1953 Deluxe 4d sdn** about 1000 **Manhattan 4d sdn** only a handful

Some aspects were makeshift, however: on the 1949-50 models, which lacked a sub-floor spare tire compartment, the left rear doors were welded shut and the spare bolted to the inside panel. (To confuse matters they dummied up a non-operable outside door handle, which must have frustrated many a passenger.) But this problem was handily cured on the handsomely restyled 1951 models.

Kaiser Travelers were offered in both the Special and Deluxe series for 1951, with two and four doors. Sales of two-door versions were minimal, and after a handful of ex-'51s were reserialed and sold off as 1952 "Virginian Travelers," Kaiser built only four-door models. These continued through 1953, almost all in the lower-end series; more luxuriously trimmed 1952-53 "Manhattan Travelers" were ostensibly offered, and at least one example has been found. Though the pre-1951 models had sold in good numbers, these later Travelers did not appeal, possibly because the new body restricted their capacity—only a few thousand were sold between 1951 and 1953.

Compared to the workaday station wagon, which still tended to be a boxy, truck-like vehicle made largely of wood in the late Forties, the Traveler was a revelation—and probably did more to popularize the civilized, all-steel wagon than most people realize. General Motors and Ford bought Travelers and tore them apart, to see if their obvious advantages were compromised by any structural shortcuts. "They were pretty good," one GM engineer told this writer. Much later, of course, the Traveler idea would lead to the modern hatchback, though not in quite the same way. One big problem that Kaiser-Frazer never licked was the seals insulating the hatches from the rest of the body—and from each other. Seal and rubber technology was not nearly so advanced then as now, and Traveler hatches leaked incessantly.

Another, minor contribution of the Traveler was its vinyl upholstery, pleated and embossed on the 1951-53 Deluxe models and the 1953 Manhattan. Working with the L. E. Carpenter Company of New Jersey, K-F interior designer Carleton Spencer developed the unique, heavy-duty upholstery, created by low-pressure refrigerated embossing. The smooth vinyl was heated and fed into a machine with refrigerated plates in the die design. The die then "kissed" the vinyl and immediately caused the design to set through heat transfer. The stuff was called "Dragon" and "Dinosaur" vinyl, Spencer said, "so no one would mistake it for real alligator or real lizard."

1954 Kaiser Darrin

By 1952, designer Howard "Dutch" Darrin had had it with Kaiser-Frazer. He'd resigned after his original design for what became the 1947 Kaiser and Frazer had been meddled with by Conrad Rehbein—the Detroit specialist hired to ready those cars for production. Then he had returned, in 1948, to design what became the brilliant 1951-55 Kaiser (see previous chapters), only to depart in disgust when the company settled on somebody else's proposal for the compact Henry J.

The Henry J chassis, though, intrigued Darrin. Around its 100-inch wheelbase, the designer thought he could hang something special in the way of a sports car—"without the authorization and knowledge of the Kaiser organization, but spending my own money." A rakish two-seat prototype took shape in Darrin's California studio. It sported sliding doors—a Darrin idea patented in 1946—a three-position top with functional landau irons, and fiberglass bodywork. The styling was beautifully proportioned, and handsome except for a small, high shell-shaped grille that "looked like it wanted to give you a kiss," as rival K-F stylist Bob Robillard put it.

Henry J. Kaiser arrived one day at Darrin's studio and promptly chewed the designer out for meddling with his sacred Henry J. "What's the idea of this," Kaiser fumed, "we're not in the business of building sports cars." Mrs. Kaiser leaped to Darrin's defense: "Henry," she purred, "this is the most beautiful thing I've ever seen...I don't think there'll be many companies after seeing this car that won't go into the sports car business." Kaiser relented. Later, when his cadre of sycophants were gathered around the table voting for the car to be named after him, Henry winked at Darrin and told them he hadn't voted: "I vote we call it the Kaiser Darrin—period."

Practical considerations dictated several changes for the production version, but only one got Darrin's dutch up: reworked front fenders that moved the headlamps to regulation height. Other alterations comprised separate lids for the trunk and top well (the prototype used a large, single, rear-hinged cover), one-piece (instead of split) windshield, a more professional interior with pleated vinyl upholstery (the prototype's leather trim became an option), and a revised dash with gauges clustered ahead of the wheel (instead of spread across the panel). Seatbelts appeared for only the second time in U.S. production, Nash having dropped them in 1951 after their appearance caused people to assume that "Nashes weren't safe." K-F also opted for an F-head Willys version of the Henry J six-cylinder engine, with a single carburetor (instead of three) and 10 more horsepower than stock. Glasspar, pioneer builder of fiberglass boat hulls and kit cars like the Woodill Wildfire, received the contract to supply Darrin bodies.

"The Sports Car the World Has Been Awaiting" had been shown as early as 1952, but the production version didn't reach showrooms until 1954 because of hesitations involving the general decline of Kaiser as a car builder, the sale of Willow Run, and the transfer of Kaiser production to Toledo. Darrins, however, were built at the Jackson, Michigan plant reserved for K-F's special projects; Jackson had, for example, built the last 1951 Frazer Manhattans.

Priced at $3668, the Darrin cost almost as much as a Cadillac or Lincoln, though it came fully equipped with tachometer, electric wipers, whitewall tires, and the novel top. With only 90 horsepower, performance wasn't earth shattering—much less than Chevy's Corvette, for example—though several supercharged examples could keep pace with 1954's quickest sports cars. The sliding doors never worked well; technology was insufficient to keep them from sticking and rattling in those days, though modern restorations work much better. The sliding door idea sounded better than it actually turned out—it didn't open all the way, for example, and getting in and out of a Darrin was a chore.

Before Darrin output could reach even 500 units, Kaiser-Willys (as the firm had become) bailed out of the U.S. market. Darrin took some of the leftover cars and installed 300-bhp Cadillac V-8s and sold them for $4350 each. The occasional Darrin went racing, but only one with distinction—by Laura (Mrs. Briggs) Cunningham. A remarkable number, close to 400, are known to survive. Had somebody other than Kaiser-Willys built it, the Darrin might have enjoyed a much brighter future.

Designer "Dutch" Darrin had his ups and downs with Kaiser-Frazer, but he was intrigued enough with the Henry J's 100-inch-wheelbase chassis to design a sports car around it. It featured sliding doors, a three-position top, nicely proportioned styling, and a curious "kiss me" grille. Alas, the Darrin's little Willys six was underpowered and its price came in near Cadillac's. With Kaiser already on the ropes, the Darrin was doomed—only 435 were built.

SPECIFICATIONS

Engine: ohv I-6, 161 cid (3.13 × 3.50), 90 bhp (supercharged about 125 bhp; with Cadillac engine 304 bhp)

Transmission:	3-speed manual, overdrive optional
Suspension, front:	independent, coil springs, tube shocks
Suspension, rear:	live axle, leaf springs, tube shocks
Brakes:	front/rear drums
Wheelbase (in.):	100.0
Weight (lbs):	2250
Top speed (mph):	**Six** 95-100 **V-8** 135
0-60 mph (sec):	**Six** 15.0 **V-8** 10.0

Production: 435; seven "split-window" prototypes were built, one of which has been discovered

CUB 235

1954-55 Kaiser Manhattan

When a well-known history of Kaiser-Frazer appeared in 1975, a wise-guy friend of the author wrote a review in *Car and Driver* calling it "a great book about a dull car." This resulted in a letter to the editor from an officer of the Kaiser-Frazer Owners Club, suggesting that the reviewer might like to "suck on a Kaiser tailpipe." All very amusing to one and all, but then one reads *Car and Driver* for entertainment, and other magazines for information.

More discerning and broad-minded car enthusiasts have long recognized that, while K-F did churn out thousands of fairly dull motorcars, the company was eccentric enough (and hired enough clever designers and engineers) to produce scores of bright ideas. From Henry J-based sports cars like the Excalibur J (which gave Jaguar XK-120s fits whenever they met on road courses) to the predictive hatchback Travelers and four-door hardtop Virginians, Kaiser-Frazer innovated and experimented. But from an industry standpoint, the most important K-F products were the radical Kaiser sedans of 1951-55—and the best of these were the 1954-55 Kaiser Manhattans.

Howard Darrin conceived the basic shape in 1948. He then took his ideas to the factory at Willow Run, Michigan and, citing a clause in his original contract to design the first K-F products, insisted on the right to submit a full-size clay model for its successor. K-F assigned Darrin a young stylist named Duncan McRae, and the result did them both credit. The 1951 Kaiser departed boldly from the ordinary, as laid down by General Motors, Ford, and Chrysler: it featured acres of glass, the lowest beltline in the industry, vast interior space for its size, and beautiful styling that relied on good lines instead of chrome (for almost the first time in anyone's memory).

Sound basic shapes usually respond well to facelifts, and the most radical for the '51 Kaiser came in 1954, when Edgar Kaiser (who liked to dabble in the styling

*Kaiser was handicapped in 1954-55 because it lacked both a V-8 and a hardtop. It compensated for the former by supercharging its venerable 226.2-cid six (bringing it to 140 bhp), for the latter with sumptuous interiors. The '55 (*opposite*) differed from the '54 (*below*) only in the hood scoop, which sported more "fins."*

department) asked his people to create something like the Buick XP-300 show car. A. B."Buzz" Grisinger worked out the front end—a concave, vertical bar grille, complemented by fender ovals surrounding the headlights and parking lights. A very tight budget precluded new bumpers, so stylist Herb Weissinger used 1951 bumper guards canted outboard—a neat trick.

Again, Kaiser abandoned Detroit convention by dropping the traditional hood ornament and badge: a simple scoop, matching the grille texture, rode atop the hood instead. In the rear, Grisinger wrapped the backlight right around, giving Kaiser an even greater lead in visibility compared to most of its rivals. He also conceived of the novel "Safety-Glo" taillights—big, rounded affairs with a lighted strip running up along the tops of the fenders. Meanwhile, Bob Robillard and Herb Weissinger redesigned the interior to resemble an aircraft cockpit, complete with toggle levers for the heating/ventilation controls and a steering column that resembled an aircraft's. And not only did they top the dash with a functional crash pad, but they put one on the back of the front seat to protect rear passengers as well. To complete the interior, Carleton Spencer crafted luxurious combinations of "Boucle vinyl" and "La Mar" fabric, set off by color-keyed "goat hair fiber" carpeting.

The Manhattan's performance badly needed a shot in the arm, and received it via a Paxton supercharger, which raised horsepower almost 20 percent. The blower made sense: at cruising speed it freewheeled economically, but depressing the accelerator advanced it from 1.5 to five pounds per square inch of boost. For the first time, a Kaiser could leap from 0 to 60 mph in less than 15 seconds, and come close to 100 mph at the top end. Not quite as good as the respected Hudson Hornet, perhaps, but certainly the Manhattan ranked as the second fastest full-size six on the American scene in 1954.

By this time, however, Kaiser production was winding down (it had already been moved from Willow Run to the Willys plant in Toledo), and only a small number of '54 Manhattans attracted buyers. A fraction of these ended up reserialed as '55s (and got a slightly different hood scoop, with a higher center "fin" and four flanking fins for quick identification). Another thousand-odd traveled to Argentina, where they became the basis for the Kaiser "Carabela." Sold sans supercharger, but otherwise unchanged, it lasted through 1962. Good designs stand the test of time.

SPECIFICATIONS

Engine:	sidevalve I-6, 226.2 cid (3.31 × 4.38), 140 bhp
Transmission:	3-speed manual; overdrive and Hydra-Matic optional
Suspension, front:	independent, coil springs, tube shocks
Suspension, rear:	live axle, leaf springs, tube shocks
Brakes:	front/rear drums
Wheelbase (in.):	118.5
Weight (lbs):	3265-3375
Top speed (mph):	95-98
0-60 mph (sec):	14.5-16.0

Production: **1954** 4110, about 3850 4d, 250 2d **1955 4d sdn** 226, plus 1021 for export to Argentina **2d sdn** 44

1950-51 Lincoln Cosmopolitan

The 1950-51 Lincolns continued the theme set down in 1949, when they were one of the few all-new postwar Ford Motor Company cars to emerge pretty much as had been originally planned. The major change, a shorter wheelbase for both the standard line and the new top-end Cosmopolitan, resulted from an August 1946 decision to cut the number of 1949 corporate platforms from six to four.

Among the casualties was a second-generation Continental on the 128-inch wheelbase originally slated for the Cosmo. E.T. "Bob" Gregorie, Ford's styling chief in the mid-'40s, recalled that "some renderings and full-size models [were made] of the Cosmo with a spare tire mounted on the trunk, but it looked too ponderous and clumsy to project the true Continental image." No doubt his heart wasn't in it, either. Company president Edsel Ford, with whom he'd collaborated on the 1939 Continental prototype, had died in 1943.

Gregorie had left Dearborn in the early '40s, but returned only to walk out again soon after management dismissed his proposed '49 Ford in favor of the George Walker/Dick Caleal design. But the smooth, "inverted-bathtub" shape that Gregorie evolved in wartime studies survived on the '49 Lincoln (and Mercury). The big Cosmopolitan was its purest expression.

"Frenched" or inset headlights and tail lamps made all '49 Lincolns immediately recognizable, but Cosmopolitans also sported stainless-steel window frames, large chrome "eyebrows" over the front wheelarches, and a predictive one-piece windshield (versus two-piece on "junior" models). Interiors featured lavish amalgams of leather and Bedford-cord cloth; instruments were a mix of round and rectangular.

Both '49 Lincoln lines offered a convertible, fastback coupe, and notchback four-door Sport Sedan (with throwback "suicide" rear-hinged back doors). Cosmopolitan added a fastback four-door oddly called Town Sedan, but the public had tired of "torpedo" styling and it wouldn't return for 1950. Cosmo prices, well up on those of recent Lincolns, ranged from $3186 for the coupe to $3948 for the convertible—around $3500-$4300 delivered.

The '49s were not only the first really new Lincolns since the pioneering 1936 Zephyr, but the first with body-on-frame construction since the last coachbuilt K-Series of 1939. They were also the first Lincolns in 17 years with V-8 power. Designed by C.C. Johnson, this was a new, but conventional, cast-iron "stroker," a fairly heavy flathead delivering 152 horsepower from 336.7 cubic inches. Though possessed of far more torque than the old V-12, Lincoln understandably avoided mentioning that it came from Ford's F7/F8 trucks. But that version's January 1948 production start allowed some 21 minor revisions to improve idling, valve and camshaft wear, and cylinder head durability, making the Lincoln unit a strong, refined, reliable engine admirably suited for luxury-car duty.

Lincoln's '49 chassis was epochal for the make, a new K-braced affair with heavy side rails, semi-floating Hotchkiss drive, and Ford-style independent front suspension with coil springs. Most customers noticed the improved ride right away, comparable if not superior to that of GM and Chrysler rivals. Tidier handling was less appreciated but just as welcome, reflecting a much lower center of gravity conferred by the new chassis and the lower-slung bodywork.

With all this, Lincoln enjoyed record 1949 production of some 73,500 units—nearly triple its previous best (due in part to a long model year). The Cosmo accounted for close to half, somewhat surprising for what amounted to a reincarnation of the lush, prewar Zephyr Custom.

Though it stayed mostly the same, this winning formula looked less like a winner over the next two years. Save for a pair of hardtop stand-ins, the Lido and Capri (see entry), the big change for 1950 was a handsome new dash designed by former coachbuilder Tom Hibbard. This was an attractive rolled affair with an oblong glass-covered gauge cluster, a motif that would persist through 1957. The '51s received more substantial trim revisions and Cosmos lost their wheelarch "eyebrows," while modest internal changes coaxed two extra horses from the flathead V-8. Lincoln volume fell dramatically, to about 28,200 and 32,600 units for 1950 and '51. The Cosmo still accounted for about half, but collectors have long noted the scarcity of coupes and soft tops, and have acted accordingly.

The Cosmopolitan became the cheaper Lincoln for 1952, part of an all-new line destined to make history. But the smooth, substantial "bathtubs" will always be remembered if for no other reason than the nine Cosmopolitan limousines that went to the White House in 1950. One would be used through 1963, serving Presidents Truman, Eisenhower, and Kennedy—and you can't get more cosmopolitan than that.

SPECIFICATIONS

Engine: L-head V-8, 336.7 cid (3.50 × 4.38) **1950** 152 bhp **1951** 154 bhp

Transmissions:	3-speed manual; overdrive and GM 4-speed Hydra-Matic optional
Suspension, front:	upper and lower A-arms, coil springs
Suspension, rear:	live axle, semi-elliptic leaf springs
Brakes:	front/rear drums
Wheelbase (in.):	125.0
Weight (lbs):	4340-4640
Top speed (mph):	95-100
0-60 mph (sec):	15.0

Production: **1950 cpe*** 1824 **4d Sport Sedan** 8341 **cvt** 536 **1951 cpe*** 2727 **4d Sport Sedan** 12,229 **cvt** 829 *includes standard and Cosmopolitan Capri models

Most people either love or hate Lincoln's 1949-51 "bathtub" styling, but at least it's memorable. Everything about the 1950 Cosmo Sport Sedan seen here was hefty: a $3240 price tag, 4410-pound curb weight, 125-inch wheelbase. Its 152-bhp, 336.7-cid flathead V-8 provided modest acceleration, but had the strength necessary for long-distance cruising.

4348

4348

1950-51 Lincoln Lido/Capri

Despite the great strides made with its new 1949 models, Ford Motor Company still had a lot of catching up to do. True, its cars now boasted contemporary flush-fender styling and fully modern chassis with independent front suspension and longitudinal semi-elliptic rear leaf springs. But years of engineering stagnation had left Dearborn with flathead engines, while rivals had begun to issue more efficient overhead-valve designs. Further, the firm lacked its own automatic transmission, now fast-becoming a sales necessity, especially in Lincoln's price class.

These deficits would be duly corrected, but Ford lacked something else in 1949: a "hardtop-convertible." General Motors surprised the entire industry that year with its airy new Buick Riviera, Cadillac Coupe de Ville, and Olds Holiday. Though sales started out modestly enough—just 9499—one didn't have to be clairvoyant to see that they could only go up. And they did with the 1950 arrival of lower-priced Chevy and Pontiac models and a trio from Chrysler Corporation, which had considered hardtops back in 1946.

Ford, still on the financial ropes in '49, found itself unable to answer GM's initiative right away. But since the first postwar Ford held the key to Dearborn's future, it naturally got the firm's first hardtop, rushed out for 1951 as the Custom Victoria V-8 (see entry). By that point, Ford had pretty much finalized an all-new 1952 corporate lineup that included Mercury and Lincoln hardtops, but there was neither money nor time for them in 1949, or even 1950-51.

Nevertheless, company pride dictated some kind of quick response, so Ford did about the only thing it could: give ordinary coupes hardtop styling flair. The result was a quartet of 1950 limited editions: Ford Crestliner, Mercury Monterey and Lincoln's Lido and Capri. The last are probably the most collectible of the bunch, being not only the most expensive and luxurious, but the rarest.

Like Ford and Mercury, Lincoln tried to compensate for the lack of a hardtop in 1950-51 by offering regular two-door models with vinyl roofs and fancy interiors. Seen here are the '51 Lido (below)*, a late '51 Lido sporting different side trim* (above)*, and a '51 Cosmopolitan Capri* (opposite)*.*

Like Crestliner and Monterey, Lincoln's hardtop stand-ins were mechanically identical with their linemates, but easily distinguished by contrasting leather-look vinyl roof coverings. Both sparkled a little more than other Lincolns, with bright drip rails, rocker moldings, and twin door mirrors, plus a gold-color Cosmopolitan hood ornament on Lido and chrome wheelarch "eyebrows" front and rear on Capri. Interiors took on a more opulent look, too, with unique door panels and premium upholstery of leather and cord cloth.

Size was the principal difference. Lido, the "junior" Lincoln coupe, shared its body with Mercury, but on a wheelbase three inches longer ahead of the cowl. The Capri bowed as an upmarket version of the senior Cosmopolitan coupe. Prices reflected this. At $2721, the Lido cost $192 more than the standard coupe, while the $3350 Capri stood $221 upstream of the regular Cosmo model. The 250-pound-lighter Lido was predictably faster and more agile than the Capri, but not much.

Dearborn also did about the only thing it could in lieu of its own automatic transmission: use somebody else's. After an unsuccessful try at buying Ultramatic from Packard, it secured GM's Hydra-Matic, which was the better choice. Lincoln first offered it beginning in June 1949, and would continue to do so through 1954.

With their smooth and reliable—but less efficient—flathead V-8, the "bathtub" Lincolns weren't as fast as ohv Cadillacs, Olds 88s, and hemi-powered Chryslers. Yet they could do a genuine 100 mph and exhibited granitic long-haul durability. As proof, Johnny Mantz drove a standard sedan to 11th overall in the 1950 Mexican Road Race, averaging 91 mph on some sections and actually leading the vaunted Olds 88 of Herschel McGriff by 11½ minutes.

But this didn't help the sales of the Lido and Capri—hampered by those stiff prices and a very late introduction (July 5, 1950)—nor Lincoln in general, whose 1950 volume reached barely half the record '49 total. Nevertheless, the pseudo-hardtops returned for '51 with the minor styling and mechanical changes applied to all Lincolns. These included longer, squared-up rear fenders for Lido, no wheelarch "eyebrows" for Capri, and identifying name script for both. Not surprisingly, demand remained very limited.

Just how limited is hard to say, because Lincoln lumped Lido/Capri production in with that of the standard coupes. It seems likely, though, that no more than 2000 Lidos and 1000 Capris left the factory each year—not the rarest cars in Detroit history, but rare enough to have made them collector's items long ago.

SPECIFICATIONS

Engine: L-head V-8, 336.7 cid (3.50 × 4.38) **1950** 152 bhp **1951** 154 bhp

Transmissions:	3-speed manual; overdrive and 4-speed GM Hydra-Matic optional
Suspension, front:	upper and lower A-arms, coil springs
Suspension, rear:	live axle, semi-elliptic leaf springs
Brakes:	front/rear drums
Wheelbase (in.):	125.0
Weight (lbs):	4100-4385
Top speed (mph):	95-100
0-60 mph (sec):	15.0
Production*:	**1950** 7592 **1951** 7209

*All Lincoln coupes, including Lido and Capri

1952-55 Lincoln

Lincoln entered 1952 with all-new styling and a 160-bhp overhead-valve V-8. The top-line Capri two-door hardtop listed at $3518. By 1955, the Lincoln had grown longer and boasted an enlarged V-8 with 225 horsepower. The Capri hardtop had also escalated in price to $3910.

In 1950, a reporter asked Ford Motor Company chief engineer Harold Youngren when he thought there'd be a new Lincoln. "Soon, please God," he replied.

The answer to Youngren's prayer arrived for 1952, and it was remarkable. Styled by George Walker with assistance from Bill Schmidt and Don DeLaRossa, this new Lincoln looked good: curvy in the right places, and clean—too clean, some said, to satisfy chrome-happy Americans. The hood now sat a bit below front-fender level for excellent forward vision, and rear fenders with a forward-raked dummy scoop on the sides, echoing Ford, provided visual interest. New features abounded, including optional four-way power seat and factory air conditioning. Fabrics and leathers, fit and finish all maintained high standards.

All '52 Lincolns rode a new 123-inch wheelbase, an apparent compromise between the previous 121- and 125-inch spans. Cosmopolitan now denoted the standard line, while the upper-class cars took the Capri name from the 1950-51 limited-edition Cosmopolitan coupe (see entry). Both lines listed a true pillarless hardtop, Lincoln's first, which sold 10,000 copies. The convertible was a Capri exclusive and Lincoln's costliest '52 at $4045. The $3517 Cosmo sedan filled the role of price leader.

Engineering changes were equally dramatic. They started with Earle S. MacPherson's new ball-joint front suspension, with rotating sockets instead of conventional kingpins and bushings that eliminated lots of unsprung weight (and 12 of 16 grease fittings). The result was a fine ride and surprisingly good handling. Said *Motor Trend:* "It doesn't heel excessively on sharp, high-speed turns, and it doesn't feel like you're guiding a couple of sponges around a turn." Also new were recirculating-ball power steering, oversize drum brakes—the first good Lincoln brakes anyone could remember—more and better body mounts, and lots of insulation.

But the capper was a brand-new V-8, Lincoln's first valve-in-head powerplant and superior to most rivals in many ways. Its crankshaft, for example, had eight counterweights instead of the usual six, plus oversize intake valves for better breathing and more output per cubic inch. Also featured was a deep-skirted crankcase extending below the crank centerline for an extremely stiff shaft support.

Like GM's ohv V-8s, but unlike its flathead forebear, the new Lincoln unit was a short-stroke, oversquare design. Displacement came in at 317.5 cubic inches,

SPECIFICATIONS

Engines: **1952-54** ohv V-8, 317.5 cid (3.80 × 3.50) **1952** 160 bhp **1953-54** 205 bhp **1955** 341 cid (3.94 × 3.50), 225 bhp

Transmissions:	**1952-54** 4-speed GM Hydra-Matic **1955** 3-speed Turbo-Drive automatic
Suspension, front:	upper and lower A-arms, coil springs
Suspension, rear:	live axle, semi-elliptic leaf springs
Brakes:	front/rear drums
Wheelbase (in.):	123.0
Weight (lbs):	4125-4415
Top speed (mph):	105-110
0-60 mph (sec):	11.0-13.0

Production: **1952 Cosmopolitan Sport Coupe 2d htp** 4545 **4d sdn** 15,854 (including Capri 4d) **Capri Sport Coupe 2d htp** 5681 **4d sdn** included with Cosmo 4d sdn **cvt** 1191 **1953 Cosmopolitan Sport Coupe 2d htp** 6562 **4d sdn** 7560 **Capri Sport Coupe 2d htp** 12,916 **4d sdn** 11,352 **cvt** 2372 **1954 Cosmopolitan Sport Coupe 2d htp** 2994 **4d sdn** 4447 **Capri Sport Coupe 2d htp** 14,003 **4d sdn** 13,598 **cvt** 1951 **1955 Custom Sport Coupe 2d htp** 1362 **4d sdn** 2187 **Capri Sport Coupe 2d htp** 11,462 **4d sdn** 10,724 **cvt** 1487

horsepower 160 with standard four-barrel carburetor and 7.5:1 compression. The one and only transmission remained GM's dual-range (four-speed) Hydra-Matic.

This fast, roadable package seemed tailor-made for competition, and tuning ace Clay Smith, helped by a bin full of heavy-duty "export" parts, made it an outstanding performer in the 1952 Mexican Road Race. High-priced European sports cars took the first six places, but next came three Smith Lincolns and a private entry that swept the new "American Stock" class. National stock-car champ Chuck Stevenson drove the top Lincoln.

Still, this probably had little to do with Lincoln's '52 fortunes, which were great for a year when the industry as a whole was still beset with allocations and material shortfalls. Lincoln was one of only two makes to see a calendar-year sales increase (the other was Willys), narrowing Cadillac's lead by some 5000 units. Although Lincoln model year *production* was down about that much compared to 1951, its '52s didn't go on sale until January and were gone by September.

Styling and chassis adjustments were minor for '53, but a host of engine tweaks—higher compression, bigger intake valves, better manifolding, higher-lift cam, and others—boosted horsepower by no less than 45. Despite having to run "more stock," Lincoln had another fine year in Mexico as Stevenson, Walt Faulkner, Jack McGrath, and Johnny Mantz finished first through fourth in class and sixth through ninth overall against everything from hemi Chryslers to Henry Js. The '54s changed little mechanically, but a heavier grille and more brightwork made them look richer. The fifth and last Mexican Road Race saw Lincoln's third consecutive sweep, with Faulkner trailing privateer Ray Crawford in the International Stock Class behind a pack of sports cars. Sadly, Clay Smith had died and, though Bill Stroppe capably relieved him, the factory team wasn't as successful against the tougher opposition. Of 14 cars entered, half by the factory, only four finished, including two privateers. For Lincoln, it was perhaps fortunate that the fabled road race ended when it did.

Lincoln also suffered in the red-hot '55 sales race, mainly because its reworked '54 wasn't as "new" as that year's Cadillac and Imperial. But it was still a top-quality item—and more powerful than ever, thanks to a newly bored 341 V-8 with 225 bhp (rivals had 25 bhp more, however). An important image point was this year's belated arrival of Lincoln's own automatic, three-speed Turbo-Drive, replacing Hydra-Matic. Model choices stayed the same, but the base group was retitled Custom. Weight changed little—one of the few '55s that didn't heavy-up a lot. Nor did prices.

Yet despite all this and a race-winning heritage, Lincoln was one of the few makes to score lower volume for '55 than '54 (the others were fast-fading Hudson, Willys, and Kaiser). But it was only temporary: Lincoln would bounce back with an altogether larger and trendier car for '56. For that story, just turn the page.

1956-57 Lincoln

The 1956 Lincoln was bigger all around, but the styling was so deftly handled that it won an award for excellence in automotive design from the Industrial Designers Institute. The top-line Premiere four-door sedan (above) listed at $4601. For 1957, the Lincoln sported fins much like those seen on the 1954 Lincoln Futura dream car. The Premiere hardtop coupe, which weighed in at a hefty 4451 pounds, retailed for an also hefty $5149.

Bigger most always meant better sales in '50s Detroit, though not necessarily better cars, as we all found out (to our sorrow). Take the 1956-57 Lincoln. After four years of capable but fairly modest cars garnering equally modest sales, Lincoln ballooned to heroic new proportions, and its sales total swelled to the second highest in the make's history. Unfortunately, this success led to even greater excess, and it would be five full years before Lincoln would return to its 1952-55 brand of restrained luxury—by which time a radically changed market left it hardly any choice.

Ads called the '56s "Unmistakably Lincoln," but you had to look twice for any vestige of '55. Gone were the trim 123-inch wheelbase, conservative styling, flat windshield, and year-old 341 V-8. In their stead came a three-inch-longer wheelbase, a new 368-cubic-inch V-8 belting out 285 horsepower—60 more than the '55 engine—and longer-lower-wider bodies with wrapped windshields. Overall length grew by no less than seven inches, width by three. Model offerings remained as before, but Capri was demoted to lower-line status, the upper series now being called Premiere.

Lincoln's '56 styling had been started by designer Bill Schmidt before he left to join Packard (then nearing its "last days in the bunker"). Like his previous work, it was simple and tasteful. What distinguished it from '55 was not glitter but size. Details and surface development were deftly handled and fit the larger proportions extremely well. As possible proof, the '56 Lincoln copped an award for excellence in automotive design from the Industrial Designers Institute.

Certain elements, especially the bodyside and rear fender shapes, had been previewed on the '54 Mercury XM-800 show car. Highlights included a clean but massive two-tier grille, headlamps nestled under large, thrust-forward hoods, and rakish vertical taillights above long exhaust ports flanking a dummy grille that duplicated the frontal motif. Two-toning was still tastefully confined to the roof. Inside, the dash continued with the basic Lincoln theme familiar since 1950, with a rectangular instrument pod above, and control switches directly ahead of and flanking

the steering column. Lincoln listed 17 basic body colors, 35 two-tone combinations, and 29 upholstery choices.

The larger '56 Lincoln V-8 was more than just a bore-and-stroke job. Block, camshaft, and oil pump were all new, as was a novel fresh-air intake feeding from the left of the grille. Compression went from 8.5:1 to a more efficient 9.0:1, while electricals switched from 6 to 12 volts.

Though overshadowed for prestige by the handsome new $10,000 Continental Mark II, Lincoln also had one of 1956's few new designs and thus did well despite an industry-wide sales decline. Calendar year output rose to nearly 50,000, and model year volume nearly doubled, also to 50,000, good for 14th place, up two from '55.

Fairly modest changes are expected in the sophomore edition of a new design, but Lincoln returned for '57 with a wild "taillift" on its '56 styling, plus a new four-door Landau hardtop in each series. Designer L. David Ash grafted on huge canted fins, while four headlamps (in vertical pairs) bowed as a "first" shared with Nash and Cadillac's Eldorado Brougham. Hiking compression to 10.0:1 added another 15 horsepower, and a newly optional "Directed Power" limited-slip differential helped put it to the road.

Lincoln had come within a third of Cadillac's sales volume in 1956; Ash's '57 styling attempted to keep it there, an appeal to what seemed to motivate luxury-car buyers, who should have been more available to Lincoln now that the big Packards were gone. More available also were features like power vent windows, electric door locks, six-way power seats, low-fuel warning light, automatic headlamp dimmer, remote-control rearview mirrors, and more efficient air conditioning. But the '57 failed its assignment. Output dropped by about 9,000 units to 41,123, while Cadillac rose to well over 150,000 units. Lincoln was doing better than in the early Fifties—but still not good enough.

The obvious solution—or so it seemed—was an even bigger 1958 Lincoln, accompanied by a less special Continental built on the same platform. Both had been evolving since 1955 at Ford Motor Company's product-planning group under Jack Reith. As for 1957, one Lincoln-Mercury executive later ruminated: "All we could [do] was hang on and try to promise the dealers a more competitive product the following year. You can better understand the decision to downgrade the Continental when you consider the failure of Lincoln Division to handle Cadillac." Perhaps, but as Dearborn would soon discover, 1958 was one year where bigger did not in any way mean better.

SPECIFICATIONS

Engine: ohv V-8, 368 cid (4.00 × 3.66) **1956** 285 bhp **1957** 300 bhp

Transmission:	3-speed Turbo-Drive automatic
Suspension, front:	upper and lower A-arms, coil springs
Suspension, rear:	live axle, semi-elliptic leaf springs
Brakes:	front/rear drums
Wheelbase (in.):	126.0
Weight (lbs):	4305-4676
Top speed (mph):	105-110
0-60 mph (sec):	10.8-11.5

Production: **1956 Capri 2d htp** 4355 **4d sdn** 4436 **Premiere 2d htp** 19,619 **4d sdn** 19,465 **cvt** 2447 **1957 Capri Landau 4d htp** 1451 **4d sdn** 1476 **2d htp** 2973 **Premiere Landau 4d htp** 11,223 **4d sdn** 5139 **2d htp** 15,185 **cvt** 3676

1958-59 Lincoln

Considering the trim, shapely Lincolns of 1952-55, it might have been hard to believe that the '58s came from the same outfit. One magazine called them "the biggest, heaviest, and newest of the mammoths"—a fair statement. The wheelbase stretched no less than 131 inches, up five from 1956-57. Overall length measured 10.5 inches greater (a full 19 feet), height four inches less (to 56.5), and track bulged an inch wider front and rear. Surprisingly, the '58s were slimmer, though by only a scant 0.2 inch. Curb weights rose by some 300 ponderous pounds.

Styling only enhanced the weighty new size. Massively square and slab-sided, it was distinguished—if that's the word—by quad headlamps in slanted oval recesses and fenders that one wag called "pre-dented," owing to heavy concave sculpturing around the wheelarches. At least the high-flying fins of '57 were trimmed down into modest blades.

As radical as its new jumbo package, the '58 debuted as the first Lincoln in 10 years with unit construction, decreed by Ford Motor Company engineering chief Earle S. MacPherson to hold the line on weight. At the time, nobody was quite sure whether a "uniframe," as Lincoln called it, would work on a car so large—and initially it didn't. Prototypes lacked rigidity so badly that numerous reinforcements had to be added, which ultimately negated the weight-savings usually realized in unitized cars.

Yet, there were improvements. Rear springing changed from the traditional semi-elliptic leafs to coils, partly to accommodate a planned air suspension that never reached production owing to development troubles. (At least one source says that about two percent of production *did* receive the air suspension.) The Lincoln's extra weight was handled by brakes with 41 percent more lining area and a big new 430-cubic-inch V-8 with an ample 375 horsepower on 10.5:1 compression. Final drive was numerically lowered in a faint gesture toward "economy" (about 10 mph around

If bigger is better, there has never been a finer car than the 1958-60 Lincoln. Measuring a full 19 feet and riding a 131-inch wheelbase, the big new Lincoln proved to be a case of the wrong car at the wrong time—out of tune in recession-wracked 1958. The '58 model (this page) *sported modest fins and canted headlights. The latter would be de-emphasized for '59, when they were integrated within the grillework. The '59* (opposite) *also sported new taillights and a longer sculpture behind the front wheels.*

town), and Lincoln's Turbo-Drive automatic was beefed up to cope with a whopping 490 pounds/feet torque.

The sole change in model offerings concerned the Premiere convertible, which transferred to the newly expanded line of near-twin Continental Mark IIIs (see entry). This left the Capri and Premiere series with a sedan and two hardtops each, all with conventional, slightly wrapped fixed rear windows instead of the Conti's reverse-slant roofline and drop-down glass. Inflation lifted prices about $200 over '57, ranging from $4803 for the Capri hardtop coupe to $5090 for either four-door Premiere.

Against all logic, these Lincolns were not clumsy, slow-moving dinosaurs. Acceleration, about the same as '57, caused tester John Preston to say it was "doubtful whether any big two-and-one-half ton car could stick any tighter in the corners, resist bottoming more on dips...or handle any better at high speed." Another myth bites the dust.

Superior passenger space was allegedly the reason for Lincoln's growth, but the '58 Cadillac actually offered four more inches of front hiproom. Though Lincoln did have substantially more shoulder room, one had to wonder how almost a foot of extra length outside translated into just an extra inch of rear legroom inside.

Regardless, buyers were less than taken with the '58 Lincolns. Production plunged from better than 41,000 to just over 17,000, not counting 12,550 Continental Mark IIIs. The sharp 1958 recession was undoubtedly a big factor and it's likely that the standard line lost a few sales to the more expensive Continentals. Cadillac volume slipped, too (as was most every Detroit producer's), but by fewer cars, so Lincoln actually lost ground against its rival.

Fortunately, Dearborn planners had already realized that these giants were as much an ill-timed mistake as the Edsel, and they duly launched a new design program that would culminate in the far more rational Lincoln Continental of 1961. Meantime, there was nothing to do but issue more of the same, so the '59s received few changes apart from styling details and a V-8 detuned to 350 bhp (via reduced compression). Though the nation's economy improved, sales didn't, dropping to slightly less than 16,000. The 1960 story was much the same, except that Lincoln managed only 13,734 standard models and some 11,000 Continentals.

But that would be the worst of it, and Lincoln's fortunes would improve dramatically with the smaller, crisply styled '61 and its successors.

SPECIFICATIONS

Engines: ohv V-8, 430 cid (4.30 × 3.70) **1958** 375 bhp **1959** 350 bhp

Transmission:	3-speed Turbo-Drive automatic
Suspension, front:	upper and lower A-arms, coil springs
Suspension, rear:	live axle, coil springs, trailing arms
Brakes:	front/rear drums
Wheelbase (in.):	131.0
Weight (lbs):	4735-4887
Top speed (mph):	110-115
0-60 mph (sec):	8.7-10.5

Production: **1958 Capri 4d sdn** 1184 **Landau 4d htp** 3084 **2d htp** 2591 **Premiere 4d sdn** 1660 **Landau 4d htp** 5572 **2d htp** 3043 **1959 Capri 4d sdn** 1312 **Landau 4d htp** 4417 **2d htp** 2200 **Premiere 4d sdn** 1282 **Landau 4d htp** 4606 **2d htp** 1963

1950-51 Mercury

Enthusiasts enshrined the 1949-51 Mercury long ago, not so much for its abilities as a production car as for its possibilities as a custom car. "Bathtub" Mercs with chopped tops, cruiser skirts, and lowered, highly decorated bodies were a common sight in the '50s. The styling may have invited such treatment: clean, rounded, and massive—a perfect canvas for any budding auto artist. Then too, film idol James Dean seared the custom Merc into a generation's collective consciousness by driving one in *Rebel Without a Cause*. Whatever the reason, no Mercury had so fired the imagination of America's youth—and it would be a long time before one would again.

The 1949-51 Mercury was something of a fluke. Ford Motor Company's initial postwar planning envisioned two separate Mercury lines on wheelbases of 120 and 123 inches. Below these came two Fords: a 100-inch-wheelbase "Light Car" compact and a 118-inch "full-size" line. At the top stood a trio of Lincolns: a 125-inch-wheelbase standard series, a pricier Cosmopolitan/Custom on a three-inch-longer span, and a new Continental and limousine on a 132-inch stretch.

Enter Ernest R. Breech, recruited in 1945 by new company president Henry Ford II as his second in command. Breech thought the proposed bathtub-style Ford too ponderous, the compact unnecessary in the booming postwar seller's market, and a new Continental questionable given scarce funds and limited potential sales. He thus "suggested" to Ford's Policy Committee in August 1946 that the two Mercurys be merged into a lower-priced Lincoln series, that the erstwhile standard Ford become a Mercury, and that a 114-inch-wheelbase Ford be developed with all due speed. Naturally, the committee went along with him.

The first all-postwar Mercury thus appeared for 1949 with a 118-inch wheelbase and a basic body shared with the new "junior" Lincolns, which rode a 121-inch wheelbase. Styling had been conceived during the war by company design chief E.T. "Bob" Gregorie. Under the hood throbbed a stroked version of the Ford/Mercury flathead V-8 venerated by hot-rodders, with an extra 16 cubic inches and 10 horsepower over 1946-48. Like other Ford Motor Company cars for 1949, Mercury got its first-ever independent front suspension and an "open" Hotchkiss rear axle (replacing torque-tube drive) on longitudinal semi-elliptic leaf springs. A single series

Although Mercury built 293,658 cars for 1950, two models were always relatively rare. The $2412 soft top (opposite page) *saw production of just 8341 units. The Monterey* (below)*, a vinyl- or canvas-topped stopgap answer to GM's hardtops, saw only 5059 copies. The Monterey listed at $2146 with a canvas roof, $2157 with vinyl.*

CALIFORNIA
003 LEW

003 LEW

continued with just four body styles: coupe, two-door wood wagon, convertible, and a four-door Sport Sedan with throwback "suicide" rear-hinged back doors.

Mercury set a production record for '49 at 301,319 units. The main reasons were the close styling relationship with Lincoln and genuine 100-mph performance. Predictably, the '50s were mostly '49 reruns. Detail appearance changes comprised larger parking lamps, "Mercury" hood letters encased in a wide chrome strip, and one-piece rear windows on coupes and sedans (replacing 1949's three-piece affairs), the last shared with Lincoln. A new dashboard similar to Tom Hibbard's Lincoln design highlighted the interior.

Two new coupe models arrived: an $1875 "stripper," to compete with the cheaper Dodges and Pontiacs, and the Monterey, available with canvas or vinyl roof covering at $2146 and $2157 respectively. The latter arrived as one of four Dearborn replies to GM's new 1949 hardtops and 1950 offerings from Chevrolet, Pontiac, Chrysler, DeSoto, and Dodge. Like Lincoln's similar Lido and Capri (see entry), the Monterey came with a luxury interior that hopefully reminded the buyer of a full-blown convertible. The Monterey was certainly more salesworthy than its Lincoln relatives, but output reached only modest levels: 5059 units for 1950, 7471 for 1951.

While Mercury had long been known as something of a "factory hot rod," the heavier '49s weren't as quick on the stock-car tracks. But the '50s held, and also did well in the first Mexican Road Race, with five of 11 entries finishing. Mercury paced the 1950 Indianapolis 500, and an overdrive-equipped Sport Sedan won the Grand Sweepstakes in that year's Mobilgas Economy Run, averaging 26.52 mpg over 751 miles from Los Angeles to the Grand Canyon.

A true Mercury hardtop would have to await Ford's 1952 corporate redesign, which means the '51s were the last "bathtub" Mercs. The "economy" coupe was canceled, but other models returned, including Monterey, wearing a toothy convex grille and longer, squared-up rear fenders. Minor engine changes brought a nominal two extra horsepower, but the big news was Mercury's first self-shift transmission. Called Merc-O-Matic, it was like that year's new Ford-O-Matic, a three-speed torque-converter unit developed with the Warner Gear Division of Borg-Warner. Priced at $159 extra, about $70 more than the still-optional overdrive, it proved highly popular right from the beginning.

Having finished ninth on 1950 model year volume of nearly 294,000 units, Mercury rose to sixth for '51 on output close to 310,400, another record. But though it was time for bigger, if not necessarily better, things, the "bathtub" Mercs would never be forgotten. Today they're enjoying a revival, as are custom cars in general. Thank goodness some have been left "stock" for us to remember as great American cars of the '50s.

SPECIFICATIONS

Engine: L-head V-8, 255.4 cid (3.19 × 4.00) **1950** 110 bhp **1951** 112 bhp

Transmission:	3-speed manual; overdrive and 3-speed Merc-O-Matic optional
Suspension, front:	upper and lower A-arms, coil springs
Suspension, rear:	live axle, semi-elliptic leaf springs
Brakes:	front/rear drums
Wheelbase (in.):	118.0
Weight (lbs):	3345-3800
Top speed (mph):	95-100
0-60 mph (sec):	16.0

Production: **1950 cpe** 146,450 **Monterey cpe** 5059 **4d Sport Sedan** 132,082 **cvt** 8341 **2d wgn** 1746 **1951 cpe** 134,697 **Monterey cpe** 7471 **4d Sport Sedan** 157,648 **cvt** 6759 **2d wgn** 3812

The '51 Mercury boasted a new grille, squared-off rear fenders, vertical taillights, and a larger rear window. The priciest model at $2530 was the woody wagon (below)*; only 3812 were built. The $1947 coupe* (opposite, top) *was more popular with 135,000 sold, but over half of total output went to the $2000 Sport Sedan* (bottom)*: 157,648 units.*

1952-54 Mercury

After being a "junior Lincoln" for 1949-51, Mercury reverted to being a "senior Ford" (as it has been through most of its 50 years to date). This was hardly bad. Lincoln became more Mercury-like for '52, and both related closely to that year's redesigned Ford.

All shared a boxy but clean new corporate look marked by one-piece windshields and full flush-fender bodysides, with thrust-forward rear-quarter sculpturing decorated to suggest an air scoop. Setting Mercury apart was what might be termed a "bulldog" grille, with a large, protruding bumper below a slim rectangular opening. Tail lamps were chrome-encased vertical units capping raked rear fenders above a simple bumper.

Mercury retained a 118-inch wheelbase for a lighter new box-section chassis sans central X-member. Suspension was basically as before, but mountings for front stabilizer bar and rear shocks were improved, as was the steering. Mercury power still came from the flathead V-8, still in the 255.4-cubic-inch form introduced for 1949, but lifted from 112 to 125 horsepower via higher compression and a more efficient carburetor. Other technical changes included a smaller (19-gallon) fuel tank with rear-center filler (concealed by the license plate, as on Ford) and revised axle ratios for the standard manual transmission and optional stick-overdrive. Self-shift Merc-O-Matic remained optional for a second year.

Besides new styling, Mercury's most obvious change for '52 was a wider assortment of models, eight in all, encompassing five body styles, up one from the "bathtub" generation. A two-door sedan was offered for the first time since 1948, and the previous part-wood two-door wagon gave way to a pair of all-steel four doors, six- and eight-passenger, with simulated wood side trim and interior-mount spare tire.

But the big attraction for '52 was the arrival of two true hardtop coupes. One inherited the Monterey moniker of Mercury's 1950-51 limited-edition coupe. The name also applied to the '52 convertible and a new uplevel four-door sedan. All other models wore "Mercury" instead of "Monterey" in rear-fender script, though some

Like Ford and Lincoln, Mercury strutted all-new styling for 1952. Though all had a "family" look about them, the Merc got a "bulldog" face, heavily chromed taillights, and its first hardtop. The '52 (top) had no chrome on the front fenders. The '53 (above and below) sported a full-length chrome strip on the sides and a modified grille. The '54 boasted yet another grille design and new taillights, plus Mercury's first modern overhead-valve V-8.

sources insist these were officially "Custom" models. In any case, the Montereys were more luxurious and more expensive, a distinction that would continue through 1954. The make's prices ranged from $1987 for the basic two-door sedan to $2570 for the eight-seat wagon.

Montereys accounted for the bulk of Mercury's '52 production, which was down by over 40 percent from record '51 owing to cutbacks in civilian manufacturing prompted by the nation's involvement in the Korean conflict. But the curbs were only temporary and Mercury would bounce back strongly for 1953, along with the rest of Detroit, recovering to beyond 300,000 units.

Mercury made no big changes for '53, but it did realign models to create its first true two-series lineup. Base-trim offerings—hardtop coupe and two sedans—were definitely Customs now, although still without identifying script. Reflecting its '52 popularity, Monterey expanded to include the eight-passenger wagon (the six-seater was dropped). Montereys featured handsome upholstery: quality broadcloth for the sedan, leather and vinyl for other models. Hardtops now carried standard two-toning, with the contrasting color confined to the roof.

Styling revisions common to all '53s included little "teeth" in the upper grille cavity, new—and prominent—bullet front bumper guards, full-length bodyside moldings, and three chrome "windsplits" on the rear fender bulges. Like Lincoln, sedans and hardtops sported one-piece backlights (still slightly wrapped). Retained from '52 was Mercury's "aircraft-inspired" dash design, with a half-moon gauge cluster atop a flat pod holding horizontal levers (with large knobs) for lights, wipers, and heater/defroster.

Like Ford, Mercury made history for 1954 by abandoning the old flathead V-8 in favor of the company's new overhead-valve Y-block engine. Befitting its upmarket status, Mercury's version ran a 0.12-inch bigger bore for 256 cid and 161 bhp versus Ford's 239.4 cid and 130 bhp. Ball-joint front suspension was also new, and appreciated for its crisper handling. The one change on the model chart involved the inevitable Mercury companion to this year's new "bubbletop" Ford Skyliner, the Monterey Sun Valley (see entry). Modest styling changes included reshaped rear fenders with wrapped, ribbed vertical tail lamps; a cleaner face with double-bar front bumper, the upper one ribbed between two bomb-like guards—making the '54 the best-looking Merc of this period.

Not the best-selling one, though, as output eased to about 259,300 units. But Mercury was on a roll—and ready for what would be the industry's best year ever. Nineteen fifty-five was at hand and, with it, a flashy new "Big M."

SPECIFICATIONS

Engines: **1952-53** L-head V-8, 255.4 cid (3.19 × 4.00), 125 bhp **1954** ohv V-8, 256 cid (3.62 × 3.10), 161 bhp

Transmissions:	3-speed manual; overdrive and 3-speed Merc-O-Matic optional
Suspension, front:	upper and lower A-arms, coil springs, anti-roll bar
Suspension, rear:	live axle, semi-elliptic leaf springs
Brakes:	front/rear drums
Wheelbase (in.):	118.0
Weight (lbs):	3335-3735
Top speed (mph):	95-100
0-60 mph (sec):	14.0-15.0

Production: **1952 2d sdn** 25,812 **4d sdn** 83,475, including Monterey 4d sdn **4d wgn** 2487 **Sport Coupe 2d htp** 30,599 **Monterey 2d htp** 24,453 **cvt** 5261 **1953 Custom 2d sdn** 50,183 **4d sdn** 59,794 **Sport Coupe 2d htp** 39,547 **Monterey 2d htp** 76,119 **4d sdn** 64,038 **cvt** 8463 **4d wgn** 7719 **1954 Custom 2d sdn** 37,146 **4d sdn** 32,687 **Sport Coupe 2d htp** 15,234 **Monterey 2d htp** 79,533 **Sun Valley 2d htp** 9761 **4d sdn** 65,995 **cvt** 7293 **4d wgn** 11,656

1954
Mercury Sun Valley

"The heart of a city at night gleams with its own stars of neon and marquee. This is a magnificent sight...All the richness and color reaches you. Yet the intensity is softened, filtered by the tint of the plastic roof...You stop for a traffic light. You glance up through the top at the overhead signal. It turns green and you continue your pleasant journey—completely, wonderfully at ease."

The honeyed words came from a brochure Mercury created for the 1954 Monterey Sun Valley. Together with its counterpart, the Ford Crestline Skyliner, it was the first production car with a roof you could see through. Between the two of them, the "glasstops" found 23,000 buyers in 1954. Though Ford's version outsold Mercury's, the Sun Valley expressed the essence of the idea, the best form it ever took.

Of course, the idea had many antecedents. Designers began thinking about "bubbletoppers" in the late 1930s, as plastic began to be accepted as a structural as well as decorative material. John Tjaarda, working for body-builder Briggs, developed the first such application—a one-piece plastic top for a 1939 Plymouth convertible sedan. At Ford after the war, show car predecessors of the Sun Valley were the X-100 and XL-500, the latter a 1953 model with a transparent top bisected by a forward-leaning rollbar. As late as 1956, when the last production Skyliners were rolling off the assembly line, Ford exhibited the Lincoln Futura with its twin plastic cockpits.

Mercury gave the Sun Valley ample publicity, claiming "A freshness of view, a new gaiety and glamour, vast new areas of visibility, a whole new concept of light and luxury...you're comfortably 'out of doors' all year long...with that wonderful feeling of being fashionably first." Actually, much of this happy puffery rang true, with certain qualifications.

The big problem was heat. To keep it down, the plexiglass section had to be tinted sun-glass green (though ads used an untinted type to show off the interior). Thus, the light that filtered inside seemed "kind of weird," according to *Motor Trend,* "and may cause many a young lady to check her makeup. She might as well switch to green lipstick." And, though desert testing claimed only a five-degree-difference between a Sun Valley and a normal hardtop interior, Mercury offered a snap-on interior shade for high summer. Air conditioning, although available in 1954, cost an arm and a leg, so few Sun Valleys had it.

The 1954 Sun Valley came in only two color combinations: yellow or mint green, both combined with a dark green top. Interiors featured yellow and dark green all-vinyl upholstery (which must have been uncomfortable), and white cloth-green vinyl. Gold "Sun Valley" script adorned the front fenders. Sun Valleys cost quite a lot—$2582 in 1954, compared to only about $2150-2250 for the Ford Skyliner.

With its bubbletop, the Sun Valley would have been merely an oddity, but the '54 Mercury was generally an exceptional car. The Ford design generation of 1952-54 was modest for the period: taut, clean, without chromium excesses, smoothly executed, and functional. The '54 emerged cleaner still, especially at the extremities. Its attractive taillights, fared into the rear fenders, could easily be seen from the sides and had fluting similar to that of today's Mercedes, and which deflected road grime. At the front rode a simple, one-bar grille under a crisp hood with a dummy airscoop (probably the only non-functional aspect). The dashboard, likewise clean and honest, featured aircraft-like toggle lever controls.

Mercury also debuted its all-new overhead valve V-8 in 1954; it displaced almost as much volume as its flathead predecessor. But whereas the flathead was a "stroker," the new Merc V-8 boasted an oversquare configuration and developed a lot more power. Its novel four-barrel carburetor featured an inlet vacuum which replaced the mechanical linkage to the two rear venturis, plus dual floats and a concentric fuel bowl. Other mechanical niceties included Mercury's first ball-joint front suspension, only four grease fittings, and more insulation than ever. But the unique feature remained that see-through top. Although all '54 Mercurys had a lot of glass, the Sun Valley offered more square inches of visibility than any other car, including the 1954 Kaiser, which of course had a solid roof.

Mercury would field another Sun Valley in 1955, but whatever market existed had already been satiated, and so it found only 1787 takers. No matter: the original stood out as the best.

Mercury introduced ball-joint front suspension and a new overhead-valve V-8 for its '54 lineup. Also featured, an attractive facelift and a new model, the Sun Valley. Like Ford's '54 Skyliner, it sported a plastic see-through roof. Though it didn't sell particularly well at the time (only 9761 units), collectors avidly seek them out now.

SPECIFICATIONS

Engine:	ohv V-8, 256 cid (3.62 × 3.10), 161 bhp
Transmissions:	3-speed manual; overdrive and Merc-O-Matic optional
Suspension, front:	independent, coil springs, tube shocks
Suspension, rear:	live axle, leaf springs, tube shocks
Brakes:	front/rear drums
Wheelbase (in.):	118.0
Weight (lbs):	3538
Top speed (mph):	100
0-60 mph (sec):	14.0-15.0
Production:	9761

1955-56 Mercury

America bought more cars in 1955 than any previous year—a boom market to rival the early postwar period. Most automakers based their late-Fifties plans on the events of 1955, none more than Ford Motor Company. The medium-price field looked especially strong that year, encouraging a resurgent Dearborn to embark on an expansive "divisionalization" program to match General Motors' five units. This involved splitting up Lincoln-Mercury and creating new divisions to handle the ritzy Continental Mark II and, from late '57, the medium-priced Edsel.

Dearborn's cars were naturally more expansive too, none more than the '55 Mercury. It not only acted like a winner, but was. As on this year's Ford, features included a dramatic facelift on the basic 1952-54 shell and larger, more potent V-8s. But Mercury also grew an inch between wheel centers, to 119 inches, the first such increase since 1942. All this helped Mercury build a whopping 435,000 cars for the calendar year, 100,000 more than its previous best. Model year volume rose by some 70,000 units to near 330,000, though Mercury remained seventh in the industry. The one disappointment was the bubbletop Sun Valley, which tapered off to just 1787 units and would never be seen again.

Reflecting the unbridled optimism of Dearborn's Executive Committee, new Mercury Division chief Jack Reith and car/truck executive vice-president Lewis Crusoe, the '55 Mercs debuted longer, lower, wider, and faster. Offerings proliferated: three series (up one from 1954) spanning 14 models ranging in delivered price from $2700 to $4000. With industry sales at record levels, Mercury had found exactly the right formula.

The new Montclair topped the line, offered as a convertible and a pair of hardtop coupes (regular and Sun Valley). Like all '55s, it carried an evolution of the '54 grille but was distinguished by a thin color panel under the side windows, color-keyed to the roof with two-toning. Next came the Monterey sedan, hardtop, and wagon, then a base Custom series with the same styles plus a price-leader two-door sedan. Like Ford, all wore newly wrapped windshields and sported more "important" lower-body sheetmetal. Mid-season brought a special new Montclair sedan with a more rakish, hardtop-style roofline, really a forecast of the hardtop sedans to come. *Motor Trend* liked it enough to call it the best-looking American sedan of 1955.

SPECIFICATIONS

Engines: ohv V-8 **1955** 292 cid (3.75 × 3.30), 188/198 bhp **1956** 312 cid (3.80 × 3.44), 210/215/225/260 bhp

Transmissions:	3-speed manual; overdrive and 3-speed Merc-O-Matic optional
Suspension, front:	upper and lower A-arms, coil springs, anti-roll bar
Suspension, rear:	live axle, semi-elliptic leaf springs
Brakes:	front/rear drums
Wheelbase (in.):	119.0
Weight (lbs):	3395-3885
Top speed (mph):	105-110
0-60 mph (sec):	10.0-12.5

Production: **1955 Custom 2d htp** 7040 **2d sdn** 31,295 **4d sdn** 21,219 **4d wgn** 14,134 **Monterey 2d htp** 69,093 **4d sdn** 70,392 **4d wgn** 11,968 **Montclair 4d sdn** 20,624 **2d htp** 71,588 **Sun Valley 2d htp** 1787 **cvt** 10,668 **1956 Medalist Phaeton 4d htp** 6685 **Sport Coupe 2d htp** 11,892 **2d sdn** 20,582 **4d sdn** 6653 **Custom Phaeton 4d htp** 12,187 **Sport Coupe 2d htp** 20,857 **2d sdn** 16,343 **4d sdn** 15,860 **cvt** 2311 **4d wgn** 17,770 **Monterey Phaeton 4d htp** 10,726 **4d Sport Sedan** 11,765 **Sport Coupe 2d htp** 42,863 **4d sdn** 26,735 **4d wgn** 13,280 **Montclair Phaeton 4d htp** 23,493 **4d Sport Sedan** 9617 **Sport Coupe 2d htp** 50,562 **cvt** 7762

Mercury adopted bolder, more "important" styling for 1955. The new top-line Montclair series included a two-door hardtop (opposite), *the most popular Merc that year with 71,588 built. Mercury listed four series in 1956, two with convertibles. The lower-price Custom soft top* (above) *listed at $2712, but production reached only 2311 units.*

Also like Ford, the Mercury V-8 was bored and stroked for '55, reaching 292 cubic inches. Custom and Monterey packed 188 bhp with 7.6:1 compression. Standard for Montclairs and optional on others was the high-compression (8.5:1) 198-bhp version teamed with Merc-O-Matic. Brakes were enlarged, and tubeless tires became standard across the board.

In all, the '55 ranked as one of Mercury's best efforts to date—arguably the best in some ways. The 1956 game plan called for more of the same. Mercury delivered, but built far fewer cars, though most other makes also declined as sales cooled off from 1955's torrid pace. Calendar year output fell to about 250,000 units, down some 180,000. However, the model year tally eased by less than 1000, though it left Mercury still stuck in seventh place.

Styling changes for '56 involved a wide "Big M" hood emblem, a bolder front end, more prominently bulged rear fenders, and full-length Z-shape bodyside moldings on Custom, Monterey, and Montclair. (The area below could be keyed to roof color with optional two-toning, though a conventional roof/lower body contrast was also available.) A new cut-rate Medalist series extended Mercury's market coverage downward but, with inflation starting to run, these models cost more than the previous year's Customs. Yet, they weren't priced far enough below this year's Customs to offset their cheaper appearance (no Z-trim, for instance) and reduced standard equipment. Only about 46,000 Medalists went out the door, while the other three lines at least doubled that figure.

Like Ford, Mercury went in for four-door hardtops this year. Arriving at mid-season and called Phaeton, they were offered in all four series. Sales seemed proportional to price: highest as a Montclair, lowest as a Medalist. Mercury also fielded a second convertible, in the Custom series. Priced at $2712, it wasn't nearly as popular as the $2900 Montclair ragtop.

Maintaining power/displacement distance with Ford, Mercury offered three versions of the 292 V-8 enlarged to 312 cid: two-barrel/210 bhp for Medalists and manual-shift Customs, four-barrel/215 bhp for Monterey and Custom automatics, and four-barrel 225 bhp for Montclair and Monterey automatics. A fourth version arrived late in the season with 260 bhp, courtesy of twin four-barrels and higher, 9.7:1 compression.

Of course, all this was necessary to keep pace with the industry's "horsepower race." Mercury moved to the fore by setting 20 new world records in NASCAR-sponsored speed trials at Kingman, Arizona. Mercury also won its class in this year's Grand National contest at Daytona. So for all its many changes over the years, and despite being overshadowed by Lincoln's prowess in the Mexican Road Races, Mercury held its ground as one of Detroit's hottest cars. Come 1957, it would be one of the glitziest.

1957-58 Mercury

Russia put the first artificial satellite into orbit in 1957; Ford gave us the Mercury Turnpike Cruiser. America's huffier social critics said the latter helped explain the former. They blamed all sorts of other things, too, but as a symbol of misapplied technology, the '57 Merc was hard to beat. Veteran tester Tom McCahill called the Cruiser a "Space Age Design for Earth Travel."

The Turnpike Cruiser made its fame as the most begadgeted version of a '57 Mercury that looked like something from another planet. Riding a 122-inch wheelbase, up three inches from 1955-56 and the longest in Merc history, this "Big M" was very big indeed. Wagons tipped the scales at close to two tons. "Bustin' out all over: lower, longer, and wider," said one magazine, and so it was—by five, three, and three inches, respectively. Despite its reduced height, the '57 gained two inches of rear headroom and four up front, thanks to a reworked chassis with side rails spread 14.5 inches further apart, permitting a new step-down floor.

Horsepower kept pace with weight. A single 312 V-8 came standard, but now packing 20 more horses than the '56; the Lincoln 368, detuned to 290 bhp, was standard on the new Turnpike Cruisers, optional elsewhere.

Speaking of which, Custom and Medalist series disappeared, but Monterey and Montclair returned along with a new Station Wagon series with no fewer than six models, all with hardtop-style pillarless rooflines and delivered prices near $5000. Topping this group was the posh ($3700 base) wood-trimmed Colony Park four-door, followed by two- and four-door Voyagers, all trimmed like Montclair. Commuter, with Monterey trim and the lowest prices, came as a nine-seat four-door and six-passenger two- and four-doors.

Styling, created under Don DeLaRossa, was busy to say the least: wild headlamp "brows;" bumpers composed of two massive oblongs; a big, concave projectile on each rear fender ending in canted, wedge-shaped tail lamps. The Cruiser looked even more contrived, previewed by the 1956 XM-Turnpike Cruiser showmobile and thus billed as "a dramatic expression of dream car design." It had, Ford thought, just about everything buyers could want: quad headlamps (where legal), "skylight dual curve windshield," a reverse-slant backlight that retracted for flow-through ventilation, and a forward-facing air intake over each A-pillar with a protruding radio antenna. The last two items applied to the two- and four-door hardtops, of course, but a Convertible Cruiser bowed at mid-year supplied with regalia decals to honor Mercury's selection as the 1957 Indy 500 pace car.

Inside, the Cruiser featured an equally futuristic "Monitor Control Panel" with a tachometer and "Average-Speed Computer Clock" set in round rubber housings, plus pushbuttons for the standard Merc-O-Matic (following Chrysler's 1956 lead). Buyers also got a map showing all U.S. turnpikes as of 1957. But the crowd-pleaser was the optional "Seat-O-Matic" memory power seat, which assumed one of 49 positions at the twist of two dials.

For all its novel glitz, and despite surprisingly good performance and roadability, the Turnpike Cruiser was a sales dud, as the production figures show. Overall, Mercury output sank from almost 328,000 units for 1956 to just over 286,000 for '57, dismal when compared to other medium priced makes (especially Chrysler Corporation's gains). Not surprisingly, the Big M slipped from seventh to eighth place.

As it turned out, the Cruiser forecast a very unpleasant 1958 in which Mercury grimly maintained eighth on 40-percent lower volume, down now to a little over 153,000 units. Sans convertible, the Cruisers became Montclair sub-models, then yielded top-line status at mid-year to the new Park Lane, a 125-inch-wheelbase convertible, hardtop coupe, and hardtop sedan powered by Lincoln's 430 V-8 and priced from $3870 to over $4000. Montclair and Monterey shared a new 383-cid big-block engine and the same minor styling changes. Undermining the junior '58 Edsels was the return of the low-line Medalist with a 235-bhp 312. A desperate effort to attract more buyers, it again failed to impress. All six wagons returned, but did even worse than in '57.

Very simply, the bottom dropped out of the medium-price market in 1958. But getting clubbed on the head gets one's attention, and it got Mercury's. The course was clear: pare down the slow-sellers and, above all, get going on a version of the new compact developing at Ford. Mercury would do both within two years.

A Mercury Convertible Cruiser (opposite, top) *paced the Indianapolis 500 race in 1957. At $4103, it was part of the three-model Turnpike Cruiser series, which also included a $3849 four-door hardtop* (bottom).

SPECIFICATIONS

Engines: ohv V-8 **1957** 312 cid (3.80 × 3.44), 255 bhp; 368 cid (4.00 × 3.66), 290 bhp **1958** 312 cid (3.80 x 3.44), 235 bhp; 383 cid (4.30 × 3.30), 312/330 bhp; 430 cid (4.30 × 3.70), 360/400 bhp

Transmissions:	3-speed manual; overdrive and 3-speed Merc-O-Matic/Multi-Matic optional
Suspension, front:	upper and lower A-arms, coil springs
Suspension, rear:	live axle, semi-elliptic leaf springs
Brakes:	front/rear drums
Wheelbase (in.):	122.0 **1958 Parklane** 125.0
Weight (lbs):	3870-4605
Top speed (mph):	100-115+
0-60 mph (sec):	8.5-13.0

Production: **1957 Monterey Phaeton 4d htp** 22,475 **4d sdn** 53,839 **Phaeton 2d htp** 42,199 **2d sdn** 33,982 **Phaeton cvt** 5033 **Montclair Phaeton 4d htp** 21,567 **4d sdn** 19,836 **Phaeton 2d htp** 30,111 **Phaeton cvt** 4248 **Turnpike Cruiser 2d htp** 7291 **4d htp** 8305 **Convertible Cruiser** 1265 **Commuter 2d wgn** 4885 **Commuter 4d wgn** 11,990 **Commuter 4d wgn 9P** 5752 **Voyager 2d wgn** 2283 **Voyager 4d wgn** 3716 **Colony Park 4d wgn 9P** 7386 **1958 Medalist 2d sdn** 7750 **4d sdn** 10,982 **Monterey Phaeton 4d htp** 26,909 **4d sdn** 28,892 **Phaeton 2d htp** 13,693 **2d sdn** 10,526 **cvt** 2292 **Montclair Phaeton 4d htp** 3609 **4d sdn** 4801 **Phaeton 2d htp** 5012 **cvt** 844 **Turnpike Cruiser 4d htp** 2864 **2d htp** 3543 **Park Lane Phaeton 4d htp** 5241 **Phaeton 2d htp** 3158 **cvt** 853 **Commuter 2d wgn** 1912 **Commuter 4d wgn** 8601 **Commuter 4d wgn 9P** 4227 **Voyager 2d wgn** 568 **Voyager 4d wgn** 2520 **Colony Park 4d wgn 9P** 4474

MERCURY
OFFICIAL
PACE CAR
INDIANAPOLIS 500-MILE RACE

1959 Mercury

Given Detroit's usual three- to four-year lead times, it's clear that the 1959 Mercury was more or less cast in the still-heady medium-price market of 1956-57. The resulting package thus turned out bigger than ever, in the spirit of those times. Yet there must have been some recognition among division planners that they'd perhaps gone too far with the 1957-58 models, for the '59 Merc seemed somehow cleaner and more tasteful overall.

It definitely loomed larger. Bodies were all-new for the second time after two years and again exclusive to Mercury (senior non-wagon '58 Edsels shared Mercury's 1957-58 shells). The existing drop-center "cow-belly" chassis was widened six inches amidships and stretched four inches between wheel centers for all but the top-shelf Park Lane, where wheelbase grew three inches.

The last, returning from '58 with the same three body styles, delivered for close to $5000 but evidently wasn't what the public wanted, as only about 12,000 buyers drove one home, including just 1254 who chose the convertible. Monterey stood pat, but the mid-range Montclair was pared down to just three models with the demise of its convertible and the ill-starred Turnpike Cruisers. Station wagons withered to four. The cheap Medalist vanished again as Edsel became part of a reformed Lincoln-Mercury Division, where it served as the price-leader line.

Big-M styling for '59 couldn't be mistaken for anything: blocky front ends, big missile-like upper-bodyside sculptures running aft from the A-posts, and sharply creased, slightly "finny" rear fenders ending in large pie-wedge tail lamps above a dummy back panel grille. The huge, compound-curve windshield boasted 60 percent more glass area than in 1957-58, so wipers were duly lengthened from 12 to 16 inches. They swept in parallel rather than "clap-hands" fashion, one of the first American cars to adopt this feature. Rear windows on the hardtops grew even larger than the new windshield, wrapped around to match reverse-angle C-pillars. Sedan backlights wrapped fully around to the C-posts beneath a heavy-looking overhang.

The Park Lane was Mercury's flagship in 1959. The two-door hardtop seen here weighed in at 4311 pounds, boasted a 430-cid V-8, and carried a list price of $3955—some $137 more than the equivalent Buick Electra. At those prices, sales were slow; only 4060 two-door hardtops found buyers.

SPECIFICATIONS

Engines:	ohv V-8, 312 cid (3.80 × 3.44), 210/280 bhp; 383 cid (4.30 × 3.30), 280/322 bhp; 430 cid (4.30 × 3.70), 345 bhp
Transmission:	3-speed manual; overdrive, Merc-O-Matic (standard on Montclair), and Multi-Drive Merc-O-Matic (standard on Park Lane) optional
Suspension, front:	upper and lower A-arms, coil springs
Suspension, rear:	live axle, semi-elliptic leaf springs
Brakes:	front/rear drums
Wheelbase (in.):	126.0 **Parklane** 128.0
Weight (lbs):	3914-4535
Top speed (mph):	95-110
0-60 mph (sec):	9.5-11.5

Production: **Monterey 4d htp** 11,355 **4d sdn** 45,370 **2d htp** 17,232 **2d sdn** 12,694 **cvt** 4426 **Montclair 4d htp** 6713 **4d sdn** 9514 **2d htp** 7375 **Park Lane 4d htp** 7206 **2d htp** 4060 **cvt** 1254 **Commuter 2d wgn** 1051 **Commuter 4d wgn** 15,122 **Voyager 4d wgn** 2496 **Colony Park 4d wgn** 5929

Mercury took advantage of its bigger '59 bodies to offer "Space-Planned" interiors. The dash, new and still imposing, sat further forward than before, opening up extra leg- and kneeroom that enhanced the '59's airier feel. Also contributing to both real and imagined spaciousness were a lower transmission hump, narrower door sills (which widened the rear footwells by 4.4 inches), wider front doors, and that monster windshield with its less severely angled "dogleg" A-pillars.

Bigger chassis aside, technical changes for the 20th-anniversary Mercurys were fairly minor. Engines remained about the same but, in a fast turnaround prompted by the '58 recession, got lower compression for improved economy. The great "horsepower race" had ended, at least temporarily. Montereys carried a 312 V-8 with 210 standard horsepower, 280 optional; Park Lane still used the Lincoln 430, detuned by 15 bhp; Commuter wagons packed a 280-bhp 383, while a 322-bhp version came standard on other models. Conventional column-lever automatic-transmission control returned as Mercury backed away from faddish pushbuttons after only two seasons (unlike Chrysler, where they'd persist for another six years). Suspension changes included wider, longer rear leaf springs, and front upper A-arms tilted downward slightly to resist nosedive in hard braking.

It's worth mentioning that the fancy Park Lane was a remnant of Jack Reith's original 1955 model-line plans that, among other things, called for a "super Mercury" to battle Chrysler and the Buick Roadmaster. But the events of the intervening four years had rendered this and the rest of Reith's "divisionalization" scheme just so much pipe dreaming. Worse, Mercury's 1959 production actually fell by about 4000 units from the dismal '58 figure despite an improving national economy. At less than 150,000, a separate Mercury body and chassis—let alone a unique "super" line—simply cost too much to sustain.

So, after a restyled 1960 reprise, and with Edsel's demise in late '59, the Big M would return to being a senior Ford. By that time the low-cost Comet compact had arrived, providing much-needed support until the medium-priced market firmed up again around 1962.

In the end, Ford overreached itself by trying to institute a GM-style five-division structure in 1957-58. Had this been inaugurated, say, three years before or three years later, when the medium-price field was healthy, the Edsel—and maybe even that "super Mercury"—might still be with us. But then, as movie mogul Sam Goldwyn said, "It's always dangerous to make predictions—especially about the future!"

1951-54 Muntz Jet

Earl "Madman" Muntz took over the Kurtis sports car, modified it, and moved production from California to Evanston, Illinois. There he built almost 500 Muntz Jets. Powered by Lincoln or Cadillac V-8s, they were quite fast for their day, and luxurious as well. Muntz lost about $1000 on each car he built, which prompted him to quit the automobile business in 1954.

The Muntz Jet was one of the many interesting "shoestring" cars that sprang up in the boom economy of the late '40s and early '50s, when most anyone with a dream and a little money thought he could make it big in the car business. The dreamer here was Earl "Madman" Muntz, the successful, irrepressible radio/TV maker whose wild-and-woolly advertising techniques had also made him Southern California's biggest—not to mention most flamboyant—used-car dealer by the early '50s. ("I wanna give 'em away but Mrs. Muntz won't let me. She's ca-RAAA-zy!")

It all started in 1948 with Frank Kurtis, famed since the late Twenties as a designer of highly competitive race cars (many of them dirt-track midgets), who decided to apply his enormous talents to a street sports car. The result, called Kurtis Sport, emerged as a slab sided two-seat convertible that was unusual for its day for having a unit body/chassis with just 10 outer panels, all aluminum except for a fiberglass hood and rear deck. Appearance was bulbous, but pleasing on a tight 100-inch wheelbase. Safety features included a full-perimeter rub rail and a large bumper/grille mounted on rubber shock absorbers (a forecast of the "safety" bumpers we'd love to hate in the Seventies). The handsomely furnished cockpit sported full instrumentation ahead of a big steering wheel on an axially adjustable column. Side windows were clumsy, clip-in Plexiglas affairs, but a removable rigid top supplemented the expected soft top.

Like interior hardware, the Kurtis' suspension and running gear were mainly proprietary components, though Frank tuned spring and damper rates for optimum handling and roadholding. The powerteam could be most anything the buyer wanted, though 239-cubic-inch Ford flathead V-8s with Edelbrock manifolds lurked under the hood of most examples. The Sport was also offered as a kit at $1495-$3495, depending on completeness.

Lightweight gave the Sport good go despite the flathead's power, and reviewers loved the car's nimbleness and stability. But Kurtis-Kraft was a small outfit, building cars largely—and slowly—by hand, so sales were as sparse as profits. Thus, after

SPECIFICATIONS

Engines: Cadillac ohv V-8, 331 cid (3.81 × 3.63), 160 bhp; Lincoln L-head V-8, 336.7 cid (3.50 × 4.38), 154 bhp; Lincoln ohv V-8, 317.5 cid (3.80 × 3.50), 160 bhp

Transmissions:	GM 4-speed Hydra-Matic; Borg-Warner 3-speed manual with overdrive optional
Suspension, front:	upper and lower A-arms, coil springs
Suspension, rear:	live axle, semi-elliptic leaf springs
Brakes:	front/rear drums
Wheelbase (in.):	113.0; 116.0
Weight (lbs):	approximately 3780
Top speed (mph):	108*
0-60 mph (sec):	12.3*
Production:	490 estimated

*with L-head Lincoln V-8 and Hydra-Matic, which were apparently fitted to most examples

seeing just 36 Sports out the door through 1950, Frank sold his Glendale, California operation to the "Madman" for $200,000.

Muntz set about making the Sport more salable, retaining its basic styling but adding 13 inches to the wheelbase, a back seat, and more conveniences. This meant extra weight, so Cadillac's new 160-horsepower, 331-cid overhead-valve V-8 replaced the Ford flathead. The result could lay claim to being America's first high-performance personal-luxury car. Muntz simply called it the Jet.

Working out of the former Kurtis plant, Muntz built 28 Jets before moving the operation to his hometown of Evanston, Illinois, just north of Chicago, and making more substantial design changes. The aluminum body—"It would dent if you leaned against it," as he told *Collectible Automobile®* in 1985—gave way to a steel shell riding a two-inch longer wheelbase. Curiously, the modern Cadillac engine was ditched for the older Lincoln flathead V-8, albeit modified with solid lifters (replacing hydraulics) from the Ford truck version. GM Hydra-Matic transmission became standard, though Borg-Warner stick-overdrive was optionally available.

"We tooled that car for $75,000," Muntz recalled. But labor costs came to a monumental $2000 per unit because body panels had to be carefully fitted, then leaded-in, and meticulous detailing was required elsewhere. "Today the labor in that s.o.b. would run 20 grand!" he said in 1985. The actual costs were bad enough. "I lost $400,000 on that project before we closed it down in 1954"—about $1000 per car. "They cost $6500 apiece to build, and at that price they wouldn't sell. At $5500 I couldn't make enough of 'em, but I couldn't afford to keep it up."

The Evanston cars weighed 400 pounds more than the Glendale Jets, but were more durable. Both versions were quite quick. Seatbelts and dash padding came standard, years before Ford tried selling safety, and the Madman proudly pointed to the Jet's fully boxed perimeter frame. "The goddamn thing was built like a tank," he proclaimed. "Had we continued, I think we'd have lightened it. If you ever had one...in a demolition derby, it'd ruin everything!" Toward the end, Muntz switched to fiberglass fenders and Lincoln's new ohv V-8.

Even Earl didn't seem to know for sure, but it's estimated that some 490 Jets were built in all, of which at least 49 have survived. Undaunted by his relative failure in the car business, Muntz again concentrated on manufacturing—and hawking—radios and TVs, ever optimistic, ever successful, ever "ca-RAAA-zy." Later he'd pioneer the stereo cartridge tape and big-screen television. "My work is my hobby, my love, my life," he once said. Sadly, that colorful life came to an end in late 1987, and we're all a little poorer for it.

1950-51 Nash Ambassador

Every once in awhile the media reiterates its theme of "Oh-but-it-was-awful-in-the-bad-old-Fifties." If you're just lucky, you might catch a docu-drama picturing a circa 1950 drive-in theater; while the narrator drones on about the horrors of Fifties cars, the camera will pan over a fleet largely composed of Nash Airflytes.

Was the Airflyte as bad as they imply? And how come there were so many of them parked at the drive-in? The answers, are "certainly not" and "read on."

Nash-Kelvinator—the company that built it—perennially marched to a different drummer, a clear-cut free thinker. Nash offered the first production postwar American sports car in 1951, the first modern compact in 1950, the first subcompact in 1954. Nash's George Mason, the only independent executive who could see beyond his nose, led an attempt to bring all the independents together before they collapsed individually. As to the Airflyte, while it wasn't the only rounded automotive shape around, it was different—radically different. For one thing, it was genuinely aerodynamic. For another, only Nash among the independents built an overhead-valve engine. For a third, with the sole exception of Hudson, Nash favored the unit body/chassis. All these concepts proved to be the wave of the future—ironically, long after Nash had disappeared from the automotive scene.

Nils Erik Wahlberg designed the Airflyte, with important input from Holden Koto and Ted Pietsch. Wahlberg, who had joined Nash in 1916, retired shortly after the car appeared; it was his final effort—wildly daring.

Think about it: nobody—but nobody—had a shape this radical in 1950: not the Big Three, not even Studebaker. Nobody had a car so honest. The look was not just

Nobody out-bathtubbed Nash in the 1949-51 era, but at least Nash could lay claim to having the most aerodynamic car on the road at the time. The top-line Nash in 1950 was the $2223 Ambassador Custom four-door sedan (this page). *It boasted a 112-bhp overhead-valve six. The '51 received a vertical-bar grille and squared-up rear fenders. The $1955 Statesman Super* (opposite) *rode a nine-inch-shorter wheelbase and was powered by a smaller 85-bhp L-head six.*

SPECIFICATIONS

Engine: ohv I-6, 234.8 cid (3.38 × 4.38) **1950** 112 bhp **1951** 115 bhp

Transmission:	3-speed manual; overdrive and 4-speed Hydra-Matic optional
Suspension, front:	independent, coil springs, tube shocks
Suspension, rear:	live axle, coil springs, tube shocks
Brakes:	front/rear drums
Wheelbase (in.):	121.0
Weight (lbs):	3325-3445
Top speed (mph):	95
0-60 mph (sec):	18.0-20.0

Production: Breakdowns not available; of model year registrations of 171,782 (1950) and 205,307 (1951), about 20 percent were Ambassadors

a look; its aerodynamics were factual: 113 pounds of drag at 60 mph, the best in the industry (compared to, say, 171 pounds for the similar looking but non-aerodynamic 1950 Packard). And who else but Nash offered seatbelts in 1950?

Then there was the Uniscope, a novel device that housed all the instruments and most controls in a teardrop-shaped unit mounted on the steering column. The only part Uniscope couldn't fit was the radio, which stayed on the dashboard. Even there, it was considered so intrusive that it came with a sliding panel to hide it from the view of aesthetic-minded Nash occupants.

Airflytes also boasted a one-piece curved windshield, when most other cars had a two-piece unit, many of them still using flat glass. And all Airflytes featured unique fully reclining front seatbacks (pneumatic mattresses were sold as accessories). The seats, together with the "Weather-Eye" fresh air heating/ventilation system, made the Nash Airflyte the most habitable long-distance touring car built in America. The reclining seats also made it the only car you could convert into a small bedroom—which explains why so many Airflytes were seen at drive-in movies.

For 1950-51, Nash offered the Airflyte in two lines, Statesman and Ambassador, on short and long wheelbases and with small and large six-cylinder engines. The Statesman, with its small six and short wheelbase, was underpowered and chunky, but the 121-inch-wheelbase Ambassador carried better proportions and could cruise all day at 90 mph. Prices started at just over $2300 and rose to about $2700 delivered for the most expensive Ambassador in 1951. There were few styling changes, although the 1951s are easily identified by their "kicked-up" rear fenders and vertical-bar grille.

The Nash Airflyte sold better than any big car in Nash history. In its first year, 1949, counting cheaper models, the Airflyte accounted for 135,000 units, which put Nash in an unaccustomed tenth place in production. Volume in 1950 and 1951 rose to the highest levels Nash had ever recorded: 172,000 and 205,000 units, respectively. Though this included increasing numbers of Ramblers, it did indicate that a car so often ridiculed today could be both popular and well ahead of the field in many areas when it was new.

1950-52 Nash Rambler

Building a small, affordable car for people who could never in the past afford to buy one new, has been the recurrent American dream since the Twenties, when the Model T Ford finally wound up production. The decade wasn't out before Nash had fielded the Ajax, Hudson the Essex, Willys the Whippet, Chrysler the Plymouth, and Studebaker the Erskine. Of these, only the Plymouth succeeded permanently, although Essex served as a strong prop to Hudson for awhile. The rest quickly foundered, unable to compete with Ford and Chevrolet, which were offering larger cars for the same money, capitalizing on their economies of scale.

After World War II, the dream took root again, although in hindsight it's obvious it was premature. As is now known, Chrysler, Ford, and General Motors successively looked at and canceled plans to build a "people's car." Two independents tried — Kaiser with the Henry J, Hudson with the Jet—and failed miserably. One other independent succeeded. To nobody's surprise, the success belonged to Nash.

As *Mechanix Illustrated*'s inimitable road tester Tom McCahill put it, Nash was "busier than a mouse in a barrel of hungry cats" after the war with its many, varied projects: the Nash-Healey, the American Motors merger, the mini-car project that resulted in the Metropolitan, the Nash-Healey, the radical Airflyte passenger cars, and the Nash Rambler. Though the last sold fewer than 10,000 copies in its first year, the Rambler came to enjoy a larger and larger share of Nash production, and by the mid-Fifties began to rocket American Motors into serious contention as the fourth component of a new "Big Four." Indeed, by 1958 AMC had forgotten all about "standard size" cars and had converted entirely to building Ramblers.

Nash's George Mason was simply smarter than all the other independent managers combined. Alone among them, he realized that his smallish company could not compete toe to toe on cost with the Big Three—that any Nash small car would

SPECIFICATIONS

Engine:	sidevalve I-6, 172.6 cid (3.13 × 3.75), 82 bhp
Transmission:	3-speed manual; overdrive optional
Suspension, front:	independent, coil springs, tube shocks
Suspension, rear:	live axle, leaf springs, tube shocks
Brakes:	front/rear drums
Wheelbase (in.):	100.0
Weight (lbs):	2420-2515
Top speed (mph):	85
0-60 mph (sec):	19.0
Production:	**1950** 9330; other figures not available

probably end up selling for roughly the price of a Chevy. This meant that a stark, detrimmed compact like the Henry J, for example, ultimately wouldn't stand a chance. Mason was the philosophic soulmate of Kaiser-Frazer's former president Joseph W. Frazer, who had wanted "to bring the Henry J out dressed up—and undress it afterwards."

So Mason opted for a different game plan: a small car that would be unique in many ways other than size. Defying all the laws of conventional logic, he brought out the Rambler—not as a cheap and basic two- or four-door sedan—but as a *convertible* and a neat little all-steel *station wagon.* A hardtop joined the line in 1951. The tactic worked brilliantly.

In retrospect it seems so obvious—but it really wasn't apparent then. The cheapest convertible on the market in 1950 (if you don't count the Willys Jeepster, and few did) was the Chevrolet at about $1850. The cheapest wagon, Plymouth's Suburban, sold for about the same price. Mason beat them both—the Rambler came in at $1808 for either the convertible or the wagon. Fifty dollars, of course, meant a lot more then than it does now, but Nash had additional weapons, too. First off, the Rambler had the advantage of being all new, whereas the others had to make do with facelifts of their '49 models. Rambler featured unit body/chassis construction, which Nash trumpeted as rattle free and far superior to the typical body-on-frame method. And finally, Nash's famous "Weather-Eye" heating/ventilating system was decidedly better than anything else around at the time.

Now 9000-odd sales wouldn't much impress Chevrolet or Plymouth—the latter accounted for about 20,000 Suburbans that same year—and it represented only about one-eighth of the Henry J's first-year sales. But as time wore on and Henry J faltered, Rambler carved out a strong and devoted public. It proved to be well built, durable, and backed by a strong dealer network (probably the best among independents). By 1955, it accounted for the lion's share of Nash/Hudson sales.

Though its styling obviously took inspiration from the then-current Airflytes, the little Rambler was the antithesis of the big bathtubs. Its wheelbase measured only 100 inches and it weighed only about 2500 pounds. And despite a small six with just 82 horsepower, it performed very well: 0-60 mph in 19 seconds and up to 30 miles per gallon when driven conservatively. Also, it would cruise happily at 80 mph, which was certainly more than the four-cylinder Henry J could do.

Nash president George W. Mason introduced the compact Rambler on April 14, 1950 with a single model, the $1808 Custom Convertible Landau (opposite). *It featured a 100-inch wheelbase and "bridge beam" rails over the windows. A small two-door wagon bowed on June 23. In June 1951, the Custom Country Club hardtop* (this page) *joined the lineup.*

1951-55 Nash-Healy

It's hard to imagine a more unlikely combination than George Mason and Donald Healey. Big George made his mark in the appliance business, came to Nash before World War II by way of the Kelvinator annexation, and in 1945 replaced Charles W. Nash as president. Donald Healey, the smiling Cornishman, was an amateur mechanic turned rally driver who dreamed about building his own ultimate sports car. After the war, Healey *did* build cars using chassis and bodies of his own design and 2.5-liter Riley engines. About 500 sedans, roadsters, convertibles, and coupes left his factory from 1946-51, 20 percent of them "Silverstones": light, fast, cycle-fendered two-seaters that performed brilliantly in European competition.

Mason and Healey met on a U.S.-bound voyage on the Queen Elizabeth, hit it off, and hatched an idea. Why not build a Nash-based two-seater powered by the big Ambassador six? The result emerged as one of the first Anglo-American sports hybrids. The Ambassador engine, a strong, modern, overhead-valve unit, took to a fair amount of "hotting up," so Healey fitted a pair of British SU carbs, hot cam, and an 8.0:1 compression aluminum cylinder head. It developed 125 bhp at 4000 rpm. Healey combined the three-speed Nash transmission with Borg-Warner overdrive, hammered out a racing body, and entered the car in Italy's Mille Miglia, finishing ninth in class. Two Healeys then competed at Le Mans, one finishing fourth overall. A year later a lone Nash-Healey took sixth overall and fourth in class.

For the production sports car, the British firm Panelcraft Limited built bodies based on Healey's roadster styling. Healey's company in Warwickshire did the rest. A Nash grille, bumpers, and headlights rode up front for identification, along with Nash badging. Output started in mid-1950, and the car was shown at the fall London and Paris shows, and in Chicago in February 1951. By that time, Healey was shipping 10 cars a week to the U.S. The '51 price tag of $4063—twice as much as an Ambassador—included an adjustable steering wheel and leather upholstery. Nash sold 104 Healeys for 1951—not many, but worth it in publicity since Nash had a sports car on the road years before the two-seaters from Ford, GM, and the other independents.

Mason didn't care much for Healey's aluminum, slab-sided British body with its two-piece, flat-pane windshield. Thus, he called on Pinin Farina, the Italian coachbuilder that had been involved with the all-new 1952 Nash Airflytes, to give the '52 model some Italian flair. The new Nash-Healey sported inboard-mounted headlights flanking a two-bar grille. Mason liked it so well that he asked his stylists to do something similar on the big Nash for 1955. The one-piece windshield on the Farina body was curved, while the rear fenders were bulged to break up the slab sides. The body, now of steel, was cheaper to make, easier to repair, and careful engineering kept weight almost the same. Although the '52 sold for much more, now $5688, production increased to 150 units for the model year.

The Nash-Healey competed in both the Mille Miglia and Le Mans again in '52. In the former, a coupe driven by Donald Healey and his son Geoff crashed, but Leslie Johnson and William McKenzie finished fourth in class and seventh overall. Le Mans really shined as Nash-Healey's finest hour, however. Donald entered two cars, an open '51 model for Johnson and Tommy Wisdom, the 1950 prototype for Pierre Veyron and Yves Giraud-Cabantous. Strategy called for the Healeys to run a conservative race, hoping that the more powerful leaders would drop out. Veyron's car retired, but the strategy worked for Johnson/Wisdom as the Talbots, Aston Martins, and Jaguars gradually quit. Two Mercedes didn't, though, leaving the Nash-Healey to finish third overall—averaging over 90 mph and 13 miles to the gallon.

Nash sold 162 Healeys for 1953, including a longer-wheelbase coupe. Probably the prettiest of all, it was named Le Mans in honor of the great 1952 performance. The convertible disappeared for '54, but the coupe received modifications: a three-piece wraparound rear window and rear side glass raked back at the top. A total of 90 coupes were built, although a few leftovers were registered as 1955 models.

Nash-Healey never achieved enough volume to warrant further development, and Nash lost about $2 for every $1 the car took in. Possibly it would have been more successful if sold by specialist sports-car dealers, and at lower prices.

Of the 506 Nash-Healeys built, well over half survive today, largely through the work of an enthusiastic Nash-Healey club. Beauty is a personal matter, but to many the '51 Nash-Healey looks purer and cleaner, if more slab-sided, than its successor. Still, the steel-bodied Pinin Farina cars are easier to repair, although more vulnerable to rust. Body differences aside, the Nash-Healey made its mark as a simple, straightforward, genuine sports car that proved its worth on the road as well as on the track—a monument to the clear thinking of the late, great George Mason and the brilliant competitive mind of Donald Healey.

The Nash-Healey, one of the first Anglo-American sports hybrids sold in the U.S., came about because British rally driver/car builder Donald Healey and George Mason of Nash hit it off on a trip across the Atlantic. The resulting car was built in England but used the Nash Ambassador overhead-valve six and other Nash components. In 1953, both a roadster (above) *and a Le Mans coupe* (opposite, bottom) *were offered, although total production came to only 162 units that year. Ultimately, 506 Nash-Healeys were built.*

SPECIFICATIONS

Engines: ohv I-6 **1951** 234.8 cid (3.38 × 4.38), 125 bhp **1952-55** 252.6 cid (3.50 × 4.38), 135 bhp

Transmission:	3-speed manual with overdrive
Suspension, front:	independent, coil springs, tube shocks
Suspension, rear:	live axle, leaf springs, tube shocks
Brakes:	front/rear drums
Wheelbase (in.):	**cvt** 102.0 **cpe** 108.0
Weight (lbs):	**1951** 2690 **1952-55 cvt** 2750 **cpe** 2990
Top speed (mph):	102-105
0-60 mph (sec):	11.0-12.0
Production:	**1951** 104 **1952** 150 **1953** 162 **1954-55** 90

NASH CAR CLUB
CALIFORNIA
CJM NH
OF AMERICA

DUAL JETFIRE

1952-54 Nash

Nash, like Packard, Lincoln, Mercury, and future partner Hudson, chose the "bathtub look" for its first postwar restyle, but its 1949 Airflyte—big, bulbous, and rather clumsy—aged as rapidly as the others. By 1951 it was as dated as last year's Paris fashions. In the heady prosperity of those times, Americans were nothing if not style-conscious.

And in particular, they were increasingly conscious of European design. Helped by a rising tide of imports, buyers were learning that cars didn't need contrived sheetmetal and tons of chrome to be attractive. Studebaker's continuing collaboration with the French-born Raymond Loewy, the prewar Packards and postwar Kaisers created by the globe-trotting Dutch Darrin and, most recently, the first Chrysler show cars executed to Virgil Exner's designs by Ghia in Italy all helped introduce Americans to the virtues of "Eurostyle."

George Mason, forever described as the cigar-chomping president of Nash-Kelvinator, had also been thinking international, cooking up a smart two-seat sports car with Englishman Donald Healey for 1951. So it was, perhaps, inevitable that Mason would seek design inspiration from a European coachbuilder.

He found it at the Turin works of Giovan Battista "Pinin" Farina, which supplied two prototypes that led to a totally restyled senior Nash for 1952 (the firm's compact Rambler had seen little change since its 1950 debut). Despite the Italian connection featured in advertising and on the cars (via discreet PF badges), the production design was largely the work of Nash's own Edmund A. Anderson. The only Farina elements retained were a square, vertical-bar grille and a three-element rear window wrapped to reverse-curve C-pillars, and the PF "signatures" seen on many of its Ferrari bodies at the time. Farina himself seemed happy to take credit for Anderson's work in public—likely to Ed's chagrin—but must have blanched at the result in private: square, slab-sided, and bearing the curious semi-skirted front wheels worn by every Nash since late 1948 save the Healey roadster. The last were dictated by Mason, who liked them for some reason. Buyers didn't, as they made for tedious tire-changing and mile-wide U-turns.

Despite all that, the "Farina" Nash was a good-looker for 1952—tastefully restrained outside, comfortably roomy inside—a good thing, as there was little else to get excited about. Models grouped into Statesman and Ambassador series as before, each offering a pair of sedans in Super and Custom trim plus a coupe. The last was now a pillarless Custom, nicely named Country Club—the big Nash had finally gotten in on the hardtop craze. Statesman had been put on a shorter wheelbase earlier and continued with same for '52, only it was now 2.3 inches longer, which together with the new styling made the junior models far less dumpy. Ambassador's span was stretched a nominal 0.3-inch.

Nash had dropped straight eights after the war to concentrate on its long-stroke sixes. These continued, too, but the Statesman's 184-cubic-incher got an even longer stroke that added 11.6 cid—and just three horsepower; a bore stretch gave the Ambassador's overhead-valve unit 18 more cubes and only five extra horses. Performance, needless to say, was tepid, but Nash's forte was long-distance comfort, thanks to exclusives like "Weather-Eye" heating/ventilation and front seatbacks that could be fully reclined to form a makeshift bed (ever worrisome to fathers with teenage daughters). Among new features for '52 were a handy full-width parcel net above the windshield, a rather overstyled symmetrical dashboard, and a fuel cap concealed behind a flip-up starboard tail lamp, a novelty that had probably been inspired by Cadillac.

Like other Detroit makes, Nash saw much lower 1952 production, owing to the government restrictions brought on by the Korean conflict, though it still ranked 10th, a position achieved the previous year. Unlike most rivals, Nash volume continued dropping, sinking to below 100,000 by 1954. An all-out Ford/Chevy sales blitz had something to do with that, but so did a relative lack of change—and the lack of a V-8 for the burgeoning horsepower race.

Nash did what it could, giving the '53 Statesman a revised "Powerflyte" six with 12 extra ponies and pumping up the Ambassador's "Super Jetfire" unit with optional twin carburetors into a 140-bhp "Dual Jetfire." The following year brought an attractive "floating" grille with concave bars, plus newly optional power steering and brakes, "Power-Lift" electric windows and, for Custom hardtops and four doors, a "continental kit."

But it was too little, too late. By April 1954, the visionary Mason had arranged a merger with Hudson to form American Motors, thus partly realizing his dream of uniting the four major independents to battle the Big Three. But Mason died in October before he could bring in Studebaker and Packard, which themselves merged that year, and his successor, George Romney, would soon bet AMC's survival entirely on compacts. Though the Farina design wasn't quite finished, Nash itself did not have long to live.

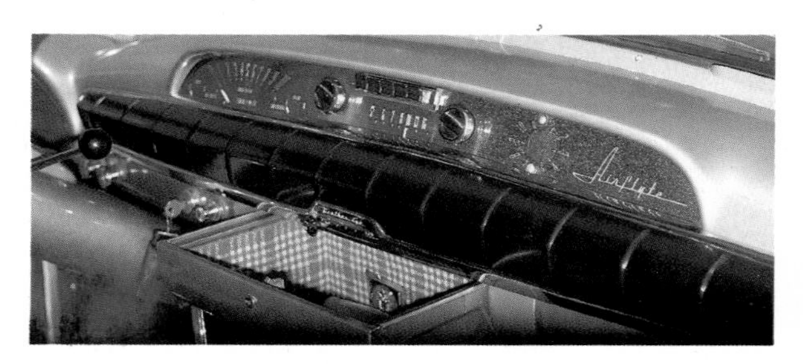

The 1952 Nash sported an all-new body, designed at least in part by Pinin Farina (and so badged). It was much squarer, but the grille and the skirted front wheels made it clearly a Nash. The Ambassador Super seen here retailed for $2557. Its 252.6-cid overhead-valve six turned out 120 horsepower, helping make it an extremely comfortable highway cruiser.

SPECIFICATIONS

Engines: **Statesman** L-head I-6, 195.6 cid (3.13 × 4.25) **1952** 88 bhp **1953** 100 bhp **1954** 110 bhp **Ambassador** ohv I-6, 252.6 cid (3.50 × 4.38) **1952-53** 120 bhp **1954** 130 bhp **1953-54** 140 bhp ("Le Mans Dual Jetfire" twin-carburetor option)

Transmission:	3-speed manual; overdrive and GM Dual-Range Hydra-Matic optional
Suspension, front:	upper and lower A-arms, coil springs
Suspension, rear:	live axle **Statesman** semi-elliptic leaf springs **Ambassador** coil springs
Brakes:	front/rear drums
Wheelbase (in.):	**Statesman** 114.3 **Ambassador** 121.3
Weight (lbs):	3025-3575
Top speed (mph):	85-95
0-60 mph (sec):	14.0-17.0

Production: **1952** 154,291* **1953** 121,793* **1954** 91,121*
*including Rambler and Nash-Healey

NASH CAR CLUB
CRUZ 52

NASH CAR CLUB
CALIFORNIA
CRUZ 52

1953-55 Nash Rambler

With the big Nash being redesigned for 1952, Nash held pat with the rounded, tubby styling on the concurrent Rambler. For 1953, though, Nash came back with a new, updated Rambler design, also claimed (with great exaggeration) to be the work of Pinin Farina. Actually, it was mainly done by Nash stylist Ed Anderson, who gets blamed for all the excesses of Nash in those years, while Pinin Farina gets the glory. The facts are that Nash hoped to benefit from the magic of the great Italian name, but that Farina had limited input on any Nash design.

Smoothly styled and obviously Nash with its skirted front wheels, the Rambler remained a four-body car in 1953—two wagons, convertible, and hardtop. But its sales soared again for the third straight year, and for 1954 it became the dominating model in the Nash lineup. No fewer than ten different variants were listed, in DeLuxe, Super, and Custom trim, broadly priced to undercut the Big Three at one end ($1550 base for the Deluxe two-door), and no higher than $2050 at the other (Custom Cross Country station wagon). Nash, doing just what Joseph W. Frazer had recommended for the Henry J, carved out a niche with the original convertible and wagon, expanded the line, then reached downmarket later with a basic two-door sedan. In fact, the two- and four-door sedans didn't come on the scene until 1954.

Another plus for this series of Ramblers is that they could be ordered with Hydra-Matic transmission ($179), supplied by General Motors. This incidentally gives lie to the perennial claim that GM worked to eliminate the independents—if there was ever an independent that might have threatened GM, it was Nash's Rambler.

Still, though, the Rambler remained true to Mason's original precepts. It didn't qualify as a true economy car, except by virtue of its fuel economy. "The word

The 1953 Nash Rambler was restyled to look more like the '52 full-size Nash, and 108-inch-wheelbase four-door sedans and wagons joined the lineup in 1954. The '55 models shown here featured a crosshatch grille and newly exposed front wheels. Note the Nash and *Hudson emblems in the grille.*

SPECIFICATIONS

Engines: sidevalve I-6 **1953 manual, 1954 2d manual** 184.0 cid (3.13 × 4.00), 85 bhp **1953 auto, 1954 2d/4d auto, 1955** 195.6 cid (3.13 × 4.25), 90 bhp **1955 Fleet** 100 bhp

Transmission:	3-speed manual, overdrive and Hydra-Matic optional
Suspension, front:	independent, coil springs, tube shocks
Suspension, rear:	live axle, leaf springs, tube shocks
Brakes:	front/rear drums
Wheelbase (in.):	100.0 **1954-55 4d** 108.0
Weight (lbs):	2400-2700
Top speed (mph):	85
0-60 mph (sec):	**manual** 18.0-19.0 **automatic** 22.0-25.0

Production: 1953 approximately 90,000 **1954** 70,000 **1955** 100,000

economy is most generally used to describe a low-priced, functional small car in which comfort, performance, and appointments have been sacrificed to keep the price down," recorded *Motor Trend*. "The Rambler does not fall into this class....You may be right in calling it a 'light car,' since it has a shipping weight of only 2655 pounds, but weight is only one factor contributing to roadability, comfort, and safety. With modern suspension systems, roadability is good in the smaller cars and little comfort is sacrificed."

That was the ticket, then, and the true key to success. Nash had managed to retain big-car feel and levels of comfort with the Rambler, whereas Kaiser's Henry J, and even Hudson's Jet, fell down in this area. The Henry J had a hard, choppy ride and limited space inside—adults were cramped in the back and almost doubled over by the fastback roofline. The Hudson Jet was certainly as roadworthy as the Rambler, but its interior had less room—and (this above all) it simply looked ugly.

Again for 1955, Rambler offered a large array of models—twelve this time, including three "Fleet" models with a dirt cheap price tag to appeal to fleet buyers (which they did). On four-door sedans and automatic-equipped cars in 1954, Rambler had provided a slightly larger engine with more horsepower; this was continued into 1955 as both engines received modest horsepower increases. The Fleet models, by the way, used the more powerful engine.

Alas, by the time the 1955s had finished their run, George Mason was gone. He died unexpectedly in October 1954, and his plans for a broad merger of four independents—Nash, Hudson, Packard, and Studebaker—died with him. But Mason had laid his plans well, having already managed to pick up Hudson. Though Studebaker and Packard did not in the end join his American Motors, Mason's successor George Romney took the Rambler ball and ran with it. By the time the 1958 recession came along, Americans realized that the compact cars the big companies were now promising them were already available at their friendly local AMC dealers. That year Rambler sales topped 185,000—and kept going. By 1961, Rambler ranked as the number three best-seller in America.

George Mason would have been proud.

1954-59 Nash Metropolitan

Along about 1952, with the Rambler solidly established in American affections, one can almost visualize the reasoning of the brilliant marketing mind of George Mason: "If they like the Rambler, why shouldn't they like something still smaller? Here's another market sector where the Big Three aren't!"

Mini-cars made no sense to anybody else in the American industry, which was exactly why Mason gave the idea some thought. The postwar boom economy had dramatically altered what latterday cliche-artists call "lifestyle." No longer did America's population want to concentrate itself in the cities; rather, the Fifties found it rapidly spreading out to vast tracts of new housing in the suburbs. This suburban swing caused the surge of popularity of the station wagon and, to a large extent, held the key to Rambler's early success. The Rambler competed not so much as an ultra-low-priced car, but as a neat second car for the rest of the family to use when the main car was otherwise engaged. If they liked Ramblers, chances are that customers in the more congested suburbs might like an even smaller but attractive runabout. Enter the Metropolitan.

The Met's origins go back to just after the war, when Mason and Nash engineer Meade F. Moore looked at a design by an independent consultant named Bill Flajole. Based on the Fiat 500 chassis-drivetrain, this prototype was named NXI (Nash eXperimental International). In a way, it was a predecessor to what we now know as the "world car," personified of late by the Ford Escort. Mason thought it might be built abroad, and get Nash seriously into the beckoning overseas markets; indeed some former associates said he thought it would sell better abroad than at home. Mason's number two man, George Romney, took the NXI to several private showings through 1950 to size up public reaction.

The public received the car well, but Mason remained cautious. He was perhaps the only independent auto executive who didn't accept the inevitable enthusiasm of postwar America for anything on wheels to color his judgement. Thus, the NXI had to wait while Mason floated the larger Rambler; if that worked, he decided, he would try the smaller car. The Rambler worked.

By the end of 1953, Nash moved ahead on the Metropolitan. Bodies, a convertible and hardtop coupe, would be built in Birmingham, England by Fisher & Ludlow. The shells would be shipped to Austin at Longbridge, where 42-bhp Austin A40 four-cylinder engines would be installed. Styling, however, would have an all-American look, and very much in the Nash image. So were the Metropolitan's bright two-tone color schemes, which one stylist likened to "Neapolitan ice cream." The target price was under $1500.

George Mason planned well. By assigning production to UK contractors he kept his own Kenosha factory free for higher volume products like the Rambler; by insisting on his own styling he gave the Met a familiar appearance (though probably condemned any chance it had to sell overseas). Best of all, if the whole project flopped, he could withdraw without losing a bundle.

But the little two-seater Metropolitan worked. Like the Rambler, it was nicely finished and offered in sporty body styles and colors. This attracted people as much as its extreme economy—40 miles per gallon under ideal conditions. Nearly 13,000 went out the door the first year, and subsequent sales remained strong enough to profitably keep the Met in production for almost a decade.

The Metropolitan 1500 arrived in mid-1956, boasting a larger 1500-cc engine and more horsepower, a larger clutch, and an oval grille bearing Nash or Hudson emblems. A newly smoothed hood eliminated the fake scoop that had adorned the original. Compared to the first Met, the 1500 would cruise at 80 instead of 70, though not with sports car efficiency. This proved a boon to commuters, who found the early car too buzzy for American highway conditions.

After the demise of the Nash and Hudson marques in 1957, the Metropolitan shed its Nash/Hudson badging and became known simply by its model name. The economy car boom brought about by the 1958 recession caused Metropolitan sales to soar, the 22,000-unit figure of 1959 it's all-time high. Arrival of Big Three compacts and additional imports brought this success to a swift halt, however, and Metropolitan sales skidded to zero by 1962. Overall, though, the Met had performed remarkably well for such a peripheral product.

The perky little Metropolitan was built in England, but carried Nash styling. The first generation (top row), *with a 42-bhp Austin four, lasted from 1954 through mid-1956. At that point, the Metropolitan received a mild restyling that included a new grille and bodyside two-toning, plus a more powerful 52-bhp engine* (bottom row).

SPECIFICATIONS

Engine: ohv I-4 **1953-56** 73.8 cid (2.56 × 3.50), 42 bhp **1956-59** 90.9 cid (2.88 × 3.50), 52 bhp

Transmission:	3-speed manual
Suspension, front:	independent, coil springs, tube shocks
Suspension, rear:	live axle, leaf springs, tube shocks
Brakes:	front/rear drums
Wheelbase (in.):	85.0
Weight (lbs):	**cvt** 1803-1835 **cpe** 1843-1875
Top speed (mph):	**1953-56** 70 **1956-59 1500** 80
0-60 mph (sec):	**1953-56** 27.0 **1956-59 1500** 22.0

Production: **1953-54** 13,095 **1955** 6096 **1956** 9068 **1957** 15,317 **1958** 13,128 **1959** 22,309

1955-57 Nash Ambassador

Most of the better-led independents had at least two restyling whacks after the war. Nash had its first shot with the 1949-51 Airflyte, its second with the 1952-57 "Pinin Farina" body, initially one of the cleanest cars of that period.

How little the house of Pinin Farina actually contributed was revealed a decade ago by John Conde, former American Motors Corporation public relations manager. Farina signed a contract to produce two prototypes a year, for Nash to do with as it pleased. The 1952-57 body was mainly designed by Kenosha stylist Edmund A. Anderson, who picked up two Farina details: the reverse dog-leg C-pillar, and the vertical blade, Ferrari-like grille. The rest came from Anderson: semi-enclosed front wheels (a fetish of chairman George Mason), rippled stamping under the beltline (inspired by classic aircraft), high hood and deck, and handsome three-way-visible taillights. Advertising, however, naturally took advantage of the Pinin Farina relationship, and Battista Farina has ever since received the credit—or blame.

Cars ought to be judged by contemporary standards, and against these the "Farina" Nash design was a good job. Though high-sided, bulky, and overbodied, so was most everything else on the market then. It offered, meanwhile, an admirable lack of unnecessary brightwork, fine visibility, and was decked out with all the famous Airflyte features: reclining seat/beds, Weather-Eye fresh-air heater/ventilator, unibody construction. The top-of-the-line Ambassador boasted interior fabrics and colors selected by Helene Rother, and a hood ornament designed by George Petty of Esquire "Petty Girl" fame. Much to the ire of Petty's followers, this was later replaced with a nondescript rocket-like motif.

To all these attributes, the big Ambassador added V-8 performance in the 1955-57 period, thanks to a deal with Packard. This brought Nash the Clipper 320 V-8 for 1955 and part of 1956, then AMC's own 327 from mid-1956 on. Both engines were

Nash encouraged 1957 new-car buyers to "Join the swing to the travel king." Alas, not many did, despite Nash's fine reputation as a comfortable long-distance traveler. Two Ambassador Custom models, both running a 327-cid, 255-bhp V-8, were offered that year: a $2763 four-door sedan (below) *and a $2847 Country Club hardtop* (opposite).

understressed, so V-8 Ambassadors were still somewhat sluggish off the line. But they were smooth cruisers at highway speeds and much better at mid-range acceleration than the sixes. (The latter departed after 1956.)

The '55s were the first Ambassadors with inboard headlamps, mounted at the edges of Farina's large oval grille. This idea was apparently inspired by Farina's treatment of the 1952 Nash-Healey. Little running lights rode on the fenders to indicate the car's actual width. But the public didn't go for it, so for 1957 the headlamps moved outboard again. The 1956 models were jazzed up with bodyside two-toning and huge "lollipop" taillights (a skinny back-up light topped by a big red one).

The 1955-57 Ambassador came in only two body styles, a four-door sedan and a Country Club two-door hardtop. This limited its sales appeal as much as anything, and in 1956 Nash sold only about 7500 copies. Two-thirds of these were the late-introduction 327 V-8s, designated the "Ambassador Special" and priced from $2350-2550, well down from the previous V-8 and a forlorn effort to improve sales.

By 1957, George Romney had made the decision to concentrate entirely on compacts, making this the final year for the big Nash. The line was restricted only to Ambassadors (the same two bodies in two levels of trim), all powered by the 327 engine— which had received a hefty boost in horsepower and now delivered really good performance. Though stuck with a now five-year-old body, Anderson and Company gave it a new look with vertical quad headlamps—the first quads in a production American car and the only ones in 1957, save for the limited-production Cadillac Eldorado Brougham. Two-tone patterns were reshuffled (some said overdone), parking lamps mounted atop the front fenders, and the front wheels were now exposed. Many Ambassadors came with "continental" spare tires.

The decision to drop the Nash and Hudson names actually came *after* Romney decided henceforth to build compact cars only. Rambler (which of course had very early antecedents, earlier even than Nash and Hudson) was by now an accepted nameplate able to stand on its own. A rather larger Rambler for 1958, initially designed to bear Nash and Hudson badges, was thus announced as the "Rambler Ambassador." It marked a sad end, though, for two distinguished names that between them shared almost a century of automotive history.

SPECIFICATIONS

Engines: **1955-56** ohv I-6, 252.6 cid (3.50 × 4.38), 130 bhp, 140 bhp optional; ohv V-8, 320.0 cid (3.81 × 3.50), 208 bhp **1956** 327.0 cid (4.00 × 3.25), 190 bhp **1957** 255 bhp

Transmission:	3-speed manual; overdrive and 4-speed Hydra-Matic optional
Suspension, front:	independent, coil springs, tube shocks
Suspension, rear:	live axle, coil springs, tube shocks
Brakes:	front/rear drums
Wheelbase (in.):	121.3
Weight (lbs):	3397-3846
Top speed (mph):	**Six** 90 **V-8** 100-105
0-60 mph (sec):	**Six** 16.0-18.0 **V-8** 12.0-16.0
Production:	**1955** 15,000* **1956** 7500* **1957** 5000*

*estimated; individual figures not available

1950 Oldsmobile 88

The original Oldsmobile 88 can lay fair claim as America's first postwar "muscle car," sounding the gun for the "horsepower race" of the Fifties. It was definitely a hit. Despite being a last-minute addition, the debut 1949 models sold more than 99,000 copies. The evolutionary 1950 racked up over a quarter-million orders. Just as quickly, the 88 began compiling an enviable competition record that firmly endowed Olds with a high-performance image, which would prove a key factor in the make's consistently high sales for most of the decade.

Like many good ideas, the 88 concept was disarmingly simple. Olds shared 1949 honors with sister division Cadillac for the industry's first high-compression overhead-valve V-8. At first, Oldsmobile's new 303.7-cubic-inch "Rocket" engine was to be limited to the senior C-body 98 series that, again with Cadillac, had ushered in General Motors' first new postwar styling the previous year. With the new look being extended to the company's junior A- and B-body models for 1949, Olds general manager Sherrod Skinner conceived the brilliant notion of slotting the compact, 135-horsepower V-8 into his lighter, Chevy-size Series 76 that still trundled around with a 105-bhp six. Voilá! Instant excitement.

The result came as a revelation to buyers accustomed to plodding L-head sixes and slow-revving straight eights. Weighing 300-500 pounds less than a 98, the typical 88 had a power-to-weight ratio of about 22.5:1, not so hot by late-Fifties standards perhaps, but sufficient to make this one of the quickest cars you could find on any showroom floor. And with prices as low as $2143 for the standard-trim fastback club coupe, the 88 offered more go for the dough than anything else on the road.

And the new Rocket V-8 was a gem, with an impressive 250 pounds-feet torque, sturdy nine-main-bearing crankshaft, modern oversquare bore/stroke dimensions, and tremendous internal strength. Though initially running on a mild 7.25:1 compression ratio, it could go as high as 12.0:1, amazing for an "everyday" Detroit engine.

Oldsmobile's new hot one had obvious potential as a stock-car racer, and it scored early by taking six of nine NASCAR Grand National events in '49, and giving Red Byron the driver's championship. The following year, an 88 broke the class record at Daytona with a two-way average of 100.28 mph. Also in 1950, an 88 won its class in the first Mexican Road Race, besting rivals such as Alfa Romeo, Cadillac, and Lincoln. On the ovals, 88s took 10 of 19 contests in 1950 and 20 of 41 in 1951. Though displaced by the amazing six-cylinder Hudson Hornet as the car to beat in 1952-54, the 88 continued to show its ability—and stamina. A 1950 model nicknamed "Roarin' Relic" was still winning the occasional modified-class stock-car race as late as 1959.

Such goings-on naturally helped Olds sales after the postwar seller's market peaked in 1950, when the division built nearly 408,000 cars for the model year—its second consecutive record. That figure wouldn't be exceeded until 1955, mainly due to production quotas caused by the Korean conflict, but after sagging to eighth in the industry for 1951, Olds returned to sixth for 1952-53, and would claim fourth for '54.

Model year 1950 brought minor styling changes to a "Futuramic 88" line that expanded via Harley Earl's pillarless hardtop coupe body style, which Olds called Holiday. Standard and Deluxe versions were offered at $2162 and $2267, respectively. Olds began giving up on fastback sedans much sooner than, say, Chevy, dropping its four-door Town Sedan this year.

Otherwise, 88 offerings for 1950 repeated those of '49: convertible, club coupe, two- and four-door notchback sedans, and four-door wagon. All but the ragtop came in Standard and Deluxe form, the latter typically costing $78 more. Prices were attractively pitched, ranging from the basic $1904 club sedan—about $375 more than a two-door Ford V-8—to $2662 for the Deluxe wagon.

Speaking of which, 1950 would see the last Olds wagons until 1957. As at other GM divisions, these all-steel models sported simulated wood trim, but at Olds sales didn't amount to much: only some 2900 of the 88s and a mere 368 of the six-cylinder Series 76 models. The 76 was on the way out, anyway, thanks to the 88, which offered far more performance for less than $170 more model for model. Olds wouldn't return to sixes until 1964, and then only on a price-leader compact.

The intervening years would bring a lot of fast Oldsmobiles, but the 88 was the first and that makes it special. Today it's revered as the granddaddy of modern muscle.

One could argue that the 1950 Olds 88 was the first "muscle car" by virtue of running the new overhead-valve Rocket V-8 in Oldsmobile's smallest, lightest body. Though the convertible was a bit heavier and more expensive than other 88s—3745 pounds and $2294—it was still a formidable performer, and a good looker to boot!

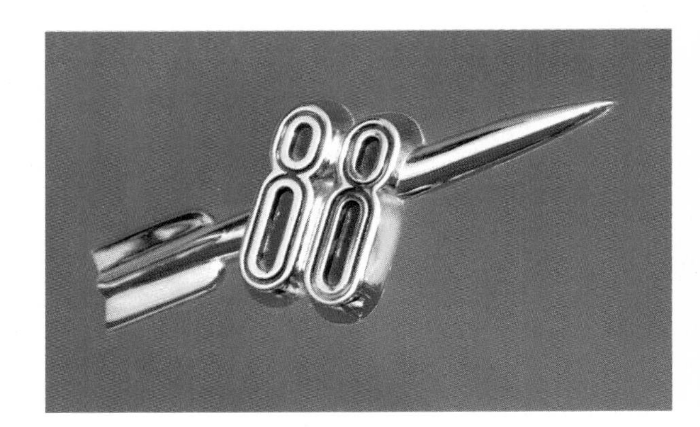

SPECIFICATIONS

Engine:	ohv V-8, 303.7 cid (3.75 × 3.44), 135 bhp
Transmission:	3-speed manual; 4-speed "Whirlaway" Hydra-Matic automatic optional
Suspension, front:	upper and lower A-arms, coil springs
Suspension, rear:	live axle, coil springs
Brakes:	front/rear drums
Wheelbase (in.):	119.5
Weight (lbs):	3435-3780
Top speed (mph):	97
0-60 mph (sec):	12.0-13.5

Production: 2d Club Sedan 14,705 **Deluxe 2d Club Sedan** 16,388 **club cpe** 10,684 **Deluxe club cpe** 10,772 **cvt** 9127 **Holiday 2d htp** 1366 **Deluxe Holiday 2d htp** 11,316 **4d sdn** 40,301 **Deluxe 4d sdn** 100,810 **2d sdn** 23,889 **Deluxe 2d sdn** 26,672 **4d wgn** 1830 **Deluxe 4d wgn** 552

1950-53 Oldsmobile 98

Both before and immediately after World War II, Oldsmobile—like Pontiac—was seen as a purveyor of sensible family cars powered by six- and eight-cylinder engines. But Olds, residing one notch above Pontiac in the General Motors pecking order, held one trump card that Pontiac didn't: a reputation for engineering innovation, built in part on the fully automatic Hydra-Matic transmission Olds had introduced in 1939.

Olds ran seventh in the industry in 1946-47. Production of its warmed-over prewar cars reached nearly 200,000 units by 1948. Style-wise, the 1946-47 models were warmed-over '42s, but the gaudy prewar grille was thankfully replaced by a simple four-bar unit for 1946-47.

In February 1948, however, a memorable new design appeared—the "Futuramic" 98. Along with a similar new style from Cadillac, it was GM's first all-new postwar design. Created by Harley Earl's Art & Colour Studio, it took inspiration from the wartime Lockheed P-38 fighter plane. The beautifully shaped 98s included sedan, club sedan (fastback), and convertible styles with standard and Deluxe trim (Deluxe only for the ragtop). Prices ranged from $2078 to $2624. Meanwhile, the 1948 series 66, 68, 76, and 78 retained the 1946-47 look. The public responded to the new Futuramics with excitement. When the model year ended, over 60,000 had been sold.

Another breakthrough innovation came in 1949 with the Rocket V-8 engine, designed by Gilbert Burrell. It was an automotive landmark—one of the first two high-compression overhead-valve V-8s. The other belonged to Cadillac. The two divisions had been encouraged to compete with each another, and in the end Cadillac raised the displacement of its V-8 from 309 to 331 cubic inches to outdo Olds' 303.7 cid.

Oldsmobile trimmed its lineup from five series to three for 1949: six-cylinder Futuramic 76, a new Futuramic 88, and the Futuramic 98. The 88, a veritable hot rod with the big V-8 in Oldsmobile's junior body, quickly established its reputation on the race track. The luxury-oriented 98 came in six models: club and four-door sedans, the same in Deluxe form, plus a Deluxe-only convertible and Oldsmobile's new

In 1950, Oldsmobile still offered fastback sedans in the 98 series, such as the club sedan (opposite). Available as a $2225 regular or $2319 Deluxe, only 11,989 were built, and so they were dropped after the model run. The 1951 Holiday hardtop (below) listed at $2882 as a Deluxe, $2545 in standard form. It weighed in at 3857 pounds.

hardtop, the Holiday. Customers apparently liked what they saw, for they snapped up 93,478 copies.

"Oldsmobile Rockets Ahead" proclaimed the 1950 brochure. And indeed it did, as Holiday hardtops were offered in all three series. The 98s now numbered nine and received fairly extensive styling changes. Featured were flush, sculptured rear fenders that were both higher and squarer. Four-door "bustle-backs" also sported a new, squarer greenhouse around the rear doors and backlight. Like most other makes, Olds did spectacularly well in 1950. Model year output shot up to 480,060 units, 106,220 of them 98s, moving Olds into sixth place.

The Super 88 was Oldsmobile's big news for 1951. It slotted between the 88 and 98. Like the 88, the 98 saw few changes for 1951 except for a simplified four-model lineup. The fastback sedans were gone now, and so were all base 98s except for the Holiday. This left three Deluxe 98s: four-door sedan, convertible, and Holiday. Production slipped to 285,615 in a down year for the industry, dropping Olds to seventh place. The 98, however, declined only slightly to 100,516 units.

The '52 big Olds carried badging on its sides that read "Ninety-Eight." The trim on the rear flanks mimicked that of the '51 Super 88, as did that on the Deluxe 88. Overall, the Ninety-Eight looked more "important" on its two-inch-longer wheelbase. For the first time since 1949, the 303.7-cid Rocket got a horsepower boost, to 145 for 88s, 160 (via a Quadri-Jet carburetor) for Super 88/98. An important new option was power steering, so anyone could "Park with just 1 finger!" Two other extras fell more into the gimmick category: the Autronic Eye automatic headlight dimmer and a self-winding car watch mounted on the steering wheel. As on some earlier 98s, electric-hydraulic windows and seat came standard on the Holiday and convertible. Government restrictions squeezed industry output in 1952. Olds fell to 213,490 units, the three Ninety-Eights (no more Deluxes) to 76,244. Still, Olds moved back into sixth.

Olds rocketed into 1953 with a "power" styled front-end and extra-cost power brakes and air conditioning. A chromy new dashboard was also featured, along with the usual trim shuffle. The three Ninety-Eights—sedan, convertible, and Holiday—were priced at $2786, $3229, and $3022. Later, they were joined by the limited-production Fiesta convertible, a $5717 image-enhancer offered only that one year. Production rose to 334,462 units for the model run, and back to six digits for the Ninety-Eight: 100,330 units, including Fiesta.

But greater things lay in store. New styling and more power jetted Olds into fourth place in 1954, and later it would take over third. The Ninety-Eight helped Olds secure its lofty position, and—unlike most of the nameplates from the Fifties—it's still with us!

SPECIFICATIONS

Engines: ohv V-8, 303.7 cid (3.75 × 3.44) **1950-51** 135 bhp **1952** 160 bhp **1953** 165 bhp

Transmission:	3-speed manual; Hydra-Matic optional
Suspension, front:	upper and lower A-arms, coil springs
Suspension, rear:	live axle, semi-elliptic leaf springs
Brakes:	front/rear drums
Wheelbase (in.):	**1950-51** 122.0 **1952-53** 124.0
Weight (lbs):	3685-4150
Top speed (mph):	95-105
0-60 mph (sec):	12.5-13.5

Production: **1950 club sdn** 2270 **Holiday htp cpe** 317 **Town Sedan** 255 **4d sdn** 7499 **Deluxe club sdn** 9719 **Holiday htp cpe** 7946 **Town Sedan** 1523 **4d sdn** 72,766 **cvt** 3925 **1951 Holiday htp cpe** 3914 **Deluxe 4d sdn** 78,122 **Holiday htp cpe** 14,012 **cvt** 4468 **1952 4d sdn** 58,550 **Holiday htp cpe** 14,150 **cvt** 3544 **1953 4d sdn** 64,431 **Holiday htp cpe** 27,920 **cvt** 7521

1953 Oldsmobile Fiesta

Glamor cars aren't supposed to make money, just news. The Oldsmobile Fiesta of 1953 is a case in point. It was the least successful of the three big limited-edition convertibles General Motors fielded that year, garnering only 458 sales to 1690 for Buick's Skylark and 532 for Cadillac's Eldorado. High price has long been cited as the reason, but the Fiesta wasn't the costliest of this trio. It was pricey to be sure at $5717, but the Skylark wasn't that much cheaper at $5000—and the Eldo cost a staggering $7750 (see entries). The latter, with more standard features and a much-reduced price, would handily outlast the other two in the marketplace. Skylark vanished after 1954; the Fiesta didn't survive past '53.

Still, the Fiesta fulfilled its main mission, that of drawing attention to an Olds line then at the end of a three-year styling cycle. It also previewed certain features of the all-new '54 models, the foundation for Oldsmobile's most profitable years of the decade.

Like the Eldo and Skylark, the Fiesta was essentially GM's big 1953 convertible—here, the 124-inch-wheelbase Olds Ninety-Eight—with a full complement of luxury extras. Fiesta and Eldorado also sported a cut-down version of the wraparound "Panoramic" windshield destined for all '54 Buicks, Caddys, and Oldsmobiles. The latter, which included small frameless ventwings, lowered the Fiesta by three inches compared to the ragtop Ninety-Eight, an easy way to give an aging, fairly bulbous design a sleeker, more "with it" look. For the same reason, and also like its sisters, the Fiesta bore the distinctive beltline "notch" or "dip" favored by GM design domo Harley Earl.

Mechanically, the Fiesta parted company with the Eldo and Skylark in having slightly more muscle than its standard counterpart: an Olds Rocket V-8, still in original 303.7-cubic-inch form, with slightly higher compression yielding 170 horsepower, five more than in the '53 Super 88 and Ninety-Eight. It was a bit extravagant for only 458 cars, but GM could afford it in those days (certainly more so than now).

General Motors was flexing its marketing muscle and demonstrating its styling leadership when it debuted a trio of super-expensive convertibles in 1953. Oldsmobile's version, the Fiesta, listed at $5717, fully $2500 more than the top-line Ninety-Eight ragtop. Aside from its rarity—only 458 were built—it served to ready the American public for an all-new '54 Olds that would borrow its "Panoramic" windshield and bodyside two-toning.

Otherwise, the Fiesta resembled the standard open Ninety-Eight except for the requisite name script, a distinctive dorsal decklid chrome strip that curved down to form a trunk handle, and special wheel covers with three-prong "spinners." The last quickly became a popular "kustom kar" item and were soon copied by any number of aftermarket accessory houses.

Olds historian Dennis Casteele notes that the Fiesta first appeared as a show car during 1952 and went into limited production by mid-1953. This suggests that it was always intended as a low-volume "showroom draw"—a reason for buyers to visit Olds dealerships and see mainstream '53s that differed from the '52s only in detail.

Since the wrapped windshield comprised the only real difference from other Olds models, Fiesta tried to add to the promise of its name by being as colorful and lavish as possible. For example, it was most always pictured with two-toning—Noel/Nile Green and Surf/Teal Blue, according to Casteele—and it's likely most came out of the factory this way, though solid black and white could also be ordered. Unlike other '53 Oldsmobiles, where the contrast color was confined to the roof, Fiesta two-toning spilled over from the rear deck onto the area above the L-shaped bodyside moldings, resulting in an attractive "saddleback" appearance that also predicted '54 Oldsmobile styling. Interiors were resplendent in hand-buffed leather, with ivory set against black, light green, or light blue upholstery. Tops came in basic black or something called "natural orlon" (tan).

No jukebox out-dazzled Oldsmobile's '53 dashboard, and few cars carried more standard goodies than the Fiesta. Besides the leather-lined interior, Rocket engine, and the expected Hydra-Matic Drive, buyers were pampered with power steering and brakes, a "super deluxe" radio, heater/defroster, wide-whitewall tires (what else in the early '50s?), back-up lights, chrome exhaust extension, and "Autronic Eye" automatic headlamp dimmer.

None of the contemporary auto magazines ever got around to testing a Fiesta, no surprise considering the late introduction and minuscule production, but it had to be the slowest '53 Olds. That's because it weighed over 300 pounds more than the Ninety-Eight convertible, rather a lot for only five extra horses to lug around.

Though the Fiesta's party didn't last long, the name would resurface on Oldsmobile's revived station wagons of 1957. But, of course, it's the very special '53 convertible that enthusiasts have come to covet—rare and interesting, a nostalgic reminder of a less troubled, more affluent Detroit where dreams went on parade like clockwork every year, and some actually made it to your local dealer. If you're too young to remember those years, too bad. You missed a great party.

SPECIFICATIONS

Engine:	ohv V-8, 303.7 cid (3.75 × 3.44), 170 bhp
Transmission:	4-speed Hydra-Matic
Suspension, front:	upper and lower A-arms, coil springs
Suspension, rear:	live axle, semi-elliptic leaf springs
Brakes:	front/rear drums
Wheelbase (in.):	124.0
Weight (lbs):	4453
Top speed (mph):	95+
0-60 mph (sec):	14.5
Production:	458

1954-56 Oldsmobile

"Classic" Chevys and two-seat T-Birds have long been admired, but how many appreciate the 1954-56 Oldsmobiles? Well, some do. In their own way, they're every bit as worthy and memorable—arguably Lansing's best efforts of the decade: smooth and solid per Olds tradition, flashy in the spirit of the times yet not overdone, surprisingly roadable. They certainly ranked as the most popular Oldsmobiles of the '50s. Consider that the division rose from sixth to fifth in industry sales with its '54 line, then claimed fourth on 1955 volume of 583,179 units—a record that would stand for the next decade.

Unlike today, everybody knew where Oldsmobile stood in the mid-Fifties—including General Motors. The redesigned '54s showed it by being mostly new but still resolutely Oldsmobile. Though clearly evolved from 1951-53, styling was blockier and more slab-sided, but pleasantly modern. Hood height dropped to near fender-level, the wrapped "Panoramic" windshield appeared on cue, and beltlines rode lower for a lighter look and better visibility.

As before, the senior Ninety-Eight employed the GM C-body, the mid-range Super 88 and base 88 series (the latter no longer "Deluxe") corporate B-body. Wheelbases went up two inches across the board with the advent of a new X-member frame that helped reduce overall height and center of gravity. New-type front coil springs and repositioned rear springs and shocks also improved handling. Performance improved via a bored-out Rocket V-8 with higher 8.25:1 compression, good for 170 horsepower with two-barrel carb for the base 88 and 185 bhp in four-barrel form for Super 88 and Ninety-Eight. The extra power was welcome, as curb weights rose some 80-120 pounds. The power steering, brakes, and optional air conditioning also came in for attention.

Olds dropped one model for '54—the Fiesta—and added two—a base 88 Holiday hardtop and a Ninety-Eight Deluxe Holiday—for a gain of one, 11 in all. Prices crept up, but not much: $10-$25. At $3249, the Ninety-Eight convertible again topped the line, but now carried the surname "Starfire," borrowed from a two-seat 1953 show car. New options included a hydraulic power window/seat system for four-door Ninety-Eights, electric windows and four-way seat for most other models, plus wire wheel covers, signal-seeking radio and, interestingly enough, padded dash.

The '54 Oldsmobile boasted an all-new body with a Panoramic windshield, an enlarged V-8, and a two-inch-longer wheelbase for all models. The Ninety-Eight Holiday two-door hardtop (this page) *listed for $3042, the Ninety-Eight Starfire ragtop* (opposite, bottom) *for $3249. The restyled '55 boasted a new grille and altered bodyside two-toning. The Super 88 convertible* (bottom) *listed at $2894.*

56 OLDS

OLDSMOBILE CLUB
CALIFORNIA
HDT 008
OF AMERICA

1957-58 Oldsmobile

Oldsmobile, like Buick, seemed to go astray in 1957-58. In retrospect, the reason isn't hard to divine. Their huge success in the booming medium-price market of 1954-55 led General Motors executives to believe that more of the same cars would bring more of the same record sales and still more profits. This prompted a conservative—if not downright complacent—approach to 1957-58 planning.

More the '57 Oldsmobiles definitely had. Billed as the most completely changed Oldsmobiles in 20 years, they came in a little longer, noticeably lower, and somewhat wider than the '56s. Wheelbases went unchanged, but spanned all-new B- and C-bodies shared with Buick. The chassis was also new: a low-riding "cowbelly" design with widely spaced side rails and Oldsmobile's first ball-joint front suspension. Curb weights tacked on some 220-300 pounds, but more cubic inches would take care of that and Olds had 'em in a Rocket V-8 punched out 371.1 cubic inches and 277 horsepower for all models—the first time since 1951, incidentally, that the same engine had been standard across the line.

Olds styling was relatively clean for a '57 GM car, and still unmistakably Olds. The "big-mouth" grille of '56, flattened now to full width, was shorn of its vertical divider and filled with a fine mesh instead of deeply inset horizontal bars. Bright sweepspears still dropped from the notch in the beltline to just below mid-body, but now shot straight back as in 1954. High-set "rocket" tail lamps, an Olds trademark since '53, gave way to semi-oval units with hooded tops that hinted at fins. As at Buick, sedans and hardtops sported three-piece rear windows, with curved triangular sections outboard of a wide center pane. Curious stamped ridges ran the length of the roof and down through the divider pillars of the rear window in some models. Not everyone approved, but at least it looked different.

Model offerings expanded with the first Olds wagons since 1950, a trio of four-doors similar to Flint's '57s: a pillared wagon in base 88 trim and pillarless 88 and Super 88 versions. All wore the Fiesta name from Oldsmobile's limited-edition 1953 convertible (see entry)—and sold quite poorly. Even convertibles did better.

Another '57 name shuffle involved prefacing the 88 and Super 88 lines with "Golden Rocket"—which made no sense at all because Oldsmobile's 50th anniversary had occurred 10 years before. And "Starfire" preceded Ninety-Eight on all four top-line models; since 1954, it had been reserved for only the top-line ragtop.

Lansing's big '57 performance news was coded J-2, a triple-carburetor package with special intake manifold, 10.0:1 compression (versus the standard 9.5:1), and new air cleaner, throttle linkage, and head gaskets. Like Dodge's D-500 option, it could be had on any model, either factory- or dealer-installed, right down to the cheapest and lightest two-door 88—which is where speed demons wanted it anyway. Cost? Just $83, a fraction of what rivals charged for fuel injection or supercharging. The J-2 was a genuine performance bargain, reducing the typical 0-60-mph time to a shade over nine seconds. Though quickly banned by NASCAR, it showed its potential when veteran stock-car ace Lee Petty blasted one to nearly 145 mph on the sands at Daytona.

But such exploits did little for sales, and Olds lost ground for '57, retaining fifth place but on 25 percent lower volume—384,390 units. Also reflecting the start of a sharp national recession that year, the standard 88 outsold the Super 88 for the first time, and by a hefty margin: better than 40,000 units.

Things went from bad to worse as the recession deepened, and the '58 Oldsmobiles—now Dynamic 88, Super 88, and Ninety-Eight—did nothing to help. We mention these over-chromed aberrations mainly for historical completeness, as they've never been considered "great" cars. Quite the opposite, in fact. Like the equally contrived "B-58" Buicks, they've long stood as symbols of everything that seemed wrong with Detroit at the time. Designer Alex Tremulis, then working for Ford but late of the celebrated Tucker debacle, satirized Oldsmobile's four horizontal rear-fender chrome strips by drawing in a treble clef and notes on a photo, as on sheet music.

Surprisingly, the '58s weren't much heavier than the '57s; they only looked it. But though the J-2 package was still nominally available, Olds performance began taking a back seat not only to glitter but gee-gaws. Among the latter was "New-Matic Ride" air suspension, which proved as unreliable as any of its ilk—and as short-lived.

Olds would get back on track for '59, but the '58s have lately attracted many younger enthusiasts who actually value their garishness as kitschy nostalgia symbolic of the age as much as the heroically finned '59 Cadillacs. That doesn't make for "great cars," of course, but it's better than nothing.

Although lavishly chrome-trimmed, the all-new 1957 Oldsmobile was tastefully designed and carried familiar Olds styling cues in the grille, side trim, and taillights. All the station wagons were called Fiesta, a name borrowed from a limited-edition 1953 Olds convertible. Fiestas in the Golden Rocket 88 line came with or without center pillars, but the top-of-the-line Fiesta, the $3541 Golden Rocket Super 88 four-door hardtop, was the best-seller of the three.

SPECIFICATIONS

Engines: ohv V-8, 371.1 cid (4.00 × 3.69) **1957** 277 bhp **J-2** 300 bhp **1958 88** 265 bhp **Super 88 and 98** 305 bhp **J-2** 312 bhp

Transmissions:	**88 and Super 88** 3-speed manual; Jetaway Hydra-Matic optional **98** Jetaway Hydra-Matic
Suspension, front:	upper and lower A-arms, coil springs
Suspension, rear:	live axle, semi-elliptic leaf springs
Brakes:	front/rear drums
Wheelbase (in.):	**88 and Super 88** 122.0 **98** 126.0
Weight (lbs):	3942-4334
Top speed (mph):	100-115
0-60 mph (sec):	9.2-10.5

Production: 1957 Golden Rocket 88 2d sdn 18,477 **Holiday 2d htp** 49,187 **Holiday 4d htp** 33,830 **cvt** 6423 **4d sdn** 53,923 **Fiesta 4d wgn** 5052 **Fiesta 4d htp wgn** 5767 **Golden Rocket Super 88 Holiday 2d htp** 31,155 **Holiday 4d htp** 39,162 **cvt** 7128 **4d sdn** 42,629 **Fiesta 4d htp wgn** 8981 **2d sdn** 2983 **Starfire 98 Holiday 2d htp** 17,971 **Holiday 4d htp** 32,099 **cvt** 8278 **4d sdn** 21,525 **1958 Dynamic 88 2d sdn** 11,833 **Holiday 2d htp** 53,036 **Holiday 4d htp** 28,241 **cvt** 4456 **4d sdn** 60,429 **Fiesta 4d wgn** 3249 **Fiesta 4d htp wgn** 3323 **Super 88 Holiday 2d htp** 18,653 **Holiday 4d htp** 27,521 **cvt** 3799 **4d sdn** 33,844 **Fiesta 4d htp wgn** 5175 **98 Holiday 2d htp** 11,012 **Holiday 4d htp** 27,603 **cvt** 5605 **4d sdn** 16,595

NEW JERSEY
QQ V643
HISTORIC

QQ V643

QQ V643

1959 Oldsmobile

Had there been a Most Improved Styling Award for 1959, Oldsmobile would have won it hands down. Of course, almost anything would have been better than the chrome-covered '58s, and the '59 definitely was: dramatically different and much cleaner. Touted as "The Linear Look," its styling earned bouquets instead of brickbats from critics and customers alike.

That ad slogan was apt. The '59 not only looked longer-lower-wider, it was. Despite fractional gains in wheelbase, overall length went up more than 10 inches on the low-line Dynamic 88 and mid-range Super 88, six inches on the posh Ninety-Eight. Bodies bulged outward to accommodate front and rear tracks widened by two and three inches, respectively (to 61 inches each) and overall height sank 1.5 inches, which also brought down the center of gravity for slightly better handling despite the increased bulk.

Stylists accentuated the new dimensions with a mile-wide grille dominated by broadly spaced horizontal quad headlamps, plus a flat, expansive hood and sculptured rear quarters that suggested fins despite straight-through fenderlines. Massively wider windshields featured more glass area and compound-curves, but without the severely angled "dogleg" A-pillars of 1957-58. Four-door hardtops, now called Holiday SportSedans, looked even more "linear" than other models because of a flat-top roof that extended just beyond a radically wrapped rear window. Two-door hardtops, now called SceniCoupes, sported a shorter greenhouse with a tall backlight that arched into the roof like the windshield.

These impressively sized structures rode atop a brand-new "Glide-Ride" chassis with perimeter side rails and a long X-member with a short tunnel in its center. A large rectangular section aft of the rear axle carried the rear of the body, which was unitized from the cowl back. Rear leaf springs for the solid axle and front coils with twin A-arm geometry continued to support the wheels. Optional air suspension returned from '58 but was as unreliable and unpopular as ever.

Olds continued to rely on its proven and potent Rocket V-8 for '59, still with the basic block introduced a decade before. The lighter Dynamic 88s retained the 371.1-cubic-inch version, with 270 horsepower in standard tune or 300 optional. New for Super 88s and Ninety-Eights was a bigger-bore, 394-cid unit rated at 315 bhp. Compression was 9.75:1 across the board. Manual transmission was still nominally available, but self-shift Hydra-Matic, standard for Ninety-Eight and optional elsewhere, remained the overwhelming buyer preference.

Priced at $4366, the Ninety-Eight convertible remained at the top of an Olds lineup comprising 15 models for '59. The Dynamic two-door remained the price-leader ($2837). Four-door sedans, now called Celebrity, continued Oldsmobile's practice of stringing model names together in tongue-twisting combinations (as it still does). Fiesta wagons were trimmed from three to two, a pillared Dynamic and Super 88 with a modern drop-down rear window instead of 1957-58's old-fashioned liftgate. It lowered manually, unless the electric lift was ordered. A rear seat split ⅓-⅔ also cost extra. The Dynamic Fiesta (odd name, that) sold somewhat better than its predecessor, but the Super Fiesta (ditto) continued to find few takers. Power vent windows appeared as the year's only new optional gadget, but six-way power seat, padded dash, air conditioning, improved "Roto-Matic" power steering, and a redesigned, take-along "Trans-portable" AM radio could all be ordered.

Though Oldsmobile's day in the racing sun was long past, Lee Petty gave the make a final bit of NASCAR glory in '59. It came at the inaugural Daytona 500 run on the then-new International Speedway in February, where Petty drove his Dynamic SceniCoupe to a virtual photo-finish with Johnny Beauchamp's Thunderbird. Petty posed for pictures in Victory Lane, but the judges looked closely at that photo and declared Beauchamp the winner four days later.

Olds, like Buick, had a mixed year in '59. Despite slightly higher model year production of close to 383,000 units, the division fell from fourth to sixth in industry rankings. Oddly, Olds had moved from fifth to fourth for '58, so maybe the brightwork brigade hadn't been so wrong after all.

Yet, the '59 came as a timely turnaround to set the stage for even greater Olds elegance—and greater Olds success—in the Sixties. Who says good taste doesn't sell?

The '59 Olds Ninety-Eight (like the Super 88) was powered by a 394-cid V-8 good for 315 bhp (above). *The two least-bought Ninety-Eights—but most sought after today—were the $4086 Scenic hardtop coupe* (opposite, top) *and the $4366 convertible* (bottom)*: 13,669 and 7514 units, respectively. Buyers preferred the four-door sedan and hardtop in '59.*

SPECIFICATIONS

Engines: ohv V-8 **Dynamic 88** 371.1 cid (4.00 × 3.69), 270 bhp; 300 bhp optional **Super 88 and 98** 394.0 cid (4.13 × 3.69), 315 bhp

Transmissions:	**88 and Super 88** 3-speed manual, Jetaway Hydra-Matic optional **98** Jetaway Hydra-Matic
Suspension, front:	upper and lower A-arms, coil springs
Suspension, rear:	live axle, semi-elliptic leaf springs
Brakes:	front/rear drums
Wheelbase (in.):	**Dynamic and Super 88** 123.0 **98** 126.3
Weight (lbs):	4040-4460
Top speed (mph):	110-115
0-60 mph (sec):	9.5-11.5

Production: **Dynamic 88 2d sdn** 16,123 **Celebrity 4d sdn** 70,995 **Fiesta 4d wgn** 11,298 **SceniCoupe 2d htp** 38,488 **Holiday SportSedan 4d htp** 48,707 **cvt** 8491 **Super 88 Celebrity 4d sdn** 37,024 **Fiesta 4d wgn** 7015 **SceniCoupe 2d htp** 20,259 **Holiday SportSedan 4d htp** 38,467 **cvt** 4895 **98 Celebrity 4d sdn** 23,106 **SceniCoupe 2d htp** 13,669 **Holiday SportSedan 4d htp** 36,813 **cvt** 7514

1959

1950 Packard

Nineteen-fifty was the final year for Packard's first all-postwar generation, with ungainly styling that has since earned them the derisive nickname "pregnant elephant," even among marque partisans. Yet these Packards merit "great car" status not only for their prestigious nameplate but as the last Packards to sell in really high numbers. The actual peak came with the initial Twenty-Second Series lineup of 1948-49: an all-time high 208,499 units. Sadly, Packard would never do so well again.

And with hindsight, the reason is obvious: Packard had abdicated its accustomed role as a strict luxury marque. Company president George Christopher had worshiped at the altar of volume ever since the Depression, and volume required medium-priced cars. The tragedy was that he kept this faith even after prosperity returned, because it ultimately squandered Packard's high-luxe image. The main beneficiary of this mistake was, of course, Cadillac.

Strictly speaking, the "elephant" models weren't all-new. Oh, there were two new engines and an expanded lineup with an extra wheelbase choice, but their basic body and chassis engineering built heavily on the 1946-47 continuation of the prewar Clipper. Introduced for 1941, the Clipper had been designed by the eminent Howard A. "Dutch" Darrin and modified for production by Packard styling chief Werner Gubitz. With flowing fenders, hidden running boards, tapered tail, and smooth overall contours, the Clipper was a dramatic departure from Packard's traditional square-rigged styling, but the new look was so well received that it was applied to almost all the 1942 models.

Beautiful though it was, the Clipper seemed somehow dated in the postwar world. No matter: Packard was hard at work on an extensive facelift. This was inspired by the final version of the Phantom, a one-off landau-roof convertible created in 1941 for design vice-president Ed Macauley, son of the famous Alvan (then in his 70s but still company chairman). Young Ed has sometimes been likened to Edsel Ford. Both were well-dressed, soft-spoken executives with a sense of style and a sensitivity unusual in Detroit. Unfortunately, Ed's aesthetic acumen must have failed him with the '48 facelift, which was debatable at best. Management dictated filling out the Clipper's body sides to give the effect of flow-through fenders, but it only added

SPECIFICATIONS

Engines: L-head straight eight **Eight/DeLuxe Eight** 288 cid (3.50 × 3.75), 135 bhp **Super/Super DeLuxe Eight** 327 cid (3.50 × 4.25), 150 bhp **Custom Eight** 356 cid (3.50 × 4.63), 160 bhp

Transmission:	3-speed manual; overdrive and Ultramatic Drive optional
Suspension, front:	upper and lower A-arms, coil springs
Suspension, rear:	live axle, semi-elliptic leaf springs
Brakes:	front/rear drums
Wheelbase (in.):	**Standard Eight** 120.0 **Super/ Super DeLuxe/Custom Eight** 127.0 **Custom Eight chassis** 148.0
Weight (lbs):	3770-4530
Top speed (mph):	85-95
0-60 mph (sec):	20.0-25.0

Production: Eight 36,471* **Super Eight** 5128, including 600 **cvt Custom Eight 4d sdn** 707 **Custom Eight cvt** 77 **Custom Eight chassis** 244
*No Station Sedans were produced in calendar year 1950; out of 472 built in 1949, an estimated 150 of these were reserialed as 1950 models.

Packard would give up on its "pregnant elephant" bathtub styling after 1950, but in 1950 its finest expression was seen on the 127-inch-wheelbase Custom Eight chassis. Offered as a convertible or a four-door sedan, the Custom boasted a 356-cid, 160-bhp straight eight. The sedan, as seen here, listed at $3975 and only 707 units were built.

some 200 needless pounds and made the car visually plump (and gave it the thickest doors in the industry)—hence the "pregnant elephant" sobriquet.

If styling wasn't its forte, the '48 was still very much a Packard for refinement, comfort, ride, and craftsmanship. Sixes were absent from the line for the first time since 1937. The new order began with Standard, DeLuxe, and Super Eight offerings on a carryover 120-inch wheelbase, with a 141-inch chassis reserved for seven-passenger Super sedans and limousines. The Super engine was a new 327-cubic-inch L-head unit with markedly undersquare dimensions, five main bearings, and a rated 145 horsepower. Lesser Eights used a "squarer" 288-cid powerplant with 130 bhp. Topping the line was the Custom Eight, distinguished by an eggcrate grille (other models used simple horizontal bars) and powered by Packard's existing—and excellent—356-cid straight eight with 160 bhp (five less than before). Model offerings comprised convertible coupe and two fastback sedans on a 127-inch wheelbase and the expected seven-seat sedan and limo on their customary 148-inch wheelbase.

But there was an intriguing newcomer: the Station Sedan. Offered only in Standard Eight trim, it was the first Packard wagon since 1941 and one of Detroit's last woodies. Like others of the breed but unlike its predecessors, it used structural wood only around the tailgate. In fact, Ed Macauley had personally won management's approval for the Station Sedan by arguing that it would require little special tooling. Real tree bark did appear on its doors and around the windows—fine-grained Northern birch—but was just bolted on. What appeared to be mahogany inserts were really painted steel panels: a brown base coat topped by a darker "grain" finish and clear enamel.

The '48 line continued into 1949 without change save a nominal 5 extra horsepower for the two smallest engines. May brought a replacement "Second Series" distinguished mainly by an extra chrome bodyside molding. At the same time, a new Super DeLuxe Eight sub-series arrived with the Custom's eggcrate grille, and long-chassis Customs were dropped. Marking Packard's 50th anniversary was Ultramatic, the only automatic fielded by an independent automaker without help from a transmission manufacturer. Combining a torque converter with multiple-disc and direct-drive clutches, it was smoother than GM's Hydra-Matic but provided only leisurely acceleration and was far less reliable.

Packard continued the mid-1949 Twenty-Third Series into 1950, after which it turned to John Rinehart's more contemporary but quickly dated "high pockets" design. But though some of its most memorable postwar cars still lay ahead, Packard had already seen its best days. In retrospect then, the "elephant" marks the beginning of the end for one of America's most revered marques, one reason it's appreciated today by collectors and enthusiasts alike.

1951-53 Packard Mayfair

The hardtop and the all-steel station wagon quickly established themselves as the two breakthroughs in postwar body design, and between them grabbed upwards of a third of domestic output by mid-decade. The hardtop stole the show with its pizzazz, however, causing automakers to jump on the bandwagon. Some hardtops looked like deft, ground-up designs; others looked like what they were: two-door sedans with hastily contrived pillarless side windows.

Packard's Mayfair was among the later arrivals, and product-wise wasn't truly satisfactory because of compromises. Packard built it on the junior short-wheelbase chassis, and attempted to sell it (and the concurrent convertible) as a prestige line. Thus it came with a "250" designation, senior-style grille teeth, 327-cid engine, full wheel covers, and pelican hood ornament. None of this disguised the fact that at $3200 to $3400, the Mayfair competed more with Buick, Chrysler, and Mercury than with Cadillac, Imperial, and Lincoln. It thus failed to buck up Packard's sagging luxury image, and added little to sales of middle-priced Packards.

None of which means it wasn't a nice car in its own right. All of the above deluxe components combined with the pillarless windowline *did* make for a sporty, upmarket Packard. "Mayfair" seemed an appropriate name, too, conjuring up images of a fashionable district in London, or a famous London coachbuilder. And the smoothly integrated styling avoided the "cobbled" look of such hastily-contrived rivals as the Hudson Hollywood and DeSoto Sportsman. Interiors, true to hardtop standards, sparkled with pretty combinations of nylon, vinyl, and leather, color keyed to the exterior hues. Full carpets and chrome plated pseudo-convertible top bows for the headliner also added a convertible touch. As long as one didn't equate it with the Coupe de Ville, the Mayfair was a perfectly attractive proposition.

Whether because it suffered by that comparison, or because of its competitive market territory, the Mayfair didn't sell very well. Packard didn't publish individual production figures, but careful analysis of serial numbers by Edward Ostrowski of the Packard Club divulges a minimum of 1258 in 1951 and 3959 in 1952. The actual 1951 figure is probably higher because Ostrowski's figures account for only 79 percent of 250 production; for 1952 his serial numbers span 95 percent of the cars.

In 1953, Packard did publish Mayfair production figures: 5150 units, the highest volume to date. The improvement probably came about because, without a price hike, Packard managed to make the '53 look more like a senior model. Bold, chrome finned housings highlighted the taillights, and a full-length strip of bright metal enlivened the body sides, as did the standard fender skirts. Six choices of nylon, leather, or nylon-and-leather enriched the interior, while options like Easamatic power brakes, power steering, power seat, electric antenna, three-way radio, underseat heater, hydraulic windows, and air conditioning helped make life a little more agreeable. And for a little more flair, one could order a Mayfair with chrome wire wheels and a "continental" exterior spare carrying either a disc or wire wheel. Finally, one could overdo things entirely by ordering bright metal "venti-ports" for the bodysides—dummy vents which Packard collectors liken to bottle openers. Thus, without much effort, the $3278 base price of a 1953 Mayfair could be run up to nearly $5000. But however bedecked, the result would still be a Mayfair, not a Coupe de Ville. That remained a problem. Cadillac, it might be noted, pushed out 14,550 Coupe de Villes that year.

Packard could not survive at volume one-third that of Cadillac—certainly not as an independent, probably not even as a cog in a multi-make corporation. Actually, Packard's total 1953 production came to two-thirds that of Cadillac, which was reasonable perhaps, but it fell to a third the following year. The hardtop carried a "Pacific" badge for 1954 and was given another ration of luxury, but fewer than 1200 left the factory. It wasn't until 1955 and the Four Hundred that Packard finally produced a genuine luxury hardtop.

Packard introduced its first hardtop along with its all-new 1951 "Contour-Styled" lineup. Based on the short-wheelbase chassis, the Mayfair nonetheless boasted trim befitting the higher-priced Packards and exterior cues such as "teeth" in the grille and "bottle openers" on the sides. The '51 Mayfair (opposite, top) *wore Packard lettering on the hood, while the little-changed '52* (center and bottom) *dropped the lettering but added a Packard crest at the top of the grille. Featured inside was a "Tele-glance" instrument panel. Prices started at $3234 and $3318 in 1951 and '52.*

SPECIFICATIONS

Engine: sidevalve I-8, 327.0 cid (3.50 × 4.25) **1951-52** 150/155 bhp **1953** 180 bhp

Transmission:	3-speed manual; overdrive and Ultramatic optional
Suspension, front:	independent, coil springs, tube shocks
Suspension, rear:	live axle, leaf springs, tube shocks
Brakes:	front/rear drums
Wheelbase (in.):	122.0
Weight (lbs):	3805-3905
Top speed (mph):	90
0-60 mph (sec):	15.0
Production:	**1951** 1500* **1952** 4000* **1953** 5150

*estimated

PACKARD

Packard

1951-54 Packard Patrician

The first Packard in ten years with its own special "name" (as opposed to a numeric or trim description), the Patrician was aptly christened after the old Roman term for an aristocrat or noble. In its first years, this designation preceded the suffix "400," which had two meanings: it placed the car a step apart and upmarket from the far less luxurious 300 and 200, and it referred to the "social four hundred" families of pre-Depression years. Back in the 1920s, Packard ads listed 400 prominent names and pointed out that they all owned Packards.

The Patrician's "Contour-Styled" body was the design of John M. Reinhart, who had been assigned to dramatically erase the much criticized "pregnant elephant" image of 1948-50, and to bring Packard into the modern idiom. Reinhart used lots of glass, including a one-piece curved windshield; a traditional grille and hood shape; and a squared-off lower body, which brought the fenders up level with the hood and deck, arguably for the first time on a mass production Detroit car.

In the luxury field, Packard introduced the only fresh design for 1951—better by far than the styled-by-engineers Chrysler Imperial and well ahead of the cow-eyed Lincoln. By comparison to arch-rival Cadillac, however, it looked conservative. Cadillacs exuded flash, even with their four-year-old 1951 body. Neither did the Patrician's interior look very inviting to luxury car clients. Though its plush broadcloths and wool carpeting met the highest quality standards, they lacked color, and many complained about the hard coil-sprung seats.

The Patrician also continued to rely on a straight-eight engine, when both Cadillac and Imperial boasted modern overhead-valve V-8s—and Lincoln would too, in 1952. But the Patrician did have smooth-shifting Ultramatic as its standard transmission, while Cadillac and Lincoln used the lumpy Hydra-Matic and Imperial made do with

Packard brought out the Patrician 400 for 1951 as its top-of-the-line sedan. The '53 model seen here (sans the 400 tag) differed from the '51 only in detail, although the straight eight saw horsepower increase from 155 to 180. Packard built 7456 Patricians that year at $3740 apiece.

PACKRO

1953-54 Packard Clipper

When an aging management chose Hotpoint appliance hotshot James J. Nance to take over Packard leadership in mid-1952, it was with the full expectation of a major shake-up in Packard's methods of doing business. Nance didn't disappoint them. He governed with a flourish, pensioning off executives who had hung on past retirement age, hired youthful new managers (many from outside the auto industry), and invigorated his team with frequent pep talks. But mainly he planned exciting new engineering and styling developments for a make that had lost both its traditional image and its sense of purpose. He didn't always make the right decision, perhaps, but it's hard to imagine Packard producing the cars it did in 1955-56 without him.

One of the tenets of Nance's philosophy was the need to separate the line of cheap Packards (that had existed at least since the Packard Six in 1937) from the traditional luxury models. Pre-Nance, the company had relied on numerical designations to do this: 200, 250, 300, 400. But these were confusing, overlapped each other (the sporty Mayfair 250 was more luxurious than the 300, for example), and did not accomplish what Nance wanted.

So Nance replaced the 200 series in 1953 with the "Clipper," a respected name from the past that had generally been linked with less expensive Packards. His ultimate plan called for evolving the Clipper into an entirely separate make, and he did in fact achieve this for 1956. But it was done over the protest of dealers, who thought it foolhardy to trade away the still-respected Packard name. "In the short run," Nance told this writer, "they were right. In the long run, this kind of thing was just handing over the luxury market to Cadillac on a silver platter."

The 1953 Clipper listed a standard and DeLuxe series, each with a four-door and club (two-door) sedan. The standard line also included a jazzed up pillared coupe called the Sportster; it sold for $114 more than the DeLuxe club coupe. Done up in two-tone color combinations and with colorful interiors, the Sportster suggested a kind of ersatz hardtop, along the lines of the Ford Crestliner (see entry), although not as elaborate. The Sportster started at $2805, while standard Clippers began at $2554. The two ranges differed only in trim details, the DeLuxe carrying bright metal moldings around the window frames, more substantial bumper guards, and a higher-grade interior.

In market orientation the Clippers took aim directly at the middle-priced field—competitive territory occupied by the likes of Oldsmobile, DeSoto, Pontiac, and Mercury. In those days, this was the most hotly contested field in the car business, but Nance's game plan worked and he claimed vindication. In the 1952 model year, Packard had built only 60,000 cars including 45,000 200s. The 1953 run totaled 90,000 units, nearly 65,000 of them Clippers, an increase of more than 40 percent for Packard's middle-priced range.

A more ambitious line of Clipper Specials, DeLuxes, and Supers, including a new Panama hardtop, saw a 1954 launch. As before, the DeLuxe received a slightly more powerful straight-eight engine. Prices hardly changed, with the detrimmed Special holding the line at $2554. The Clipper Super made a bid for the elusive upper-middle-priced territory held by Chrysler and Buick, with the Panama starting at $3125. An additional 120 Clipper chassis were produced for commercial bodies built by the Henney Company. Styling was similar to 1953, but distinguished by designer Dick Teague's novel taillights tucked into the fender tops; Teague referred to their design as the "sore thumb look."

Unfortunately, what had worked in 1953 refused to work again. The Ford-GM sales wars wreaked disaster on the independents, who could not discount their cars to the extent that the big companies did. Furthermore, the public increasingly insisted on V-8 engines, and the Clipper—like the senior Packards—still labored along with the old-fashioned straight eight. Gear-start Ultramatic, a revision of the original Packard automatic designed to give better acceleration, was an improvement, but not enough in and of itself to stem sales losses to V-8 rivals. Clipper production fell drastically, barely exceeding 23,000 units. But plans were afoot to turn this around with an extensively revised '55 Clipper.

Packard marked time in 1954 while awaiting a major redesign and a V-8 for 1955. Meanwhile, the lower-priced '54 Clippers came in three flavors, the tastiest being the Super. The four-door sedan shown here listed at $2815, and ran Packard's mid-size 327-cid straight eight with 165 horsepower. A total of 6270 were built for the year.

SPECIFICATIONS

Engine: sidevalve I-8 **1953 standard and 1954 Special** 288 cid (3.50 × 3.75), 150 bhp **1953 DeLuxe** 327 cid (3.50 × 4.25), 160 bhp **1954 DeLuxe and Super** 165 bhp

Transmission:	3-speed manual; overdrive and Ultramatic optional
Suspension, front:	independent, coil springs, tube shocks
Suspension, rear:	live axle, leaf springs, tube shocks
Brakes:	front/rear drums
Wheelbase (in.):	122.0
Weight (lbs):	3585-3750
Top speed (mph):	90-95
0-60 mph (sec):	15.0-17.0

Production: **1953 standard 4d sdn** 23,126 **club sdn** 6370 **Sportster** 3672 **DeLuxe 4d sdn** 26,027 **club sdn** 4678 **commercial** 380 **1954 Special 4d sdn** 970 **club sdn** 912 **DeLuxe 4d sdn** 7610 **club sdn** 1470 **Sportster** 1336 **Super 4d sdn** 6270 **club sdn** 887 **Panama 2d htp** 3618 **commercial** 120

SUPER CLIPPER
MICHIGAN
HISTORIC VEHICLE

1955-56 Packard Caribbean

The last Caribbeans stood proudly as the most luxurious cars built by Packard since the 1948-50 Custom Eights, direct descendants of the great open Packards of the "golden age," the Twenties and early Thirties. Base-priced around $6000, a hair below the Cadillac Eldorado, they were certainly meant to be profitable, and to serve as proof that the Packard marque had returned to its heritage of undiluted luxury. Sadly, they were built by a company skirting financial disaster, without friends among the banks and insurance companies that backed car builders in those days, and destined for the scrap heap of history—despite ambitious plans to succeed them with a dashing line of even longer, lower, wider, and more powerful land yachts in 1957.

In 1955, Packard was poised to produce a tremendously impressive Caribbean, since all its plans had finally come to fruition: V-8 engine, Torsion-Level suspension, Twin-Ultramatic Drive, and a gee-whiz facelift courtesy of Dick Teague. The two-year problem of having only the junior wheelbase for its convertible was solved when Packard turned to plastic tooling for a five-inch-longer-wheelbase body. This new method took half the time and cost 60 percent less than the traditional steel tooling, allowing Packard to produce a long-wheelbase Four Hundred hardtop, as well as the Caribbean convertible.

Equipped with Teague's massive eggcrate grille, three-tone paint job, a bejeweled dashboard, and cushy leather upholstery, the '55 Caribbean came with Ultramatic, Torsion-Level, dual antennas/exhausts/hood scoops, radio, heater, and power-everything. The only options were wire wheels ($325), tinted ($32) or shaded ($45) glass, and air conditioning. The mighty flagship also sported the most powerful Packard V-8 engine: 275 horsepower, provided by twin Rochester 4GC carburetors with progressive linkage (four barrels in operation full time, the other four kicking

SPECIFICATIONS

Engine: ohv V-8 **1955** 352.0 cid (4.00 × 3.50), 275 bhp **1956** 374.0 cid (4.13 × 3.50), 310 bhp

Transmission:	Twin-Ultramatic
Suspension, front:	independent, longitudinal torsion bars
Suspension, rear:	live axle, longitudinal torsion bars
Brakes:	front/rear drums
Wheelbase (in.):	127.0
Weight (lbs):	4590-4960
Top speed (mph):	120
0-60 mph (sec):	11.0-12.0
Production:	**1955 cvt** 500 **1956 cvt** 276 **htp cpe** 263

in as required). This meant fuel mileage on the order of 8-12 mpg, but nobody in the Caribbean's price league worried about such trifles anyway.

Despite Packard's claim that it was purposely limiting production to 500, James Nance (at least) would have given his left arm for more, since the 500 sold out within four months of announcement. Nance urgently memoed his sales manager to try to get disappointed customers into Four Hundreds, which dealers might trade back later for '56 Caribbeans: "You might save some of these people by fixing up the Four Hundred with dual aerials to give it a little Caribbean flavor." A few dealers actually did "convert" Four Hundreds, and far more ambitiously, by ordering Caribbean hoods, side trim, and leather upholstery and affixing Caribbean script.

Looking back, it seems that Packard missed a chance to sell more Caribbeans than the planned run. Unlike the 1953-54 models, which had to be specially finished by Mitchell-Bentley, the '55 was basically just a trim option, albeit a convertible, built alongside the other Packards at the Conner Avenue factory. The actual hardware involved the special hood, mainly; holes for script could have been drilled with templates. Spare parts had to be stocked; why were they so miserly in banging Caribbeans out? With a hard-driving salesman like Nance at the helm, the decision is difficult to fathom. By comparison, Cadillac sold 3950 Eldorados, and production there continued to climb upward.

Both the Eldo and Caribbean added a hardtop model in 1956, but Cadillac's flagship outsold the Caribbean ten to one that year. Mainly this was owed to Packard's 1955 service problems, and public fear that the make would soon disappear—as mentioned in earlier chapters. But it was a shame, because the '56 Caribbean, powered by a mighty 310 horsepower, 374 cubic-inch V-8, was the best yet.

The facelift involved a new grille, deeply hooded fenders, and a minor trim shuffle. Most novel was the interior, which featured electronic push-buttons for the Twin-Ultramatic, and two-way removable seat cushions. The former soon proved problem-prone, less reliable than Chrysler's mechanical buttons; the latter was truly brilliant. Owners had the option of jacquard cloth upholstery on one side, leather on the other. It is a mystery why this novel treatment, so useful in areas of wide climatic changes, wasn't more widely used during the bench seat era.

The '55 Caribbean was uprated to Packard's 127-inch senior wheelbase, and was heavily restyled, like the rest of the line. The '55 (opposite) listed at $5932 and saw output of 500 units. The '56 (this page) received a modest facelift and sold for $5995, and was joined by a $5495 hardtop. Sales came in at 276 and 263, respectively.

1955 Packard Clipper/ 1956 Clipper

The Clipper officially became a make in its own right for 1956—separate from Packard in style, marketing, and "official" industry records. It received as many alterations as did Packard in these years, with stylists working to visually separate it as much as possible from the Patrician and Four Hundred. Product planners, meanwhile, tried to separate the two lines by as many dollars as possible. Thus, while Packard kept its 1954 prices about the same for '55, Clippers actually dropped $100 or so—despite being radically restyled, equipped with V-8 engines and, in some cases, with Torsion-Level suspension.

Bill Schmidt and his designers did an amazing job of disguising the Clipper's aged body, while making it nevertheless different-looking than the Packard. Clippers, for example, received less elaborate grillework and did without the "Reynolds Wrap" anodized aluminum along the body sides. Two-toning took on a radical pattern: the hood and front fender color swept downward across the doors and flowed back along the lower rear fenders. In retrospect, solid-color Clippers look better, but in 1955 with two-toning all the rage, this seemed a logical approach to the problem. Dick Teague's "sore thumb" taillight from 1954 remained, with back-up lamps fitted underneath the red lenses.

The Torsion-Level Clipper Custom comprised a four-door sedan and the Constellation (nee Pacific) hardtop coupe; the club sedan body style was eliminated. At lower prices, initially with conventional suspension, came the DeLuxe and Super sedan and Super Panama hardtop. These used a smaller 225-bhp V-8, while the Custom was powered by a detuned 245-bhp version of the Packard 352. A colorful array of interiors in nylons, vinyls, or jacquards was offered. Despite their higher price, Customs sold better, their Torsion-Level suspension impressing buyers who

SPECIFICATIONS

Engine: ohv V-8 **1955 DeLuxe and Super** 320.0 cid (3.81 × 3.50), 225 bhp **1955 Custom** 352.0 cid (4.00 × 3.50), 245 bhp **1956 DeLuxe and Super** 352.0 cid, 240 bhp **1956 Custom** 275 bhp

Transmission:	3-speed manual; overdrive and Twin-Ultramatic optional
Suspension, front:	**1955 DeLuxe and Super** coil springs, tube shocks **Custom** independent, longitudinal torsion bars, tube shocks (optional Super) **1956** torsion bars (DeLuxe delete option)
Suspension rear:	**1955 DeLuxe and Super** live axle, leaf springs, tube shocks **Custom** live axle, longitudinal torsion bars (optional Super) **1956** torsion bars (DeLuxe delete option)
Brakes:	front/rear drums
Wheelbase (in.):	122.0
Weight (lbs):	3680-3885
Top speed (mph):	100-110
0-60 mph (sec):	10.0-14.0

Production: **1955 DeLuxe 4d sdn** 8039 **Super 4d sdn** 7979 **Super Panama 2d htp** 7016 **Custom 4d sdn** 8708 **Custom Constellation htp cpe** 6672 **1956 DeLuxe 4d sdn** 5715 **Super 4d sdn** 5173 **Super htp cpe** 3999 **Custom 4d sdn** 2129 **Super Constellation htp cpe** 1466

hadn't expected anything this exotic in a middle-priced model. In fact, the torsion bars were so impressive that Packard made them optional on the Super in mid-1955 and standard across the board on the 1956 Clipper, though conventional suspension was a delete-option on the DeLuxe.

This attractive range of sedans and hardtops sold close to 40,000 units for the model year, good considering that the lineup lacked station wagons, coupes, and four-door hardtops to expand the market base. And it was certainly a lot more Clippers than had been sold in 1954. Claiming the Clipper name could stand on its own, management brought out the facelifted '56s with no Packard name anywhere on the exterior—but dealers protested and a small script nameplate was grudgingly applied to the decklid.

The 1956 Clipper line was a re-run of the five 1955 models, except that the "Panama" name was dropped from the Super hardtop and all cars now had the 352 engine. Styling was strictly a reshuffle of 1955, grilles going from vertical to horizontal bars, "candy cane" two-toning being replaced by a less complicated bodyside color sweep to match the roof tone. Dick Teague freshened the rear end with tall, sharply raked "slipper" taillights surmounting horizontal back-up lamps. Prices remained about the same, but Clipper had suffered in 1955 from the same problems Packard did: quality control, Ultramatic nits, troublesome Torsion-Level motors—and a public increasingly convinced that this make would soon become an "orphan." Besides, sales in general receded after setting an industry record in 1955. It all added up to fewer than 20,000 model year sales. A 1957 Clipper would appear, but based entirely on the Studebaker President.

Clippers were built alongside Packards at the Conner Avenue, Detroit plant where the company installed its production line for 1955. Conner was selected because Packard's longtime body builder, Briggs, had been bought by Chrysler in 1954; Packard had not built its own bodies since it had contracted with Briggs for the prewar Clipper. President Nance figured the job could be done better by the modern, one-story Conner plant than the aging Packard factory on East Grand Boulevard. Alas, Conner wasn't nearly large enough, causing production-line tie-ups; and the sheer newness of the place produced quality control problems.

In retrospect, Nance would have probably done better to bring the body building operation into Grand Boulevard. But hindsight is cheap, and Conner looked very tempting back in 1954. But after 1956 it wouldn't matter anyway, since neither would be in operation.

In 1955, a vertical-bar grille, "sore thumb" taillights, and unique side trim and two-toning set the Clipper Custom Constellation hardtop (opposite) *apart from the big Packards. The '56 edition* (this page) *sported a horizontal-bar grille, new taillights, and more tasteful two-toning. List price was $3076 in 1955, $3164 in '56.*

1955-56 Packard Patrician/Four Hundred/Executive

The 1955 Packard looked all-new; in fact, it used a heavily restyled 1951-54 bodyshell. New also for the big 127-inch-wheelbase Packards was a 260-bhp version of the 352-cid overhead-valve V-8 and "Torsion Level" suspension. The Packard Four Hundred two-door hardtop shown here listed at $3930 and saw a production run of 7206 units.

Though far from completely new, the 1955-56 Packard received probably the most revolutionary facelift of the Fifties. It represented a significant departure from previous practices, not only in styling, but in engineering as well. Those who condemn James Nance as a wrecker of the company are obliged to tell us what the old management he replaced would have delivered by 1955: as one Packard writer put it, there would probably have been nothing left but a $2300 Clipper sedan, powered by the only straight-eight engine left in the world.

The new cars were committee-engineered—but what a committee: Bill Graves, chief engineer, headed the V-8 project, staffed by J.R. Ferguson, Bill Schwieder, and E.A. Weiss; Forest MacFarland and Herb Misch developed the new Twin Ultramatic transmission; Bill Allison created the "Torsion Level" suspension.

SPECIFICATIONS

Engine: ohv V-8 **1955** 352.0 cid (4.00 × 3.50), 260 bhp **1956 Executive** 275 bhp **1956 Patrician and Four Hundred** 374.0 cid (4.13 x 3.50), 290 bhp

Transmission:	Twin-Ultramatic
Suspension, front:	independent, longitudinal torsion bars
Suspension, rear:	live axle, longitudinal torsion bars
Brakes:	front/rear drums
Wheelbase (in.):	127.0 **1956 Executive** 122.0
Weight (lbs):	4045-4275
Top speed (mph):	115
0-60 mph (sec):	10.5-11.5

Production: **1955 Patrician 4d sdn** 9127 **Four Hundred htp cpe** 7206 **1956 Executive 4d sdn** 1784 **htp cpe** 1031 **Patrician 4d sdn** 3775 **Four Hundred 2d htp** 3224

It was on this last feature that Packard hung its 1955 advertising slogan, "Let the Ride Decide." Torsion bars had been tried before, but never had they been mounted longitudinally, without anchor points, working on all four wheels. They provided a remarkable combination of ride and handling, scaling even car-breaking railroad crossings with aplomb. And as one Packard enthusiast likes to point out, "most of them are still leveling away 33 years later."

The new V-8, a solid design, boasted the highest horsepower in the industry save for the Chrysler 300. Enlarged to 374 cubic inches in 1956, the big Packard V-8 saw use in the Studebaker Golden Hawk, several drag racers, and even marine applications. More controversial was Twin-Ultramatic transmission, named for its combination of gear-start and torque converter, designed to handle the V-8's formidable power.

With Twin-Ultramatic the car started in low, then shifted to high via a band release and clutches; at cruising speed the converter locked up (as became common in the Eighties). Its weakness centered on the complicated linkage used for the low-to-high shift. Unless properly set up—tricky for most independent garages, and for owners once Packard dealers began disappearing—the high clutches would burn up. Also, Twin-Ultramatic kicked down too slowly at mid-range rpm, which caused lugging and resultant engine problems.

Though serious Packard collectors would have nothing else, most defenses of Twin Ultramatic seem to contend that it would have worked fine if it had the kind of factory service and support enjoyed by TorqueFlite or Hydra-Matic. Most judicious is this comment by a respected Packard writer: "Properly set up, properly driven, and

properly maintained, it was among the best available. But it was unforgiving of a lapse in any one of these requirements."

Styling of the '55 Packards, which after all were still based on the aging Reinhart shell dating back to 1951, reflected the wizardry of Bill Schmidt's design department, chiefly Dick Teague. A glitzy mid-Fifties eggcrate grille, hooded headlamps, a ribbed chrome molding for the sides to break up the tall appearance, enormous "cathedral" taillights and dual exhausts at the rear, and a wraparound windshield touched all the bases for mid-Fifties buyers. Most important, the Patrician sedan was at last joined by a hardtop worthy of the first rank, named the Four Hundred—a designation Packard had used before, but now spelled out.

Performance, good looks, a truly innovative suspension system, and luxury brought Packard modest success in 1955. Sales nearly doubled 1954 levels, and the company enthusiastically released a mild facelift for 1956. In addition to the Patrician and Four Hundred—and with Clipper now officially a separate make—Packard added a lower-priced "Executive" sedan and hardtop on the Clipper wheelbase, priced about $700 below the flagships and distinguished by the Clipper's pointed "slipper" taillights.

Unfortunately, the 1955 recovery had not been sufficient, nor nearly what Packard needed. Output, after all, still remained far below most pre-1954 figures. A spate of service troubles involving rear axles, Torsion-Level motors, Twin Ultramatic, and assembly quality, did further damage in the marketplace. Sales, counting Clipper, fell again—to lower than the '54 level. Financing for future models dried up, Nance left, and Studebaker-Packard signed a management agreement with the Curtiss-Wright aircraft company. Future Packards would be in fact merely deluxe Studebakers: the '56 was destined to be the last of the big Packard luxury cars.

Packard spun off the Clipper as a separate make for 1956, and gave the senior models modified grillework, a front bumper with more widely spaced "Dagmars," and more deeply hooded headlights. The Four Hundred hardtop (opposite, top) *and Patrician sedan* (bottom) *boasted a 374-cid, 290-bhp V-8. The less-expensive Executive* (this page), *available as a hardtop or four-door sedan, rode the shorter 122-inch wheelbase and used the 352-cid, 275-bhp V-8.*

CALIFORNIA
BAE 192

CALIFORNIA
BMC 986

1957 Packard Clipper/1958 Packard

Without sources to finance his all-new line of 1957 Packards, middle-priced Clippers, and Studebakers, James Nance resigned as chief executive officer. Studebaker-Packard was then picked up by Curtiss-Wright Corporation, as a dalliance of its president Roy Hurley, who thought he could show Detroit a few things.

It is commonly said that Hurley wanted Studebaker-Packard because its losses would help minimize corporate taxes on profitable Curtiss-Wright. In the short term this may have been an attraction, but Hurley had every intention of making S-P profitable. One way to do that, he figured, was to sell off Packard's Michigan factories and concentrate all production at the Studebaker plant in South Bend, Indiana.

This was duly arranged for 1957, but it created a problem: Packard dealers held franchises which promised them a Packard to sell as long as S-P remained in business. Without Grand Boulevard or Conner Avenue, a traditional big Packard was not possible; anyway, Packard had cried for a full restyle for years and the proposed '57 designs were moribund. Solution? A Studebaker with Packard labels, of course! Thus emerged the 1957 Packard Clipper, cleverly designed by Dick Teague to mimic 1956 Packard styling, but built entirely around a Studebaker President bodyshell.

As far as it went, it turned out fairly well. Teague transferred the rakish '56 Clipper taillights to the rear end, applied some "Reynolds Wrap" trim to the sides, and crafted a grille and dashboard reminiscent of the '56. Upholstery, while not quite up to Packard quality, was as luxurious as they could make it. Two body styles, a four-door "Town Sedan" and a shorter-wheelbase "Country Sedan" wagon, were chosen, being two of the most popular body styles at the time. A hardtop would have been helpful, but incredibly, Studebaker had no hardtops at the time, aside from the sporty Hawk.

SPECIFICATIONS

Engine: ohv V-8, 289.0 cid (3.56 × 3.63) **1957** 275 bhp **1958** 210 bhp, 225 bhp optional

Transmission:	3-speed manual; overdrive and Flight-O-Matic optional
Suspension, front:	independent, coil springs, tube shocks
Suspension, rear:	live axle, leaf springs, tube shocks
Brakes:	front/rear drums
Wheelbase (in.):	**4d sdn** 120.5 **4d wgn and htp cpe** 116.5
Weight (lbs):	3480-3650
Top speed (mph):	**1957** 120 **1958** 105
0-60 mph (sec):	**1957** 9.0-10.0 **1958** 11.0-12.0

Production: 1957 4d Town Sedan 3940 **Country Sedan 4d wgn** 869 **1958 4d sdn** 1200 **4d wgn** 159 **htp cpe** 675

The '57 Packard Clipper (opposite) *was clearly based on the '56 Studebaker President Classic, but it wore its Packard styling "cues" better than one could have reasonably expected. With its contrived quad headlights and fin-on-a-fin rear end, the '58 redesign* (this page) *was a disaster—a sad end, as it proved, to a noble name. In all, 7431 "Packardbakers" were built during the two-year period.*

Along with the sale of the Utica engine plant went Packard's V-8, but South Bend contributed its fine 289-cid small-block Studebaker V-8, which in supercharged form gave the '57 almost as much horsepower as the '56 Packards. Base prices started at $3212 for the sedan, $3384 for the wagon, about $700 upstream of the comparable Studebaker President. With its 120.5-inch wheelbase, the Clipper Town Sedan had actually lost only 1.5 inches between the wheels compared to the '56 Clipper, but it weighed some 300 pounds less and lacked the "presence" of the earlier Clipper.

The worst problem the new Packard faced was its name. People recognized it on sight as a Studebaker. Traditional Packard buyers took one look and went over to Cadillac or Lincoln; traditional Studebaker buyers found them too expensive. Thus, nice as they were, the '57s accounted for only about 5000 sales.

The decision then turned to the '58 models. Though Packard franchises had by now all been dualled to handle Studebakers, the company still entertained hopes for an eventual revival of the luxury Packard. S-P's president, Harold Churchill, decided to keep the present charade going. A Studebaker hardtop was planned for 1958, so the '58 Packard (sans "Clipper") consisted of the previous sedan and wagon, plus a new two-door hardtop (and a Packard version of the Studebaker Hawk—see next chapter). Prices remained in the low $3000s.

The unenviable task of designing the '58 Packards fell on Duncan McRae. Somehow, he had to keep up with the styling trends set down by the competition, but S-P couldn't afford to tool anything besides the new hardtop. So McRae resorted to welded-on tailfins, so hastily contrived that they actually formed a kind of double-fin at the rear. Because quad headlights were all the rage, he also had to develop awkward bulging pods to fit them on the 1958 Packards. Gold mylar side trim, another popular fetish of the time, added to the freaky look. The supercharged engine was left off the sedan, wagon and hardtop, so the Packard now ran with the same power as a Studebaker President.

The result could almost have been predicted—a travesty, and a sad end, as it proved, to a noble name. Sales of the 1958s amounted to only 2622 units, counting the Hawk. The bizarre wagon, priced too high at $3600, came in lowest, accounting for a grand total of 159 vehicles.

This sort of situation simply couldn't go on. With S-P now basing all its hopes on the compact Lark for 1959, and franchise obligations met with Studebakers, the Packard automobile came to an end. The name did find itself used briefly on some export trucks, and was finally dropped from the corporate title in 1962.

1958 Packard Hawk

The most bizarre and interesting 1958 Packard most certainly had to be the Hawk, a $4000 supercharged line-leader based on the Studebaker Golden Hawk, with special styling by Duncan McRae. Like the luxury Golden Hawk 400, the Packard Hawk featured a full leather interior. Its front end design, however, stood apart—completely unique and unforgettable: a wide-mouth grille that looked as if it had been inspired by Electrolux. Other odd features included exterior vinyl armrests along the side windows, a spare tire outline on the rear deck, and gaudy gold mylar inserts for the flared tailfins. McRae did manage to avoid quad headlamps, considered so essential on the other '58 Packards. But the car's styling wasn't entirely McRae's doing. Studebaker-Packard chairman Roy Hurley had to bear much of the responsibility; in fact, there probably wouldn't have been a Packard Hawk were it not for him.

"Mr. Hurley had seen a Ferrari and a Mercedes 300SL during one of his European trips," McRae recalled, "and insisted that a special Hawk be designed to imitate them. The result was what we smilingly called the 'Hurley Hawk'...a perfect example of the wrong idea, overpriced, uncompetitive, overdecorated. Together with the other 1958 Packards it proved a sad end to the marque which expired in mid-year in Studebaker clothing."

Hurley's fascination with the likes of Ferrari and Mercedes explain the Packard's broad scoop grille. Duncan McRae's understanding of the Packard heritage likewise explains the hood indentations or "cusps," which represented the Packard hood shape dating back to the 1904 Model L. McRae, also a flying enthusiast, accepts credit for the padded exterior armrests, which reminded him of classic airplanes. The gold mylar tailfins and spare tire impression (likened by stylists to a toilet seat) were simply attempts to set off the Packard Hawk from the Studebaker versions, which cost at least $700 less.

In Roy Hurley's defense, we ought to remember that he was desperately trying to retain an image of Packard distinct and separate from Studebaker, in the hopes that a big luxury Packard line might still be viable. Hurley had engineered an agreement through which Studebaker-Packard became the North American agent for Mercedes-Benz, and many S-P dealers sold the German luxury cars; but evidently he saw this as a sideline to the luxury business that a future Packard might enjoy.

A letter from Hurley to S-P president Harold Churchill is illuminating. "If you are cautious and come up with a more conventional style [of Studebaker-based Packards for 1958], I am quite sure it will be labeled a Studebaker and will fail, and I doubt that Packard can stand another year of that atmosphere.... You must avoid any action that would cause the public to feel that Studebaker-Packard is going to dry up and that you will be an importer of foreign cars. The new Packard is the best answer to this kind of skepticism." Unfortunately, all the company had to work with *were* Studebakers, and no amount of glorification or special trim could prevent them from being labeled as such.

On the inside, the beautifully finished Packard Hawk sported tan pleated leather. The driver faced an array of business-like white-on-black instruments set into an engine-turned metal dashboard. Flight-O-Matic automatic transmission and a supercharged 289 came standard, providing vivid performance. The Packard Hawk also benefited from 1958 chassis modifications: new rates for the variable-rate front coil springs, revised shock valving, and asymmetrical leaf springs lengthened toward the rear. These changes eliminated the tendency of the 1957 [Studebaker] Hawks to oversteer. Most observers concluded that the '58s rode and handled better than the '57s.

The Packard Hawk remains a curiosity—an outgrowth of last-ditch attempts to preserve the Packard name, as hastily abandoned as they were conceived. Not surprisingly, production was very low, and the scarcity of surviving examples has made the Hawks the most collectible of that 1957-58 range of cars known to enthusiasts—quite accurately—as "Packardbakers."

The Packard Hawk came about because Studebaker-Packard chairman Roy Hurley wanted a car to emulate the Ferrari and Mercedes-Benz 300SL he had seen while in Europe. While it didn't look like either, the Hawk did have a high level of performance—its supercharged 275-horsepower V-8 could accelerate it from 0-60 mph in as little as eight seconds.

SPECIFICATIONS

Engine:	ohv V-8, 289.0 cid (3.56 × 3.63), 275 bhp
Transmission:	3-speed Flight-O-Matic
Suspension, front:	independent, coil springs, tube shocks
Suspension, rear:	live axle, leaf springs, tube shocks
Brakes:	front/rear drums
Wheelbase (in.):	120.5
Weight (lbs):	3470
Top speed (mph):	125
0-60 mph (sec):	8.0-9.0
Production:	588

1951-52 Plymouth Belvedere

Plymouth had the dubious distinction of being the last Chrysler Corporation make to field a hardtop. Its Cranbrook Belvedere arrived a year behind the pillarless Dodge, DeSoto, and Chrysler models—and Chevrolet's sporty 1950 Styleline DeLuxe Bel Air. Even hard-pressed Ford got the jump on Plymouth by bringing out its new Custom V-8 Victoria about three months earlier in the 1951 model year.

It seemed rather curious for a make that had long been the industry's number-three seller, and it reflected a kind of benign neglect that hampered Plymouth in the closing years of the K.T. Keller era. Keller had taken over as company president upon Walter Chrysler's death in 1940. With his practical bent, the cars produced under his aegis were uniformly orthodox and quite dull. Plymouth was no exception.

Though enlarged from 201.3 to 217.8 cubic inches for 1942, Plymouth's plodding L-head six hadn't changed much since its previous enlargement in 1934. With 95 horsepower through the early-'49 models and 97 bhp thereafter, it barely stayed competitive with Chevrolet's "Stovebolt" six, but not the flathead Ford V-8, the traditional low-price performance leader. But where Ford and Chevy offered glamorous new 1949 styling, Plymouth's "new" look made it just another one of Keller's postwar boxes: roomy but conservatively upright at a time when the public wanted low-slung torpedoes. This miscalculation would cost Chrysler dearly. By 1952 the firm would surrender to Ford as Detroit's number-two producer; by 1954, Plymouth would fall from third to fifth in sales, behind Buick and Olds.

Plymouth had other problems too. Where Chevy and Ford responded fairly quickly to the public's growing preference for automatic transmissions—in 1950 and '51, respectively—Plymouth wouldn't get one until late 1954. Then too, Plymouth lost some important sales momentum in the huge late-Forties seller's market as Dodge Division, where Keller had been general manager in the early Thirties, got preference in the allocation of postwar-scarce materials, which forced Plymouth to make do with lower production.

Plymouth also got short-shifted by dealers. Arch Brown, writing in *Collectible Automobile,* quoted this recollection of a former Dodge-Plymouth agent: "We advertised Plymouth heavily as our price-leader...But over on the next street were the Chrysler and DeSoto dealers [who also] carried Plymouth [and were thus] ready to shave a few dollars off our price to make a sale. So our people were instructed to...focus the prospect's attention on Dodge." As Chrysler and DeSoto dealers did the same, Plymouth sales suffered.

It's ironic that Plymouth fielded the last low-priced hardtop, because Chrysler had built seven prototype Town & Country hardtops a full three years before GM's first 1949 production models. But for reasons no one seems to recall, Chrysler held back on this instantly popular innovation, and thus had to play catch-up in 1950-51.

Nevertheless, the Belvedere signaled that things were beginning to change at Plymouth, and Highland Park in general—as indeed they were. In 1950, Keller moved up to chairman and the aggressive L.L. "Tex" Colbert replaced him as president. It would take a few years for this and other personnel changes to affect Chrysler products, but at least the Belvedere could lay claim to being the sportiest closed Plymouth in a long time. Naturally, it was offered only in the top-line series, newly Cranbrook (previously Special DeLuxe), and bore the same revised styling that made all '51 Plymouths look a bit more "important" than the 1949-50 models. It arrived quite late—March 31—but added a lot of spiff to a line that needed all it could get.

There certainly wasn't much else to talk about for '51. Ditto '52: just bolder "Plymouth" grille lettering and a revised rear license lamp/holder. But the Belvedere gained some added distinction in new "saddleback" two-toning, with downward-curved rear-quarter chrome moldings defining a contrast-color area matching the roof.

Later Plymouth hardtops, like most everyone else's, were priced about the same as comparably trimmed four-door sedans, but the first Belvedere came at a premium price. At $2114, the '51 cost nearly $300 more than the Cranbrook four-door and only $108 less than the convertible. This may explain why Plymouth moved only 51,266 Belvederes for 1951-52 (Chrysler didn't separate production for these model years), far adrift of Ford's 187,606 Victorias and Chevy's 177,890 Bel Airs. Though better times were coming, they were still a few years away.

Chevy had a hardtop in 1950, Ford got one a couple of months into the 1951 model year. Plymouth had one for '51, too, but not until March 31. It was properly known as the Cranbrook Belvedere (above) *and it listed at $2222. The '52 Plymouth was a carbon copy of the '51, but the Belvedere* (opposite) *sported an interesting—and attractive—"saddleback" two-tone paint job that saw the roof color sweep down over the rear deck.*

SPECIFICATIONS

Engine:	L-head I-6, 217.8 cid (3.25 × 4.38), 97 bhp
Transmission:	3-speed manual; overdrive optional
Suspension, front:	upper and lower A-arms, coil springs
Suspension, rear:	live axle, semi-elliptic leaf springs
Brakes:	front/rear drums
Wheelbase (in.):	118.5
Weight (lbs):	3105-3182
Top speed (mph):	80-85
0-60 mph (sec):	15.0
Production:	51,266

1130

1953-54 Plymouth Belvedere

Nothing sold cars in the Fifties like styling, as it still does. Though performance became more important as the decade wore on, especially after 1954, a car needed the right looks if its maker hoped to stay in business—let alone turn a profit—and more than a few makes fell victim to odd or outmoded styling. One thinks of Kaiser-Frazer, Nash and Hudson, Studebaker-Packard—and, of course, Edsel.

If not exactly terminal, Plymouth sales charts certainly looked anemic by 1953, reflecting too many years of pedestrian people-movers in a market gone mad for power and pizzazz. But Plymouth, like Chevrolet, would undergo a memorable metamorphosis for 1955, with fully contemporary styling and hot new V-8 performance. Still, such wholesale changes took time even in that freewheeling age, when major design overhauls came as an almost annual fall ritual, so both makes issued transitional models for 1953-54, basically their familiar fare with a little more go and a lot more show.

Plymouth needed styling help in the worst way by 1953. Compared with Chevy and Ford, which had become far prettier with their first postwar redesigns of 1949—and thus more popular—Plymouth still looked like your grandmother's car, and sales had been withering. But Virgil Exner had come aboard as Chrysler styling chief, and the '53 corporate line was the first to reflect his influence. It couldn't have come at a better time for Plymouth, which had little else to talk about that year, for it still lacked the V-8 performance accorded Chrysler and DeSoto for 1951-52, and with which Dodge would make hay for '53.

Still, hopes ran high in Plymouth's 25th anniversary year—but the results came in mixed. Offerings were regrouped from three series into two by dropping the low-end, 111-inch-wheelbase Concord, including its dated fastback model, and putting the 118-inch-wheelbase Cambridge and Cranbrook on a new 114-inch chassis. Exner penned fully flush fenders, a smoother front, a lower deck, the now-obligatory one-

SPECIFICATIONS

Engines: L-head I-6 **1953-early 1954** 217.8 cid (3.25 × 4.38), 100 bhp **late 1954** 230.2 cid (3.25 × 4.63), 110 bhp

Transmission:	3-speed manual; overdrive optional **1953-early 1954** Hy-Drive semi-automatic optional **late 1954** 2-speed Powerflite automatic optional
Suspension, front:	upper and lower A-arms, coil springs
Suspension, rear:	live axle, semi-elliptic leaf springs
Brakes:	front/rear drums
Wheelbase (in.):	114.0
Weight (lbs):	2888-3273
Top speed (mph):	80-90
0-60 mph (sec):	15.0-16.0

Production: **1953 htp cpe** 35,185 **1954 4d sdn** 106,601 **Sport Coupe 2d htp** 25,592 **cvt** 6900 **Suburban 2d wgn** 9241 **chassis** 2031

Plymouth received chunky, more compact styling for 1953. The Cranbrook Belvedere hardtop (below) *listed at $2064 and 35,185 were sold. For 1954, Plymouth made the Belvedere a four-model series. The $1953 four-door sedan* (opposite, top) *was the most popular with 106,601 built, the $2301 ragtop the least chosen with just 6900 built.*

piece windshield and, on the top-line Belvedere hardtop, stylish reverse-curve C-pillars. Yet despite a wheelbase just an inch shorter than that of Ford and Chevrolet, the new design looked stubby, almost homely in fact.

Worse, mechanical changes were few. A slight compression boost lifted Plymouth's hoary six from 97 to an even 100 horsepower—hardly earthshaking. And a new transmission option, Hy-Drive, arrived. But instead of a full automatic like Chevy and Ford had been touting for two and three years, this was merely a semi-automatic of the sort previously reserved for Chrysler's senior makes. Left in High range, it made for, shall we say, stately acceleration; for best performance one had to move off in second (the high ratio in Low range), then shift to High by lifting off the gas.

Plymouth volume rose by almost two-thirds for 1953, but only because restrictions caused by the Korean conflict had curtailed '52 production (to an estimated 396,000 units). But even at some 650,500 units, Highland Park's breadwinner remained a distant third behind Ford and Chevrolet, both of which saw production easily exceed 1.2 million. Worse, Buick was fast-closing in on Plymouth's traditional number-three spot.

The modestly facelifted '54s wouldn't stave off the attack. The Belvedere moniker expanded from the glamor-leading hardtop to encompass the entire top-range series. Next came the mid-priced Savoy and low-end Plaza, reinstating a three-series lineup. All Belvederes save the Suburban wagon wore little chrome fins on their rear fenders, a forecast of literally bigger things to come. But though Plymouth called them "Hy Style," the '54s really weren't. The problem was size, or rather the lack of it: a full five inches shorter than the '54 Ford, for example, even though all '54 Plymouths (except wagons) stretched beyond the '53s by nearly the same amount. But the difference showed, and it hurt.

Mechanical changes were again limited. Chrysler's fully automatic two-speed PowerFlite transmission became optionally available at mid-season, when the old six was stroked to deliver 110 bhp. But both were too little, too late. Chevy bumped its six to 115/125 bhp, while Ford boasted about its new 130-horsepower overhead-valve V-8, and both had offered automatics for several years. All these factors contributed to a sales tumble so severe that Plymouth finished fifth behind Buick and Oldsmobile.

But better times were almost at hand. Beginning with the hot new '55, the next four years would produce some of the best—and best-selling—Plymouths in history.

1955-56 Plymouth

Chrysler Corporation's historic postwar turn from staid styling and pedestrian performance to hot cars with high style began with the 1950 arrival of "Tex" Colbert as company president and Virgil Exner as chief stylist. It culminated in a dramatically new and eminently more successful corporate line for 1955. All five Chrysler makes, including the newly separate Imperial, were good-looking, well-built, and speedy. But if anyone had been giving out a "Most Improved" award, Plymouth would surely have been in contention as much as that year's equally transformed Chevrolet.

Styled under Exner's direction by Maury Baldwin, the "Forward Look" '55 bowed as the most exciting Plymouth ever: sleek, well proportioned, and appreciably quicker. Wheelbase gained only an inch, thus matching Ford and Chevy, but overall height came down 1.5 inches, while overall length stretched an extra 10.3 inches more than the '54, up now to 203.8 inches. With "fall-away" front fenders, hooded headlamps, wrapped windshield, vastly expanded glass areas, shapely rear fenders, and optional two-color "Sportone" paint, Plymouth aptly billed the '55 as "a great new car for the young at heart."

Plymouth's other big news for '55 was its first-ever V-8. Called "Hy-Fire," it was a modern, oversquare overhead-valve design with efficient polyspherical combustion chambers and aluminum pistons. It went into 61 percent of total production, though the figure would have undoubtedly been higher had it been more readily available. It came in three versions: a 241-cubic-inch unit with 157 horsepower; a bigger-bore 260 cid boasting 167 bhp; and the same with optional "PowerPak" (four-barrel carb and dual exhausts), good for 177 horses. Even the old PowerFlow six was tweaked, via higher 7.4:1 compression, to 117 bhp. Transmission comprised the three-speed column-shift manual, the same with optional overdrive, and fully automatic Powerflite. The last, now controlled by a willowy wand protruding from the dash to the right of the steering wheel, ended up on 46 percent of production.

Handling, already one of Plymouth's better features, came in for further improvement for '55 via wider rear leaf springs and front coils newly wrapped around the shock absorbers. *Motor Trend* magazine rated Plymouth "the easiest car to drive in 1955." Air conditioning, power steering and brakes, and electric windows, and power front seat all appeared on the options list; suspended foot pedals and tubeless tires were standard.

Plymouth retained its three 1954 series but shuffled body styles. These comprised a club coupe and four-door sedan in each line, a bottom-rung Plaza business coupe at $1639, and two- and four-door Suburban wagons. The top-line Belvedere added a convertible, Sport Coupe hardtop, and four-door Suburban. All, save the business coupe, were available with the V-8, which came standard on the $2478 ragtop.

With all this, Plymouth did exceptionally well in record-setting '55. Model year production jumped from a little over 463,000 to a gratifying 705,455, a healthy 52 percent gain that put Plymouth in fourth place, ousting Oldsmobile but still behind Buick.

Plymouth remained fourth for 1956 despite an industry-wide sales retreat that saw volume drop some 39 percent. A deft facelift brought a reshaped grille and side trim, plus uplifted rear fenders that took the "Forward Look" to new heights and looked good on the '55 bodies. Models expanded as a four-door hardtop, pioneered the previous season at GM, joined the Belvedere line as the Sport Sedan; Savoy picked up a Sport Coupe hardtop. Wagons were now a separate Suburban series, with DeLuxe, Custom, and Sport models paralleling Plaza, Savoy, and Belvedere trim.

Engineering changes included a switch from six- to 12-volt electrics and the controversial pushbutton Powerflite controls (four, in a pod to the driver's left) that would be a fixture at Highland Park for the next nine years. And a gimmicky—but unpopular—new innovation joined the options list: the Chrysler/RCA "Highway Hi Fi" record player.

With the horsepower race at full gallop, performance again got Plymouth's major emphasis for '56. Still-higher compression took the old six to 125/131 bhp; the base Plaza/Savoy V-8 was bored to 270 cid and 180 bhp with two-barrel carb. Belvedere/Suburban got a new 277-cid Hy-Fire with 187 bhp as standard; PowerPak took it to an even 200 bhp.

But Plymouth had something even hotter for '56: a dashing new limited-edition hardtop that banished the make's fuddy-duddy image almost as fast as it ran at Daytona. It bore a perfect name—Fury—and it's the subject of our next installment.

After a dismal sales year in 1954, Plymouth burst into 1955 with all-new styling and an equally new V-8 engine. Buyers approved as production took a 52-percent jump. The top-line Belvedere series included Plymouth's only convertible (opposite, top), *which sold for $2351 and saw 8473 built. The '56 facelift was actually a tail-lift. The Belvedere club sedan* (above) *retailed at $2008, while the two-door hardtop went out the door for $2214* (opposite, bottom).

SPECIFICATIONS

Engines: 1955 L-head I-6, 230.2 cid (3.25 × 4.63), 117 bhp; ohv V-8, 241 cid (3.44 × 3.25), 157 bhp; 260 cid (3.56 x 3.25), 167/177 bhp (standard/Powerpak option) **1956** L-head I-6, 230.2 cid (3.25 × 4.63), 125/131 bhp; ohv V-8, 270 cid (3.63 x 3.25), 180 bhp; 277 cid (3.75 × 3.13), 187/200 bhp (standard/Powerpak option)

Transmission:	3-speed manual; overdrive and 2-speed PowerFlite optional
Suspension, front:	upper and lower A-arms, coil springs
Suspension, rear:	live axle, semi-elliptic leaf springs
Brakes:	front/rear drums
Wheelbase (in.):	115.0
Weight (lbs):	3025-3513
Top speed (mph):	80-95
0-60 mph (sec):	12.0-14.5

Production: 1955 Plaza 4d sdn 84,156 **club cpe** 53,610 **Suburban 2d wgn** 31,788 **Suburban 4d wgn** 15,422 **business cpe** 4882 **Savoy 4d sdn** 162,741 **club cpe** 74,880 **Belvedere 4d sdn** 160,984 **club cpe** 41,645 **Sport Coupe 2d htp** 47,375 **cvt** 8473 **Suburban 4d wgn** 18,488 **1956 Plaza business cpe** 3728 **4d sdn** 60,197 **club sdn** 43,022 **Savoy 4d sdn** 151,762 **club sdn** 57,927 **Sport Coupe 2d htp** 16,473 **Belvedere 4d sdn** 84,218 **Sport Sedan 4d htp** 17,515 **Sport Coupe 2d htp** 24,723 **cvt** 6735 **DeLuxe Suburban 2d wgn** 23,866 **Custom Suburban 2d wgn** 9489 **Custom Suburban 4d wgn** 33,333 **Sport Suburban 4d wgn** 15,104

17289

PLYMOUTH
MINNESOTA
635-774
COLLECTOR

1956 Plymouth Fury

Part of a quartet of high-performance limited editions from Chrysler, the Plymouth Fury was introduced at the Chicago Automobile Show on January 10, 1956. While it shared the same hardtop body used for the conventional Savoy and Belvedere, it was immediately recognizable via its standard eggshell white finish and full-length bodyside sweepspear of gold anodized aluminum. Anodized gold also decorated the grille center and the special "spoke" wheel covers, which bore a close resemblance to Cadillac's "Sabre Spokes." (Chrysler cleverly used these same covers on the 1956 DeSoto Adventurer, except that the hubs were plain on the Fury, monogrammed "DeS" on the Adventurer.)

Inside, the Fury sported a special interior in colors to match the vivid exterior: vinyl bolsters with black jacquard inserts. The dashboard looked like a conventional '56, except that a tachometer filled in the blank space to the right of the speedometer. All this fancy trim was arresting, and looked very good on the mildly finned 1956 hardtop body. But what really made the Fury memorable was what happened when someone floored its accelerator pedal.

In addressing performance, Fury engineers didn't soup up an existing V-8, like Ford or Chevy. They felt that the standard 277-cubic-inch polyspherical-head V-8 needed more displacement for this application, having decided against taking any chances with reliability by bolting on a supercharger. Unexpectedly, they also avoided a hemi transplant from one of the other Chrysler divisions—though it's not known whether this was out of choice or because sister divisions wouldn't coöperate.

What they *did* choose was an engine from across the river: the 303-cubic-inch poly-head V-8 from the Canadian Chrysler Windsor/Dodge Royal. This happened to be a good pick because it fell right at the top of the displacement limit for Class 5 (259-305 cid) in the National Association for Stock Car Auto Racing (NASCAR).

To this basic block engineers applied a high-lift cam, solid valve lifters, domed pistons, four-barrel carburetor, free-flow dual exhausts, and 9.25:1 compression heads. The result: 240 horsepower, about .8 bhp per cubic inch. It's a comment on the pace of the Fifties "horsepower race" that Chevrolet achieved a full 1.0-bhp per cubic inch just one year later with fuel injection, though the Chrysler 300B also managed this magic mark in 1956 with its optional high compression heads, and so did DeSoto for that matter.

To handle the extra poke, Furys came equipped with heavy-duty springs and shocks, jumbo Dodge brakes with 11-inch diameters, wide 7.10 × 15 tires, and a front anti-sway bar. A heavy-duty three-speed manual transmission with a beefy clutch put the power to the road. Chrysler two-speed Powerflite automatic, now with pushbutton control, could be had as an option. The chassis gave the Fury a low, hunkered-down appearance that contrasted with the rather tall, high-sided appearance of conventional models.

If anybody doubted that the Fury could blow away the cobwebs accumulated from Plymouth's three-decade history as an economy car, they had only to read the papers. On the same day the new Fury debuted in Chicago, a pre-production prototype driven by Phil Walters tore up the sands of Daytona Beach, Florida. Fresh from campaigns in his Chrysler-powered Cunningham racing cars, Walters blasted through the flying mile at 124 mph, with a best one-way speed of 124.611 mph, and covered the standing mile at 82.54 mph—extraordinary for a near-stock passenger car weighing 3650 pounds.

Just as the Fury was preparing to dominate its class at the Daytona Speed Weeks in February, NASCAR ruled that it had not been in production the required 90 days to qualify as "stock." Plymouth replied by running it as a Factory Experimental, using a higher-lift cam, new heads with 9.8:1 compression, and a Chrysler manifold carrying twin four-barrel carbs. Thus equipped the Fury scorched through the traps at 143.596 mph—a speed beaten by a Mercury, but nonetheless impressive.

Despite a base price of $2866, the Fury sold fairly well for a specialty model. Almost as hot in "street" guise as modified, it impressed everyone with its combination of speed and agility. The only regret was that it didn't come as a convertible—though at least one collector has recently built his own from a Fury found wrecked in a junkyard!

Plymouth jumped into the high-performance market at the Chicago Auto Show in January 1956 with the introduction of the Fury. It was basically a Belvedere two-door hardtop with its own unique touches in gold: side trim, "spoke" hubcaps, and grille center. A special 303-cid poly-head V-8 with 240 bhp gave 0-60-mph times of about nine seconds.

SPECIFICATIONS

Engine:	ohv V-8, 303.0 cid (3.82 × 3.31), 240 bhp
Transmission:	3-speed manual; Powerflite 2-speed automatic optional
Suspension, front:	independent, coil springs, tube shocks
Suspension, rear:	live axle, leaf springs, tube shocks
Brakes:	front/rear drums
Wheelbase (in.):	115.0
Weight (lbs):	3650
Top speed (mph):	120
0-60 mph (sec):	9.0
Production:	4485

P L Y M O U T H
56 FURY

1957-58 Plymouth Fury

For 1957 the Chrysler corporate line was fully redesigned at a cost of $300 million, under the direction of Virgil Exner. "Ex" altered the cars so dramatically that Chrysler temporarily took design leadership away from market leader General Motors. Plymouth, perhaps, emerged as the most radical 1957 Chrysler product, and said as much in its ads: "Suddenly It's 1960!" And to enhance the new image, the Fury boosted its reputation as the most exciting Plymouth.

A daringly low beltline and acres of glass, fenders brought level with the hood and deck, and prominent but well integrated tailfins stood out as the chief design components. The fins were actually aerodynamic, adding directional stability, but only at very high speeds. It's doubtful even Fury drivers noticed.

The '57 Fury again came only as a hardtop, and with the same ivory paint and gold side trim as before. It made its entrance after the rest of the line, and was built in limited numbers, but it hardly mattered as Plymouth could barely meet orders for its regular models in the early part of the '57 model run. On the new body with its smooth hardtop roofline, Fury hallmarks looked better than ever. The anodized gold wheel covers of 1956 were dropped, but gold now appeared on the grille bars. Bumper extenders, optional on lesser Plymouths, came standard on the Fury, adding 1.5 inches to overall length. Like its lesser linemates, the '57 Fury rode a three-inch-longer wheelbase and stood an astonishing 5.5 inches lower than the '56 model. Wheel diameter shrank an inch, and tire size increased to 8.00 × 14.

As in 1956, options included "Full-Time" power steering, power brakes, air conditioning, electric seat and windows, whitewalls, and (though not prominently advertised) dealer-installed seatbelts. Standard Fury goodies encompassed a two-tone steering wheel, variable-speed electric wipers, padded dash and sun visors, foam-rubber seat cushions, and a "sweep-second self-regulating watch."

The '57 came out the chute faster than ever, too, as Chrysler engineers massaged the Canadian 303 V-8 by boring it out to 318 cubic inches. That number would soon become familiar to Mopar enthusiasts, as would the other hot-rodders' tricks employed: dual four-barrel carburetors, high-compression heads, domed pistons, free-flow dual exhausts, high-lift cam, and heavy-duty valve springs. Dubbed the "V-800," this engine delivered a hefty 325 lbs/ft torque. Incidentally, the V-800 could be ordered for *any* Plymouth, from the luxurious Belvedere right down to the unprepossessing two-door Plaza—which made the latter quite a Q-ship and inspired many an impromptu drag race.

Two other developments went into making the '57 Fury memorable. One was Chrysler's new three-speed TorqueFlite automatic transmission, which gained a reputation as America's best automatic, bar none. Still with pushbutton control, it pulled a 3.36:1 rear axle ratio, with other ratios available both for the axle and the standard heavy-duty three-speed manual gearbox.

The second development was torsion-bar independent front suspension, which put Chrysler Corporation cars at the top of the heap for handling. It provided effortless high speed cruising, competent handling over rough surfaces, and a new level of handling precision. "The Fury will power through hard turns, can be drifted by a true believer," wrote test driver Joe Wherry. "The only handling minus was the lack of self-centering action inherent in the power steering system, but the fast steering (a shade under 3.5 turns lock-to-lock) allowed quick corrections."

Plymouth model year production shot up by better than 200,000 units for 1957, to 762,231. Like other Plymouths, the '58 carried over the established '57 package. Again, Fury sported the distinctive color scheme and gold anodized grille (repeated on the sub-bumper stone shield), but quad headlights and "lollipop" taillights were distinguishing features, as were the stock wheel covers with their gold centers. The V-800 engine remained the same as in 1957, but a new option, the "Golden Commando" 350 V-8, pumped out up to 315 horsepower with fuel injection.

Unfortunately, 1958 would the last year for the limited-edition Fury. The economic recession that occurred this year set production far back, for Plymouth generally as well as for Fury. The result was a 1959 series of "standard" Fury models, displacing Belvedere at the top of the line, but topped in turn by a new Sport Fury hardtop and convertible, the lineal successors to the 1956-58 original. Another factor contributing to the "hot" Fury's demise was the 1957 Auto Manufacturers Association decision to cease overt factory support and advertising of racing efforts. Though the Fury name would live on into the front-wheel-drive age, it's the 1956-58 original collectors seek out today.

The 1957 Plymouth was so new that the ads proclaimed: "Suddenly It's 1960!" And indeed, it was new from its heavily browed headlights to its soaring tailfins. As in 1956, the '57 Fury, as seen here, was Plymouth's costliest model ($2925), and the fastest, too. Distinguishing the Fury from other '57s were gold grille bars, gold side trim, standard bumper extensions, and ivory paint. Power came from a 318-cid V-8 that sported dual four-barrel carbs and cranked out a whopping 290 horsepower.

SPECIFICATIONS

Engine: ohv V-8 **1957-58** 318 cid (3.91 × 3.31), 290 bhp **1958** 350.0 cid (4.06 × 3.38), 305 bhp (315 bhp with fuel injection) optional

Transmission:	three-speed manual; 3-speed Torqueflite automatic optional
Suspension, front:	independent, torsion bar
Suspension, rear:	live axle, leaf springs, tube shocks
Brakes:	front/rear drums
Wheelbase (in.):	118.0
Weight (lbs):	**1957** 3595 **1958** 3510
Top speed (mph):	**318 V-8** 120 **350 V-8** 125
0-60 mph (sec):	**318 V-8** 8.0-9.0 **350 V-8** 7.0-8.0
Production:	**1957** 7438 **1958** 5303

Fury
57 FURY

Fury

Fury

1959 Plymouth Sport Fury

Detroit has long played name games, often to the great confusion of car buyers. Thus have the automakers trotted out all-new models with old handles, to cash in on past glories, or created new titles to make old cars seem new.

In the '50s, the industry hit upon a variation that's still in widespread use. Its called the "trickle-down game." A new name appears on a top-end model or series, then filters to the bottom of the line via elimination of older and/or lower-status names. History is full of examples: Bel Air and Impala at Chevrolet, Fairlane and Galaxie at Ford.

Chrysler Corporation is a past master at the sport, and it added an interesting twist with Plymouth's '59 Sport Fury. As chronicled elsewhere in this book, the Fury began as a speedy, limited-edition 1956 hardtop, and continued as such for the next two years. Though never a big seller, it cast a performance image over the entire Plymouth line with obvious sales implications, and division marketers just couldn't resist trying to capitalize on it.

Accordingly, they put the Fury label on all top-of-the-line '59 Plymouths except Suburban wagons, removed Plaza nameplates from low-end models, and pushed Belvedere and Savoy down a notch. The only problem this created was what to call the limited edition. Well, the 1956-58 Fury had definitely been sporty, so why not name its '59 successor Sport Fury? That they did. And for the first time they offered their hottest car as a convertible as well as the customary hardtop coupe. Curiously, though, the new standard Fury line didn't list a ragtop, just a pair of hardtops and a four-door sedan.

For all the name shuffling, the '59 Furys, standard and Sport, were far less "limited" than the high-powered stormers of 1956-58. Where the latter had seen only 4500-7500 copies a year, the Sport Fury ran close to 24,000 units all by itself, and standard Fury reached nearly 65,000. Of course, this was just what the sales

SPECIFICATIONS

Engines: ohv V-8, 318 cid (3.91 × 3.31), 260 bhp; 361 cid (4.12 × 3.38), 305 bhp

Transmission:	3-speed manual; overdrive and 3-speed TorqueFlite automatic optional
Suspension, front:	trailing arms, longitudinal torsion bars
Suspension, rear:	live axle, semi-elliptic leaf springs
Brakes:	front/rear drums
Wheelbase (in.):	118.0
Weight (lbs):	3475-3670
Top speed:	90-110
0-60 mph (sec):	10.5-14.0
Production:	**2d htp** 17,867 **cvt** 5990

department wanted, and it helped Plymouth hold onto third place in recovery '59 despite total volume that rose by only 15,000 units—while Chevy gained over 300,000 units, Ford nearly half a million.

Plymouth had roared back into third on the strength of its handsome 1957 models. Chrysler wanted to keep it there, so after detail changes for 1958, Plymouth received a more substantial restyling for the last iteration of its three-year design cycle. As facelifts go, the '59 wasn't bad, but it wasn't great either, just different. Curiously, Sport Furys wore no identifying script, just a large circular crest above a broad swath of anodized aluminum on the rear flanks.

Chrysler design chief Virgil Exner had been taken with the idea of translating classic-era motifs to modern cars, and his first attempt appeared this year in a new Plymouth option: a trunklid appliqué that supposedly suggested an outside spare tire but looked more like a trash-can lid. Chrysler laid on a lot of other gimmicks for '59, and even Plymouth buyers could order an electronic headlight dimmer, self-dipping rearview mirror (unpopular then, but destined for greater success in its '80s reincarnation) and, for convertibles and hardtop coupes, individual bucket seats that swiveled outward when a door was opened to assist entry/exit.

Mechanically, Plymouth mostly marked time for '59. The ancient "PowerFlow" L-head six was in its final year and basically unchanged. V-8s began with the 318 first seen in the '57 Fury, now producing 230 horsepower in base V-800 trim or 260 bhp with optional "Superpak" four-barrel carb and dual exhausts. A bore job took the top "Golden Commando" engine from 350 to 361 cid, but horsepower remained 305 on the same 10.0:1 compression. Fuel injection, a brief and troublesome 1958 flirtation, was no more. Plymouth belatedly joined Detroit's short-lived fling with air suspension by offering an optional rear-only setup for '59. This used both air bags and lighter leaf springs, plus modified front-torsion-bar geometry. Installations are unknown, but couldn't have been significant.

And for about six years after 1959, neither was Plymouth. With 1960's all-new "Unibody" line began a dark period of oddball styling, abortive downsizing, sloppy workmanship, halting corrective measures, and disappointing sales. Not until the '70s would Plymouth regain third place, and it didn't hold onto it for long. The Sport Fury proved somewhat hardier: temporarily abandoned but reinstated for 1962 as the most youthful full-size Plymouth, which it remained through 1971, when Chrysler started playing name games again.

The Fury was demoted one notch for 1959 to make room for the new top-line Sport Fury. As its name implied, it came in two sporty models: a $2927 hardtop and a $3125 ragtop. The base 318-cid, 260-bhp V-8 provided lively performance, but a 361-cid, 305-bhp powerhouse made it even more sporty.

1950-52 Pontiac Catalina

Anyone born after 1960 may find this hard to believe, but there was a time when hardtops were quite exotic. That time, of course, harks back to 1949, when General Motors pioneered the pillarless idea with a trio of low-volume "hardtop-convertibles."

To enhance their allure, product planners looked to faraway places with strange-sounding names. Thus did Buick offer a Riviera, named after the famed French and Italian coastlines, and Cadillac the Gallic-sounding Coupe de Ville. Oldsmobile, though a bit more prosaic with Holiday, managed to capture the spirit of the thing.

Nineteen forty-nine also saw GM complete its first postwar restyle, issuing redesigned A- and B-bodies in the image of the new-for-1948 C-body Cadillacs and Olds 98. This mainly involved Chevrolet and Pontiac, both of which fared quite well stylistically. They fared well commercially, too, with record production that went up again for 1950, bolstered by their first hardtops.

But where Chevy fielded a single pillarless coupe, the natty Styleline DeLuxe Bel Air (see entry), Pontiac proffered no fewer than four Catalinas, named for the romantic island 26 miles off the Southern California shore. (Bel Air referred to that same area, though a little further inland: the exclusive residential district near Beverly Hills.) DeLuxe and Super trim and six- and eight-cylinder engines accounted for the variations, all in the Chieftain lines composed of strictly notchback styles. Pontiac also offered Streamliner Six and Eight series, each with standard- and DeLuxe-trim fastback sedans and, oddly enough, a wagon.

Interestingly, at least one *1949* Catalina was built. Though strictly for show, it previewed the rakish production roofline with its modestly wrapped, three-element rear window.

Like Chevrolet's, Pontiac's successful '49 package involved mainly a styling job, its basic engineering being of prewar origin, but it was good enough to last through 1952 with only evolutionary changes. The '50s wore a toothier grille, while the 1950-51 sported a horizontal divider bar with a deep central vee cradling a large Pontiac crest.

Pontiac names were nothing if not confusing in 1951: Streamliner, Chieftain, Six, Eight, standard, DeLuxe, Super. The car you see here is a Chieftain Eight Super DeLuxe Catalina, which sold for $2271. Exclusive to Super DeLuxes was a Sapphire Blue over Malibu Ivory color scheme (or the reverse). The straight eight was good for 122 bhp.

SPECIFICATIONS

Engines: L-head I-6, 239.2 cid (3.56 × 4.00) **1950** 90 bhp **1951** 96/100 bhp **1952** 100/102 bhp; L-head I-8, 268.4 cid (3.38 x 3.75) **1950** 108 bhp **1951** 116/120 bhp **1952** 118/122 bhp

Transmission:	3-speed manual; 4-speed Hydra-Matic optional
Suspension, front:	upper and lower A-arms, coil springs
Suspension, rear:	live axle, semi-elliptic leaf springs
Brakes:	front/rear drums
Wheelbase (in.):	120.0
Weight (lbs):	3469-3573
Top speed (mph):	80-95
0-60 mph (sec):	13.0-15.5
Production:	NA

"Silver Streak" hood and rear deck stripes, a Pontiac fixture since the Thirties, remained much in evidence. So did the stern countenance of Chief Pontiac as a mascot. Like all proper hood ornaments in those days, it glowed with the headlamps on.

Gimmicky feature names were *de rigueur* at the time, and Pontiac had its fair share. Interiors featured "Vision-Aire," at least partly because of a larger, slightly curved (but still divided) "Safe-T-View" windshield. Also touted were a "Carry-More" trunk, wider "Easy-Access" doors, dash-mounted "Finger-Tip" starter, and "Tru-Arc Safety Steering" (which was actually slower than before).

Pontiac's main mechanical developments for 1949 included adoption of a 120-inch wheelbase for all models (replacing the 119/122-inch split used since '41), slimmer channel-section side rails for the X-member chassis, and telescopic shock absorbers all-round (which yielded a "Travelux Ride"). Pontiac's old L-head six and eight soldiered on, smooth running as ever and reliable as the tides. Respective horsepower for 1950 was 90 and 108. For 1951, the six was stepped up to 96 bhp, the eight to 116. An optional high-compression head (necessitating premium fuel) added four horses to each. Respective '52 ratings came in at 100/102 and 118/122.

Optional Hydra-Matic Drive gave Pontiac popularity a big boost during this period. First offered for 1948 at $185, it was reduced to $159 the following year and went into 78 percent of total production. Fastbacks were fading from favor, and Pontiac was even quicker to abandon those, dumping the Streamliner series for 1952 and putting wagons into the Chieftain lines.

The Catalinas were another story. Like hardtops everywhere, they sold strongly from the start, and went nowhere but up despite being less than $100 cheaper than Pontiac's true convertibles. The division didn't record individual body-style production, but it's known that two out of every three Catalinas sold in this period were Eights. This suggested that buyers wanted hardtops with maximum power as well as maximum luxury.

Luxury they got. Like other early GM hardtops, Pontiac's came handsomely upholstered in vinyl and leather. Bright horizontal strips over the headliner seams added to the "convertible feel," an idea contributed by GM's legendary chief designer, Harley Earl.

In all, the first Catalinas stand as elegant symbols of Pontiac's postwar turn from "super Chevy" to a more luxurious car with its own identity. In time, that trend would prove as profitable as hardtops and automatics.

1953-54 Pontiac

Time marches on, but its tempo never seemed quicker than in '50s Detroit. Take Pontiac. By 1953, the successful basic design the division had been plying since 1949 now looked quite dated—never mind its '30s-era L-head straight eight, a glaring anachronism in an age of compact, high-compression V-8s. But Pontiac had a V-8 coming, not to mention an all-new car for it to power. Trouble was, both were still a few years away, so there was nothing to do but freshen the existing package and hope for the best.

That view, however, is with the 20/20 clarity of hindsight, which never fully explains the future but makes it easy to predict the more recent past. Given Detroit's usual lead times, it's clear that the 1953 Pontiac resulted from decisions taken in 1950-51, when the end of the postwar seller's market made bigger, shinier, more luxurious cars a must. More power was a must, too, but the V-8, which Pontiac had been working on since the late Forties, ran into development troubles and wouldn't be available for 1953 as originally planned.

For a time, though, stylish new size was enough. Wheelbase, for example, grew two inches for identical groups of longer, slightly lower Chieftain Sixes and Eights bearing reskinned Uni-Steel bodies with new "Dual Streak" styling. The last encompassed a one-piece windshield, a wrapped rear window (except on Catalina hardtops, which already had one), bi-level bodyside moldings, a more imposing grille and, wagons excepted, rear fenders that kicked up into stubby little fins to flank a bulkier rear deck.

Model choices remained broadly the same, but the pricier Catalinas became Customs, instead of Supers. Wagons, all-steel four-doors since late '49, were still offered with optional pseudo-wood side trim of Di-Noc decals.

Pontiac received a major facelift for 1953 while awaiting the all-new 1955 models. Wheelbase was stretched two inches on all models, and the styling took advantage of this by trying to make the '53s look more "important." Among the 26 models offered were the DeLuxe Chieftain wagon (above), *the Chieftain convertible* (below), *and the Chieftain Catalina hardtop* (opposite). *All Chieftains could be had with a six or straight-eight engine.*

SPECIFICATIONS

Engines: **1953-54** L-head six, 239.2 cid (3.56 × 4.00), 115/118 bhp (manual/automatic); L-head eight, 268.4 cid (3.38 × 3.75) **1953** 118/122 bhp (manual/automatic) **1954** 122/127 bhp (manual/automatic)

Transmission:	3-speed manual; overdrive and Dual-Range Hydra-Matic optional
Suspension, front:	upper and lower A-arms, coil springs
Suspension, rear:	live axle, semi-elliptic leaf springs
Brakes:	front/rear drums
Wheelbase (in.):	122.0 **1954 Star Chief** 124.0
Weight (lbs):	3466-3776
Top speed (mph):	90-105
0-60 mph (sec):	12.5-14.5

Production: **1953 Chieftain Six** 38,914 **Chieftain Eight** 379,705 **1954 Chieftain Six** 22,670 **Chieftain Eight** 149,986 **Star Chief** 115,088

Mechanical changes included a "Curve-Control" suspension with revised geometry, plus recalibrated springs and shocks said to confer a "Comfort-Master" ride. Also new were "Key-Quick" combined starter/ignition (replacing a dashboard button), uprated generator, and a larger fuel tank and oil pump. Power steering and GM's "Autronic Eye" headlamp dimmer joined the options list. Hydra-Matic, now with "Dual Range" control, ended up on some 71 percent of 1953 production, this despite a late-summer fire at the Hydra-Matic plant that cost Pontiac an estimated 30,000 sales and forced it to substitute Chevrolet's Powerglide on some 18,500 cars.

With all this, plus the end of the Korean conflict and government-mandated production cutbacks, Pontiac stood to do well in 1953. It did. Helped further by stable prices in the $2000-$2750 range, Pontiac notched a volume gain of more than 50 percent, reaching near 419,000 units, the second highest total in division history.

But the lack of a V-8 really hurt in '54, when Pontiac remained one of only two Detroit makes still saddled with side-valve straight-eight engines. (Faltering Packard was the other.) Thus, after finishing fifth in the production race every year since 1948, Pontiac slipped to sixth on much lower volume of just under 288,000 units.

Mind you, neither Pontiac engine was bad, but increasing weight taxed the old eight, let alone the six, which also remained basically unchanged. Underscoring their burden was a new top-of-the-line luxury series, the Star Chief. Built on Pontiac's longest-ever wheelbase (124 inches) and pushing 3700 pounds, it was sensibly offered only with the eight. Delivering Oldsmobile size and luxury for somewhat less money ($2300-$2600), the Star Chief could be termed a fair success, its four models accounting for about 115,000 sales against 150,000 Chieftain Eights and just 23,000 Sixes. A smooth, detail reworking of 1953 styling gave all models revised side trim and a slim scoop in the central grille bar. Adding a Star Chief Catalina brought Pontiac hardtops to five.

Again in the brilliance of retrospect, 1953-54 turned out to be a transition period for Pontiac. And a very important transition it was. Like Chevrolet, the division was preparing its customers for a dramatic turnaround that would open a new performance era while producing some of the most memorable cars in Detroit history. As the saying goes, you have to crawl before you can run. With its '55s, Pontiac started to run—hard. It hasn't stopped yet.

Pontiac debuted a new top-line series for 1954, the Star Chief. It rode a 124-inch wheelbase, two inches longer than other Pontiacs, and came only with the straight-eight engine. The Custom Catalina hardtop seen here listed at $2557, only $73 less than the ragtop. In total, Pontiac built 115,088 Star Chiefs during its inaugural year.

CALIFORNIA
JTH 126

1955-56 Pontiac

Most of what's been said for Chevrolet's startling 1955 metamorphosis (see entry) applies to that year's equally altered Pontiac—only the latter's changes were relatively more important, given Pontiac's traditionally lower volume. Of course, *higher* volume was the reason both makes changed so dramatically, and their means to that end were basically the same: new V-8 power in a more modern chassis topped by flashier, more colorful styling.

As a low-price car, Chevy achieved somewhat better results than its lower-medium sister. But Pontiac could hardly be unhappy with model year production of over 553,000 units, a record it wouldn't break until 1963.

It's often been true that Pontiac follows where Chevrolet leads, and so it was with 1955 styling. Superstructure, including GM's trendy "Panoramic" wrapped windshield, was dictated by Chevy's all-new A-body, but stylist Paul Gillan gave Pontiac its own distinct look below the beltline. The result was generally pleasing, save for the rather unfortunate blunt front. Ever-quotable veteran auto tester Tom McCahill said it made the car look "like it was born on its nose."

Like Chevy, Pontiac didn't alter wheelbases, but the new styling and a 2.75-inch height reduction made the '55s seem a lot sleeker, though they were little wider than the '54s and only a tad longer. The big Star Chiefs, in fact, actually measured 3.4 inches *shorter*.

Model offerings thinned from 22 to 13. The low-end series was the new Chieftain 860, offering sedans and wagons with two or four doors. The mid-range Chieftain 870 substituted a Catalina hardtop for the two-door wagon (the latter a new Pontiac body type). Star Chief returned to top the line with plain and Custom four-door sedans, a Catalina hardtop and a convertible, and the singular Safari, a lush hardtop-styled wagon *á la* Chevy's Bel Air Nomad, built on the shorter Chieftain chassis (and covered in the next entry).

Pontiac's other big '55 bombshell came in the form of a modern overhead-valve V-8. Called Strato-Streak, it had evolved from experimental work begun as early as 1946. Originally planned for 1953, it had been delayed by development and production problems.

But it ended up being worth the wait. Some of its features, such as the innovative ball-stud rocker-arm mounts, found their way into Chevy's new '55 V-8. However, the 287-cubic-inch Pontiac unit was unique in having the right cylinder bank cast slightly forward of the left to simplify distributor positioning and drive. Other exclusives included efficient "gusher valve" cooling, a harmonic vibration damper, tapered valve guides, fully machined combustion chambers and, per GM practice, hydraulic valve lifters.

The product of some three million development miles, the Strato-Streak delivered 180 horsepower standard, or 200 bhp with the $35 four-barrel-carburetor option—gains of at least 52 and 41 percent over the last L-head six and eight. It mated to the usual "three-on-the-tree" manual transmission or optional self-shift Hydra-Matic. Installations of the latter rose to a remarkable 90-plus percent of production.

Again like Chevy, Pontiac improved its chassis for '55. A lowered center of gravity and rear springs mounted outboard of the side rails, instead of inboard, contributed to better roadholding, if not ride. Other changes included revised front geometry, larger brakes, 12-volt electrics, standard tubeless tires, and refinements to the optional air conditioning and power steering. Power windows joined the options list at $40.

In all, 1955 turned out to be a vintage Pontiac year—which only made the modestly facelifted '56s seem something of a letdown. Yet, there was no lack of good news. Each series gained a four-door Catalina hardtop (which proved quite popular), a simplified "Strato-Flight" Hydra-Matic offered smoother shifting, and the V-8, bored out to 316.6 cid, now developed either 205 bhp (Chieftains) or 227 bhp (Star Chief). Pontiac also listed a newly stroked 347-cid version with a rollicking 285 bhp "for those who wish to race professionally or who vie with each other in having a 'hot' performing car." Alas, complaints about the 1955's "hard" ride prompted softer shock valving that did nothing for handling; neither did lighter power steering.

But though output slipped back to sixth on '56 volume of near 405,500 units, Pontiac built its 6,000,000th car late in the model run, and it wouldn't be long before Pontiac would work its way up to third. In these two short years, Pontiac had laid the groundwork to become a force to be reckoned with in the showroom or on the street. Enthusiasts have been grateful ever since.

Pontiac boasted all-new styling and an overhead-valve V-8 for 1955. The top-line Star Chief series included the $2691 convertible (top row)*; 19,762 were built. The '56 Pontiac sported a revised grille and side trim; the mid- range 870 Chieftain Catalina* (opposite, bottom) *sold for $2840 and enjoyed a production run of 24,744 units.*

SPECIFICATIONS

Engines: ohv V-8 **1955** 287.2 cid (3.75 × 3.25), 180/200 bhp (2-/4-barrel carburetor) **1956** 316.6 cid (3.94 × 3.25), 205/227 bhp (Chieftain/Star Chief); 347 cid (3.94 × 3.56), 285 bhp (optional racing engine; limited availability)

Transmission:	3-speed manual **1955-56** Dual Range Hydra-Matic optional **1956 Star Chief** Strato-Flight Hydra-Matic optional
Suspension, front:	upper and lower A-arms, coil springs
Suspension, rear:	live axle, semi-elliptic leaf springs
Brakes:	front/rear drums
Wheelbase (in.):	**Chieftains** 122.0 **Star Chief** 124.0
Weight (lbs):	3476-3797
Top speed (mph):	100-115
0-60 mph (sec):	12.0-14.0

Production: **1955 Chieftain 860 4d sdn** 65,155 **2d sdn** 58,654 **4d wgn** 6091 **2d wgn** 8620 **Chieftain 870 4d sdn** 91,187 **2d sdn** 28,950 **Catalina 2d htp** 72,608 **4d wgn** 19,439 **Star Chief 4d sdn** 44,800 **cvt** 19,762 **Custom 4d sdn** 35,153 **Custom Catalina 2d htp** 99,629 **1956 Chieftain 860 4d sdn** 41,987 **2d sdn** 41,908 **Catalina 2d htp** 46,335 **Catalina 4d htp** 35,201 **4d wgn** 12,702 **2d wgn** 6099 **Chieftain 870 4d sdn** 22,082 **Catalina 2d htp** 24,744 **Catalina 4d htp** 25,372 **4d wgn** 21,674 **Star Chief 4d sdn** 18,346 **cvt** 13,510 **Custom Catalina 2d htp** 43,392 **Custom Catalina 4d htp** 48,035

Pontiac
2907907

1955-57 Pontiac Safari

The 1956 Pontiac Safari was officially listed as a Star Chief Custom even though it rode a wheelbase two inches shorter than other Star Chiefs. Like them, however, it received top-grade trim and, at $3129, outpriced them all. Maybe that's why only 4042 were built that year.

It's easy to dismiss the original 1955-57 Safari as "Pontiac's Nomad," but that hardly does justice to either of these handsome wagons. Though both have the same origin, the Pontiac differed sufficiently from the Chevrolet (see entry) to be very desirable in its own right—maybe even *more* desirable, as fewer Safaris were built and thus survive today.

The story begins with the 1954 Corvette Nomad, one of three one-offs inspired by Chevy's new fiberglass-bodied sports car for that year's GM Motorama. Riding a stock '53 Chevy station wagon chassis, it combined the Corvette's lower-body lines with a distinctive hardtop-style wagon roof, a tasteful blending of the two body types then accounting for a third of all new-car sales. This greenhouse made for an uncommonly pretty wagon: wide, rakishly angled B-pillars; thin, forward-sloping rear pillars; wrapped side glass; horizontal rooftop "fluting." Chiefly the work of young Carl Renner, it so impressed company design chief Harley Earl that, at the last minute, he ordered it to be adapted to Chevy's all-new '55 passenger-car styling, resulting in the production Bel Air Nomad.

At first, this unique two-door wagon belonged to Chevy alone—until Pontiac found out and lobbied for its own version. As both makes shared the same new '55 A-body, this posed no real problem. But "Chevrolet didn't like that," as Renner recalled later. "Chevrolet always wanted things exclusively. However, management wanted [a Nomad] for the Pontiac line, too, so it worked out."

Despite appearances, the Safari shared precious little with other '55 Pontiacs aft of the cowl, but *did* share the Nomad's inner wheelhousings, glass, doors, roof, and tailgate. Its drivetrain, of course, came strictly from Pontiac, and stylists retained as much stock body hardware as possible, including taillights, minor trim, dashboard, and front end. Chassis and floorpan came from the lowly Chieftain 860 two-door wagon, which meant a wheelbase of 122 inches, seven inches longer than Nomad's

SPECIFICATIONS

Engines: ohv V-8 **1955** 287.2 cid (3.75 × 3.25), 180/200 bhp (2-/4-barrel carburetor) **1956** 316.6 cid (3.94 × 3.25), 227 bhp; 347 cid (3.94 × 3.56), 285 bhp (optional racing engine; Safari installations doubtful) **1957** 347 cid (3.94 × 3.56), 270/290/320 bhp (2-/4-barrel carburetor/3x2-barrel Tri-Power carburetion)

Transmission:	**1955** Dual-Range Hydra-Matic **1956-57** Strato-Flight Hydra-Matic
Suspension, front:	upper and lower A-arms, coil springs
Suspension, rear:	live axle, semi-elliptic leaf springs
Brakes:	front/rear drums
Wheelbase (in.):	122.0
Weight (lbs):	3636-3750
Top speed (mph):	100-115
0-60 mph (sec):	10.5-12.5
Production:	**1955** 3076 **1956** 4042 **1957** 1292

but two inches shorter than for other models in the top-line Star Chief series, where the Safari was naturally placed.

We say "naturally," because the Safari was intended as a larger, costlier, cushier, and more powerful Nomad. It thus arrived with V-8 and Hydra-Matic included in its $3047 base price, though a few options could push that over $4000. By contrast, the Nomad listed for $2571 with V-8 (a six could be specified, but few were built). This put the Safari at the high end of the wagon price spectrum and, as with the Nomad, surely limited sales as much as its relative impracticality as a wagon.

Indeed, the Safari was downright luxurious, somewhat more so than the Nomad, with standard leather upholstery and cargo-deck carpeting instead of vinyl seats and a linoleum floor. Greater size and weight offset a bigger, more powerful V-8, so the Safari had no performance advantage over a comparably equipped Nomad. Still, as the accompanying figures show, it was quite fast by any standard.

Continuing the comparisons, the Safari's rear seat initially had a different folding arrangement and was larger and more comfortable, but became just like Nomad's after 1955. Of course, the Safari inherited the Nomad's panoramic outward vision—and, unfortunately, its water-leaking tendencies around the tailgate. Inherited from other Pontiacs was a hard-riding chassis that, curiously enough, provided little, if any, margin of handling superiority. In fact, one writer describes the Safari as a car that "constantly seems to be seeking some place on the road other than where you want it to be." But thanks to larger brakes, the Safari stopped better—at least through 1956. A switch from 15- to 14-inch wheels and tires left Pontiac's '57 brakes just that much smaller to be inadequate for severe conditions.

A final, if obvious, comparison: Safari and Nomad shared in the styling and engineering changes applied to their linemates, and both expired after 1957, the year Pontiac watered down the Safari name by using it on all its conventional wagons as well. At least Chevy had the decency to wait a year before doing the same with Nomad.

It's sad these two lovely wagons had to die so young and that more weren't built. Happily, after years of languishing in the Nomad's shadow—and too often being used for Nomad restorations—the Safari has at last stepped into the collector-car sunlight. Its fans say that, as a bigger and brighter Pontiac, it actually interpreted the original Nomad idea better than Chevrolet. Some might argue that, but few would dispute the Safari's standing as a great American car of the '50s.

1957 Pontiac Bonneville

History sometimes repeats itself by working in reverse. Take Pontiac's once-famous "Silver Streak" trim. Division general manager William S. "Big Bill" Knudsen had put the distinctive chrome strips on the hoods of his 1935 models (as suggested by stylist Virgil Exner) to spiff up their styling and improve sales. They remained a Pontiac trademark until his son yanked them off 20 years later—for the same reason.

"We had to get rid of that 'Indian concept,' " said Semon E. "Bunkie" Knudsen in 1978. "No reflection on the American Indian, but old chief Pontiac had been associated in the public mind with a prosaic, family-toting sedan from the time Pontiacs were first built."

Pontiac's image definitely needed rejuvenating when Bunkie took on his father's old job in mid-1956, and he hustled. There had already been timely shots in the sales arm with fresh new styling and the division's first ohv V-8 for 1955, followed by more flash, cubic inches, and horsepower for '56. There wasn't much Bunkie could do about 1957 styling (other than yanking off that "pair of suspenders," which required a minor tooling change for the hood), but he could give the make another infusion of youthfulness by again stepping up performance.

Knudsen quickly secured a new chief engineer, future GM president Elliot M. "Pete" Estes, and put him to work on extra carburetors and higher compression. One of the first fruits of his labors appeared during model year '57 in the legendary Tri-Power setup, a trio of two-barrel instruments atop a newly enlarged 347-cubic-inch version of Pontiac's versatile 1955 V-8. Next Bunkie hired famed Daytona Beach speed merchant Smokey Yunick to prepare it for the track, and a Knudsen-sponsored car ran a record 131.747-mph at that year's Speed Weeks. When the Automobile Manufacturers Association agreed to its anti-racing "edict" in early '57, Knudsen took Pontiac performance underground, retaining Yunick for development work and later resuming ties with tuner Ray Nichels.

Bunkie had something else up his sleeve for '57: a hot limited edition to bring throngs of performance-seekers into Pontiac showrooms. It bowed in February with a perfect name: Bonneville, after the Utah salt flats where most everybody went to assault speed records.

Knudsen later termed the Bonneville "the car I was counting on to bring the new message to the public. And it did. I remember sitting in the grandstand at Daytona...at its first race. Somebody...shouted, 'Look what's happened to Grandma!'" No wonder: "Grandma" had been to Vic Tanny.

Announced at $5782—when a Star Chief ragtop listed at $3105—and mainly "for dealer use only," the Bonneville debuted as the costliest and most muscular Pontiac yet. The most luxurious too. Offered only as a convertible on the top-line Star Chief series' 124-inch wheelbase, it came with Strato-Flight Hydra-Matic, power steering and brakes, heater/defroster, and numerous accessories that cost extra on lesser models. These ran to a light package, "Wonderbar" signal-seeking radio with electric antenna, eight-way power seat, power windows, and power top. Trim was naturally Pontiac's best, including leather upholstery and deluxe carpeting.

Setting Bonneville apart outside were anodized-aluminum gravel shields on the lower rear fenders, "hash mark" front-fender trim, chrome-plated bullets set within the spear-like bodyside moldings adopted as part of this year's restyle, and unique spinner wheel covers. The result looked longer and lower than other '57 Pontiacs.

The Bonneville's main technical attraction was advertised in bold front-fender nameplates that read "Fuel Injection." This referred to a 347 V-8 that achieved 310 bhp via the new Rochester system designed by GM Engineering and shepherded into production by Harry Barr and Corvette wizard Zora Arkus-Duntov. Though similar to the Ramjet option introduced that same year at Chevrolet (with Rambler, the only other domestic make to offer fuel injection on a production model), it was a tidier setup allegedly designed for maximum low-range torque rather than top-end power. It consisted of separate fuel and air meters on a special assembly sitting where the carburetor and intake manifold normally would. Fuel was injected directly into each port, making this what we'd now call a mechanical "multi-point" system.

For all that, the weighty Bonneville ended up slightly slower in all-out acceleration than one of the light Chieftain two-doors with Tri-Power. One magazine timed it at 18 seconds in the standing quarter-mile—fast but not breathtaking.

But it didn't matter, because the '57 Bonneville existed mainly as a promotional exercise. That's why only 630 were built. But it provided just the sort of sales tonic old "Grandma" had needed, and it worked.

"You can sell an old man a young man's car," Bunkie once said, "but you can never sell a young man an old man's car." With the '57 Bonneville, Pontiac wouldn't do that again for a long, long time.

The 1957 Bonneville was intended to boost Pontiac's image with the youth market. At $5872, $2677 more than a Star Chief ragtop, not many young buyers could afford one—nor could their folks either! But with fuel injection and 310 horsepower, the Bonneville made its mark, and thereby eliminated forever Pontiac's old "Grandma" image.

SPECIFICATIONS

Engine:	ohv V-8, 347 cid (3.94 × 356), 310 bhp
Transmission:	4-speed Strato-Flight Hydra-Matic
Suspension, front:	upper and lower A-arms, coil springs
Suspension, rear:	live axle, semi-elliptic leaf springs
Brakes:	front/rear drums
Wheelbase (in.):	124.0
Weight (lbs):	4285
Top speed (mph):	125+
0-60 mph (sec):	8.1
Production:	630

57BONNE

57BONNE

1958
Pontiac Bonneville

The debut 1957 Bonneville had given staid old Chief Pontiac a slightly racy reputation, just as division chief Bunkie Knudsen had planned. Yet barely four months after Pontiac's hot new ragtop wowed the crowd at Daytona, the Automobile Manufacturers Association entered into its "gentlemen's agreement," whereby automakers would no longer support racing or emphasize performance in advertising. Suddenly, the Bonneville seemed without a mission.

But not to Bunkie, who knew that the mission had already been accomplished. His task now turned to maintaining the renewed public interest in Pontiac fired by the '57 Bonneville, and plans for '58 played right into his hands.

Though not fully influenced by Knudsen or division chief engineer Pete Estes, the '58 Pontiacs were new from the ground up, with completely restyled bodyshells on a Cadillac-inspired X-member frame. Pontiac claimed greater rigidity for the new chassis, which would be retained through 1960, and it facilitated the use of coils instead of semi-elliptic leaf springs at the rear for a better ride. (It also afforded precious little protection in a side impact.) Wheelbases and the twin-A-arm/coil-spring front suspension stayed the same, but Bonneville switched to the shorter Chieftain platform in the interest of better handling, and a hardtop coupe version joined the lineup. Though trim remained top grade, most of the '57 Bonnie's lavish equipment now appeared on the option sheet, cutting base price by some $2300.

Pontiac's most fascinating new '58 feature was optional "Ever-Level" air suspension, modeled after Cadillac's system on the '57 Eldorado Brougham and offered across the board at $175. However, not too many orders came in at that price, and the setup proved so troublesome that Pontiac dropped it after only a year, about as quickly as other makes gave up on their equally problem-plagued systems.

Overt racing support was out (officially, GM would abide by the AMA racing "ban" even after rivals returned to the tracks) but performance remained a major thrust. Accordingly, all '58 Pontiacs got a V-8 bored out to 370 cubic inches. Called "Tempest," it was offered in no fewer than six forms. Most Bonnevilles carried the single-four-barrel unit, boasting 10.0:1 compression and 285 bhp with Hydra-Matic. Fuel injection was still available—and still troublesome—and a formidable $500 asking price discouraged all but about 400 buyers before the system exited during the year.

This left the 300-bhp Tri-Power engine as the darling of the leadfoot crowd—and a performance bargain at just $93.50. *Motor Trend* timed one at a creditable 8.2 seconds in the 0-60 mph sprint and 18.8 seconds at 88 mph in the standing quarter-mile. *Mechanix Illustrated's* Tom McCahill hit 125 mph with a 285-bhp car, moving him to exclaim: "The 1958 Pontiacs are hotter than a blowtorch."

They should have been slower: four inches longer, two inches wider, and some 100-200 pounds heavier than the '57s. This was dictated in part by the "New Direction" styling, which looked better than the '57, but still not the best—though it could have been worse. Yet even the Bonneville, the most sparkling of the line, doesn't look too bad now next to some other '58s, notably Buick, Olds, and Mercury.

Being more readily available, the Bonneville sold much better in '58—better than 19 to 1 over the '57, in fact. But that was scant consolation in a year when most everybody except AMC's Rambler skidded downward. While Chevy sales fell by 17.5 percent and Oldsmobile's by 20 percent, Pontiac dropped by more than a third, though it again finished sixth (as it had since 1956).

Yet, the Bonneville proved that Knudsen knew what he was doing. "There was no point competing against Chevrolet," he said later. "They had their market sewn up tight. But setting out after Buick and Oldsmobile *was* possible." Like Chevy that year, the '58 Pontiac ended up a one-year-only design, because the company had decided to share bodies more closely from 1959 on. But in line with his plan of moving Pontiac upmarket, Knudsen managed to exchange Chevrolet's forthcoming A-body for the larger, equally new Buick/Olds B-body. "Up until then," he observed, "Pontiac had used the Chevy body, maybe with an extended rear deck. There was no point in that, and I think the results bear out our decision."

Indeed they did. You can see for yourself in the next section.

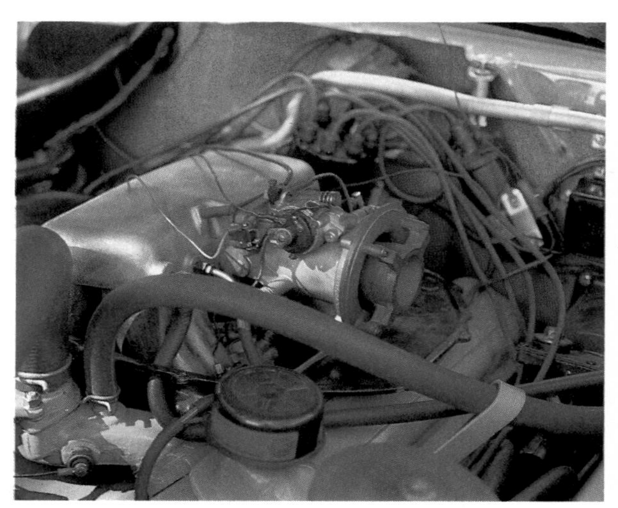

The first Bonneville bowed in mid-1957 as an ultra-expensive, limited-production convertible. Pontiac wanted to expand on that base for 1958, so the price was cut $2300 and a hardtop added. All Pontiacs ran with a 370-cid V-8 in '58, available in a number of horsepower ratings, the top two choices fed via Tri-Power triple carbs or fuel injection.

SPECIFICATIONS

Engines: ohv V-8, 370 cid (4.06 × 3.56), 240/255/270/285/300/310 bhp (Chieftain and Super Chief with manual shift/Star Chief and Bonneville with manual/Chieftain and Super Chief with automatic/Star Chief and Bonneville with automatic/optional Tri-Power/optional fuel injection)

Transmissions:	3-speed manual; Super Hydra-Matic optional
Suspension, front:	upper and lower A-arms, coil springs
Suspension, rear:	live axle, coil springs
Brakes:	front/rear drums
Wheelbase (in.):	122.0
Weight (lbs):	3481-3586
Top speed (mph):	100-130
0-60 mph (sec):	8.2-11.0
Production:	**2d htp** 9144 **cvt** 3096

1959 Pontiac

Bunkie Knudsen was never swayed by tradition as Pontiac general manager, but he started one of his own with the 1959 models. Not long after he'd erased "Silver Streaks" from the '57s—the trademark trim his father had originated over 20 years before—Bunkie looked at a near-final '59 styling model and pronounced it akin to "a football player wearing ballet slippers." For the more broad-shouldered appearance he demanded, engineers hastily widened track from 58.7 to 63.7 inches in front and from 59.4 to 64.0 inches in back. This resulted in the first "Wide-Track" Pontiac—and a big upsurge in division fortunes.

Knudsen thought the "Wide-Track" designation corny, but it caught on with the public. So did the cars. After years of being mired in fifth or sixth, Pontiac moved smartly up to fourth place by building some 383,000 of its '59s. Though not a production record, it represented a healthy 77 percent gain over the depressed 1958 total in a year when the market as a whole rose only some 31 percent. It also came as a moral victory: the first time Pontiac had finished ahead of both intramural rivals Buick and Olds. As with the 1957-58 Bonneville, Bunkie had obviously chosen the right track.

It was the "Wide Track," of course, a moniker that had more behind it than mere Madison Avenue hype. Pontiac immodestly proclaimed itself "America's No. 1 Road Car" in 1959, and most critics agreed that the new spread-tread chassis made for terrific cornering and a smoother ride. Alas, it also made the cars too wide for the neighborhood car wash.

But there was pleasure in doing that job yourself, because the new bodies looked sensational. Though the two wheelbase lengths stayed the same, the '59s were predictably longer (by up to nine inches), wider (by some three inches overall), and lower. This made them both roomier and heavier, but they also wore more sculpturing and looked much cleaner. Acres of extra glass, thin-pillar rooflines, a

The Bonneville consisted of one model in 1957, two in 1958. By 1959, there were four Bonnevilles: convertible, Vista hardtop sedan, Custom Safari wagon, and Sport hardtop coupe (seen here). At $3257, the last was the least expensive Bonneville, and at 3985 pounds the only one with a curb weight under the two-ton mark.

broad hood and rear deck, and the first of Pontiac's distinctive split grilles added up to styling uncommonly tasteful for its time. One writer termed the '59 package "a long, long way from the old-maidish Pontiac of a few years ago."

Engineering had come a long way too. Besides the Wide-Track chassis, the big news was a V-8 stroked to 389 cubic inches, a figure destined for performance fame. It initially came in no fewer than six versions, all called "Tempest" (a name adopted for '58). These ranged from the "420-E," a low-compression economy mill with 215 horsepower, to the rip-roaring Tri-Power unit with a rated 310 bhp. A 330-bhp four-barrel engine and a 345-bhp Tri-Power were added during the year.

Other technical changes were less obvious but just as praiseworthy. Brakes gained cooling flanges in front and 10 percent more lining area to correct the 1957-58 models' lack of stopping power, and GM's Saginaw Division contributed new rotary-valve power steering that preserved driver control in the event of hydraulic failure. Other new features included rear-seat heater ducts, electric windshield wipers (replacing vacuum-operated) and, on wagons (all four-doors now), a roll-down rear window instead of a clumsy liftgate.

Like Chevy with the Impala and Plymouth with its Fury, Pontiac turned the limited-edition Bonneville into a full-fledged series for '59, rendering it somewhat less exclusive but far more salable. A flat-top "Vista-roof" hardtop sedan joined the convertible and hardtop coupe, all on the longer Star Chief wheelbase, and there was even a six-passenger Bonneville Safari wagon on the shorter platform of this year's new low-end Catalina series; it garnered the fewest orders of any '59 Pontiac. Catalina took over for the old Chieftain, while the Bonneville line pushed Star Chief down a notch to substitute for the previous Super Chief.

Overwhelming public acceptance confirmed the shrewdness of these and other product moves. *Car Life* picked Bonneville as the best buy in its price range, and *Motor Trend* named the entire Pontiac line its 1959 "Car of the Year." Though the price-leading Catalina quickly established itself as the division's best-seller, Bonneville actually outsold the mid-range Star Chief. Bunkie had been right again.

This basic formula would boost Pontiac into third place for 1960, where the make would finish every year from 1962 to 1971. So, in a sense, Bunkie started another tradition with the '59s— which only goes to show that those who make history are sometimes the ones who disregard it.

SPECIFICATIONS

Engines: ohv V-8, 389 cid (4.06 × 3.75), 215/245/260/280/300/310/330/345 bhp

Transmission:	3-speed manual; 4-speed Super Hydra-Matic optional
Suspension, front:	upper and lower A-arms, coil springs
Suspension, rear:	live axle, coil springs
Brakes:	front/rear drums
Wheelbase (in.):	**Catalina/all wagons** 122.0 **Star Chief/Bonneville** 124.0
Weight (lbs):	3870-4370
Top speed (mph):	110-125
0-60 mph (sec):	9.0-11.5

Production: **Catalina 2d Sport Sedan** 26,102 **4d sdn** 72,377 **Sport Coupe 2d htp** 38,309 **Vista 4d htp** 45,012 **cvt** 14,515 **Safari 4d wgn 6P** 21,162 **Safari 4d wgn 9P** 14,084 **Star Chief 2d Sport Sedan** 10,254 **4d sdn** 27,872 **Vista 4d htp** 30,689 **Bonneville Sport Coupe 2d htp** 27,769 **Vista 4d htp** 38,696 **cvt** 11,426 **Custom Safari 4d wgn 6P** 4673

1956-57 Rambler

Conventional wisdom in Fifties Detroit held that you couldn't build a car with four decent-size doors on anything less than a 100-inch wheelbase. Thus, when Nash decided to add four-door sedans and wagons to its Rambler line for 1954, it put them on an eight-inch longer wheelbase. Though hardly an earthshaking development, this 108-inch platform would loom important as the foundation for the bigger Ramblers of 1956 and beyond.

As America's first truly successful postwar compact, Rambler already loomed as Nash's mainstay by 1954, when the venerable Kenosha, Wisconsin, firm joined up with Hudson to form American Motors. Packard absorbed Studebaker that same year, another combination that, as one S-P veteran later recalled, was "like two drunks trying to help each other across the road." But George Mason, the former Nash-Kelvinator president who first headed AMC, had long recognized that the independents needed to combine for survival in the postwar world, and these initial linkups fit his long-time dream of merging all four companies. Sadly, Mason died soon after AMC was born, leaving Studebaker-Packard to continue its long, slow slide toward oblivion and AMC to rely increasingly on compacts for near-term salvation.

The first postwar Rambler of 1950 had been mainly Mason's idea. Mason loved small cars, so it came as no surprise that his successor as AMC president did too. If anything, George Romney preached the compact gospel with even more fervor. But Romney knew the public wanted more impressive cars, even economy compacts, so he okayed bold new styling on the "big" 108-inch chassis for all '56 Ramblers.

The result was not only attractive but quite popular despite the market's general cool-down from torrid '55. Of course, it helped that Lincoln had 1956's only other really new car, and that Rambler prices started as low as $1829. As in '55, AMC sold Ramblers with both Nash and Hudson emblems at the respective dealerships, moving just under 80,000 of the '56s. Significantly, that came to more than five times the year's volume for the senior Nash *and* Hudson, which were now basically twins under the skin—and not long for this world.

Much of Rambler's early success had come from its popular, pioneering all-steel station wagons, and AMC continued emphasizing them for '56. Still called Cross Country, but now limited to four-door models only, it was offered alongside a four-door sedan in mid-range Super and top-line Custom trim (the base Deluxe series had just the sedan). Customs also included a new pillarless Cross Country—Detroit's first hardtop wagon—as well as a pillarless sedan.

Rambler's new '56 styling featured a square, but pleasing, look. Hard to believe it came from the same Ed Anderson who did that year's garish "V-line" Hudson. Highlights included a Nash-style oval grille with inboard headlamps, a newly wrapped windshield, and chrome upper bodyside moldings swept up onto the roof's rear end, forming a distinctive "basket handle" with optional two-toning. One could even order tri-tone paint on Custom sedans and hardtops. Custom Cross Countrys were available with simulated woodgrain bodyside trim instead of two-toning. As before, the wagon roof dipped slightly at the C-pillar, providing a platform for the rear rooftop luggage rack that had become a popular Rambler accessory.

Dimensionally, the '56 Ramblers measured about five inches longer than the four-door '55s. Surprisingly, they were a bit narrower, although rear track boasted a five-inch-wider stance. Inside, rear-seat passengers found 2.5 inches more legroom, while luggage capacity expanded by 25 percent, or by one-third in wagons. Engineering was orthodox, apart from Nash's usual unit construction and all-coil suspension. New-for-1956 features included torque-tube drive as well as an overhead-valve version of the old 195.6-cubic-inch six, the only engine available.

With only 120 horsepower, the '56 wasn't any faster than previous Ramblers, but Romney and his buyers didn't seem to care. They wanted good mileage, and the '56 delivered. Rambler won the Mobilgas Economy Run for the second year in a row, averaging over 24 miles per gallon with optional Hydra-Matic (purchased from GM).

Things became a bit more interesting for '57, when AMC's new 250-cid V-8, a late-1956 Nash/Hudson option, became available across the board in an otherwise little-changed Rambler. It was a good move, providing 190 bhp and livelier acceleration while using only a little more fuel. Confirmed misers stuck with the base six, which gained 15 bhp but still delivered over 20 mpg.

With Nash and Hudson looking terminal, AMC made Rambler a separate make for '57 and watched model year production shoot above 91,000. But literally bigger things were at hand, including a Rambler no one expected: a hot limited edition. It wasn't a wagon, and it wasn't the sort of thing Romney favored—which may be why they called it a Rebel. You can read all about it in the next section.

AMC fielded its first all-new car with the 1956 Rambler. It rode a 108-inch wheelbase and featured chunky, though modern, styling. Featured were inboard headlights and a "basket handle" above the rear window. Among the models offered were the $1939 Super four-door sedan (opposite page), the $2239 Custom Cross Country wagon (this page, top), and the $2224 Custom hardtop sedan (center). The '57 got a slightly modified grille and parking lights, plus two-toning that de-emphasized the basket handle. It is seen here as the Custom four-door hardtop.

SPECIFICATIONS

Engines: ohv I-6, 195.6 cid (3.13 × 4.25) **1956** 120 bhp **1957** 135 bhp; ohv V-8, 250 cid (3.50 × 3.25), 190 bhp

Transmission:	3-speed manual; overdrive and GM Hydra-Matic optional
Suspension, front:	upper and lower A-arms, coil springs
Suspension, rear:	live axle, coil springs
Brakes:	front/rear drums
Wheelbase (in.):	108.0
Weight (lbs):	2992-3392
Top speed (mph):	80-100+
0-60 mph (sec):	11.0-13.5
Production:	**1956** 79,166 **1957** 91,469

1957 Rambler Rebel

The Rebel was hardly the type of car one would have expected from Rambler. But there it was, with its 327-cubic-inch, 255-horsepower V-8: bigger than anything from Chevy, Ford, or Plymouth. It could accelerate from 0-60 mph in about 7.5 seconds—Corvette territory that!

As some might recall, the first Rambler Rebel prompted a lot of head-scratching in 1957. Wasn't "Rambler" that little Nash, the one that had become almost synonymous with affordable, no-nonsense transportation since 1950? Sure. *Everybody* knew what a Rambler was: slow but thrifty, small but comfortable, reliable and dull. Yet suddenly, AMC sprung on an unsuspecting public a flashy four-door hardtop Rambler with a bigger V-8 than anything found at Chevrolet, Ford, or Plymouth. What in the world was going on?

With hindsight, the answer's easy. The Rebel came as a subtle sign that American Motors would soon give up on Nash and Hudson—at least in name—and put all its chips on Rambler. As only 1500 samples were built, the '57 Rebel was obviously never intended to make money, especially at its $2786 base price. But it did introduce the public to a new name—and the idea that at least some future Ramblers might *not* be economy compacts.

The car itself was straightforward enough. Its big attraction lurked under the hood: AMC's new 327-cubic-inch V-8, designed by David Potter and first seen in late '56 as a Nash/Hudson option. As used in the Rebel—and the final Nashes and Hudsons of 1957—it developed 255 horsepower via dual exhausts and a four-barrel carburetor (the early version produced 240 bhp). Design-wise, it was as modern as most anything from the Big Three: five-main-bearing crankshaft, cast-iron heads, aluminum-alloy pistons with three steel-insert rings. These features, as well as the basic block and a short 3.25-inch stroke were shared with the smaller 250-cid V-8 offered optionally in lesser '57 Ramblers. A half-inch-larger bore (from 3.50 inches) accounted for the increased displacement.

Co-author Richard M. Langworth, who interviewed Potter in the Seventies, learned that the 327 might well have evolved from the V-8 that Kaiser had envisioned but never could get into production (thus hastening its demise). "Some of the design ideas for a proposed Kaiser 288-cubic-inch V-8 did become the industry design some

SPECIFICATIONS

Engine:	ohv V-8, 327 cid (4.00 × 3.25), 255 bhp
Transmission:	GM Dual-Range Hydra-Matic
Suspension, front:	upper and lower A-arms, coil springs, anti-roll bar
Suspension, rear:	live axle, coil springs, anti-roll bar
Brakes:	front/rear drums
Wheelbase (in.):	108.0
Weight (lbs):	3353
Top speed (mph):	115+
0-60 mph (sec):	7.2
Production:	1500

years later," Potter said. "Whether this was carried by Kaiser engineers to other companies when Kaiser closed or was just the natural progress of the best way is hard to say. Some design ideas I used in the AMC V-8 are found in all modern designs: green-sand casting (instead of baked-oil sand core) for the tapper chamber and front face to achieve greater dimensional accuracy as well as low foundry cost, for example."

Whatever its origins, this engine made the Rebel one of 1957's hottest performers. No wonder. It resulted in a power-to-weight ratio of about 13 lbs/bhp, which would have looked good in the muscle-car Sixties. To handle it, AMC fitted Gabriel adjustable shocks and heavy-duty springs all-round, plus an anti-roll bar at each end. Power steering came standard, as did the power brakes that all Rambler Customs received. Bendix fuel injection had been planned, but never materialized.

Not that it was needed. AMC sent a Rebel down for press evaluation on the sands at Daytona Beach, where auto tester Joe Wherry recorded an average of just 7.5 seconds for the benchmark 0-60-mph sprint. "From a steady 50 mph in overdrive," he wrote, "the needle hits a corrected 80, with sudden kickdown slapping the box back into third, in just 7.2 seconds. That is high performance, believe me, when family cars are under discussion."

Wherry judged Rebel handling "fine—not superb, but improved over the regular Rambler line...[the suspension changes] minimize roll, make nose-diving on fast stops very slight indeed, and prevent bottoming except...where speed is extreme. The torque-tube driveline prevents rear-axle wind-up on fast takeoffs. [Road feel] is good even with power steering...although the lock is too great (nearly four turns)." Joe reported some brake fade in repeated high-speed applications, but said "the Rebel sho-'nuff ain't the only power-packed critter with brakes that need beefing up..."

Like most '50s specials, it wasn't exactly subtle, either. AMC stylist Ed Anderson gave it silver paint set off by gold-anodized side trim, plus a padded dash and sunvisors, Rebel name script, and the "continental" outside spare tire that cost extra on lesser Rambler hardtop sedans.

In retrospect, the '57 Rebel was an aberration, a performance car from an economy-car outfit, a short toot of the corporate horn. Not until the mid-Sixties would AMC field anything quite so sporty. The Rebel's true significance is in helping to make V-8 power a part of the Rambler image. That it also happened to be one of America's quickest and more interesting cars of the Fifties is only a bonus for those lucky enough to own one today.

1958-59 Rambler Ambassador

Nash and Hudson saw more setbacks than successes in the postwar years, prompting the shotgun wedding that formed American Motors Corporation in 1954. But mergers alone don't improve products or sales, so after struggling along for another three years, these two once-great nameplates were finally put to rest. But they lived on in spirit in a new line named after Nash's best: Ambassador.

Arriving for 1958, the Ambassador was basically what Nash and Hudson would have been had they continued. Well, not quite, because there's evidence that the Ambassador looked infinitely better than the stillborn '58 Nash and Hudson. As something of a rush job, the Ambassador simply borrowed the '58 Rambler's restyled bodyshell, but spliced in an extra nine inches ahead of the firewall for a 117-inch wheelbase. The resulting longer hood made for better proportions, but nobody was fooled into thinking this was anything other than gussied-up Rambler.

Still, AMC stylist Ed Anderson did a good job in reskinning the basic unitized structure of the 1956-57 Rambler. Aside from hood length, grilles, taillights and such, Ambassadors and Ramblers shared the same square-lined appearance, relieved only by trendy canted tailfins that seemed quite modest compared to the wings sprouting elsewhere. Grilles, by the way, were die-cast, not stamped—more expensive but more durable too.

All 1958 AMC models came with four doors, except for the reborn 100-inch-wheelbase Rambler Americans (see entry). Ambassador—marketed as a separate make, not a Rambler—offered a single series comprising sedans and Cross Country wagons in Super and Custom trim, plus a pillarless Cross Country and a Country Club hardtop sedan, both Customs. The Rambler line found itself newly divided into Six and Rebel V-8 series comprising Deluxe, Super, and Custom sedans and wagons, plus six-cylinder Super and eight-cylinder Custom Country Clubs.

Befitting its higher station, the Ambassador carried AMC's new 327 V-8, with higher compression adding 15 horsepower to the '57 figure. Rambler Sixes went up 3 bhp, to 138, while the 250-cubic-inch Rebel V-8 also got a tighter squeeze and switched from two- to four-barrel carburetion for a gain of 25 bhp to 215.

Otherwise, these cars were much like AMC's '57 products, though there was no lack of technical change. For example, optional GM Hydra-Matic got the boot in favor of Borg-Warner's new three-speed "Flight-O-Matic" transmission, complete with Chrysler-style pushbutton controls (in a panel to the lower left of the steering wheel). The all-coil suspension went basically unchanged, but rear shocks got revised rates, wheels shrunk an inch to 14, and a front anti-roll bar was made standard for Ambassadors and optional on Ramblers. "Power-Lok" limited-slip differential was a new $40 extra, and a Ford-style safety package (padded dash and sunvisors) also joined the options list. AMC even got in on the air suspension fad with an optional rear-only setup, though few buyers ordered it.

Nash, and then AMC, had long led the way in automotive heating, ventilation, and air conditioning. For 1958, a fully integrated version of the famous "Weather Eye" factory system debuted. Yet another industry first was the new "deep-dip" rustproofing given all AMC cars before painting. Dunking their bare body/chassis structures in a big bath of special chemicals was claimed to forestall the dreaded tinworm, which can wreak earlier and more damaging havoc to unit-body cars (another Nash/AMC tradition) than body-on-frame construction.

Road-testers gave generally high marks to AMC's new "big one," calling it surprisingly quick, decently roomy, fairly luxurious, and not nearly as thirsty as the outsized Detroiters that AMC president George Romney kept calling "dinosaurs." It was even fair value at prices in the $2500-$3100 range. But the public literally didn't buy any of this. Though Rambler was one of the few makes to tally higher volume in recession-wracked 1958—reaching a record 217,000 units—only 1340 of them wore Ambassador nameplates, according to one source (another with production listings by wheelbase suggests that output hit 7000 units, probably more likely).

The story for recovery '59 was much the same for AMC as output continued to climb and the corporation enjoyed a record $60 million profit. But AMC didn't separate Rambler/Ambassador production that year, although the proportion likely was about the same as in 1958, with the small American and the Six/Rebel again garnering the vast majority of sales. Changes that year included thicker brake linings, a gaudier grille, the usual trim shuffles, rear doors recontoured to blend more smoothly with the tailfinned fenderlines, and optional front-seat head restraints.

Though the Ambassador would survive all the way through 1974, it would always be too much like mid-size AMC cars to attract much of a following—and rather stuffy in the bargain. In that sense, it was very much like the Nash whose name it inherited, a car with little place in an age when it definitely wasn't hip to be square.

The '58 Ambassador replaced the big Nash and Hudson, but was basically a Rambler stretched nine inches ahead of the cowl. It alone used AMC's 327-cid V-8. At $3116, the Custom Cross Country four-door hardtop wagon (opposite, top) *topped the '58 lineup. The '59 received a new grille; the four-door sedan* (bottom) *sold for $2587 to $2732.*

SPECIFICATIONS

Engine:	ohv V-8, 327 cid (4.00 × 3.25), 270 bhp
Transmissions:	3-speed manual; overdrive and 3-speed Borg-Warner Flight-O-Matic optional
Suspension, front:	upper and lower A-arms, coil springs, anti-roll bar
Suspension, rear:	live axle, coil springs; rear air springs optional
Brakes:	front/rear drums
Wheelbase (in.):	117.0
Weight (lbs):	3456-3591
Top speed (mph):	105+
0-60 mph (sec):	10.6
Production:	**1958** 7000* **1959** 10,000*

*estimates

AMBASSADOR

1958-59 Rambler American

You'll get some argument as to whether the Rambler American is really a "great" car of the Fifties. Plain, unimposing, and dull, it was anachronistic even when new—which is precisely why it fascinates today. For this was the first—and so far only—instance when a U.S. automaker dared resurrect one of its old models.

The car in question was the original Nash-designed, 100-inch-wheelbase Rambler of 1950-55. For a time, its bigger and bolder 1956 replacement seemed sufficient to see American Motors (heir to both Nash and Hudson) through the rest of the decade at least. But AMC president George Romney had noted the growing popularity of small economy imports. When a recession began making itself felt in 1957, he decided that AMC might need a smaller, budget-priced car of its own to compete with the foreigners at the bottom end of the market.

Alas, neither time nor money allowed for an all-new design. AMC was busy making its sensible 1956-57 Rambler somewhat less so for '58, and readying a stretched Ambassador version (see entry) to replace the moribund big Nash and Hudson. But Romney, nothing if not a maverick, had an idea: Why not just take the little Rambler out of mothballs?

Reviving an obsolete design was unheard of in those days (and still is, come to that), but it made sense. AMC still had the original Nash tooling, and it had long since been paid for. This allowed the firm to field its import-fighter quickly and cheaply, which promised handsome profits even with low list prices. And the size slotted in perfectly: a bit bigger than the top-selling foreigners, smaller and thriftier than anything offered by the Big Three.

When the recession deepened, Romney put the rush on his new/old car, which arrived late in the '58 model year as the American. The name was right, too: a patriotic pitch to those cash-short buyers who'd plunk for a domestic econocar where given a choice.

The outmoded styling couldn't be hidden, but AMC freshened it up a little by adding a mesh grille and opening up the odd, semi-enclosed front wheelarches that had made for tricky tire changing and a yacht-like turning circle on the 1950-54 Ramblers. Naturally, AMC had no choice but to use the veteran Nash-designed 195.6-cubic-inch six, rated at 90 horsepower and teamed with a standard three-speed column-shift manual transmission. To keep prices down, only a two-door sedan was offered, in basic DeLuxe and slightly fancier Super trim, plus a DeLuxe business sedan *sans* back seat, a $1775 price leader. Options were restricted for the same reason; overdrive and "Flash-O-Matic" automatic transmission, radio, heater, and whitewall tires being the main choices.

No-nonsense simplicity, near 30-mpg fuel economy, and a made-in-America label constituted strong selling points in recession '58, and the American found close to 31,000 buyers despite its late start. If it caused the larger Ramblers to seem almost pretentious, it also made a good many imports seem cramped, underpowered, and overpriced—which some were.

Even though there wasn't much need for change, the American saw a few for 1959. A two-door station wagon returned from '55, still offering 52 cubic feet of cargo space with the back seat folded. DeLuxe and Super trim continued, the latter distinguished by bright window frames and nicer upholstery. Brakes were now self-adjusting on all models. Options expanded to include the inevitable rooftop luggage rack for the Super wagon, plus tasteful two-tone paint and a $59 continental kit for sedans. The last looked incongruous on the dowdy American, but it opened up more trunk space, just as it had in 1950-55.

Despite new competition from Studebaker's Lark, AMC's Truman-era compact had a field day in the twilight of the Eisenhower age. Helped by a full selling season and the 1959 market's general recovery, the American soared to over 90,000 sales, far ahead of DeSoto, Chrysler—and Edsel.

Though the American became sportier, somewhat faster, and much prettier in later years, it's the 1958-60 generation that's lately become something of a minor collectible. Like the VW Beetle, it made its fame as a "reverse-status" car that succeeded by flying in the face of most everything Detroit stood for at the time. That may not make it a great car—but it's one you've got to respect.

When George Romney took the old 100-inch-wheelbase Rambler out of mothballs in 1958, some thought him crazy. Buyers in that recession year didn't, though—they liked the $1789 and $1874 price tags for the two-door sedan and wagon.

SPECIFICATIONS

Engine: ohv I-6, 195.6 cid (3.13 × 4.25), 90 bhp

Transmission:	3-speed manual; overdrive and Borg-Warner 3-speed "Flash-O-Matic" optional
Suspension, front:	upper and lower A-arms, coil springs
Suspension, rear:	live axle, semi-elliptic leaf springs
Brakes:	front/rear drums
Wheelbase (in.):	100.0
Weight (lbs):	2439-2554
Top speed (mph):	85
0-60 mph (sec):	14.0

Production: **1958 DeLuxe 2d business sdn** 184 **2d sdn** 15,765 **Super 2d sdn** 14,691 **1959 DeLuxe 2d business sdn** 443 **2d sdn** 29,954 **2d wgn** 15,256 **Super 2d sdn** 28,449 **2d wgn** 17,383 **panel delivery** 6 prototypes

1950-51 Studebaker Commander

Studebaker entered the Fifties riding high. The one-time wagonmaker had been "first by far with a postwar car," the dramatic and dashing 1947 models that attracted customers in numbers unheard of in South Bend. Despite labor troubles, material shortages, and the drain of heavy investments for new-model development and new facilities, Studebaker built over 191,000 cars and trucks in 1947, earning more than $9 million in profits. The following year, volume swelled to nearly a quarter-million units, profits to a record $19 million. Things looked even better in '49 as sales jumped 30 percent, to about 305,000 vehicles, and profits leaped above $27.5 million.

But troubles were brewing. Though still popular, Studebaker's "New Look" '47 styling hadn't changed much, and by 1950 it no longer looked so new. Not so the competition, whose first postwar models had arrived in force, mostly for '49. South Bend again hoped to move out front with brand-new styling that year, but it was delayed by internal dissention between the Raymond Loewy consultant team and an in-house faction led by designer Virgil Exner, engineer Roy Cole, and production manager Ralph Vail. Studebaker also needed to respond to Big Three initiatives like high-compression V-8s, automatic transmissions, and "hardtop convertibles."

Ultimately, Exner departed for Chrysler, Cole and Vail were diffused, and engineers continued working overtime on the aforementioned innovations. Meantime, Loewy staffer Bob Bourke, who'd helped shaped the '47, came up with one of history's most bizarre facelifts: the infamous "bullet nose" 1950-51 Studie. It resulted from a personal directive by the French-born Loewy: "Now, Bob, eet has to look like zee aeroplane."

It did, but the record shows it might have turned out better. And though Studebaker called it the "Next Look," nobody rushed to copy it. Still, the new bullet-nose styling helped Studebaker ride the crest of the postwar seller's market to another volume record: over 343,000 cars. Alas, it would never again do so well.

Besides that outrageous front, the 1950 Studebakers boasted an extra inch in wheelbase, reshaped rear fenders, and redesigned instrument panels. More significant was a switch to front coil springs, ousting an antiquated single transverse leaf. The broad range of Champion and Commander coupes, sedans, and convertibles offered since 1947 gained four closed Champion Customs; starting at $1419, they returned Studebaker to the low-price field for the first time since 1939. A half-point compression

The "bullet nose" 1950 Studebaker Commander stirred up controversy where ever it went, but it sold well. The Regal DeLuxe convertible (below) listed at $2328, while the Regal DeLuxe coupe with its four-piece wraparound rear window went out the door for $2018 (plain DeLuxe, $1897).

boost added five horsepower to the old Champ six; Commander's larger six gained 2 bhp to 102. As befit its higher station, Commander rode a 120-inch wheelbase, seven inches longer than the Champ, and prices ranged from $1871 to $2328 for a Regal DeLuxe convertible.

Spring 1950 brought Studebaker's most important postwar engineering advance yet: "Automatic Drive." A line-wide option developed in concert with Borg-Warner's Detroit Gear Division, it was the only automatic transmission designed and built by an independent other than Packard. And several features made it one of the best anywhere: no-slip torque-converter; a safety that prevented in-gear starting and damage should reverse be accidentally selected on the move; no-creep operation; and a "hill-holder" that kept the car from rolling backward down an incline. Ford wanted to buy Automatic Drive for its cars, but Studebaker refused to sell—in retrospect, a serious mistake.

The big ammunition for '51 arrived as the much needed overhead-valve V-8, exclusive to the Commander. Besides being a fine engine and the first modern V-8 from an independent, it put Studebaker at least three years ahead of Chevy/Ford/Plymouth. Its greater compactness prompted a five-inch cut in Commander wheelbase. Rising production costs dictated putting the Champion on this platform, too, so it inherited the Commander's new-for-1950 center-point steering and coil-over front shocks.

Otherwise, the '51s were much like the '50 Studebakers. The "bullet nose" was toned down a bit by painting its large, chrome outer ring, series were renamed and trim reshuffled, Commanders got improved electric wipers (optional on Champions), and prices went up a little. The long-wheelbase Commander Land Cruiser sedan, alone on a four-inch-longer wheelbase, remained the pride of the South Bend fleet at $2289, although the Commander State convertible outpriced it by a few dollars.

With less weight and nearly 18 percent more horsepower, the V-8 Commander caused a mild sensation. Gushed tester "Uncle Tom" McCahill: "This powerplant transforms the maidenly Studie of recent years into a rip-roaring, hell-for-leather performer that can belt the starch out of practically every other American car...." Still, a Commander won its class in the '51 Mobilgas Economy Run, averaging 28 mpg with overdrive over 840 miles. Commanders were highly respected cars of their day for long-distance travel, especially the V-8 Land Cruiser. Of course, at just $75 below a Buick Super, they had to be.

Nonetheless, an abbreviated model year and the beginning of government-ordered production cutbacks (due to the Korean conflict) hampered Studebaker output, which dropped to below 269,000 units for '51, 124,280 of them Commanders. South Bend was still riding pretty high and some of its most memorable cars lay ahead, but the long, slow slide to oblivion had already begun. Ultimately, being "first by far" would cost Studebaker its life.

SPECIFICATIONS

Engines: **1950** L-head six, 245.6 cid (3.31 × 4.75), 102 bhp **1951** ohv V-8, 232.6 cid (3.38 × 3.25), 120 bhp

Transmission:	3-speed manual; overdrive and 2-speed "Automatic Drive" (from mid-1950) optional
Suspension, front:	upper and lower A-arms, coil springs
Suspension, rear:	live axle, semi-elliptic leaf springs
Brakes:	front/rear drums
Wheelbase (in.):	**1950** 120.0 **Land Cruiser** 124.0 **1951** 115.0 **Land Cruiser** 119.0
Weight (lbs):	3215-3375
Top speed (mph):	**1950** 85 **1951** 100
0-60 mph (sec):	**1950** 16.0 **1951** 13.0
Production:	**1950** 72,562 **1951** 124,280

1952 Studebaker Starliner

If the 1950 Studebakers had the "Next Look," as the ads said, what was going to follow it? That became the question as America's oldest vehicle maker prepared to celebrate its 100th birthday in 1952. And once again, no one seemed to have a clear answer. But 1952 called for *some* sort of styling change—car companies don't observe centennials every day, you know—and South Bend didn't suffer from any shortage of ideas.

The one most favored was the Model N (allegedly for "New"), basically a rebodied version of the existing 1947-51 design, developed by Bob Bourke of the Raymond Loewy studios. Several other proposals envisioned lower, sleeker, and more sculptured lines, but still recognizably Studebaker. The only point of controversy arose over whether to continue the 1950-51 "bullet nose," which the public seemed to like—even if the Loewy team and some Studebaker executives didn't.

Events soon rendered the matter academic. The Korean conflict intervened, and so Studebaker had military contracts to fill, and the government meantime had limited civilian auto production, all of which forced the Model N to be abandoned—literally, in the woods surrounding the South Bend proving grounds. Besides, Loewy had come up with something far better, though because he did so in early 1951 there was no hope of having it ready in time for the '52 centenary. (It did appear for '53, however, as the next section relates). All this left another major facelift the only option, and it duly arrived, marking the sixth and final appearance of the basic 1947 design.

Co-author Richard Langworth once asked Loewy if adverse dealer reaction forced Studebaker to forsake the bullet nose after only two years. "Yes," he replied. "[1952] was a typical facelift, and most welcome, as it made it possible to lower the [hood]. I always objected to [its] high hood."

The main visual change centered on a nose that looked bulbous rather than pointy, plus a more conventional grille—a low, toothy, split affair dubbed the "clam digger" by some stylists. Two-toning became available for the first time since the war, but the glamor news had to wait for the belated arrival of a pillarless hardtop coupe in Champion Regal and Commander State trim. Called Starliner, it appeared one to four years behind similar offerings from the Big Three and independent rivals Packard and Hudson. But at least Studebaker beat out Kaiser-Frazer, which never would field this popular body style (to its ultimate disadvantage), and was no later than Nash (which also issued its first hardtops for '52). "I don't know why it took so long to get into production," Loewy told Langworth. "We had made scale models before, and quite attractive ones, as well as dozens of renderings."

These developments aside, the '52 Studebakers didn't differ too much from the '51s. Champions retained their old 169.6-cubic-inch L-head six, still at 85 horsepower, while the uplevel Commander line returned with the efficient 232.6-cid overhead-valve V-8 introduced the previous year, also unchanged at 120 bhp. "Automatic Drive" transmission remained an across-the-board option.

With its wraparound backlight and airier look, most observers found the Starliner quite attractive. And like hardtops everywhere, it found immediate popularity, accounting for fully 15 percent of total 1952 Studebaker sales. Price was evidently not a negative factor in this. At $2220, the Champ version ran only $53 below the Regal convertible; in the Commander line, only the State convertible cost more ($2548 versus $2488 for the hardtop).

In a double dose of promotional puffery, a Starliner was selected to mark the end of Studebaker's first 100 years of production, rolling out the door at 3:20 p.m. on February 15, 1952: Studebaker number 7,130,874. Perhaps predictably, officials in nearby Indianapolis selected a Studebaker to pace that year's Memorial Day 500 race, but a Commander convertible did the honors there, closed bodies being less suitable for parade chores. Two more class wins in the Mobilgas Economy Run iced South Bend's centennial cake, where a Champ averaged 27.8 mpg and a Commander returned 25.6 mpg.

Studebaker's first hardtop must have been a rather costly proposition, as it ended up being a one-year-only model, replaced by the rakish all-new Loewy design of 1953. Not that it mattered much. Studebaker could afford to indulge itself a little in 1952, though this would be about the last time it could. The rosy nostalgia and optimistic predictions of that centennial year would soon be washed away by a river of troubles, most of which the company would bring on itself. Ultimately, they'd force Studebaker to leave the car business barely 14 years into its second century.

Studebaker introduced its modern overhead-valve V-8 in 1951, and followed that up with its first hardtop in 1952, the Starliner. It was a perfect mate to the lively 120-horsepower V-8; so equipped it was called the Commander State Starliner and sold for $2488. Six-cylinder partisans could save a few dollars by ordering the Champion Regal Starliner, which came in at a more modest $2220.

SPECIFICATIONS

Engines: Champion L-head I-6, 169.6 cid (3.00 × 4.00), 85 bhp **Commander** ohv V-8, 232.6 cid (3.38 × 3.25), 120 bhp

Transmission:	3-speed manual; overdrive and 2-speed "Automatic Drive" optional
Suspension, front:	upper and lower A-arms, coil springs
Suspension, rear:	live axle, semi-elliptic leaf springs
Brakes:	front/rear drums
Wheelbase (in.):	115.0
Weight (lbs):	**Champion** 2860 **Commander** 3220
Top speed (mph):	**Champion** 85 **Commander** 100
0-60 mph (sec):	**Champion** 16.0 **Commander** 13.0
Production:	26,667

ONTARIO
HVJ 285

ONTARIO
HVJ 285

1953-54 Studebaker Starliner

In the judgment of qualified observers, the 1953 Starliner emerged as the finest piece of automotive styling from an American manufacturer during the Fifties. Some thought that ironic in a way, since it came from Studebaker, a make known for bizarre, but certainly not state-of-the-art design. Its predecessors had included two years of weird looking, pointed-nose jobs and a 1952 facelift that resembled a big anteater. Nobody expected what Studebaker dished out in 1953.

On the other hand, such pure and beautiful lines (most of them by Bob Bourke, head of the Raymond Loewy Studios styling team at Studebaker) probably wouldn't have survived had they originated with one of the Big Three. They were too radical for Ford and Chrysler, not blowzy enough for General Motors. Studebaker, reaching for a difference, adopted the Starliner with a minimum of protest, though the sedans based on it didn't look nearly as inspired. The selling job was performed on management by Raymond Loewy, the brilliant French designer whose entire career had been built upon the selling of advanced ideas to recalcitrant businessmen. To Loewy and Bourke, a debt is owed.

Bob Bourke told this writer that his inspiration came from the Lockheed Constellation aircraft: "The general nose-down feel of the fuselage in particular was reflected in the front fender and hood contours." The angle termination of the rear fenders, with the taillights buried within, and bumpers which appeared almost integral with the sheetmetal, were purely automotive touches, elegantly handled. For side definition, Bourke created a sweeping "character line" running from the forward part of the front fenders through the door, then bending down to the rocker panel in a reverse angle, duplicating that of the rear fenders.

The coupe thus created bowed as a "Starlight" (with rigid "B" pillars and door window frames), but the finest workout appeared on the "Starliner" hardtop, available as either a six-cylinder Champion or a Commander V-8. Bourke had actually wanted a single piece of side glass—like the post-1969 Camaro—but this created an immense door span, and he didn't like the alternative of a huge "blind" rear quarterpost either.

Of course, other shapes were considered for the 1953 Studebaker, many of them far more conventional. But Raymond Loewy felt that Studebaker would not succeed by aping Detroit—give the public a low, lithe, European design, he said. It was nip and tuck for some weeks, Bourke remembered. "But sure enough, finally we were told the 'European style' was to go into production. It was an emotional moment."

Wisely, Studebaker chief engineer Eugene Hardig allowed the designers to put both the Starliner and Starlight on the 1953 Land Cruiser's extended 120.5-inch wheelbase (itself based on the 120.0-inch stretch of the then-present 1950 Commander). The '53 sedans used a four-inch-shorter wheelbase. This gave the coupes proportions equal to their smooth, clean styling—they would not have looked nearly as nice on the shorter chassis.

The Champion ran an underpowered six and sported a cleaner, less contrived dashboard. The Commander, however, used Studebaker's excellent small-block V-8, lively and durable, and the only overhead-valve V-8 in the near-low-price field at the time—at $2374, it cost $300 more than a Ford Victoria, $300 less than an Olds Super 88 Holiday hardtop. Both models were available with overdrive, or the Borg-Warner automatic, which Studebaker had offered since 1950.

By far the most interesting drivetrain feature was Studie's new mechanical powered steering, offered initially as an option, but soon withdrawn. Developed by Warner Gear Division of Borg-Warner, it required only two pounds of wheel effort to become operative, but required an excessive 4½ turns lock-to-lock. Resistant to road shock, it provided good wheel-to-unit control. But at $161 it proved too expensive, and a GM hydraulic system replaced it after only 100 had been installed.

Response to what everyone called the "Loewy coupes" was good—too good. Studebaker endured problems, which delayed production. Worse, the build plan called for four sedans to each coupe; demand turned out to be the opposite. Thus, Studebaker lost a good many customers in 1953. In haste to turn the production mix around, Studebaker cut corners and quality control suffered. The '54s debuted virtually the same in all respects, but with eggcrate grilles. Unfortunately, the lovely Starliner had already lost its initial sales momentum.

To many eyes, the 1953 Studebaker Starliner was the most beautiful automotive design to emerge during the Fifties. The Champion Regal Starliner listed at $2116, weighed 2760 pounds, and was powered by an 85-horsepower L-head six. Performance was modest, but fuel economy was excellent.

SPECIFICATIONS

Engine: **Champion** sidevalve I-6, 169.6 cid (3.00 × 4.00), 85 bhp **Commander** ohv V-8, 232.6 cid (3.38 × 3.25), 120 bhp

Transmission:	3-speed manual, overdrive and "Automatic Drive" optional
Suspension, front:	independent, coil springs, tube shocks
Suspension, rear:	live axle, leaf springs, tube shocks
Brakes:	front/rear drums
Wheelbase:	120.5
Weight (lbs):	**Champion** 2760-2825 **Commander** 3120-3175
Top speed (mph):	**Champion** 85 **Commander** 100
0-60 mph (sec):	**Champion** 20.0 **Commander** 13.0-16.0
Production:	**1953** 32,294 **1954** 9342

ONTARIO
HVH 426

ONTARIO
HVH 426

1955 Studebaker Speedster

In designing the 1955 Studebakers, as one magazine put it, "a chrome-happy kid had a holiday." Actually, the kid was a grown man, Bob Bourke of the Loewy design group, and he didn't like what he had to do. "The chromed front end was to have been painted the body color, forming a long, smooth snout, with mesh grille insert," Bourke told this writer. "Ken Elliott [Sales Manager] was convinced that more chrome was the way to go." Bourke had also planned a short-wheelbase two-seat convertible based on the Starliner, which looked superb in full-size clay, but management decided (probably rightly) that its appeal would be too limited, and canned this project.

Though a true sports car didn't make it, a relatively inexpensive, sporty confection did. The President Speedster, with its 185-bhp V-8, dual exhausts, "tri-level" paint job, and full instrumentation including tachometer, appealed to the sporting instincts surfacing among buyers in 1955. Originally, 20 Speedsters were run off for the round of early 1955 auto shows; they proved so popular that the Speedster went into limited production for the balance of the model year.

To create a Speedster, Studebaker began with a President hardtop (rarely called "Starliner" in 1955). The outside received special badging, simulated wire wheels, heavy combination bumper guard/foglamps, and the aforementioned three-tone paint jobs, which often came in wild combinations like "Lemon and Lime" or pink and gray. A broad, bright band followed the roof curvature ahead of the backlight. On the inside, diamond quilted leather and vinyl upholstery in color-keyed shades was combined with a magnificent, engine-turned dashboard with purposeful white-on-black instruments. Standard equipment included power steering and brakes, radio, clock, tach, whitewalls, back-up lights, and foglamps—all for a list price of $3253.

According to *Motor Life*, the Speedster acted "more like a sports car than any other hardtop." The wheel sat flat in one's lap, the seats were low, and the driver's legs stretched out almost horizontally. The rev counter was useful even on automatic-equipped cars: "One time I started in *LOW*, moved the lever to *DRIVE*, but no shift came," said *ML*'s tester. "A glance at the tach showed the needle rapidly climbing over 5000, so I backed off on the throttle. Without the tach I might have dangerously overrevved the engine."

Motor Trend only reluctantly returned its test Speedster after a brief 300-mile encounter: "It's fun to drive, both from a performance and handling standpoint. It should make an ideal automobile for anyone who wants a car with semi-sports car characteristics and a 'different' appearance, but who needs room for four or five people. The many custom touches and'extras' which are ordinarily added cost items—power steering, power brakes, special paint job—combine to make it a high performer ideal for family driving."

Speedsters delivered outstanding performance right off the showroom floor, but Los Angeles dealer John McKusick wasn't satisfied with that. He offered a $390 option consisting of a McCulloch supercharged engine, hooked to a conventional manual gearbox. The effect was electrifying, as these comparisons show:

	Supercharged Speedster	Speedster Automatic	President Automatic
Horsepower:	210 (est.)	185	175
0-30 mph (sec):	3.0	3.5	3.8
0-60 mph (sec):	7.7	10.2	13.4
¼-mile (sec):	86.0	83.0	79.8
Top speed (mph):	120 (est.)	110	106

The Speedster was not built in vain, or simply to cream off a few high-end sales for Studebaker. Many of its features are now recognizable as having evolved into the 1956-58 Golden Hawk, including the sporty dashboard, deluxe interior, wild two-tone paint jobs—and McKusick's McCulloch supercharged engine.

Yet another Los Angeles dealer, Belmont Sanchez, got tired of waiting for the oft-promised Studebaker convertible. So he devised a $500 option called the "Sahara," a hardtop with the roof cut off and reworked for a snap-on fitting, like a removable-top 1955-57 Thunderbird. The price seemed a bargain, but probably did not include much strengthening of the body and frame to handle the added flex; the expense of such modifications was in fact the reason Studebaker never built a production convertible out of these good-looking coupes. Too bad, but at least they *did* build the Speedster hardtop; collectors today wish they had built more.

The Studebaker President Speedster started out as a show car during the early part of the 1955 model year, but ended up going into limited production. Although the Speedster shared its basic styling with the President hardtop, it was distinguished by its 185-bhp V-8, dual exhausts, "tri-level" paint, simulated wire-wheel covers, full instrumentation, and special badging. Performance was marvelous, but the $3253 price tag was a bit on the high side, and so ultimately only 2215 copies were built.

SPECIFICATIONS

Engine: ohv V-8, 259.2 cid (3.56 × 3.25), 185 bhp

Transmission:	3-speed manual with overdrive or "Automatic Drive" standard
Suspension, front:	independent, coil springs, tube shocks
Suspension, rear:	live axle, leaf springs, tube shocks
Brakes:	front/rear drums
Wheelbase (in.):	120.5
Weight (lbs):	3301
Top speed (mph):	110
0-60 mph (sec):	9.0-10.5
Production:	2215

TYP 282
Studebaker

1956-58 Studebaker

Studebaker-Packard, founded with so much optimism in 1954, had fallen into total disarray by 1956. By then, the '56 Studebakers had necessarily long been finalized, designed by S-P styling under Bill Schmidt and a consultant Schmidt admired: Vince Gardner. The Loewy team departed after finalizing the 1956 Hawk.

"Vince modeled the front and rear of the 1956 Studebakers," Loewy's Bob Bourke recalled. "He created a very nice, squared-off deck and a clean grille, and carried over the two flanking grilles from earlier designs. He worked like hell [but was paid] next to nothing—about $7500....Vince was pretty much a loner, but when fired up he'd put roller skates on his feet."

The new look was adopted to erase what had been a broadly unsuccessful Loewy design—except for the coupes. The sedans, Studebaker's traditional mainstay, had fared particularly poorly in the 1953-55 design cycle. So for 1956 they got all new side moldings to define the two-tone area on more expensive models. The interior, by Duncan McRae, included a novel "cyclops eye" speedometer—a small drum, rotating to show only current speed, changing color from green to orange to red as speed increased. The model range included the six-cylinder Champion, the V-8 Commander and President, along with the Hawks mentioned earlier.

But there were curious anomalies—really bad planning by S-P management, which should have seen and filled important gaps in the Studebaker body range long before. For instance, the station wagon—a facelift of the body style introduced in 1954—still had only two doors, despite overwhelming public preference for four-door wagons; and there was still, at this late date, no mainstream Studebaker hardtop.

S-P president James Nance, who gets so much blame for what happened, saw this need from the time Packard and Studebaker came together, and repeatedly urged four-door wagons and hardtops upon his reluctant partner, Harold Vance of Studebaker. Thanks to Nance, the four-door Provincial (Commander) and Broadmoor (President) wagons made it into the lineup for 1957, and a hardtop (Commander and President Starlight) debuted in 1958, the latter described as being "Hawk-inspired." But these came very late—and not in time to change the results, which were grim. A restyled grille and taillights didn't help for '57, either, and tacked-on fins and weird-looking pod-mounted quad headlights did nothing to further the "completely new luxury look for 1958!" that the brochure promised. Thus, Studebaker's model year output fell steadily: 70,000 in 1956, 63,000 in 1957, 45,000 in 1958.

One has to conclude that Studebaker, in planning these models, almost always made precisely the wrong decision. For 1956, the Champion and Commander included a stripped two-door sedan called the "sedanet," which didn't sell; yet in 1957-58 they kept pounding this dead horse by producing the Scotsman line of dirt cheap sedans and two-door wagons, minus almost all exterior bright trim, upholstered in cheap cloth and cardboard, and with as much allure as a garbage scow. In 1955, Studebaker had finally brought the entire President line up to a 120-inch wheelbase; but the very next year the President dropped back to the short wheelbase, except for a single four-door sedan, the Classic. When it had the option of the 1956 Packard V-8 and the supercharged 1957-58 Studebaker 289 V-8, which would have transformed the President from a plug-ordinary car to a really exciting one, Studebaker settled for conventional smallblocks.

Sure—by dumb luck—the Scotsman turned out to be the right idea in recession year 1958. But the public didn't want this ugly, stripped duckling—it wanted the brightly colored, nicely finished Rambler. The Scotsman did sell 20,000 units in 1958, which was about twice as many as the Champion, Commander, or President. But think how many more copies it would have sold if it had offered a little more chrome and a nice, bright interior.

Frankly, it was a wonder that this benighted company survived at all after 1956-58—years when none of the plant's employees knew from one day to the next whether they'd have a job next week. Boy scouts could have managed Studebaker better than the men who ran it, and each of the few smart ideas—the sporty Hawks, the supercharger, the 1959 Lark—had to be clubbed into top management by the designers and engineers they were lucky enough to have, but didn't deserve.

Studebaker went through hard times in the 1956-58 era because of a lack of money for a complete restyle. The '56 was a continuation of the 1953 bodyshell, but new sheetmetal saw the design squared up both front and rear. The President Classic (this page and opposite top and center left) *rode a 120.5-inch wheelbase, four inches longer than standard models. The '57* (center right) *received a new grille, the '58* (bottom) *yet another trim shuffle.*

SPECIFICATIONS

Engines: **1956** sidevalve I-6, 185.6 cid (3.00 × 4.38), 101 bhp; ohv V-8, 259.2 cid (3.56 × 3.25), 170/185 bhp; 289.0 cid (3.56 × 3.63), 195/210/225 bhp **1957** 185.6 cid, 101 bhp; 259.2 cid, 180/195 bhp; 289.0 cid, 210/225 bhp **1958** 185.6 cid, 101 bhp; 259.2 cid, 180 bhp; 289.0 cid, 210/225 bhp

Transmission:	3-speed manual; overdrive and Flight-O-Matic optional
Suspension, front:	independent, coil springs, tube shocks
Suspension, rear:	live axle, leaf springs, tube shocks
Brakes:	front/rear drums (finned on President)
Wheelbase (in.):	116.5 **1956-57 President Classic and 1958 President** 120.5
Weight (lbs):	2680-3420
Top speed (mph):	**Six** 90 **259 V-8s** 100-105 **289 V-8s** 110-115
0-60 mph (sec):	**Six** 17-18 **259 V-8s** 14-15 **289 V-8s** 11-12

Production: **1956** **Champion** 23,000* **Commander** 25,000* **President** 18,209 **1957** **Scotsman** 10,000* **Champion** 14,000* **Commander** 18,000* **President** 13,000* **1958** **Scotsman** 20,870 **Champion** 10,325 **Commander** 12,249 **President** 10,422
*estimate

PARISIAN
CLASSIC CARS

ONTARIO
TXS 999

1956 Studebaker Hawk

Evolving from the Speedster concept—a four- or five-seater featuring sports-car characteristics—Studebaker's Hawks preceded the Mustang by eight years as the original "ponycar," but have never been recognized for this because they had far less influence on the market. The Mustang sold 680,000 copies in its first eight months; the Hawks sold 79,000 copies over eight years.

Nonetheless, the Hawk is significant historically, and a fine car in its own right, logically taking the "Loewy coupe" a step further in evolution—and packing performance, at least in supercharged form—that the Starliners could only hint at.

In 1956, their initial year, Studebaker built the Hawk in four flavors, which together accounted for about 20,000 sales, nearly one-fourth of Studebaker's model year total. The Flight Hawk served as the price leader, a pillared six-cylinder coupe (nee Starlight) starting at just $1986. The Golden Hawk hardtop soared over the rest of the line with the help of a big Packard V-8 with optional Ultramatic Drive. At lower altitudes came the Power Hawk pillared coupe and Sky Hawk hardtop, with 259- and 289-cid Studebaker V-8s, respectively, and optional Borg-Warner automatic. Product planners had certainly produced as broad a variety of Hawks for '56 as possible.

The Golden Hawk, with its distinctive fiberglass tailfins and luxurious interior in vinyl or vinyl-and-cloth, naturally attracted the most attention with auto buffs. Definitely in the hot car class, it competed with two-seaters like the Thunderbird, and even with Ultramatic Drive it proved only slightly slower than with stickshift.

Unfortunately, the Golden Hawk had one major drawback—it was nose heavy. The Packard engine weighed about 100 pounds more than the Studebaker 289, itself no lightweight. This caused the car to understeer with single-minded consistency, and sometimes even interfered with acceleration. "Due to the tremendous torque of the engine (380 lbs/ft at 2800 rpm) *and* due to the [heavy engine], it is almost impossible to make a fast getaway start on any surface without considerable wheel spinning," wrote the veteran road tester Tom McCahill. "If I'd shoved 200 or 300 pounds of sand in the trunk to equalize the weight distribution, my times would have been considerably better." Few other testers condemned this nose-heavy characteristic at the time, but in 1957, when the Packard engine gave way to a Studebaker, they outdid each other by noting what an improvement it was.

For those who found balance and finesse as important as brute force, the Sky Hawk provided a reasonable alternative. At $500 less than the Golden Hawk, it had to be one of the best buys of 1956. Like the Golden Hawk (but not the Power and Flight Hawks), it used finned brake drums, which were highly resistant to fade. It handled beautifully, and with 210 horsepower could hardly be considered a slouch in performance. It sported a vinyl interior of luxurious design, the same tooled metal dash as the Golden Hawk (tachometer optional), and much cleaner exterior styling. The Sky Hawk flew without the aid of what Bob Bourke called "those damnable fiberglass fins." Further, it lacked the Golden Hawk's bright metal rocker panel covers and its band across the rear roofline. Like the Golden Hawk, however, its plumage included colorful two-toning, with a beltline divider causing the beak to come in a different color than the tail. But the determined conservative could order one in a solid color.

The Power and Flight Hawks received more modest trim and offered two-toning only on their roofs. Both were clean-lined, good-looking, finless cars, and the Power Hawk's smaller V-8 provided excellent performance for only $2100 base. Though produced in greater numbers than their hardtop brethren, they have not been as carefully preserved, and are rare today. Like many models before and since, they've been overlooked by collectors who seek out their more glittery peacock linemates—but they are well respected by those who know and appreciate their quiet merits.

All four Hawks were designed by the Loewy Studios under Bob Bourke, who is most proud of the classic, square grille, which did so much to freshen the 1955 body. Shortly after the '56s were firmed up, however, the merged Studebaker-Packard management terminated Loewy's contract. But the Frenchman would return in the Sixties, this time to design the memorable Avanti.

Studebaker listed four Hawks for 1956: Flight Hawk (opposite, center left) *and Power Hawk* (center right)*, both pillared coupes, plus the Sky Hawk* (bottom) *and the top-line Golden Hawk* (top)*, both hardtops. Engine offerings comprised a 185.6-cid six, Studebaker 259.2- and 289.0-cid V-8s, and—for the Golden Hawk—a Packard-built 352-cid, 275-bhp V-8. Prices started at $1986.*

SPECIFICATIONS

Engines: **Flight Hawk** sidevalve I-6, 185.6 cid (3.00 × 4.38), 101 bhp; ohv V-8 **Power Hawk** 259.2 cid (3.56 × 3.25), 170 bhp **Sky Hawk** 289.0 cid (3.56 × 3.63), 210 bhp; 225 bhp optional **Golden Hawk** 352.0 cid (4.00 × 3.50), 275 bhp

Transmissions:	3-speed manual, overdrive optional **Flight, Power, and Sky Hawk** 3-speed Flight-O-Matic optional **Golden Hawk** Gear-Start Ultramatic optional
Suspension, front:	independent, coil springs, tube shocks
Suspension, rear:	live axle, leaf springs, tube shocks
Brakes:	front/rear drums **Sky and Golden Hawk** finned drums
Wheelbase (in.):	120.5
Weight (lbs):	**Flight Hawk** 2780 **Power Hawk** 3095 **Sky Hawk** 3215 **Golden Hawk** 3360
Top speed (mph):	**Flight Hawk** 90 **Power Hawk** 100 **Sky Hawk** 110-115 **Golden Hawk** 120
0-60 mph (sec):	**Flight Hawk** 18.0 **Power Hawk** 15.0 **Sky Hawk** 11.0-12.0 **Golden Hawk** 9.0-10.0

Production: **Flight and Power Hawk** 11,484 **Sky Hawk** 3610 **Golden Hawk** 4071

1957-58 Studebaker Golden Hawk

Facelifted afresh, now by Duncan McRae of Studebaker-Packard's in-house design team, the 1957 Golden Hawk tried to keep pace with styling trends by adding tall, steel, concave fins to replace the little fiberglass ones of 1956. McRae also cleaned up the bright metal trim without altering Bob Bourke's classic square mesh radiator, ribbed rear deck, or purposeful instrument panel. Instead of the shape-concealing two-tone paint jobs of 1956, McRae restricted Golden Hawk second colors to the fins, leaving the roof the same color as the rest of the body.

Under the skin, many differences quickly became apparent. First off, the Studebaker 289 V-8 replaced the 1956 model's Packard engine. The Golden Hawk also shared two notable developments with the full range of 1957 Studebakers: variable-rate front coil springs and optional Twin Traction (limited-slip) differential. Twin Traction conducted drive force to one rear wheel even if the other wheel lost traction, providing up to 80 percent of engine power to the one with the best grip. With the new springs, the front coil compressed at an equal rate, coil by coil, helping to equalize spring action under load and surface conditions. Golden Hawks also continued the 1956 finned brake drums, important in reducing fade under heavy usage. One good idea, unfortunately not adopted, was rack-and-pinion steering. The Monroe Corporation had experimented with it on a 1956 Studebaker, but high costs prohibited its use.

Probably the most interesting feature of the '57 Golden Hawk was its McCulloch centrifugal supercharger, which had recently also seen use on the 1954-55 Kaiser Manhattan. Designed in 1951 by Robert Paxton McCulloch, who had built both Roots-type and centrifugal blowers since the 1930s, it represented $700,000 in research and development.

The supercharger was driven by a belt taken off the crankshaft pulley, through a planetary ball mechanism, which increased impeller speed 4.4 times over belt speed.

The '57 Golden Hawk traded Packard's 352-cid, 275-bhp V-8 for Studebaker's 289-cubic-inch V-8. With standard supercharger, it too boasted 275 horses. Style-wise, the '57 Golden Hawk (both pages) sported taller fins and altered two-toning. The '58 added mesh grillework to the front vents and saw the trim shuffled around a bit.

The impeller was activated by a solenoid built into the accelerator linkage and its speed was variable—controlled by the position of the pedal. At medium cruise, the blower freewheeled, delivering only about 1.5 pounds per square inch of boost. Depressing the accelerator increased boost pressure to 5.0 psi. Although impeller speed did not exceed 30,000 rpm, McCulloch claimed 60,000 rpm could be sustained without damage. The supercharger had its own built-in oil reservoir (using automatic transmission fluid) and independent pressure lubrication, which did not require service. On the 289 V-8, the blower boosted horsepower by 22 percent.

One little known Hawk variation was the Golden Hawk "400," introduced in April 1957 to spark the spring sales season. The designation was snitched from Packard, which had used it since 1951 to define some of its higher priced models, ending with the Four Hundred hardtop of 1956. Originally the term referred to the social 400, America's most prominent families.

In 1957, with the big Packard gone, the 400 became the finest and most expensive model in the Studebaker-Packard lineup. The interior stood out as the most significant feature of the 400, sporting full-pleated leather (identical to that of the later Packard Hawk). Other special features included a fully carpeted trunk and flared armrests, like those on the 1956 Hawks. When two-toned, which was usual, the forward air intake openings flanking the grille were painted the second color to match the tailfins. The interior was available only in white or tan, and non-wearing surfaces like door panels, sun visors, headliner, and instrument panel padding were finished in vinyl. The 400 cost about $300 more than the standard Golden Hawk.

With the Hawks being one of Studebaker's few sales successes in 1957, little change occurred in 1958. A switch to 14-inch wheels gave a one-inch lower height and a circular "Hawk" badge adorned the lower grille for easy recognition. Eliminating the rear seat armrest allowed three people to squeeze into the back seat. The Golden Hawk 400 disappeared, but a wide range of fabrics and vinyls, stretched over foam-padded, coil-sprung seats were available.

The 1957-58 Golden Hawk proved even faster than the 1956 version, and a much better handling car—"as far removed from its '56 namesake," *Hot Rod* stated, "as it is from a Sherman tank. [It] can cut a pretty fancy corner without any of the front end 'wash out' displayed by the '56." It's too bad that only 4356 buyers took advantage of this $3182 bargain in 1957 to find out, and a shame that just 878 individualistic souls did so in 1958.

SPECIFICATIONS

Engine:	ohv V-8, 289.0 cid (3.56 × 3.63), 275 bhp
Transmission:	3-speed manual; overdrive and 3-speed Flight-O-Matic optional
Suspension, front:	independent, coil springs, tube shocks
Suspension, rear:	live axle, leaf springs, tube shocks
Brakes:	front/rear finned drums
Wheelbase (in.):	120.5
Weight (lbs):	3250
Top speed (mph):	125
0-60 mph (sec):	8.5-9.5
Production:	**1957** 4356 **1958** 878

1959 Studebaker Lark

The end of Studebaker-Packard would have surely come after the disastrous 1958 model year had it not been for the compact Lark, carved out of body panels and mechanical components dating back to 1953, but arriving just in time for the public's sudden shift to economy cars in light of the 1958 recession. While General Motors, Ford, and Chrysler rushed to get their "compacts" into production for 1960, Studebaker already had exactly what people wanted to drive off the showroom floor—and this time the body style lineup left no gaping holes. The Lark came as a two-door sedan, four-door sedan, two-door wagon, and hardtop right off the bat. It wasn't on the market a year before a four-door wagon and convertible made their debut, and the Lark could be had with either an economy six or a sprightly V-8. Studebaker product planners had finally learned some lessons.

The Lark's success was owed chiefly to three men: S-P president Harold Churchill, now finally on his own after the Curtiss-Wright management contract lapsed and Roy Hurley went away; stylist Duncan McRae, now finally free to do something really good without being prodded by chrome- and tailfin-happy would-be marketing experts; and chief engineer Eugene Hardig, who had plenty of talent when they'd let him use it. "Church" inspired his minions with old films of Studebaker's great 1939 success, the Champion. McRae put together a track team of designers—Bob Doehler, Ted Pietsch, and Bill Bonner among them. Hardig tackled the job of building a new, compact body with what tools and dies he had. "Without Gene," McRae said later, "the Lark would not have been possible....I believe that Gene and his people took less than nine months from clay approval to introduction—unheard of in those days. A comparable program today would take about 22 months."

"Its basis was a '58 sawed off at both ends—just a seating buck to show how much room there'd be inside and to illustrate minimum overall length....We wanted a small car, so a lot had to be taken off ahead of the front wheels. We were allowed to flatten the 1953-style roof, and it was the first time in my three years with the company that we were given new fenders, hood and grille, deck lid, rear quarters, lower deck panel, new bumpers, and instrument panel to work with. We developed two full-sized clay models, with Bill Bonner in charge of one and Bob Doehler the other, and Bill's was selected." Hardig's engine engineers were readying a new overhead-valve six for 1961, but Gene meanwhile improved what he had for 1959. Churchill wanted a "smaller, stiffer engine" for maximum economy and durability, so Hardig destroked the L-head from 4.375 to 4.00 inches, lowering displacement to the pre-1955 level, and horsepower to 90—but hardly affecting torque, which dropped from 152 lbs/ft to 145. In consideration of the Lark's lightness (as low as 2600 pounds with the six), the 259 seemed a better V-8 option than the 289. Even so, it could be ordered with the 1957 "Power Pack" of four-barrel carburetor and dual exhausts, good for 195 horsepower.

The Lark's effect on Studebaker was electric. As of June 30, 1958, the balance sheet showed cash and securities of $27 million, against accounts payable of $24 million and a 3½-year combined loss of nearly $100 million. Payments on loans from 20 banks and three insurance companies couldn't be met, and stockholder equity was nil. The first year of the Lark engendered sales of $387 million (the best since 1953), and the company earned over $28 million. Employment increased over 60 percent to 12,000 by mid-1959. Production kept building as the '60 model year arrived, and total production for the 12 months of 1959 exceeded 150,000 units. Studebaker shot past Cadillac into tenth place in the industry, a position it hadn't held since 1953.

In the end, however, it all proved in vain. The Lark itself gained a reputation for slipshod assembly and poor dealer service. People used to crackerjack Big Three agencies were put off by what passed for the typical Studebaker dealership of 1959. Then too, despite its high 1959 profits, Studebaker barely stayed in the black the next year, and never did manage to raise the money to completely revamp the Lark. So when the onslaught of the Big Three compacts began in 1960, the Lark was clearly in trouble.

And so the Lark, cleverly conceived as it was, ended up a case of too little, too late, and one more proof of an aged Detroit dictum: you can be small and succeed; but if you come up with something entirely new, before you know it you have elephant footprints all over you.

The 1959 Studebaker Lark wasn't as new as it looked. A clever hatchet job shortened the '58 Studie's front and rear overhang and the wheelbase by eight inches, while a tiny budget yielded some new sheetmetal. The result saved Studebaker—temporarily, as it turned out—and put it into the profit column, also temporarily. Among the models offered were a six-cylinder Lark VI Regal hardtop at $2275 (opposite, bottom) *and a Lark VI two-door wagon* (top), *available as a $2295 DeLuxe or $2455 Regal.*

SPECIFICATIONS

Engines: **Lark VI** sidevalve I-6, 169.6 cid (3.00 × 4.00), 90 bhp **Lark VIII** ohv V-8, 259.2 cid (3.56 × 3.25), 180 bhp; 195 bhp optional

Transmission:	3-speed manual; overdrive and 3-speed Flight-O-Matic optional
Suspension, front:	independent, coil springs, tube shocks
Suspension, rear:	live axle, leaf springs, tube shocks
Brakes:	front/rear drums
Wheelbase (in.):	108.5 **Regal wgn** 113.5
Weight (lbs):	**Six** 2577-2815 **V-8** 2924-3148
Top speed (mph):	**Six** 90 **V-8** 100-105
0-60 mph (sec):	**Six** 17.0-18.0 **V-8** 12.0-13.0
Production:	**Lark VI** 98,744 **Lark VIII** 32,334

59 STUDEBAKER
173 AOB

1959 Studebaker Silver Hawk

Pretend to be a fly on the wall during the planning conference for the 1959 Studebakers. You can almost hear President Harold Churchill, that car-wise veteran now freed from the direction of people who didn't know his business, reasoning like this: "In '59 we'll have the all-new Lark to replace all this unsuccessful 1956-58 stuff."

"What about the Hawk?" his colleagues ask. Churchill replies: "The $3300 Golden Hawk is consistently outsold by the $2300 Silver Hawk. In 1957 the margin was four to one; in 1958 the margin's nine to one. If we keep anything, it should be the latter."

Basically, this was the right decision. In the clear light of hindsight, one can perhaps suggest one refinement: They should have kept the Golden Hawk hardtop body, but used the down-market Silver Hawk drivetrain. The "Loewy coupe," after six years in the marketplace, had become fairly long-in-the-tooth by the late Fifties. The use of six-cylinder and non-supercharged V-8s (which Churchill did opt for) combined with the hardtop body style would have been the most salable package. As it turned out, the pillared coupe they chose over the hardtop accounted for about 8000 sales in 1959.

The company's actual thinking was explained to this writer by former manager Ed Reynolds, who recalled that his seniors would have preferred to drop the Hawk altogether. They got talked out of it, Reynolds said, by the dealers, who "had to have the Hawk to maintain floor traffic. The Hawk was expensive to build, a low-profit car with insufficient volume, and the dies were beginning to wear out. As a compromise we dropped the hardtop, which we could produce less cheaply. The theory was that the other [Lark] hardtops would take up the appeal slack lost by the demise of the Golden Hawk."

The larger V-8 having been dropped, the Silver Hawk had to settle for the 259-cubic-inch unit. A six-cylinder engine was added to broaden appeal, and in deference to the public's new interest in fuel economy. But the record showed that Hawk buyers preferred the V-8 by a two-to-one margin, and the following year Studebaker built Hawk sixes for the export market only.

A trim shuffling took place for recognition purposes, the circular grille badge of 1958 being eliminated in favor of a small hawk emblem on a black background, affixed to the lower left corner of the square grille. The straight-through beltline molding of 1958's Silver Hawk was replaced by a piece of bright metal on the front fenders and doors, and a separate piece of brightwork ran under the tailfins. The fins also bore the black hawk emblem and the model name in chrome script.

The parking/directional lights, which had ridden atop the front fenders since Bob Bourke designed the first '56 Hawks, now moved back into the little side openings that flanked the grille, where they had been on the original 1953-55 coupes. "High fashion interiors commended by *Harper's Bazaar*" came in combinations of cloth and vinyl, and reclining seats joined the options list for the first time. The traditional engine-turned dashboard, with its white-on-black, sports car instruments, was retained.

The Silver Hawk occupied a market niche pretty much to itself in 1959, there being no comparable sport coupes offered by the Big Three. The six sold for $2360, the V-8 for $2495. Nine dollars more would buy a 1959 Chevy Bel Air two-door sedan with a V-8 and its infamous "batwing" styling, but it hardly qualified as a car for the sporting set.

With Studebaker's promotional focus on the Lark, the Silver Hawk moved down to secondary product status in the merchandising department's eyes. It appeared almost as a sidebar, a corner in the catalog otherwise fully devoted to the Lark.

"There's no car quite like the Silver Hawk," read the brief advertising pitch. "Long, lithe, suave and charmingly continental...a superb example of styling that relies on purity of line rather than ornamentation....Its performance is as distinguished as its appearance. For *this* car revels in the delight of driving. It appreciates a knowledgeable hand on its wheel and ready feet on its pedals—and shows it by responding with precision and alacrity. It is an unusually distinctive automobile, crafted for the owner who has a zest for life and the imagination to live it."

All puffery aside, this really summarized quite accurately the virtues of the Silver Hawk. Though by no means the powerhouse that the blown Golden Hawk had been, it had enough zip to suit most owners' whims; for those who wanted sporty lines coupled with economy, a six-cylinder alternative could be ordered for the first time since 1956. Ultimately, it made sense to keep the Hawk going until Studebaker could finally recast it as the Gran Turismo Hawk in 1962.

After a dismal sales year in 1958, Studebaker dropped the Golden Hawk. For 1959, this left only the Silver Hawk pillared coupe, offered either as a $2360 six or a $2495 V-8. Buyers chose the 3140-pound V-8 model by a two-to-one margin. Horsepower ratings came in at 90 for the 169.6-cid six, 180 or 195 for the peppy 259.2-cid V-8.

SPECIFICATIONS

Engines: sidevalve I-6, 169.6 cid (3.00 × 4.00), 90 bhp; ohv V-8, 259.2 cid (3.56 × 3.25), 180 bhp; 195 bhp optional

Transmission:	3-speed manual; overdrive and 3-speed Flight-O-Matic optional
Suspension, front:	independent, coil springs, tube shocks
Suspension, rear:	live axle, leaf springs, tube shocks
Brakes:	front/rear drums (finned)
Wheelbase (in.):	120.5
Weight (lbs):	**Six** 2795 **V-8** 3140
Top speed (mph):	**Six** 90 **V-8** 100
0-60 mph (sec):	**Six** 18.0 **V-8** 12.0-13.0
Production:	**Six** 2417 **V-8** 5371

IND-59
BN 92
LINCOLN YEAR

20
40
60
80
100
120
MILES

1950-51 Willys Jeepster

The civilian line of postwar Jeeps had their origins in the advanced thinking of Joe Frazer, Willys-Overland's prewar president, and his successor Charlie Sorensen—Henry Ford's longtime production boss, hired by Willys chairman Ward Canaday when Frazer left to set up Graham-Paige. All three executives feared relying solely on conventional passenger cars after the war, realizing that a small independent needed unique products to survive the crunch of Big Three competition.

During Frazer's tenure, Milwaukee designer Brooks Stevens had published articles in the *Journal of the Society of Automotive Engineers* about civilian uses of the Jeep. One of his radical ideas suggested giving the vehicle pastel colors, fresh upholstery, a softer ride, and rakish styling, thereby transforming it into a snappy touring car. This impressed Frazer and Willys engineer Barney Roos, who hired Stevens as a design consultant in 1943. The first result, a proposal known as the "6/66," emerged as an envelope-bodied passenger car! This wasn't quite what Frazer had in mind, but he named it "Jeepster," a title that stuck. When Sorensen arrived, he put Stevens back on the track of designing what ultimately became the production Jeepster, a vehicle that could justly be called America's last touring car.

Sorensen was greatly influenced by his friend John Tjaarda, designer of the 1936 Lincoln Zephyr, who had suggested Sorensen's name to Canaday when Frazer resigned. According to writer Michael Lamm, Tjaarda wanted five companies to "market the Jeep globally in three versions. The 'International Car Co.' was to be made up of Willys-Overland in the U.S., Mathis of France, Industrias Basicas Mexicanas in Mexico, Briggs Bodies Ltd. and Daimler in England, and the Swedish Automobile Company of Stockholm. Tjaarda further proposed that, with military stockpiles of Jeep parts and assembled cars already all over the world, at war's end the International Car Co. should sell: (1) the military Jeep, painted more brightly and with softer springs; (2) a longer Jeep station wagon with a plywood body; and (3) a passenger car version on a lowered frame, using mostly Jeep running gear but without four-wheel-drive."

Though the Tjaarda proposals came to naught, they bear a remarkable resemblance to Lee Iacocca's proposals 40 years later. And some of the ideas did prevail in Sorensen's postwar revival of Jeep-based designs. Accordingly, Brooks Stevens' Jeep station wagon and pick-up truck line appeared in 1946, the former acquiring stylist Art Kibiger's "canework" trim panels.

The first Jeepsters—called phaeton convertibles—began in 1948, and through early 1950 they were powered by Willys' four-cylinder Whippet L-heads; in 1949 an optional L-head six joined the four. Finally, in mid-1950, the L-heads were replaced by overhead valve F-heads, converted from the old engines by Barney Roos. He pulled off a neat trick by bypassing the intake valve seats and installing new heads and camshafts; he also raised the six-cylinder engine's displacement by about 10 percent, raising horsepower slightly in the process.

Physical changes between the early 1950 and late 1950/1951 Jeepster were minimal, though a definite edge in quality exists on the former, which had upright grilles, more chrome, and better trim. Production never reached high levels. According to the Mid-States Jeepster Association, the best year came in 1948, when just over 10,000 Jeepsters were produced. The initial price, close to $1800, put many buyers off (a '48 Ford Super DeLuxe V-8 convertible sold for $1740 base) and had to be drastically cut in 1949. In 1951, Jeepsters sold for $1426 base for the four-cylinder model, $1529 for the six-cylinder. But even the lower prices didn't help sales.

The Jeepster was, after all, a highly peripheral, specialty product. In the Sixties an updated version called the "Jeepster 2" did carve out a reasonable following, but by then America had grown affluent enough to afford the kind of rough and ready, sunny-day vehicle the Jeepster was. In the early Fifties, it was just slightly ahead of its time.

Before reentering the automobile business in 1952, Willys sold a specialty model, the Jeepster phaeton convertible. It bowed in 1948 as an offshoot of the Jeep station wagon that had made its debut in 1946. Although a four was standard, the 1950 model seen here came equipped with a six-cylinder engine. It weighed 2485 pounds and sold for $1490, down from an initial price of $1765 in 1948. Sales were slow even at the lower price.

SPECIFICATIONS

Engines: **Early 1950** sidevalve I-4, 134.2 cid (3.13 × 4.38), 63 bhp; sidevalve I-6, 148.5 cid (3.00 × 3.50), 70 bhp **late 1950/1951** the same I-4 converted to ohv, 72 bhp; ohv I-6, 161.0 cid (3.13 x 4.38), 75 bhp

Transmission:	3-speed manual; overdrive optional
Suspension, front:	planadyne independent, transverse leaf spring, tube shocks
Suspension, rear:	live axle, longitudinal leaf springs, tube shocks
Brakes:	front/rear drums
Wheelbase (in.):	104.0
Weight (lbs):	2459-2485
Top speed (mph):	80
0-60 mph (sec):	**Four** 28.0 **Six** 25.0
Production:	5844

GG 3935

BEAM
FUEL
OIL
AMP
TEMP

1952-55 Willys Aero-Eagle/ Bermuda

Despite the phenomenal success of the wartime Jeep, Willys-Overland chairman Ward Canaday never doubted that his company would get back into production of passenger cars after the war. A variety of ideas were conceived, including designs from Brooks Stevens, Bob Andrews, Art Kibiger, and Clyde R. Paton. But only the last, with collaboration from stylist Phil Wright, succeeded.

Paton had been Packard's chief engineer from 1930 to 1942, when he went on a leave of absence to join GM's Allison Division; he returned in 1944 to develop an aircraft engine plant, and after the war joined Ford, where he helped reorganize the engineering department. Like many others, Paton became intrigued with the idea of an inexpensive car people could buy new, and hired Phil Wright as his designer. Their ideas dovetailed so well with those of Canaday that he gladly hired them on.

The result, in due course, would be the 1952 Aero-Willys, a handsome, unit-body car possessing very clean lines and providing excellent ride characteristics and good handling despite its relatively low weight. Four separate two-door models debuted, offering the Willys L-head and F-head six-cylinder engines. The only hardtop offered, the Aero-Eagle, slotted in at the top of the line. Fitted with handsome, color keyed upholstery, and sold only with the 90-bhp overhead-valve six, the Eagle listed at $2155—by far the most expensive Aero in a lineup that started at $1731.

Veteran observers of the postwar scene will know immediately why the Aero-Willys failed: the price was simply far too high. Against it were arrayed the formidable wares of the Big Three. The Eagle's price problem becomes clearly visible when compared with competitive hardtops. The 1952 Chevy Bel Air, for example, started at $2006, the Ford Victoria at $1925, and the Plymouth Belvedere at $2216. Only the Plymouth cost more, but hardly enough to entice away loyal Plymouth partisans. And one can scarcely imagine a Ford or Chevy loyalist paying more for the smaller, lighter Willys.

Pricing continued to plague the Aero-Eagle through 1953 and '54, during which period Willys-Overland was bought out by Kaiser—another company hardly known for competitive prices. The car itself remained essentially unchanged. The 1953 Willys—now offering seven models, including three four-door sedans—could be told at a glance by a gold "W" mounted in the center of the grille, signifying the Golden Anniversary of Willys-Overland. The Aero-Eagle hardtop, now listing at $2157, saw output increase from 2155 units in 1952 to 7018, one-sixth of Willys' 1953 output.

The '54s sprouted an extra red lens under the flush-fitting taillights, and hardtop offerings increased to five: base Eagle plus Custom, Special, DeLuxe, and DeLuxe Custom. The "Custom" referred to a continental spare tire, but this only added to the price tag and it sold poorly. Despite all the offerings, Eagle hardtop output slipped to just 1556 units out of total Willys production of 11,856.

In an attempt to broaden the Aero's appeal in 1954, the L-head six from the big Kaiser was made available—at a higher price, of course. Though dealers couldn't give the top-line Eagle DeLuxe Custom away at $2411 base, this version did pack extraordinary performance, at least for Willys. Griff Borgeson, writing in *Motor Life*, described it as "torrid," a factual enough exaggeration relative to most of Willys' competition. His 0-60 time came in at 13.9 seconds, better than any 1954 Plymouth or Chevy, and almost on par with Ford's new overhead-valve V-8.

In a rump effort that came far too late, Kaiser brought out a drastically rationalized 1955 Willys line at highly competitive prices, scrubbed the "Aero" name, and christened the hardtop "Bermuda." With it came the postwar Willys' only major facelift, crafted by stylist Herb Weissinger. It featured a broad, vertical-bar grille striking a family resemblance to that of the 1954-55 Kaiser, a hood strip ending in a chrome and plastic "sail" ornament, curious two-toning along the bodysides and deck (which AMC's little Metropolitan would copy for 1956), and big chrome cappings below the taillights—anything to make it look different.

The big-engined Bermuda sold at a base price of just under $2000, while the 161-cid F-head came in at $1895, and was advertised—correctly—as "America's lowest priced hardtop." But it was too late. Only about 2000 Bermudas rolled off the assembly line, all except 59 of them equipped with the 226-cid six. After building these, and approximately 3000 sedans, Willys gave up on passenger cars, discontinuing production in Toledo. But the tooling found its way to South America, where a very nice version along 1954 lines, built by Willys-Overland do Brasil, found willing buyers into the 1960s. In all, the Aero actually lasted over 10 years—which attests to its basically good design.

Last ditch efforts rarely succeed, but Willys gamely tried to buck the odds with a 1955 facelift. The Aero-Eagle hardtop, renamed Bermuda, featured a new Kaiser-inspired grille, bodyside two-toning, big chrome blobs under the taillights, and lower prices. None of it helped, but the Willys went on to become a big hit in Brazil.

SPECIFICATIONS

Engines: **1952-55** ohv I-6, 161.0 cid (3.13 × 4.38), 90 bhp **1952-53** sidevalve I-6, 161.0 cid, 75 bhp **1953-54** F-head I-4, 134.2 cid (3.13 × 4.38), 72 bhp **1954-55** sidevalve I-6, 226.2 cid (3.31 x 4.38), 115 bhp

Transmission:	3-speed manual, overdrive optional **1954-55** GM Hydra-Matic optional
Suspension, front:	independent, coil springs, tube shocks
Suspension, rear:	live axle, leaf springs, tube shocks
Brakes:	front/rear drums
Wheelbase (in.):	108.0
Weight (lbs):	2487-2904
Top speed (mph):	**161 Six** 85 **226 Six** 90
0-60 mph (sec):	**161 Six** 20.0-22.0 **226 Six** 14.0-15.0

Production: **1952 Aero-Eagle** 2364 **1953** 7018 **1954 Aero-Eagle** 660 **Custom** 11 **Special** 302 **DeLuxe** 84 **Custom DeLuxe** 499 **1955 Bermuda** 2215

ONTARIO
WYB 701

ONTARIO
WYB 701

Index